KASHMIR
Ethnic Conflict
International Dispute

KASHMIR
Ethnic Conflict
International Dispute

Iffat Malik

OXFORD
UNIVERSITY PRESS

OXFORD
UNIVERSITY PRESS

Great Clarendon Street, Oxford OX2 6DP

Oxford University Press is a department of the University of Oxford.
It furthers the University's objective of excellence in research, scholarship,
and education by publishing worldwide in

Oxford New York

Auckland Bangkok Buenos Aires Cape Town Chennai
Dar es Salaam Delhi Hong Kong Istanbul Karachi Kolkata
Kuala Lumpur Madrid Melbourne Mexico City Mumbai Nairobi
São Paulo Shanghai Singapore Taipei Tokyo Toronto

Oxford is a registered trade mark of Oxford University Press
in the UK and in certain other countries

ISBN 0 19 579622 5

Typeset in Times
Printed in Pakistan by
Mas Printers, Karachi.
Published by
Ameena Saiyid, Oxford University Press
5-Bangalore Town, Sharae Faisal
PO Box 13033, Karachi-75350, Pakistan.

To

My Parents

With Love

CONTENTS

FOREWORD

Few of the contemporary world's regional conflicts have been as protracted and complex as the Kashmir dispute between India and Pakistan. Dating from 1947, when Pakistan and India secured their independence from Britain, it has evolved through several stages and taken on additional political and strategic characteristics that make it today a fundamentally different—and, in a number of important respects, more perplexing—conflict from what it was when it began over half a century ago. One of the most obvious of these newer characteristics is, of course, the evolution of India and Pakistan into overt nuclear weapon states. That has wrought a change in the military-strategic equation between them whose impact on the Kashmir dispute's interstate or *external* circumstances can scarcely be exaggerated. Without question, this change has grafted an element of sheer menace to the dispute—that of a so-called 'nuclear flashpoint'—that it did not have before.

Almost equally conspicuous among the Kashmir dispute's newer characteristics, however, are changes in the *internal* circumstances enveloping it in the Indian-administered state of Jammu and Kashmir. One of these changes occurred in the last years of the 1980s with the emergence of a powerful Kashmiri Muslim separatist movement. The violence stemming from this change in the situation has turned the state into a bloodstained battleground not only between India and Pakistan but also between Indian security forces and India's own Kashmiri citizens.

Some of the Kashmir dispute's newer characteristics have both internal *and* external dimensions. One of these is the arrival in the last two decades or so of a profound change in its *ideological* colouration. By this I mean that it has acquired a radicalized religious dimension, that of religious nationalism, reaching far beyond the state's borders, which has supplemented and dramatically transformed Kashmir's already complicated pattern of ethno-linguistic identities. Whatever may have been the underlying motivations at the outset of the Kashmir dispute, there can be no doubt that Kashmir is today, among other things, a rallying point for the forces of militant Islam as well as for its militant Hindu adversaries.

It is this multi-dimensional and steadily evolving aspect of the Kashmir dispute that supplies the motivation for Iffat Malik's study. Taking as her starting point that the unraveling of Kashmir's meaning today requires making a distinction between its internal and international dimensions, she maintains that both of these dimensions must be considered in conjunction with one another. She makes the provocative argument, however, that it is the *internal* politics of Jammu and Kashmir State that is of greatest importance today and, moreover, that *internal* political issues are increasingly determining the *international* character of the Kashmir dispute. She acknowledges that deep hostility has always been emblematic of the India-Pakistan relationship; but it has grown even deeper, she contends, as the relationship between them—in all its economic, political, cultural, military and strategic dimensions—has increasingly been held hostage to the domestic political compulsions of India, Pakistan, and Kashmir itself. As Iffat sees it, the gradual convergence of the dispute's internal and international aspects has materially increased the risk of war while at the same time vastly complicating the search for resolution.

This enormously thoughtful, sobering, and refreshingly balanced discussion of the Kashmir dispute's politically inter-linked internal and international dimensions offers no solutions. No less valuable, however, is what it does offer—greater understanding of the dispute at a particularly momentous, and potentially calamitous, point in its history.

Professor Robert G. Wirsing
Asia-Pacific Center for Security Studies
Honolulu, Hawaii
18 May 2001

ACKNOWLEDGEMENTS

Lots of people helped in the preparation of this book, some in a professional capacity, others in a personal one. It would be impossible to list all of them, but those I owe an especial debt to, include: Bikku Parekh, Tahir Amin, Subrata Mitra, Robert Wirsing, Vernon Hewitt, Ershad Mehmood, Akbar Ahmed, Ayub Thakkar, and Alexander Evans. Especial thanks to my brothers Ijaz and Sajjad for their personal support, and also to Asma Akhtar, Sadaf Abdullah, Abda Ashraf, Azmat Nisa and Ayesha Siddiqua-Agha. A very big thank you to Zubair Idris for making my transition to life in Islamabad so pleasurable. Finally, this book is also dedicated to the memory of my uncle, Abdur-Rehman Malik.

INTRODUCTION

Kashmir is one of those trouble zones that periodically, and increasingly frequently, dominate news headlines. Often it does so in the context of Indo-Pak antagonism: the two chronically hostile neighbours poised to go to war over the disputed region yet again. But, somewhat confusingly, it also appears in the context of domestic Indian politics: westerners taken hostage or attacks by militants against the State Assembly, to give two examples.

Why the diversity? Is Kashmir an international problem or an internal domestic one?

In fact, it is both. The Kashmir problem is best understood as not one, but two long-running disputes. The first and longer running one is that between India and Pakistan. It is a relatively straightforward dispute over territory and dates back to the partition of the subcontinent in 1947. The more recent one is that within Indian Kashmir. It is essentially an ethnic conflict between, on the one hand, different ethnic groups within the state, and on the other between these and the Indian government.

The basic premise of this book is that only when Kashmir is considered as these two quite distinct problems, can events there and their impact on the wider region be properly understood. Kashmir as a problem in South Asia has to be considered separately from Kashmir as a problem within India.

Separately but not in isolation; this is the other important point to appreciate. There are two distinct Kashmir problems, but there is a great deal of parallel and overlap between them. Each influences and determines the other. Hence they also need to be considered in conjunction. That is what this book attempts to do.

Traditional writing on Kashmir focuses on the international dimension—competing Indian and Pakistani claims to the state, their efforts to gain control of it, and the varied and numerous attempts made to resolve the dispute over it. Robert Wirsing's excellent *India, Pakistan and the Kashmir Dispute* is an obvious example. Where the internal dimension is mentioned it is usually as an aside to the international dispute, or it is discussed from highly partisan perspectives: the official Indian and Pakistani lines given a veneer of objectivity.

This book looks at both international and internal problems, but deliberately stresses the latter. The reason is partly because, as mentioned, the international dispute has been exhaustively covered by other writers. But it is also because, increasingly, the internal Kashmir conflict is dominant and driving the international Indo-Pak dispute.

The internal Kashmir conflict is considered an ethnic struggle because, as will become apparent through the book, ethnicity and politics in the Valley are closely interlinked. Ethnic identification and consciousness are influenced by political developments; ethnic identification and consciousness determine political choices; there is negligible cross-ethnic politics. In examining Kashmir as an ethnic conflict, therefore, the book looks at ethnic identification and consciousness, factors influencing these, relations between different ethnic groups, and between these and the Indian state. Through this it traces the roots of conflict.

In looking at the kinds of factors that influence ethnic identification and consciousness within Kashmir, a division is made into 'internal' and 'external' factors. The former include state government policies, socio-economic changes, local politics, etc. The latter refer to developments taking place outside Kashmir—in India, Pakistan and elsewhere—but having an impact on people within it. The reason for this division is simply ease of analysis. It is not meant to imply that these two sets of factors are completely discrete.

Having examined the factors influencing ethnicity in the Valley, the political manifestations of this are assessed. What do the different ethnic groups in the state want? How have their demands changed over time? How divergent are their political views and demands? Most important, how have ethnic and political differences led to ethnic conflict?

As stressed above, Kashmir the international dispute is considered separately but in conjunction with the ethnic one. Thus, at appropriate points, the reasons why India and Pakistan are both so desperate to control the state, their traditional stances on Kashmir in international forums, Indo-Pak conflicts and efforts at resolution are all reviewed.

One final point: developments within Jammu and Kashmir are considered across the whole of the state. But ethnic identification is only assessed in detail in the Kashmir Valley. This is partly because of the massive ethnic diversity across the state, but more importantly, because it is the Valley that is the real epicentre of ethnic conflict.

Some Theoretical Points

Since one of the basic premises of this book is that Kashmir's development as an Indian state should be viewed as essentially an ethnic issue, it would be useful to clarify at the outset the concept of ethnicity.

There has been much debate among scholars of ethnicity as to whether it should be viewed as a primordialist or an instrumentalist phenomenon. Proponents of the primordial approach see ethnic attachments as one of the 'givens' of human existence, and ethnicity as a natural instinctive phenomenon. They can be subdivided into socio-biologists such as Pierre Van den Berghe who believe it has a biological, genetic basis, and those like Clifford Geertz who view it as more sociological. Instrumentalists reject this 'natural' view of ethnicity, preferring to root it firmly in behaviour. Eller and Coughlan for example write: 'claims to ethnic membership arise and change according to situationally variable circumstances and interests.' Ethnicity, in other words, is a tool constructed to gain material, political or other advantage. There are yet more scholars who see both the above as partially correct. They see ethnic attachments arising both from primordial bonds and from the desire to achieve specific social/economic/political objectives. This book follows this third school of thought: 'ethnicity is best understood in terms of a rational=non-rational continuum rather than as an either/or dichotomy.'

So what exactly is an ethnic group? Does it refer to a linguistic group, a religious community, all people living within the same region, or a racial group? The definition used in this book is actually based on none of these: rather, it follows Smith's view that the essential condition for shared ethnicity is belief in common descent. An ethnic group is thus: 'A group of people who believe they have a common origin and descent, hold shared historical memories, and in addition will usually have one or more characteristics in common (e.g. language, religion, culture) which serve to differentiate members from outsiders.'

The other point to stress about ethnic groups is their subjective nature. This applies to both membership of the group and its identifying traits. With respect to the latter, just because the members of a particular group have a certain trait in common it does not automatically follow that that trait must be an identifying feature of the group. The significance—or lack of it—of a shared trait is determined not by outside observers, but by members of a group themselves. And it is generally the case that they will assign importance to those traits that distinguish them from outsiders. Horowitz notes: 'It is not the attribute that makes the group, but the group and group differences that make the attribute important.'

Turning to the former, outsiders cannot bunch people together into ethnic groups: they must themselves have a sense of belonging to that group, they must possess ethnic consciousness. Without it, even if they speak the same language, follow the same religion and have identical cultural traits, they cannot be regarded as an ethnic group. The level of ethnic consciousness in a group can be regarded as a measure of how strongly members are aware of their ethnic identity, how strongly they feel themselves to be part of a group, and how important membership of that group is to them. Ethnic consciousness will vary from one group to the next.

From the generally subjective nature of ethnicity outlined above, it will be apparent that ethnic groups possess considerable potential for change: identifying markers, levels of ethnic consciousness and group membership can all be subject to flux. The range of possible factors inducing such fluxes is considerable. This book is concerned largely with the ways in which political developments affect ethnic identification in Kashmir. Hence the review below is confined to political factors that can influence ethnic identity.

Political Contextual Factors

Mobilizational Theories

Greater ethnic consciousness can be a consequence of the spread of democracy and electoral politics. States are supposedly 'composed of congeries of free-floating individuals' equal before the law, who form the units of political action. But in practice the effective unit of political action is the group rather than the individual. This is where ethnicity comes in: it is a source of ready-made groups which can be mobilized for political action and/or be a secure source of votes. Ethnic groups are particularly suited for political mobilization because of the primordial element in ethnic consciousness. This gives members of an ethnic group a greater sense of unity and collectiveness, plus a stronger commitment to the group, than members of an interest group united solely by common economic/political goals.

A subtle variant of this mass politics theory is that of economic/political advantage. Whereas in the former, ethnic mobilization results from the need for groups, in the latter, it is generated by the desire to achieve specific political and/or economic goals. Ethnicity here is a means to achieve a clear end. This could range from extracting more funds from the state, higher job quotas, better educational opportunities, acquiring political power at the centre, wrestling concessions for the ethnie from those in power, etc.

Another variant is based on ethnic elites. Brass is probably the keenest advocate of this view—that ethnic mobilization results from the ambitions of ethnic elites. In the case of political leaders these ambitions will obviously be centred around gaining power—either absolute power or as great a share of it as possible. Their reasons for playing the ethnic card to secure votes become apparent when one compares the situation in civic 'individual-based' nations with that in 'ethnic group-based' ones. In the former, political leaders must win over each person individually. Since they will obviously have different priorities and interests, the politician is put in the difficult position of having to adjust his message to suit different listeners, or else of deciding whose support he can afford to sacrifice. In ethnic-based societies members of a single ethnie will—admittedly to varying degrees—have the same priorities and interests. Thus if he can find a message that will appeal to the group identity the ethnic political leader can save himself considerable time and effort. Alternatively, the ethnic leader need have no specific ideology at all: the mere fact of his belonging to a particular ethnic group could be enough to win him the votes of its members.

The important point to stress is that ethnic politicians can only attract the ethnic vote [or other elites' such as religious leaders' group support] if members of their ethnic group have a high degree of ethnic consciousness. While this might well be present already, where it is not, politicians will try and instil it. This is particularly the case when ethnic elites know they have little/no chance of winning support from members of other ethnic groups. The need for them to solidify the support of their own group becomes correspondingly greater.

Furthermore, elites can influence the salience of ethnic markers; depending on what best serves their interests they could stress one particular trait and suppress another. Brass has clearly highlighted this phenomenon among the Muslims of India. The interests of ethnic elites can therefore be a very important factor both in inducing (greater) ethnic consciousness and in determining what this may be based upon.

Oppositional Theories

Spicer accounts for the persistence of ethnic groups, such as the Jews, Basques, and Irish, as a result of each facing pressure to assimilate into larger societies and each resisting that pressure and developing well-defined symbols to distinguish themselves from the larger society.[1] Scott has extended Spicer's explanation of continuous opposition accounting for 'persistent identity systems', to produce the following general rule:

> The greater the opposition—economic, political, social, religious, or some combination thereof—perceived by an ethnic group, the greater the degree to which its historical sense of distinctiveness will be aroused, and hence the greater its solidarity or the more intense its movement towards redress.[2]

Ethnic groups can experience different kinds of opposition. Among the most common as an inducer of greater ethnic consciousness is economic/political discrimination. This economic/political discrimination theory differs from the 'economic/political advantage' theory discussed above, in that groups are not mobilizing simply to improve their lot. Rather, the greater sense of ethnic identity is a psychological response to being discriminated against because of that identity. Such 'reactionary' ethnic identification will be greater, where it is practised by other, clearly differentiated, ethnic groups, than where it is conducted by an 'anonymous' ('non-ethnic') state.

The other form of opposition ethnic groups tend to face, is pressure to assimilate with other ethnic groups in the society. The most frequent source of such pressure is the state. In their efforts to become nation-states, many states promote an 'official nationalism', i.e. what they regard as the 'national' culture, language, history, etc. The aim behind such an exercise is to mould a homogenized population with a greater sense of unity and loyalty to the state.[3] Where the state government is non-ethnic, the official nationalism is likely to be based upon a composite culture, but where one particular ethnic group is dominant, it is the culture and language of that group which will be promoted. Other ethnic groups in the state will either accept the official/dominant group culture/language, or, as is more likely, will reject it and hold more firmly to their own ethnic traditions.

The need to homogenize, and the consequent ethnic backlash, is most evident in former colonies such as many African states, which were formed with little regard for whether state boundaries matched the distribution of ethnic groups. This led to the creation of multi-ethnic states in which, on the one hand, inhabitants feel little loyalty to the state—a totally new entity— and on the other hand, it is trying to mould them into a homogenous population in order to prevent its own break-up.

The State

When looking at the influence of political contextual factors on ethnic consciousness (mobilization), the single most important factor is undoubtedly the state. This has already been mentioned above in the context of other political factors influencing ethnicity, e.g., erosion of identity and economic/political discrimination, but there are many other (potential) reasons for the state to impinge on ethnicity.

The position of the state in a multi-ethnic society can be very significant. It has a multiplicity of possible roles. Brass has identified three broad theories of the state that see it as, respectively: a neutral arena of interest group competition ('viewed neither as dominated by the groups that contest in its arena, nor as an autonomous force in relation to them'); an instrument of group domination; or, thirdly, as a relatively autonomous entity with interests and strategies of its own (e.g. 'local control, administrative convenience, the gathering of popular support').[4]

Of these, modern states generally correspond to the second and third theories. Neutrality, assuming the intention is there (which it rarely is!), is very difficult to implement in practice. Not only do groups try to gain the support of the state, but the pursuit of a neutral policy 'often means, in effect, support for the status quo, a refusal to rectify an existing imbalance between groups'. Brass concludes: 'the state can be and is most often a relatively independent, if not a dominant actor, [but] this is not to deny that it can also be captured by particular groups or segments of society for long periods of time.'[5]

The position of the state, in relation to the various ethnic groups in a plural society, will obviously affect its treatment of those groups. A state dominated by one particular group is likely to pursue policies favourable to that group, with the frequent consequence of arousing resentment in less favoured groups. This was seen clearly in the apartheid-era South Africa. On the other hand, a state with its own 'non-ethnic' interests will put those first; where these non-ethnic interests oppose those of its constituent ethnic groups the result could well be resentment against the state. In both cases—though more in the former than the latter—resentment is likely to be manifested in heightened ethnic consciousness and mobilization. The kinds of policies most likely to arouse such an 'ethnic backlash' have been discussed above, i.e. the allocation of funding, location of development programmes, educational opportunities and job quotas, access to/denial of power, etc.

A state can also influence ethnic consciousness if it acts as a population classifier. This particular role of the state was seen most clearly in colonial times. Colonial rulers classified and divided their populations up into specific (ethnic) groupings. In modern societies, this role tends to be undertaken by states in which there are 'ethnic' quotas for things like university places and government jobs. [Quotas are usually set to overcome a disadvantage, to bring backward groups up to the level of more advanced ones.] Apart from the relative levels set for various groups, possibly arousing resentment, the important point is that by making ethnic background a criterion for the allocation of such places, the state promotes ethnic identification.

The structure of the state and the kind of government it has can also be a major factor in ethnic identification. Skocpol writes:

> states matter because their organizational configurations, along with their overall patterns of activity, affect political culture, encourage some kinds of group formation and political actions (but not others), and make possible the raising of certain political issues (but not others).[6]

Sticking with the example of India, by ruling out religion as a legitimate basis for group demands but allowing language, the Indian state encouraged the formation of language-based communities rather than communal ethnicities. With respect to the kind of government, one could make the very broad generalization that in non-western countries the more democracy there is—the more power is up for grabs—the more likely one is to see politically motivated ethnic mobilization. [The caveat of 'non-western countries' has been added because ethnicity must be at least moderately salient in a society before it can be dragged into the political arena: ethnicity tends to be far more salient outside the West.] Conversely, the more hegemonic and undemocratic the rule, the less political incentive there is for ethnic mobilization. [Though one could, of course, present a strong case for resentment at lack of democracy being manifested in greater ethnic consciousness.]

Finally, state legitimacy can be a factor in inducing ethnic consciousness. Legitimacy, here, refers not to democracy or the lack of it, but to the very boundaries and existence of the state itself. Is this acknowledged and accepted by its population? This question is particularly relevant for 'new' multi-ethnic states in which the citizens have no previous history of forming a political unit. If they accept the sovereignty of the state in which they find themselves, then it has a chance of moving forward and establishing itself, and of instilling in people the sense of being citizens of that state. But, if the sovereignty of the state itself is not acknowledged by (even some of) its citizens, this has grave implications for its survival, or at a minimum, for peace.

The attitude of states to their diverse populations and their approach to moulding them into a 'nation' can be tremendously significant in promoting or discouraging ethnic identification. Homogenization policies pursued by states have been alluded to above. As mentioned there, while these might succeed in bringing diverse peoples together, they are more likely to cause them to hold onto their distinct identities more strongly, i.e. to promote ethnic consciousness. But states which encourage their constituent ethnicities to retain their respective identities (e.g. using their own language) run the constant risk of those groups 'opting out' of the state whenever they feel their staying within is no longer of benefit. Ethnicity-based political mobilization remains available as a means of expressing opposition to the state.

Whether ethnies accept the authority of the political unit in which they are situated will also depend on the regional context. A minority border group in state A, with neighbouring state B in which fellow 'ethnics' form the majority, is likely to be ambiguous about accepting the authority of A. There will always be an underlying option to secede to B—something that will come to the fore whenever the group feels neglected or discriminated against by state A. The attitude of state B in such situations will also be significant—whether it encourages ethnic identification across the border, or whether it supports secessionist tendencies.

Overall then, we see that the state has enormous potential to influence ethnic identification. So much so, that in assessing what causes ethnic mobilization, it is almost as important as looking at the ethnic group and what makes it tick, to look at the state in which it is situated and see what makes it tick. Specifically, one should look at who controls the state, whether its authority is acknowledged by all its citizens, the kind of government and political structure it has, its economic policies, and its attitude to ethnic heterogeneity.

Outline

Chapter one attempts to assess the 'original' identity of the Kashmiri people. In examining how ethnic identification and consciousness have evolved in line with political and other developments, one must have some idea of what they were to start with. There are two main population groups in the Valley: Pandits and Kashmiri Muslims. The chapter examines the similarities and differences between them, their interaction and perceptions of each other. In particular, it addresses the issue of *Kashmiriyat*, an identity that, according to some, was once shared by Pandits and Muslims in Kashmir. Did such a common ethnic identity really exist? The chapter concludes that Pandits and Muslims formed two quite distinct groups, but that they co-existed in harmony. Furthermore, the potential was definitely present for *Kashmiriyat* to evolve.

The next three chapters look at political developments within Jammu and Kashmir. Chapter two covers the period up to 1947; Chapter Three that up to 1965; and Chapter Four the period between the 1965 Indo-Pak War and the onset of the current Kashmir conflict. The evolution of the international Kashmir dispute is also reviewed in these chapters. The approach taken is to outline political and other developments and show how these impacted ethnic consciousness and identification in the Valley, and Indian and Pakistani attitudes to the state.

The next three chapters look at external developments. The external political arena which has undoubtedly had the most influence on Kashmiri thinking is that of India. Many Indian political developments are given in Chapters Two to Four because they also involve Kashmir, e.g. the 1965 Indo-Pak War. Chapter Five, on Indian politics, does not go over these events again but it does explain the background to them. For example, why India was not able to grant Jammu and Kashmir genuine autonomy. Its other focus is on developments within India that have not directly involved the state but have possibly influenced events there. Most notable among these is the rise of Hinduism as a major political force within India.

The second most significant political arena, from the Kashmiri perspective, is that of Pakistan. Pakistani politics are discussed in Chapter Six. Again, those events mentioned already in previous chapters are not repeated, but the background to them is explained. Pakistan's appeal as an alternative homeland for 'Indian' Kashmiris is also assessed.

Chapter Seven looks at the influence of political developments across a far wider area—the Muslim world. The current resurgence (emergence) of Islam as both personal faith and political ideology in many Muslim countries is reviewed in terms of its causes and manifestations. This is followed by an assessment of the role of Islam in Kashmir: is the Valley also seeing a rise in Islam as a political force?

Chapter Eight examines the conflict in Kashmir. Militant groups involved in the insurgency, their goals, the response of the Indian government, its efforts to quell the militancy, the impact of the conflict on the Valley's civilian population and (so far as possible) their political views are all assessed. Efforts at political resolution are also reviewed. Pakistan too is involved in the ethnic conflict, e.g. selectively supporting some militant groups, playing a major role in Kargil. The Kashmir conflict thus, in many ways, marks the convergence of the two Kashmir disputes: ethnic and international.

The concluding chapter sums up the findings about the causes of the Kashmir disputes, ethnic and international, and assesses the prospects of their resolution.

NOTES

1. See Scott Jr., George, 'A resynthesis of the primordial and circumstantial approaches to ethnic group solidarity: towards an explanatory model', *Ethnic and Racial Studies* (13:2, April 1990), p. 158.
2. Ibid., p. 164.
3. Smith argues that the need for homogenization is a consequence of the modern inter-state system, which demands civic mobilization: 'Once regional, and later global, systems of state are in place, their demands on individual state elites are such as to compel rapid incorporation of all classes and ethnie...As far as the "outside" is concerned, citizens must be sharply differentiated from foreigners, and citizens must be as little differentiated internally as possible'. 'Ethnie and Nation in the Modern World', *Millenium Journal of International Studies* (14:2), p. 134.
4. See Brass, Paul, 'Ethnic Groups and the State' in Brass (ed.), *Ethnic Groups and the State* (London, Croom Helm, 1985), pp. 3–10.
5. Ibid., p. 9.
6. Skocpol, Theda, 'Bringing the State Back In: Strategies of Analysis in Current Research', in Evans, P., Rueschemeyer, D., and Skocpol, T., (eds.), *Bringing the State Back In* (Cambridge, Cambridge University Press), p. 21.

1

ETHNIC IDENTIFICATIONS IN KASHMIR

Two main population groups can be identified as traditionally inhabiting the Kashmir Valley: Kashmiri Muslims and Pandits (Kashmiri Brahmans). The divisions between the two are today very pronounced. As discussed in later chapters, Pandits and Muslims no longer live in the same regions, they have different aspirations, separate political organizations, etc. The issue addressed in this chapter is whether this current wide gulf reflects a long-standing reality in Kashmiri society or is it of more recent origin?

Several writers (e.g. Akbar, Bhattacharjea, Puri) claim that only in this century have the Muslims and Hindus of Kashmir developed distinct communal identities—originally they were united by a common 'Kashmiri' identity, referred to as *Kashmiriyat*, and formed a single Kashmiri community. Munshi vividly describes this single community:

Truly was it said that the Pandits and Muslims were two brothers, pursuing two different faiths in perfect mutual affection, respect and trust. They shared each others joys and sorrows, respected equally the sufis, saints and sages, traditions and rituals and places of worship, and merrily participated in each others' festivals. In essence, they lived a common community life, keeping the core of religion outside the circle of day-to-day social life...These shared values were rooted in common stock, ethnicity and perceptions of good and evil which they took pride in as an invaluable inheritance from the past.[1]

Advocates of a common Kashmiri identity such as Balraj Puri attribute it largely to geographical and historical factors. Puri argues that the Valley's being surrounded by a series of mountain ranges served on the one hand to cut its inhabitants off from the outside world, and on the other helped them form a close knit community. This latter process was encouraged by their scenic surroundings: 'The fabled beauty of Kashmir... further inspires a deep love for the land.'[2]

Historically, Puri writes that *Kashmiriyat* has persisted and been strengthened by the Kashmiris' ability to absorb new ideas and traditions. They have over the centuries undergone mass conversions successively to Buddhism, Hinduism and Islam. But Puri claims that each conversion did not entail the negation of what had gone before, but rather an addition:

> Kashmir has been a melting pot of ideas and races. It received every new creed with discrimination and enriched it with its own contribution, without throwing away its earlier accretions. As Sufi observes..., 'It has imbibed the best of Buddhism, the best of Hinduism and the best of Islam.'[3]

This process of integrating new religious traditions with existing ones extended into other aspects of life. Bamzai writes that, 'As in religion, so in philosophy, art and literature Kashmir evolved a composite culture.' The culmination of this was an identity unique to the natives of the Valley—'the fusion and assimilation of varied faiths and cultures had resulted in their particular and specific ethnicity'[4]—*Kashmiriyat*.

In order to verify or otherwise the authenticity of this claim one must look at the similarities and differences between Kashmiri Muslims and Pandits, and between them and their co-religionists in other parts of the subcontinent. From these one can establish whether Kashmir 'originally' had one Hindu-Muslim Kashmiri community or two separate ones.

Cultural Practices

There were, and are still, undoubtedly many similarities between Pandit and Muslim cultures in the Kashmir Valley. In dress, for example, both wore the loose, baggy-sleeved *pheran*. Similarly, both communities used an earthenware bowl filled with charcoal, called a *kanghri*, to keep warm in the harsh Kashmiri winter. Kashmiri tea could be found brewing throughout the day in every Kashmiri household—be it Muslim or Pandit. The dietary habits of Hindus and Muslims were less differentiated in Kashmir than in other parts of India. Muslims generally avoided eating beef, while mutton was a regular part of the Pandits' diet. And of course, followers of both religions spoke Kashmiri.

To an outsider then, all Kashmiris would appear to share a common culture, or at least have large elements in common. A closer inspection, however, would reveal that the similarities were not as great as first appeared. Take food, for example: Muslim and Pandit dishes were different, and even more so was their manner of eating. Muslims, particularly at social functions such as weddings, would eat three to four sharing the same plate but among Pandits, 'not even a father and son would share'.

Turning to clothes, while both Pandits and Muslims would wear the *pheran*, there were differences between the kinds they wore; these differences were especially marked among women's *pherans*. Furthermore, the clothes worn under the *pheran* were completely different: Muslims wore the *shalwar*, Pandits the *pajama*, 'No Kashmiri Pandit ever uses the *shalwar*; they will never use it. They say it is Muslim dress.'[5] Sender claims that Hindu and Muslim dress in Kashmir has actually been different since the late thirteenth century, when Sayyid Hamadani admonished the Muslim king for wearing Hindu clothes.[6]

Pandits and Muslims could also be visibly distinguished by their hair: Pandit men had a quite distinct style of cutting their hair and were clean-shaven, while among Muslims, a beard was a sign of piety. A further visible distinguishing feature was the *tyok* worn by many Pandits on their foreheads. Made using saffron or some other coloured paste, the mark was elongated in

Pandit men and round in Pandit women. No Muslim would ever have a *tyok* on his/her forehead.

The language of Muslims and Pandits was differentiated not by accent but by vocabulary. Certain words and phrases would only be used by Muslims; others only by Pandits. These included the obvious religion-based expressions (*W'Allah, Bhagwan*), but also terms referring to general things. Muslims tended to use words derived from Persian, Pandits from Sanskrit. The distinction in their vocabulary was quite marked. Mir Abdul Aziz cites the example of water: Kashmiri Muslims called this *aab*, Pandits *poan*. Aziz claims that a Muslim who said *poan* would immediately be asked 'Have you left Islam?'

The differences between Pandit and Muslim culture in Kashmir are summarized by Madan:

> The traditional clothing of Pandit men, women and children is different from that of their Muslim co-villagers...Pandit houses look different from those of other Kashmiris both from inside and outside. Their places of worship are also distinctive in appearance as are their religious, wedding and funeral gatherings. The sight of flowers (particularly marigolds) and the sound of conch shells are characteristic of these events. Though they speak Kashmiri, like the others, the Pandits' speech is more laden with Sanskrit than that of the Muslims. Personal and family names, with a few exceptions are also different.[7]

In summary then, the inhabitants of the Kashmir Valley did have a distinct regional culture. Furthermore, there was a great deal in common between Kashmiri Muslim and Pandit culture and language. But there were also differences that clearly distinguished the two.

Religious Worship

To what extent, if any, was religious worship common among Kashmiri Muslims and Pandits? To what extent, if any, was the practice of religion in the Kashmir Valley different from that in other parts of the Indian subcontinent? Taking common religious practices first, most Muslims in Kashmir were originally Hindus. The claim made by proponents of *Kashmiriyat* is that Kashmiri Muslims retained many of their Hindu ancestral religious practices, albeit modified to fit within an Islamic framework. The widespread tradition of 'saint worship', manifested for instance in the reverence of shrines, is particularly cited as a hangover from the Hindu era: 'The Kashmiri Muslim has transferred reverence from Hindu stones to Muslim relics...Muslim saints are worshipped like Hindu gods and godlings.'[8] Bazaz, a prominent Pandit, summed up the 'Hindu' element of Kashmiri Islam:

> Islam as practised in the Valley, though it surely stands on the basis of the cardinal principles taught by the Quran, has been deeply influenced by the ancient Kashmir culture...A Kashmiri Muslim shares with his Hindu compatriots many inhibitions, superstitions, idolatrous practises as well as social liberties and intellectual freedoms which are unknown to Islam.[9]

There is some evidence to suggest that a small section of Kashmiri society did achieve a high degree of synthesis between Hindu and Muslim traditions. The famous poetess and saint Lal Ded exemplified this synthesis ['Truth is not a prisoner of mosques and temples and is all-pervading'[10]]. She was followed by Sheikh Nur-ud-Din, commonly referred to as Nand Rishi, whose *rishi* order included both Muslim and Hindu mystics. Sender claims that 'the composite religious strain in Kashmir was still strong' well into the seventeenth century. He cites the *Dabistan-i-Mazahab* of Fani which mentions several sects that welcomed both Hindus and Muslims.[11]

In modern times too perhaps the most obvious example of Kashmiri Hindu-Muslim synthesis is their common reverence of the shrines of the founders of such sects. Tremblay writes that Charar-i-Sharif, Nand Rishi's shrine, 'is regularly visited by Hindus as well as Muslims'.[12] She goes on to say that another reason for religious sites being mutually revered was the fact that many Muslim mosques/shrines were constructed on Hindu sites, and that a place was retained in these for Hindus to worship:

> For example, Kashmiri Pandits are allotted a place outside the Shah-i-Hamdan mosque, near the spring (originally dedicated to the goddess Kali) to offer their prayers. Similarly, the Baha-ud-Din shrine built on the premises of the temple of Pravaresvara still contains a small polished black stone pavilion, supposedly a remnant of the original temple.[13]

With the exception referred to above—revering certain common saints and sites, and possibly participating in Muslim religious celebrations[14]—there is little evidence to suggest that the Brahmans of Kashmir (the only caste not to convert to Islam) adopted any Islamic religious practises. The very fact of their refusal to convert to Islam (many fled the Valley while others opted for death rather than become Muslim) shows how strong their attachment was to their ancestral religion—and this in turn accounts for their resistance to the influence of another faith. A further explanation for the Pandits' impermeability to Islam is that of all the Hindu castes, the Brahmans have traditionally taken their religious duties most seriously (felt most bound by them).

How big a factor was religion in the Kashmiri regional identity? Tremblay argues it was a significant factor: 'The concept of Kashmiriyat does not exclude religion...its emphasis on syncretism and tolerance for other religions has led to the development of indigenous philosophies, practices and traditions of Hinduism and Islam in the Valley, which tend to differentiate both religious communities from their counterparts elsewhere.'[15]

Taking Kashmiri Muslims first, specifically in terms of religious worship (i.e. distinct from culture, language, etc.), there were few major differences between them and non-Kashmiri Muslims. Mosques were constructed somewhat differently in the Valley, and during prayers a portion was (is?) recited aloud which the rest of the Muslim *ummah* read quietly. Purdah was traditionally less rigorously enforced among women in Kashmir than among their sisters elsewhere; rather than covering themselves completely from head to foot they made do with a shawl pushed back behind their ears, i.e. leaving the face exposed. (Note this is not necessarily the case today.) Being *pir parast* ('saint worshippers') was not something unique to Kashmiri Muslims: *pir parast* were—and still are—found in many other parts of the Muslim world, and particularly so in the Indian subcontinent, though, of course, the particular saints revered vary from region to region.[16]

Kashmiri Islam thus differed little from that practised outside the Valley, but the differences between Kashmiri Hinduism—or rather 'Brahmanism'—and that of the rest of India were more pronounced. Sender writes:

> That the Pandits were 'Hindu' was only meaningful in a limited way. That they were 'Hindus' did not mean that there was much in their religious beliefs that they shared with other 'Hindus'. The Kashmiri form of Hinduism was distinctive. Kashmiri Shaivism incorporated numerous Tantric rituals that would be considered unorthodox even in the broad range of permissibly religious behaviour traditionally sanctioned for Brahmans. The carnivorous diet to which the Kashmiris insistently (but later somewhat defensively) clung, for example, was anathema to the vegetarian Brahmans of the plains. In culture as well as in religion, the Pandits of Kashmir differed from the Brahmans *(of the plains)*.[17]

Indeed, according to Sender the differences between Pandits and other Brahmans were so great that 'to view the Pandits as Kashmiris *(is)* more sensible than to view them as "Brahmins".'[18] The laxity of Kashmir's Brahmans was lamented by Hindu visitors to the Valley. Srivara, writing in the sixteenth century, for example, referred to 'some merchants of the city...who followed the customs of the Hindus from their birth [yet] killed cows within the city', and Shuka criticized the Pandits for not carrying out 'the duties of their caste'.[19]

The Pandits' lack of orthodoxy had its origins in the reign of Zain-ul-Abidin, a Muslim ruler who did not discriminate on the basis of religion, but tried to promote the interests of all his citizens. Brahmans who had fled from the persecution of his father, Sikander, were encouraged by Abidin to return to the Valley. Those that did so found themselves facing something of a dilemma: in order to take advantage of the employment opportunities being opened to them they would have to breach some of their traditional religious taboos—in particular those restricting contact with Muslims. They overcame this dilemma by effectively dividing into two groups—those continuing the 'sacred' traditions, and those engaging in more 'secular' pursuits.[20] This functional differentiation initially took place within the same family, e.g. one son would learn Sanskrit while another would learn the court language (Persian), but later it extended to whole families and was enforced by endogamy. This resulted in the emergence of two 'sub-castes' within the Pandit community—gor (from guru) and karkun (workers).

Sender notes that the 'secularisation' of the majority of the community—the karkun soon outnumbered the gor—was facilitated by two factors: 'The geographic isolation of Kashmir from Hindustan made compromise easier. Departure from the orthodox standards of the plains could go unnoticed. Moreover, the Kashmiri Brahmans were priests only to their own community. Outside restraints were not, therefore, forthcoming.'[21]

A point that should be stressed is that while karkun Pandits did certainly relax some of the religious rules governing their behaviour, they did not go so far as to adopt any specifically Islamic practises, 'The behavioural code of the Pandits is permissive but not absolutely so'.[22] In other words, the growing gulf between Pandits and non-Kashmiri Brahmans was not accompanied by a narrowing in the gulf between them and the Valley's Muslims.

In summary, religion played a stronger role in differentiating Pandits from other Hindus, than Kashmiri Muslims from other

Muslims. But it could not be described as a unifying factor between Pandits and Kashmiri Muslims.

Inter-Communal Tolerance and Interaction

The Kashmir Valley was historically renowned for its absence of communal conflict. While other parts of the Indian subcontinent periodically succumbed to serious religious violence, Kashmir remained largely immune to this disease. The lack of Hindu-Muslim fighting has also been taken as proof of *Kashmiriyat*—the conclusion being drawn from it that in Kashmir regional identification was stronger than religious identification; people were Kashmiri first and then Hindu or Muslim.

Four factors can be identified as accounting for the absence of communal conflict in Kashmir. The first of these was the difference in socio-economic niches occupied by Pandits and Muslims. The former were known for their high standard of education and enjoyed a virtual monopoly on court and later government service. Kashmiri Muslims, by contrast, were very poorly educated; they were typically occupied as labourers, agricultural workers and craftsmen. Pandits and Muslims were not, therefore, competing for the same kinds of jobs—had they been doing so the chances of maintaining communal tolerance would have been much reduced. This latter point was demonstrated early in the last century when Kashmiri Muslims started acquiring university education and threatened the Pandits' traditional monopoly on government service—Pandit-Muslim relations deteriorated.

The second factor inhibiting communal conflict in Kashmir was the relative distribution of power and population among Muslims and Hindus. While the Pandits were vastly outnumbered by Kashmiri Muslims, the vulnerability induced by their minority status was mitigated by their priviliged position in the state. As just mentioned, Pandits were highly educated and held most of the administrative posts in the Valley. This advantage was enhanced by the favourable treatment they received from the state's Dogra rulers. Madan writes that when Gulab Singh became ruler of Kashmir in 1846, following almost 500 years of Muslim and Sikh rule, the fortunes of the Pandits significantly improved:

> They were in many respects favoured by the Hindu government as against the Muslims, and were quick to take advantage of these favourable circumstances. By 1947, when Dogra rule came to an abrupt end, the Pandits had improved their political and economic position to such an extent as to be identified with the ruling class of Dogra Hindus in the eyes of Muslims.[23]

One could, therefore, conclude that the reason Kashmiri Pandits never (before the present conflict) came under attack from the majority Muslim population was not the latter's tolerance induced by shared *Kashmiriyat*, but rather their impotence.

The third and perhaps most important reason for greater communal tolerance in Kashmir as compared to the rest of India, was the fact that there was only one Hindu caste in the Valley— that of the Brahmans. The Kashmir Valley was unique in the Indian subcontinent in not having any of the lower castes, these having long ago converted to Islam. Their absence forced the Pandits to make use of Muslims to do those tasks which would have been polluting for them to do themselves. Since the list of jobs which were polluting for Pandits was quite extensive— 'barbers, blacksmiths, cobblers, carpenters, oil-pressers, potters, tonga-drivers, washermen, weavers, etc.'...in fact any kind of manual labour—this produced a high degree of interaction between them and local Muslims. In order to get their hair cut, their houses cleaned, their clothes washed, etc., the Pandits *had* to deal with Muslims. In his study, Madan highlights the forced nature of such contact:

> Though the Pandits avoid intimate physical contact of all kinds with the Muslims, indirect contact is either unavoidable (for example the services of the barber or of the attendant at the cremation ground) or is tolerated (for example, acceptance of milk

from a Muslim cowherd or having one's house cleaned by a Muslim servant)...unavoidability of physical contact with Muslims in certain situations can be taken care of by the performance of routine corrective actions, such as the washing of one's hands.[24]

Such functional interaction was a necessity. The indicator of a sense of shared community would be if there was also social interaction. While the *Kashmiriyat* 'lobby' claim that Pandits and Kashmiri Muslims would commonly visit each other's houses, eat together, attend weddings, etc., T. N. Madan's detailed study of rural Pandits suggests this is painting a somewhat rosy picture:

> The Pandits and Muslims...do not intermarry, nor do they interdine...(they) are linked by co-residence in villages (or urban neighbourhoods) and by economic transactions. There are no marriage or commensal relations between them and physical contact between them is severely restricted.[25]
>
> One loses it (Pandit identity) by totally abandoning the traditional way of life, or the crucial elements of it, as when one eats and lives with Muslims or marries among them.[26]

Education and modernization did break down some of the barriers preventing Hindu-Muslim socialization. The impact of these was obviously greater in cities than villages. Madan, for instance, acknowledges that adherence to food (eating) restrictions was weaker in Srinagar than in the villages he studied. But in both rural and urban settings Pandit-Muslim marriage—the most intimate form of social interaction—was a strict taboo:

> For a Pandit, marriage with a Muslim is permanently polluting, and therefore, out of the question, unless he is willing to leave his household, sever all ties of kinship, and renounce his religion. Such renunciation entails the loss of property rights...The Koran forbids a Muslim to marry a follower of such religions as permit idol worship and do not have a revealed book; and Hinduism falls in this category.[27]

The extent to which Pandit-Muslim marriage was taboo became evident as recently as 1967. A Pandit girl called Parmeshwari converted to Islam and married a Muslim boy, leading to outrage among the Pandit community: 'The Valley became the scene of strong protests and demonstrations in which the Muslims were accused of forcefully converting and kidnapping the girl'.[28]

The fourth factor accounting for the absence of communal violence in Kashmir was the fact that the practice of both Islam and Hinduism there were less orthodox than in the rest of India. It has been commonly observed that as people become more orthodox in their beliefs—'fundamentalist'—their level of tolerance towards others different from themselves decreases. [An obvious illustration of this correlation would be the rise in popular support for the BJP and the destruction of the Babri Masjid at Ayodhya.]

In all of the above reasons there is little to suggest that Kashmiri Muslims and Pandits lived together in harmony because they saw each other as part of the same community or ethnic group.

Descent

The definition of an ethnic group given in the introduction listed language, culture, religion, language, etc., as features that members may well share in common, but not necessarily so. The one element that was considered essential for a group of people to constitute an ethnic group was a belief in common origin and descent. Did Kashmiri Muslims and Pandits see themselves as having a common descent?

Until the advent of Islam to Kashmir the majority of the Valley's population were Hindu. Despite being divided into castes that did not inter-marry, in terms of ethnic identity they saw each other as one. This situation changed after Islam came to the Valley, and particularly after the rule of Sikander—a Muslim king who gave his Hindu subjects the choice of converting to Islam, exile or death. Most non-Brahman Hindus opted for Islam, but among Brahmans this course was generally rejected. Many of them opted to leave the Valley, while many others chose death rather than give up their traditional faith. Madan writes that at the time of Sikander's death (1414) there were reputed to be only eleven Brahmans left alive in Kashmir.[29] Sikander's son, Zain-ul-Abidin, was a more enlightened ruler; he promised his Hindu subjects freedom of worship. As a result many Brahmans returned to Kashmir. Today's Pandits are the descendants of the eleven Brahmans left in Kashmir in 1414 and of the others who returned there from exile. They have carefully preserved their original 'gene pool', neither marrying out of their caste nor out of their ethnic group.

No such exclusivity was maintained by Muslims in the Valley. Throughout Kashmir's history, as new peoples settled in the Valley, they inter-married with the Muslims already there. The result is that present-day Kashmiri Muslims are the descendants of Kashmiri Hindus, but also of Arabs, Persians, etc.

Today, Pandits view themselves as the only 'true' Kashmiris. They see Kashmiri Muslims as of mixed stock, with perhaps some Kashmiri element but also lots of non-Kashmiri ones. They do not accept them as having the same ancestry.

Relations with Non-Kashmiris

In the case of both Kashmiri Muslims and Pandits, they were closer to their non-Kashmiri co-religionists than to each other. Inter-marriage is a good indicator of closeness. [Enloe describes it as the 'bottom line' of ethnicity.[30]] We have already seen that Pandits and Kashmiri Muslims did not inter-marry. Kashmiri Muslims would, however, marry Muslims from other regions of the state. Such inter-regional marriages occurred when suitable marriage partners could not be found locally, or between migrants and locals. While they were by no means the norm, there was no taboo against their taking place.

In the case of Pandits, marriage gives little indication of relative closeness since they would marry neither Kashmiri Muslims nor non-Kashmiri Hindus. However, the favoured treatment they received from the state's Dogra rulers—alluded to above—and the fact that they consistently opposed the political demands of the Kashmiri Muslims, siding instead with Jammu Hindus (discussed in later chapters), suggests they were closer to the latter than the former.

Conclusion

There is much to support the notion of a single Kashmiri community embracing Muslims and Pandits, united by a shared *Kashmiriyat*. There was definitely much that the two groups had in common and that differentiated them from non-Kashmiris: culture, language, religious unorthodoxy, etc.

But when one looks at the critical indicators of shared ethnicity or even community spirit, i.e. social interaction, common descent, mutual regard, it is quite clear that Pandits and Kashmiri Muslims did not see each other as one. The interaction between them was of a purely functional nature, necessitated by the social profile of the Valley. Pandits saw Kashmiri Muslims as the descendants of 'outsiders'. Both Muslims and Pandits were closer to other Muslims and Hindus than to each other. In short, they formed two quite distinct communities, with their own social order, practises and values.

However, the gap between them was far narrower than that between corresponding communities in other parts of the Indian subcontinent. A variety of factors combined to minimize communal conflict in the Valley. One could, therefore, best sum up by saying that Kashmiri Muslims and Pandits formed a harmonious plural society. The essential characteristic of a plural society is that it is comprised of groups that are different but that manage to accommodate their differences and live together amicably. 'Agreement between the two communities is built upon an explicit recognition of differences between them. For the Pandits the Muslims are the "others" or "outsiders" but not strangers and vice versa.'[31]

This then is the 'starting point' when examining the ethnic conflict in Kashmir: two communities who saw each other as different but lived together in harmony. Both had a strong regional as well as religious sense of identity. The many things they had in common could have led to the evolution of a common Kashmiri identity and nationalism. That obviously did not happen. Subsequent chapters will examine what caused the initial differences between Kashmiri Muslims and Pandits to be accentuated and the political manifestations of these.

NOTES

1. Kaul, L.K., and Teng, M.K., 'Human Rights Violations of Kashmiri Hindus', in Thomas, R., (ed), *Perspectives on Kashmir: The Roots of Conflict in South Asia* (Boulder, Westview Press, 1992), p. 178.

2. Puri, Balraj, 'Kashmiriyat: the vitality of Kashmiri identity', *Contemporary South Asia* (4:1, 1995), p. 61.

3. Ibid., p. 61.

4. Punjabi, Riyaz, 'Kashmir: The Bruised Identity' in Thomas, *op. cit.*, p. 137.

5. Mir Abdul Aziz, freelance journalist; interview with author, February 1997, Islamabad.

6. Sender, H., *The Kashmiri Pandits: A Study of Cultural Choice in North India* (Delhi, Oxford Univ. Press, 1988), p. 12.

7. Madan, T.N., *Family and Kinship: A Study of the Pandits of Rural Kashmir* (2nd edition, Delhi, Oxford Univ. Press, 1989), pp. 235–6.

8. Neve and O'Molley cited in Puri, *op. cit.*, p. 61.

9. Bazaz, P. N., *The History of the Struggle for Freedom in Kashmir* (New Delhi, Pamposh, 1954), pp. 91–2, cited in Bhattacharjea, Ajit, *Kashmir: The Wounded Valley* (New Delhi, UBSPD, 1994), p. 36.

10. Ibid., p. 31.

11. Sender, *op. cit.*, p. 37.

12. Tremblay, R.C., 'Kashmir: the Valley's political dynamics', *Contemporary South Asia* (4:1, 1995), p. 87.

13. Ibid.

14. This is suggested by Sender's comment, referring to Pandits, that 'today's Kashmiri children no longer take part in the *tazia* processions in Muharram as their parents once did'. *Op. cit.*, p. xxii.

15.   Tremblay, *op. cit.*, p. 86.

16.   Among the more famous saints revered in the Indian subcontinent are Khwaja Moinuddin Chishti, whose shrine is at Ajmer; Data Ganj Baksh (Ali Hajweiri) who is buried at Lahore; and Khwaja Nizamuddin Awlia whose shrine is in Delhi.

17.   Sender, *op. cit.*, p. 32.

18.   Ibid.

19.   Ibid., p. 26.

20.   'Polarisation meant that the secular world would not threaten the ritual world...Because the two spheres were divorced, a more liberal definition of pollution was made possible for those not engaged in ritual functions.' Ibid., p. 23.

21.   Ibid., p. 23.

22.   Ibid., p. xv.

23.   Madan, *op. cit.*, p. 19.

24.   Ibid., p. 244.

25.   Ibid., p. 192 and p. 236.

26.   Ibid., p. 237.

27.   Ibid., p. 90.

28.   Tremblay, *op. cit.*, p. 87.

29.   Madan, T. N., 'The Social Construction of Cultural Identities in Rural Kashmir', in Madan (ed.), *Muslim Communities of South Asia: Culture, Society and Power* (Revised edition, New Delhi, Manohar, 1995), p. 256.

30.   Enloe, Cynthia, 'Religion and Ethnicity' in Hutchinson and Smith (eds.), *op. cit.* (1996), p. 199.

31.   Ibid., p. 236.

2

HISTORY AND POLITICAL DEVELOPMENTS UP TO 1947

Early History

Rule up to the Dogra Period

Very early Kashmiri history was chronicled by Kalhana, writing in the twelfth century, in his *Rajatarangini* (River of Kings). According to this Kashmir was originally ruled by Buddhists, starting with Ashoka (r. 274–237 BC), a convert from Hinduism, who founded the Kashmiri capital, Srinagar. By the seventh century Buddhist rule had given way to Hindu rule. The two major Hindu dynasties were the Karkota dynasty which ruled until AD 855, and the Utpala dynasty which directly succeeded it. Notable rulers were Lalitaditya (AD 724–760)—who expanded his influence into parts of India and Central Asia, and who built the great sun temple at Martand—and Avantivarman (AD 855–883), first of the Utpalas, who introduced extensive drainage and irrigation systems, in addition to being another great builder and town planner. Hindu rule withstood two attempts by Mahmud of Ghazni (in 1015 and 1021) to bring the Valley under Islamic control. The surrounding mountains and cold climate considerably helped Hindu resistance.

However, by the beginning of the fourteenth century Hindu rule had totally degenerated, and foreign invaders could no longer be repelled. In 1320, Kashmir was conquered by the Mongols, led by Dulacha, who laid it to waste. The Mongols held control only briefly, losing power in the same year to a

Buddhist chief originally from Baltistan, Rinchin. Under the influence of a Sufi divine, Sayyid Bilal Shah (a.k.a. Bulbul Shah), Rinchin converted to Islam and took the name Sultan Sadruddin. His conversion paved the way for the first of three periods of Muslim rule.

In 1339, some time after Sadruddin's death, an adventurer from Swat called Shah Miri seized power and crowned himself Sultan Shamsuddin. The Shah Miri dynasty formed the first major period of Muslim rule, lasting until 1586. In that year Kashmir was conquered by the Mughal Emperor Akbar, and remained in Mughal hands until 1752. The collapse of Mughal power in India permitted the Afghan warlord, Ahmed Shah Durrani, to conquer the Valley. This final Afghan period of Muslim rule was by far the bloodiest and most oppressive. So much so that the—by now predominantly Muslim—population, asked the Punjabi Sikh King, Ranjit Singh, to take over their land. Although Ranjit Singh took Kashmir from the Afghans in 1819, Sikh rule proved to be hardly less bloody. It was to last only twenty-seven years. In 1846, the British defeated Ranjit Singh's successors at the Battle of Sabraon, and captured Lahore. This created a power vacuum in Kashmir, since the British had no desire to administer such a remote territory directly.

In 1820, Ranjit Singh had made a Dogra Rajput, Gulab Singh, Raja of the state of Jammu. At the same time he had given Poonch as a *jagir* to Gulab Singh's brother, Dhyan Singh. Gulab Singh was able to build a small 'empire' on this base: he conquered Ladakh in the 1830s, followed by Baltistan, and later extended his authority into the north-western regions of Gilgit, Hunza, etc., now known as the Northern Areas.

In 1846, Gulab Singh, by then Prime Minister of the Sikh government in Lahore, helped the British cause by failing to send his troops to fight with the Sikhs. Gulab Singh was rewarded, and the British dilemma about the administration of Kashmir solved, by the 1846 Treaty of Amritsar. Under the terms of this Treaty, the British awarded Kashmir to Gulab Singh, together with the title of Maharaja, and in return received from him 7,500,000 Rupees. They also retained supreme control of the Valley.

Gulab Singh died in 1847, and was succeeded by his son, Ranbir Singh, who after his death in 1885, was in turn succeeded by his son, Pratap Singh. Pratap Singh had no sons of his own, and therefore tried to appoint one of Dhyan Singh's Poonch descendants as his heir. The British, however, preferred his nephew, Hari Singh. Their support ensured that when Pratap Singh died in 1925, it was indeed Hari Singh who became Maharaja of Jammu and Kashmir.

In 1935–36 Poonch, which had almost been a State in its own right, became an integral part of Jammu and Kashmir. Its integration was the result of a successful lawsuit in British Indian courts, motivated in large measure by resentment at Pratap Singh's attempt to deny Hari Singh the throne. The acquisition of Poonch marked the last stage in the formation of the pre-Partition state of Jammu and Kashmir.

Religious Development

Kalhana, in the *Rajatarangini*, writes that under the influence of Nagarjuna—a Buddhist philosopher who founded Madhyamika or the Middle Way of Buddhism, and who settled in the Vale in the first century BC—the indigenous people gave up their primitive religious practices and adopted Buddhism. In the eighth century, Vasagupta founded a new religious philosophy called Shaivism or Trikha. This was essentially a fusion of Buddhism with an ancient Vedic faith, and laid stress on monotheism and egalitarianism.

Islam acquired a significant following in Kashmir after the rule of Rinchin Shah in the fourteenth century. Contrary to what one might expect, most conversions did not result from the Muslim rulers using force, but rather were achieved by the preaching of foreign Sufis (mystics), notably the Persian Syed Ali Hamdani. Since most new believers had converted from Hinduism, it is not surprising that Kashmiri Islam retained some

Hindu practices, e.g. as a concession to the former Hindu tradition of audible prayer, the Muslim prayers were also recited aloud—a practice not found anywhere else in the Islamic world.[1] Islam, in turn, exerted an influence on native Hinduism.[2] This 'semi-synthesis' of Hinduism and Islam was personified in Lal Ded, a hermit-poetess who preached the oneness of all religions, the need for communion with God, and renunciation, and was revered by Hindus and Muslims alike. One of Lal Ded's followers, Nand Rishi, founded the *rishi* order which consisted of both Hindu and Muslim devotees united by a common asceticism and love of humanity.

Conversion from Hinduism to Islam was generally painless, but there were some exceptions. Sultan Sikander (r. 1389–1413) tried to force conversions to Islam, and attempted to destroy all vestiges of Hinduism in Kashmir. During his reign many Kashmiri Brahmans (Pandits) fled to other parts of India. But they were enticed back to the Vale by Sikander's son and successor, Zain-ul-Abidin (r. 1420–1470), more commonly referred to as Bud Shah (the Great King). In contrast to his father, Bud Shah welcomed thinkers of all religions to Kashmir, and he rebuilt many temples and shrines.

In summary, over the centuries the Kashmiri population underwent several changes of faith, but these generally came about voluntarily, and were not accompanied by persecution of other religions. Thus, although Buddhism died out in the Valley, a community of Brahmans persisted even after the conversion of most of the population to Islam.

Pre-partition Jammu and Kashmir

Before looking at the history of modern Kashmir and political developments in it, it would be useful to build up a picture of the Valley and the state of which it was part, in the early half of this century. This will be done by examining in turn the state's geography, demography and socio-economic conditions.

Geography

Situated in the northeast of the Indian subcontinent, the state of Jammu and Kashmir occupied a territory of 222,800 sq. km. Comparable in size to Great Britain, it was one of the largest states in India. It consisted of the Valley in the centre, encircled by the regions—clockwise from north—Gilgit, Baltistan, Ladakh, Jammu and Poonch. Its neighbours were Afghanistan (and the Soviet Union, separated only by the small Wakhan tract of Afghan territory) to the north-west, China's Sinkiang Province to the north, Tibet to the east, and British India to the south.

Several mountain ranges cut across Jammu and Kashmir. To the north it is traversed by those ranges that link the Pamirs and Hindu Kush in the west with the Himalayas in the east. The Karakoram range in Baltistan includes the world's second highest mountain, K2. The Tibetan and semi-Tibetan tracts extend into a corner of Ladakh. Finally, cutting across the southeast corner of the state, and separating Kashmir Valley from the level plateaus of Jammu, is the Pir Panjal range.

The Indus River and two of its tributaries pass through the state. The Indus does so in an arc from its Tibetan source in the east towards the Punjab in the west. The Jhelum River actually has its source in Jammu, passing from there into the Kashmir Valley. The Chenab, third of the Punjab's 'five rivers', originates elsewhere in India but passes through Jammu and Poonch. Another Indus tributary, the Ravi, for part of its length marks the border between Jammu and Punjab. These rivers are, of course, the life-blood of the Punjab.

Turning to major highways, the only road within the state linking Jammu and Srinagar was the Banihal Road. Since this had to go over the Banihal Pass in the Pir Panjals, it used to be snowbound in winter. Srinagar was linked to Rawalpindi (now in Pakistan) via the Jhelum Valley Road. Besides the Banihal Road two other main roads led from Jammu, one towards Sialkot (now in Pakistan) and the other towards Pathankot (now in Indian Punjab). The latter was the only road from post-1947

India to the state. The only rail link was a short line from Jammu to Sialkot.

Owing to its cool climate the Kashmir Valley attracted many tourists in the summer. It was also the principal area of cultivation in the state, the main agricultural produce being rice and fruit. Much of the state's timber and other exports passed through the Valley to what is now Pakistani Punjab. Kashmir was renowned for its crafts, notably shawl-making and carpet-weaving, as well as walnut wood carving and *papier mache*.

Demography

The population of Jammu and Kashmir was very heterogeneous—mostly as a consequence of the state's piecemeal formation. According to the 1941 Census, the total population of the state was 4,021,616.[3] In terms of religion this divided into:

Muslims	3,073,450 (>75%)
Hindus	807,549 (¬20%)
Sikhs	50,662[4]
Buddhists	38,074
Christians	3,079
Tribals	29,374

Jammu and Kashmir's population was heterogeneous not only in terms of religion, but also linguistically, culturally and racially. Consider its different regions in turn:

Kashmir Valley

With a total population of 1,728,600, the Valley was predominantly (over 90 per cent) Muslim, but had a significant Pandit (Kashmiri Brahman) community. The main language spoken was Kashmiri, part of the Dardic linguistic family unique to the mountainous areas of the north-west. The Valley had its own culture—wearing the *pheran*, Kashmiri tea, using a *kangri* to keep warm, etc. The Muslims mostly followed the Sunni sect, but some of their religious practices were unique to Kashmir, e.g. the absence of domes on mosques. Approximately 5 per cent of the Valley's Muslims were Shia, and there was also a small Ahmadiyya community.

Jammu Province

Jammu was the ruling Dogra dynasty's heartland, with a population of 1,561,580. The centre of the province was dominated by Hindus and Sikhs, but Muslim populations in the periphery (Mirpur and Riasi districts) constituted a majority (61.3 per cent). These Muslims were ethnically and culturally closer to those of the neighbouring Punjab, than to those in the Vale. The Hindus of Jammu, unlike those of Kashmir who were virtually all Brahman, were of various castes and races.[5] Dogri and Punjabi were the main languages spoken in Jammu.

Poonch

The population of this region was predominantly Muslim. Separated from Kashmir by the Pir Panjals, the inhabitants racially, linguistically, and culturally resembled Punjabi Muslims. Like the Punjabis, and unlike the Kashmiris, Poonchis were traditional soldiers.

Baltistan

The 160,000 inhabitants of this region were almost all Muslim as well. However, they differed from the state's other Muslims in that they followed the Twelver branch of Shi'ism, and racially were of Tibetan stock. They also spoke their own language, Balti.

Ladakh

This was the most sparsely populated region of Jammu and Kashmir, with a population of just 40,000 spread over a considerable area. Most of the inhabitants were again of Tibetan stock, but were Buddhist.

'Northern Areas'

This term is actually of relatively recent origin: it refers to the regions of Astor, Gilgit, Hunza, Iskhuman, Nagar and Yasin. The total population of these regions was 40,000. The majority were Muslim but like the Baltistanis followed Twelver Shi'ism rather than Sunni-ism, with the exception of Hunza where most were Ismaili. Apart from speaking Dardic languages there were no significant cultural links between these people and the Kashmiris.

Socio-economic Conditions at the Turn of the Century

Dogras

Concentrated in Jammu, the Dogras naturally benefitted from their kinship with the ruling family. They held the best positions in both the Military and Civil Services. While traditionally renowned for their fighting ability, they possessed few skills to justify the latter positions.[6] Second to the State, they were also the major landowners. Dogra domination was resented both by Muslims, and somewhat surprisingly, by Kashmiri Pandits (see below). Muslim and Pandit resentment of the Dogras was reciprocated: 'The Dogras have always regarded Jammu as their home and Kashmir as the conquered country…they established a sort of Dogra oligarchy in the state in which all non-Dogra communities and classes were given the humble places of inferiors.'[7]

Pandits

In contrast to the martial Dogras, the Pandits were renowned for their intelligence. When a bureaucratic form of administration was introduced in the state by Ranbir Singh, and developed by his son Pratap, officials had to be drawn from the Punjab because so few locals possessed the necessary qualifications. But the Pandits were quick to make up for this weakness—Pandit Hargopal Kaul, together with Annie Besant, founded the Hindu College (later renamed Sri Pratap College) at Srinagar in 1906— and then campaigned successfully for state employment to be restricted to state subjects only.[8] But they never managed to overcome Dogra domination of the most senior positions, remaining confined to the minor, clerical administrative posts. This led them to have a resentful attitude towards the Dogras: 'The Pandits…do not consider him (Hari Singh) as one of their own. In language, in mode of living, and in his descent he has nothing in common with the people of Kashmir. They have always felt aggrieved and felt discontented with the policy of the Government which excessively favoured the people of Jammu Province, especially the Rajputs, at their expense.'[9] The *Manchester Guardian* noted, however, that the gulf between Pandits and Dogras 'is bridged by the Pandits' feeling that Dogra (Hindu) rule is better anyhow than Moslem rule, and that the Dogras are their bulwark against the danger of Muslim aggression.'[10] Note that in the minor positions occupied by the Pandits they faced little competition.

Muslims

The Muslims of Jammu and Kashmir were backward in almost every sense. Militarily, after years of foreign domination, they were notorious for their lack of fighting spirit. To ensure this never re-emerged, the Dogras followed the example of their Sikh predecessors and barred Kashmiris from military service.[11] They were also forbidden to possess arms.

Economically, the combination of the State's exorbitant tax collection policy, the ban on Kashmiri land ownership, and widespread corruption by minor officials, ensured that the Muslims never advanced above a 'mere survival' level. The trend for exorbitant tax collection had been set by Gulab Singh, determined to recover the Rs 75 lakhs he had payed the British for Kashmir,[12] and continued by his successors. Not only were tax levels very high, but virtually nothing was exempt from taxation: crops, fruit, grazing for animals, handicrafts (shawls, carpets, etc.), marriage ceremonies, labour services—including grave-digging and even prostitution!

In education also, the Muslims lagged far behind the Hindu communities. There were few opportunities for them to acquire an education, and even where these existed the Muslims were— at least initially—very slow to make use of them. As a consequence very few were employed in the State administration.[13] By the mid-twenties this situation had improved somewhat in that the Muslims had become aware of the importance of education, and were clamouring for greater opportunities to acquire this, and for a higher proportion of State jobs. Initially, Muslim demands for more educational facilities were rejected, but in 1916 an Educational Officer with the Government of India, Sharp, was asked by the State to examine Muslim grievances. Although the recommendations of Sharp's report were accepted by the Maharaja, this was of little practical effect because his ministers refused to implement them.

Among the other forms of official discrimination Muslims faced were a ban on cow slaughter, which was generally tolerated, and a ban on the *khutba*[14] and property disqualification for apostasy[15] which were much resented. Of greater practical consequence were the numerous forms of 'unofficial' discrimination. These included hindrance in public religious worship, especially ceremonies, and the notorious *begar* system whereby the State could force its subjects to work on State projects such as road-building. Those 'recruited' had no right to refuse and received little or no payment for their services. Further, most such work could only be carried out during the summer months—when the peasants most needed to be at home to tend their crops. *Begar* was officially abolished in accordance with the recommendations of Sir Walter Lawrence (Settlement Officer 1889–95), but in practice, the system continued virtually unabated. Perhaps the greatest Muslim grievance was against something 'for which it is impossible to quote chapter and verse, and difficult even to produce adequate evidence'[16]—the general bias of Hindu officials towards their co-religionists. The *Times* of 5 December 1931 writes:

> The grievances of Kashmiri Muslims are of long standing...State ownership of all agricultural land, the forest administration, police severities, official control over the sale of silk cocoons, unequal taxation, and the partial payment of land revenue in kind instead of cash—all these are matters of dispute...[*But*] the pinch of the shoe is felt in its daily use...when the village schoolmasters, the civil and criminal judges, the revenue and forest officers—in fact, the local representation of every department are predominantly Hindu among a Moslem population, friction is inevitable, and is generated by every word of asperity and every inconsiderate action.[17]

Early Political Activity

Hindus

Early Hindu political activity had a definite regional basis, with that in Jammu being separate from that in the Valley. Considering Jammu first, under the influence of various social and religious reform movements active within British India, notably the Arya Samaj, the Dogra Sabha[22] formed there in 1903. This body was very conservative in its outlook, both with respect to religion and to politics. The only 'radical' demands it made were for the Government to employ natives of the state rather than outsiders, and for tighter definitions of the term 'State Subject'. With the fulfilment of these demands by the mid-1920s, the Dogra Sabha effectively died out.

Turning to Kashmir, the Pandits success in acquiring education, and their campaign for State Subject—only employment, have already been mentioned. The employment campaign was principally conducted by a group formed in 1915 called the Yuvak Sabha. This was ostensibly a 'religious' organization, but its main purpose—as demonstrated by the employment campaign—was to safeguard the 'material' interests of the Pandit community. The Yuvak Sabha, though it did engage in politics, did not advocate radical reform. On the contrary, it wished to retain the status quo, and neither it nor the Dogra Sabha attacked the Maharaja.

In addition, also largely influenced by the Arya Samaj, a number of reform movements emerged towards the end of the nineteenth century. The Bishen Sabha, named after the social reform activist Pandit Bishen Narayan Dar, reflected his liberal views on some religious practices, e.g. advocated an end to the 'taboo' on foreign travel. The main organization—and the one that persisted into the twentieth century—was the Dharma Sabha. Pandit Hargopal Kaul was the driving force behind this movement. In contrast to the Bishen Sabha, it was strictly orthodox in its approach to religion. However, it was strongly in favour of Hindus (including women) acquiring education (Kaul co-founded the Hindu College in 1906), and it pushed for certain social reforms. Of the latter the most significant in terms of political consequences, was the Dharma Sabha's campaign to allow widow re-marriage. This campaign aroused strong emotions, and prompted the formation of two well-organized groups of mainly young men—one in favour, the other opposed. The latter was the Dharma Sabha, which after Kaul's death had become far more conservative. The former was referred to as the 'Fraternity'. Founded in 1930, it initially aimed to reform Hindu society, not only by allowing widow re-marriage but also, for example, by encouraging women's education. The Fraternity was later to change both its aims, and its name (to Sanatan Dharma Young Men's Association); the background to these transformations will be considered below.

Muslims

Mirwaiz-i-Kashmir

The Muslims of Jammu and Kashmir could be divided into two groups, on the basis of the two prominent traditional religious leaders they followed. These were the Mirwaiz of the Jama Masjid in Srinagar (Ahmed Ullah d. 1931, followed by Muhammad Yusuf Shah) and the (lesser) Mirwaiz of the Khanqah-i-Moalla, the shrine of Syed Ali Hamdani (Ahmed Hamadani). The first of these positions emerged at the turn of the century as a consequence of the preaching of Rasul Shah, a 'Wahabi'ist' who condemned the widespread practice of deifying saints and paying homage at their shrines. Eventually, this preaching became a movement, by 1901, with a hereditary leader referred to as Mirwaiz. The Mirwaiz-i-Kashmir rapidly became the most influential Muslim leader in the State. Some idea of the position's importance can be gauged from the fact that over 100,000 people were reported to have taken part in Ahmed Ullah's funeral procession in 1931.

The second 'Mirwaiz-ship' emerged when Rasul Shah's puritanism was resisted by those who wanted to maintain the old traditions. These *ahli-aitqad* (believers in six shrines) were led by the head of the most famous shrine, the Khanqah-i-Moalla, who also came to be referred to as Mirwaiz. Followers of the Mirwaiz of the Jama Masjid were known as *Kota*, those of the Khanqah-i-Moalla Mirwaiz as *Khanqahshia* or *Cheka*.

A certain amount of rivalry probably always marked relations between the holders of these positions—competing as they were for control of the same community—but this became very intense during the time of Mirwaiz Hamadani, after he permitted an Ahmadiyya leader to preach from the Khanqah-i-Moalla. Mirza Kamalul-Din was the head of the Ahmadiyya community, and he visited Jammu and Kashmir in 1924.[18] Orthodox Muslims generally view the Ahmadis (Qadianis) as heretics and Ahmed Ullah, the Mirwaiz-i-Kashmir at that time, had forbidden Kamalul-Din from preaching at the Jama Masjid. In addition, he ordered Mirwaiz Hamadani to ban him from the Khanqah-i-Moalla. Perhaps swayed by Kamalul-Din's stress on the unity of the Muslims, or perhaps simply because he was unwilling to obey his rival, Hamadani ignored this order—thereby arousing Ahmed Ullah's anger and intensifying Kota-Cheka rivalry.

What was the relevance of all this to politics? Its indirect relevance was two-fold. Firstly, Rasul Shah's reform—or rather revivalist—movement gave Muslims a greater sense of self-consciousness as a religious community. And since his purification drive was not targeted against just saint-worship, but also against all 'idolatrous' (i.e. Hindu) religious practices, it made Muslims more aware of their distinctiveness from Hindus (non-Muslims generally). Secondly, for perhaps the first time in Jammu and Kashmir's history, the State's Muslims were united behind a single leader (more accurately, behind one of two influential leaders). Previously they had followed numerous lesser *Pirs*. This unification laid the foundations for later communal political activity.

Rasul Shah's other activities had the same indirect effect of promoting group unity and organization among Muslims—characteristics which could later be used for political purposes. These other activities were primarily educational. The Anjuman-i-Nusratul-Islam was formed in 1905 to promote both religious and modern (non-religious) education among Muslims. Organized into committees and councils, the Anjuman either set up new schools or took over the running of existing institutions. In all of these, Islamic and modern subjects were taught side by side. In the 1920s, the Anjuman turned its efforts towards social reform, but achieved little success. It did, however, set a precedent of group organization as a means to achieve Muslim demands. It was succeeded by numerous other associations active within the Muslim community: Anjuman-i-Hamdard-i-Islam founded by Punjabi-speaking Muslims, and the Anjuman-i-Islamia in Jammu to name two.

Turning to direct relevance, neither the Mirwaiz-i-Kashmir nor the Khanqah-i-Moalla Mirwaiz were content to remain as religious leaders, pronouncing only on religious matters. Both soon became directly involved in Kashmiri politics. Ahmed Ullah, for example, was one of the signatories of the 1924 Memorandum by 'Representatives of Kashmiri Muslims' to the Viceroy, Lord Reading. This was a list of 'non-religious' demands for better opportunities and rights for Muslims.[19] The Mirwaiz' involvement in politics was to increase over time and the rivalry between their followers carried into the political arena.

'Representatives of Kashmiri Muslims'

This was not an official organization; rather it consisted of growing numbers of leading Muslims who periodically put forward lists of demands for the betterment of the Muslim community. The first Memorandum issued by the Representatives (then five in number) concerned the educational backwardness of Muslims. This was blamed on Hindu officers, whom they accused of failing to promote, and further, of actively suppressing Muslim education. Their main demand was that a Muslim officer, or failing that a European, be appointed head of the Education Department—at the time a Hindu, Narayan Das, was in charge. The following year, the Representatives (expanded to thirty-seven) issued a second Memorandum. This was presented to the Viceroy's Private Secretary. Besides better education, it pressed for greater Muslim employment in the State Services, and for the appointment of two Muslim ministers. The Representatives' third Memorandum in 1924 was presented to the Viceroy himself, then Lord Reading, during his visit to Jammu and Kashmir. A recent strike at the State Silk Factory in Srinagar[20] had already drawn the attention of the British (through their Resident in Kashmir) to grievances felt by the State's Muslims. The third Memorandum articulated these grievances. Apart from changes in the Silk Factory, and long-standing complaints about education and employment, it demanded land reform, abolition of the *begar* system, hand-over of all Government-held mosques to the community, and the setting up of a representative Legislative Assembly. The

Government's response was to punish three of the Representatives, by either exiling them or by confiscating their property.[21] The significance of the Representatives lay not so much in the practical results they were able to achieve—quite frankly, pretty negligible—but in the fact that they put forward *political, non-religious* demands on behalf of a *religious* community.

Reading Room

The various efforts to promote education among Muslims bore fruit in the 1920s when the first Kashmiri degree-holders began returning to the State, having graduated from institutions in British India such as the Aligarh Muslim University. During the course of their education many of these young men had been exposed to new, liberal ideas, as well as to the various political movements sweeping across India.[22] Returning to Jammu and Kashmir they found themselves back under a 'semi-feudal' regime, and with access to jobs—which their qualifications should have opened up—denied to them. A group of these graduates started meeting regularly at a house in Fateh Kadal, Srinagar, and from this evolved the 'Fateh Kadal Reading Room Party.' 'The Reading Room Party served as a rendezvous where we discussed national issues, and amongst other things, deplored the existing conditions.... We wanted to open a window to the world to apprise it of the wretched conditions in Kashmir.'[23] Articles written by members, highlighting Muslim grievances, were published in British Indian Muslim newspapers such as *Siyasat* and *Muslim Outlook*. When the Government banned these from the State, they used another paper, *Inqilab*, and after that was also banned they started printing pamphlets.

In 1930, while the Maharaja was abroad, the Reading Room issued a Memorandum to the Regency Council running Jammu and Kashmir. In it they complained of 'discriminatory' practices, designed to keep Muslims out of State employment.[24] The Council responded by inviting them to present their case. One of the group's two representatives chosen for this purpose was Muhammed Abdullah.[28]

Sheikh Muhammed Abdullah was born in 1905, the son of a Kashmiri *pashmena* (wool) merchant. After obtaining his F.Sc. he hoped to study medicine, but failed to win a State scholarship. So instead he did his B.Sc. from Islamia College, Lahore, and secured a second division M.Sc. in chemistry from Lahore. On returning to Jammu and Kashmir he again failed to win a scholarship, this time for further study abroad, and also could not get a gazetted appointment in the State Service. Abdullah saw both these failures as examples of Government discrimination against Muslims. His political activism had started in Lahore with the publication of a letter listing Muslim grievances in *Muslim Outlook*, but really took off when he became involved in the Fateh Kadal Reading Room meetings.

A large measure of Abdullah's initial popularity among Muslims was due not to his political speeches, but to his skilled recitation of the Quran. He writes in his autobiography: 'My style of recitation had become very popular...People were thrilled to hear my voice...I [also] used to recite Iqbal's poetry which moved them deeply.'[25] Schofield cites a contemporary of Abdullah: 'The masses were too downtrodden, too ignorant to be awakened by mere politics. They followed him as a religious leader, who, in the early days lived amongst them. This is how he was so successful in motivating them.'[26]

While the 1930 meeting with the Regency Council produced no results, the Reading Room and even more so, Sheikh Abdullah, went on to play a very prominent role in Kashmiri politics.

A similar organization to the Fateh Kadal Reading Room Party was formed in Jammu in 1922. Called the Young Men's Muslim Association, its aims were identical to those of the Reading Room, namely to improve the conditions of the Muslim community. One of its leading figures was Chaudhri Ghulam Abbas who, like Abdullah, was to feature prominently in later developments.

13 July 1931: Turning Point

The events of this day were the culmination both of a number of recent incidents mainly involving Jammu Muslims, and of the longer-term sense of grievance among Muslims throughout the State. Causes of the latter have been described above. The incidents in Jammu included the alleged demolition of a mosque in Riasi by the Government; at another site Muslims being prevented from praying; banning of the *khutba* in a Jammu mosque by police on 29 April 1931; and an incident on 4 July between a Muslim police constable and his Hindu superior, in which the latter allegedly threw/tore up a copy of the Quran. Taken together, these incidents produced the impression within the Kashmir Valley, that in neighbouring Jammu Islam was being deliberately attacked by the State—'Islam in danger!'[27] Posters describing the events in Jammu, issued by the Young Men's Muslim Association, and denunciations by religious leaders helped fuel the Kashmiri Muslims' sense of outrage. The result was widespread public protests.

In response to the Muslims' protests G. Wakefield, Senior Member of the State Council, invited representatives of both Kashmiri and Jammu Muslims to put their demands before the Maharaja. After a public meeting on 25 June, at which seven Kashmir representatives were selected, and after they had departed,[28] a Pathan cook named Abdul Qadir made an impromptu, highly 'inflammatory' speech condemning Hindus in general, and Hari Singh's rule in particular. He was immediately arrested on charges of sedition. Qadir's trial provided a fresh focus for Muslim anger. Such were the crowds when proceedings started at the Srinagar Sessions Court on 6 July, that the Government ordered the session to be moved to Srinagar Central Jail and held in camera. When the session resumed there on 13 July, a crowd of some 7000 gathered outside and demanded entry into the jail. Scuffles broke out between the crowd and the police; the latter eventually opened fire on the crowd killing twenty-one.[31] As the bodies of the dead were being carried in a procession to the Jama Masjid, anti-

Hindu riots broke out in some other parts of Srinagar. The worst violence took place at Maharaj Ganj where Hindu shops were looted and three Hindus killed. Altogether some 163 people were injured.[29]

Before considering the consequences of the events of 13 July 1931, some attention should be paid to the underlying causes of those events. Though on the surface these events were prompted by religious concerns, it would really be more accurate to describe their causes as socio-economic in nature. The Muslims' educational backwardness and their lack of both socio-economic and political clout has already been described. So too has the community's early forays into politics, which showed that dissatisfaction at their situation had been building up among the Muslims for some time. It was inevitable that at some point something would have triggered this dissatisfaction into looking for more concrete, outward expression. Furthermore, it would not be unreasonable to assert that this trigger could just as likely have been a 'secular' issue as a religious one—a repetition of the shooting at demonstrators involved in the 1924 Silk Factory Strike, for instance. Certainly, the intensity of protest over a secular issue would not have been as great as that over 'Islam in danger,' but that some kind of popular protest would have occurred is beyond doubt. Therefore, the fact that the actual trigger—the alleged abuses in Jammu—was religious in nature, was almost coincidental.

In summary, the real underlying cause of the demonstrations in Kashmir, that culminated in the Jail protest, was Muslim anger and frustration at their community's poor socio-economic status. And the real target of their anger was not the Hindu community—despite the attacks on them—but the State. As the British Resident in Kashmir at the time noted: 'The tenseness of Muhammedan feeling is rather anti-Darbar than anti-Hindu.'[30]

Turning to the consequences of the demonstrations and Jail protest, 13 July 1931 could be described as marking a turning point in the history of Jammu and Kashmir with respect to: one, relations between the Maharaja and his people, and, two, Hindu-Muslim relations. The date was also to prove highly significant with respect to external (British Indian) interest in the affairs of Jammu and Kashmir—considered separately below. Finally, the events of July 1931 had a profound influence on the course of politics in Jammu and Kashmir. This aspect will also later be considered separately.

Maharaja-People Relations

The events of 13 July showed that the notorious 'docility' of the Kashmiri people could no longer be taken for granted. Mere use of force and repressive measures by the State would not suffice to control the population. Instead, it was obvious that the State would have to make some concessions. The Government began on 14 July by announcing the setting up of a Commission of Enquiry into the previous day's incidents.[31] The Dalal Commission, named after its chairman Barjor Dalal, was to examine the appropriateness of the actions taken by the authorities to deal with the disturbances.[32] The enquiry was boycotted by the Muslims, who argued that their imprisoned leaders should be released first, but they did take part in another Commission set up in November 1931. Chaired this time by a British officer, the Glancy Commission was to enquire into the general grievances of Muslims in Kashmir.[33] In its report, submitted on 22 March 1932, the Commission dismissed some Muslim complaints, e.g. concerning the apostasy law,[34] but generally upheld those concerning taxes (especially land revenue), the *begar* system, corruption among officials and the lack of State employment. On the subject of education it urged Muslims to take greater advantage of the opportunities provided by the Government. Its most important recommendation was that the Government make efforts to ensure all communities were fairly represented in the State Service. The Maharaja accepted all the Commission's recommendations.

Following the submission of his report, Glancy again found himself in the position of chairman, this time of the Kashmir Conference on Constitutional Reforms. In its report it recommended the setting up of a legislative assembly, the main features of which were to be: limited powers to make laws; a mixture of elected and nominated members with election of the former for three years by 10 per cent of the population; and separate electorates with seat numbers weighted in favour of Hindus.[35] These recommendations for limited popular representation were also accepted by the Maharaja. Elections were held on 3 September, and the 'Praja Sabha' duly inaugurated on 17 October 1934. In February 1939, the Assembly's composition was changed such that elected members, for the first time, formed a majority.

We thus see that over a period of less than ten years, the Maharaja suffered marked erosion of his powers—at least theoretically—in favour of the people.[36] Obviously, Jammu and Kashmir was still far from an ideal democracy, indeed it was distant even from the power 'sharing' arrangements of British India, but compared to the earlier days of autocratic Dogra rule it had come a long way. Note that virtually all concessions were made by the Maharaja under force of public pressure—a trend initiated by the 13 July protests against the State.

Hindu-Muslim Relations

It was stated above that the real target of Muslim anger in the July 1931 protests was the Government of Jammu and Kashmir. Some of that anger was, however, taken out on Kashmir's Hindu community, and 13 July could therefore be said to mark the beginning of inter-communal violence in the Kashmir Valley. Until that time Pandits and Kashmiri Muslims had largely lived together in harmony, and Hindu-Muslim clashes of the kind so often seen in parts of British India were unknown there. Such clashes did not become commonplace after 13 July, but they did periodically recur—there was further Hindu-Muslim rioting in September and again in November 1931. Communal violence had entered the vocabulary of Hindu-Muslim relations in Kashmir.

It could be argued that Hindu-Muslim clashes in the Valley were inevitable once Muslim political agitation started. The reasons for this are twofold: one, the rule against which the Muslims were protesting was that of a Hindu dynasty; two, the educational and employment opportunities that the Muslims coveted were enjoyed by the Pandits. Put another way, class and religious cleavages in Kashmir coincided. The consequence of such coincidence was that a conflict between 'haves' and 'have nots' would—did—also come to be seen as one between 'oppressed' Muslims and 'exploitative' Hindus. Bazaz writes:

> The movement of 1931 was a spontaneous mass uprising. It had political and economic causes behind it...[But] People are religion ridden. It was therefore not difficult for the Muslim bourgeoisie to give the movement a religious colouring and make the Muslim masses believe that they had suffered because the unbelievers were the rulers of the State and dominated in every walk of life.[37]

That the trigger sparking off Muslim protests was a *religious* issue, served as a catalyst for inter-communal violence—it speeded up the onset of a phenomenon that would have appeared sooner or later anyway.

Finally, though the principle reason for inter-communal rivalry in Kashmir was socio-economic grievances, it was exacerbated by a number of other factors. Most notable of these was encouragement by Muslim and later Hindu groups in British India. Also significant was the fact that the nationalist movement within British India—despite the efforts of the Congress—was characterized as much by Hindu versus Muslim as by anti-British feelings. A third factor was the reaction (resistance) to Muslim demands for better opportunities by the Hindu community.

External Interest

All-India Muslim Kashmir Committee

Muslims of Kashmiri origin living in the Punjab had been taking a keen interest in developments in their native state for some time. After the crisis of 13 July they organized themselves into a formal group called the All-India Muslim Kashmir Committee. The President of the new organization was Mirza Bashir Ahmed, head of the Ahmadiyya community at Qadian. Its other leading member was Muhammad Iqbal, the Muslim poet-philosopher and drafter of what later became known as the 'Pakistan Resolution'. The principle aim of the Kashmir Committee was to draw the attention of the British Indian Government to the grievances of Muslims within Jammu and Kashmir, in the hope that it would then exert pressure on the Darbar to carry out reforms.[38] Specifically with respect to the events of 13 July, the Committee demanded the setting up of an independent Commission of Enquiry, and it decided to commemorate 'Kashmir Day' on 14 August, to express sympathy with the jailed 'martyrs.'[39]

The All-India Muslim Kashmir Committee was prevented from becoming a major force by the fact that—like the Muslim community in Jammu and Kashmir itself—it was plagued by the Qadiani problem. With the head of the Qadianis as its President, it was viewed by Mirwaiz Yusuf Shah and his followers as a Qadiani organization. (That Sheikh Abdullah was in close touch with the Kashmir Committee, was taken by Mirwaiz Yusuf Shah as further 'proof' that he was a member of the Ahmadi sect.) Iqbal eventually resigned from the Committee over the Qadiani question, returning a month later to become its President only after Mirza Bashir Ahmed had been forced to vacate the post. But by then the Committee had largely lost its influence.

The main significance of the All-India Muslim Kashmir Committee lay in its encouragement of the Muslims of Jammu and Kashmir to mobilize politically *as Muslims*—it was one of the driving forces behind the formation of the Muslim Conference (see below). In doing so, the Committee was merely passing on what had by then become an established concept in British India, namely that Hindus, Muslims, etc., formed not only distinct religious but also *political* communities. Just as Iqbal and an increasing number of his co-religionists in British India view the Muslims there as a single political constituency, so did they see Jammu and Kashmir's Muslims as both a religious community and a political group. More importantly, they passed this perception on to the Jammu and Kashmir Muslims themselves.

Anjuman Ahrar-i-Islam

In contrast to the All-India Muslim Kashmir Committee which favoured a constitutional approach in its efforts to improve conditions for the state's Muslim community, this second Punjabi organization opted for more direct—and violent—action. Also referred to as the Majlis-i-Ahrar, its leader was Mazhar Ali. The Anjuman was formed well before 13 July 1931, but until then had largely confined its activities to British India. After the jail incident it became active in Jammu and Kashmir as well. It seems unlikely that in doing so, the group (or at least its leaders) were motivated by heart-felt concern for the state's Muslims. For the Ahrars, involvement in Kashmir was a purely religious affair—an opportunity for them to demonstrate what devout Muslims they were, by helping 'their brothers fight Hindu oppression'.[40]

One consequence of this was that their activities were sometimes resented just as much by the Muslim Conference as by the Maharaja's Government.[41] For instance, after the Glancy Commission's recommendations were accepted by the Maharaja, Muslims within the State welcomed the move and suspended their agitation. The Ahrars, however, continued organizing *jathas* (bands of Muslim demonstrators) to enter Jammu Province from the Punjab.[42] Another reason for the rivalry between the Anjuman and the Muslim Conference was, for the most part, the perennial Qadiani issue. The highly orthodox Ahrars shared the Mirwaiz-i-Kashmir's hatred of the sect. They believed that Muslim agitation from within Jammu and Kashmir was instigated by Qadianis, and thus could never bring themselves to wholly endorse it.

The Majlis-i-Ahrar mobilized its followers in Punjab by telling them that demonstrations by their 'Muslim brothers' in Jammu and Kashmir were being brutally suppressed. This reinforced the impression already given by the Punjabi Muslim press that Muslims within the state were suffering all kinds of discrimination. Alleged restrictions on religious worship, e.g. banning of the *khutba* and *azan*, and the tearing up of the Quran, had received widespread publicity in the province, and predictably, aroused great anger among Punjabi Muslims. Thus, the Ahrars had no difficulty recruiting for their *jathas*. These *jathas* began entering Jammu Province from early October 1931, but the most incursions took place in November. Their presence served to encourage anti-Government demonstrations by Jammu Muslims, as well as to incite communal violence. The killing of twenty-five Muslims by State troops on 21 January 1932, inflamed what was already a very tense situation. The Maharaja was forced to ask for British military assistance in suppressing the disturbances and expelling the Ahrars. This was readily given, and the situation brought under control.

The role of the Anjuman-i-Islam in encouraging Muslim antagonism towards Hindus within Jammu and Kashmir is thus quite apparent. Since communalism breeds itself, Muslim communalism and anti-Hindu violence provoked a reaction of *Hindu* communalism and *anti-Muslim* violence, which in turn provoked further Muslim communalism and so on. The Ahrars could, therefore, be described as having acted as catalysts in a 'chain reaction' of communalization—one which continued to 'run' long after they themselves had been removed from the state.

Nehru; Indian National Congress;
All-India States People's Conference

During the early 1930s, those involved in the nationalist movement in British India began taking an interest in political developments in Jammu and Kashmir. The events of 13 July, of course helped draw their attention to the state. Probably the greatest interest was evinced by the leader of the Indian National Congress, Pandit Jawaharlal Nehru. The reason for his interest will be apparent from his name: Nehru came from a family of Kashmiri Brahmans who had migrated to Delhi, but had 'preserved' their Pandit blood intact. Though he himself had never lived in the State, and hardly ever visited it, Nehru nevertheless identified strongly with his ancestral homeland.[43]

Initially, the Indian National Congress' policy was one of non-interference in the affairs of the Indian States. This policy was dictated by the practical difficulties of campaigning on two fronts simultaneously, i.e. against both the British and the Indian Princes. It was also based on the consideration that while the States' rulers were far from democratic, they were at least Indian. Direct Congress involvement was, therefore, ruled out, but the party did help found, and lent its support to, a separate organization, the All-India States People's Conference. Set up in 1927, the aim of this organization was to achieve responsible government in the states through representative institutions, and to retain the ruling Princes as nominal Heads of State.[44]

But as the nationalist struggle in British India proceeded it became apparent to those involved that—since the Indian States were interspersed throughout the British Provinces—any scheme for future government of the latter would not be feasible unless the former were also taken into consideration. Various proposals for a federal arrangement were put forward, notably the Government of India Act of 1935.[45] But when these were frustrated, largely by the Princes' refusal to make concessions to a federal government, Congress changed its policy with respect to the States. From that point, freedom for the people of the States became just as much a Congress goal as freedom for

Indians under British rule. Nehru made clear the party's new approach in his presidential address at the annual session of the People's Conference:

> there is no independence in the States and there is going to be none, for it is hardly possible geographically and it is entirely opposed to the conception of a united, free India...the time approaches when the final solution has to come—a Constituent Assembly of all the Indian people, framing the Constitution of a free and democratic India.[46]

Thus, after 1938, Congress workers were allowed to actively participate in political movements in the Indian States. Not surprisingly, Nehru became most active in the politics of Jammu and Kashmir. The Indian National Congress', and especially Nehru's, role will be considered in more detail below. Suffice it to say for now that—in contrast to the Punjabi organizations just described which promoted communal politics—the Congress encouraged Kashmiris to join them in the pursuit of non-communal, Indian nationalist politics.

Hindu Mahasabha

The 'ideology' of this organization was *Hindutva*, a doctrine developed by Vinayak Savarkar. *Hindutva's* basic creed was that all those whose religion originated in the Indian subcontinent were Hindus; and, further, that they should have their own country where they could flourish as 'Hindus'. Such a definition of 'Hindu' automatically excluded Muslims (also Christians), and consequently—as articulated in Golwalkar's 1940 revised version of *Hindutva*—denied them the right to live in India.[47]

In the context of Jammu and Kashmir, in keeping with its desire that India become a Hindu *rashtra*, the Mahasabha urged the Hindus of the state to keep it a Hindu-controlled one, i.e. to preserve the Maharaja's rule and Hindu socio-economic domination. It called, for instance, for harsh measures to curb anti-Government Muslim agitation, and it condemned Gandhi for calling for Hari Singh's abdication. The Mahasabha also increased fears among Jammu and Kashmir's Hindus of suppression by the Muslim majority. During a visit to Jammu in July 1942, Sarvarkar condemned 'Pakistan' and those who were 'sacrificing Hindu interests to satisfy Muslims'—a reference to Congress and Gandhi.

The Hindu Mahasabha thus had the same influence on the Hindus of Jammu and Kashmir as that of the Punjabi Muslim organizations on the state's Muslims—namely, promoting religious identification and inter-religious rivalry.

Post-1931 Politics

The events of 13 July 1931 radically altered both the pace and direction of political mobilization in Jammu and Kashmir. The immediate effect on the Muslims was the formation of a political 'party', the Muslim Conference, while among the Pandits political priorities were re-assessed.

Muslim Politics: Formation of the Muslim Conference

Following the events of 13 July, a political organization was formed to specifically promote the interests of Jammu and Kashmir's Muslims. Called the All-India Jammu and Kashmir Muslim Conference, its first session was held in October 1932. Sheikh Abdullah was elected President of the new party. When it was formed, the Muslim Conference enjoyed the support of all the major Muslim groups in Jammu and Kashmir: young graduates formerly of the Reading Room or the Jammu Young Men's Association; Mirwaiz-i-Kashmir Yusuf Shah; Mirwaiz of the Khanqah-i-Moalla Hamadani; and the small but politically active Ahmadi/Qadiani community. All these diverse elements had been brought together by a shared hatred of Hari Singh's rule and a common perception that the Muslims were being exploited by the Hindu community. Muslim political unification had thus been achieved, but almost from the outset it was threatened by divisive forces.

The most obvious of these was Yusuf Shah's hatred of the Qadianis, and his belief that Sheikh Abdullah was (if not one of them) at least strongly linked to them. It is unlikely that Sheikh Abdullah ever believed in Ahmadiyyat, but he was initially very close to the Ahmadi community, both within Jammu and Kashmir and in British India (Qadian). This connection developed in the days of the Reading Room. While the Ahmadis had had little success preaching to the masses, they had acquired some influence over the young men at Fateh Kadal. Abdullah's first public appearance, for example, was at an *Eid-Milad-ul-Nabi* (Prophet's birthday) meeting organized by Maulvi Abdullah, a leading member of the Ahmadiyya community in the state.[48] Sheikh Abdullah did eventually expel all Qadianis from the Muslim Conference, not because of any personal aversion to them, but apparently in response to the propaganda spread by Yusuf Shah, included in some Punjabi newspapers, that he too belonged to the sect. By that time, however, relations between the leading Muslims within the Conference had deteriorated to such an extent that expelling the Qadianis had little effect.

A less apparent, but probably equally important, factor was the Mirwaiz-i-Kashmir's resentment of Abdullah's growing popularity.[49] No doubt he saw this as a challenge to his own position within the Muslim community. It is quite possible that Yusuf Shah never genuinely believed Abdullah was a Qadiani, but persisted with such claims in public in the hope of discrediting his young rival. Whatever Yusuf Shah's motives, the net result was that the Muslim Conference developed two rival factions—one led by Abdullah and supported, not surprisingly, by Mirwaiz Hamadani; the other by the Mirwaiz-i-Kashmir. Although the 'official' split did not occur until much later, the rivalry between these two factions soon became so intense that it erupted into violence.[50]

The disunity within the Muslim Conference was to prove very significant. Its immediate effect was, of course, to prevent the Muslims presenting a united front in opposition to the Maharaja's Government and the Hindu community. In the longer term it was to be a factor in Abdullah's decision to change course and adopt secular, non-communal politics. And in the very long-term it was to lead to the Muslim community being divided on the question of Jammu and Kashmir's future.

Hindu Politics

A number of factors promoted communalism among Hindus. The first was their position as a minority group (in terms of population) in the state. Not unnaturally, they feared Muslim domination. The anti-Hindu rioting following the Jail protest of 13 July, and subsequent similar incidents, served to vindicate and increase their sense of vulnerability. Bazaz writes that after this rioting:

> The Hindus became definitely hostile to the (Muslim) movement and openly and solidly joined the Government forces to get it suppressed.... The idea of Hindu rights and Muslim rights, characteristic of the bourgeoisie politics in India, began to assume greater significance.[51]

The second reason was 'material'. As described earlier, the Hindus had long held the upper hand in Kashmir—the Dogras in power, the Pandits in education and employment. When the Muslims began agitating for better educational and employment opportunities, this Hindu domination was threatened. It was quite obvious to the Pandits in particular that any concessions to Muslim demands could only be made at the expense of their own jobs. Thus, in the words of Premnath Bazaz: 'as soon as the middle class Muslims...demanded a share in Government services on the basis of population, and communalism, Pandits took fright and became the champions of Hindu communalism and defenders of the Hindu Raj.'[52]

The Sanatan Dharma Young Men's Association—formerly the Fraternity—made the preservation of educational opportunities for Pandits and even more so jobs, its priority.[53] Similarly, the Yuvak Sabha, which had earlier successfully campaigned for State subjects (in effect Pandits) to be employed in Jammu and Kashmir instead of outsiders, now worked to protect those jobs from Muslim encroachment. When the Glancy Commission Report was issued in March 1932, Kashmiri Hindus strongly opposed its recommendations.[54] Government acceptance of the Commission's recommendations and its—highly limited—implementation of them, caused the Pandits to accuse it of being pro-Muslim, and to some extent turn against it.[55]

Thirdly, greater self-consciousness and communalism among the state's Hindu community, was a reflection of—and reaction to—what was happening in the Muslim community. Operating in a vicious circle, communalism in one community led to communalism in the other, leading to more so in the former, and so on. The Middleton Commission Report on the later Hindu-Muslim distrubances in Jammu in 1932, highlighted the 'knock-on' effect of communalism:

It appears to me that the Mussalman allegation concerning the non-communal nature of their agitation was substantially correct in the earlier stages thereof. In Jammu, however, it led to communal distrust and tension during the summer; the desire to obtain more official posts necessarily implied diminution in the number of posts available for other communities and the demand for severe punishment of individuals concerned in the alleged insults to religion was also a feature of introducing a communal element. The posters issued by Rajput and Hindu Associations show that members of those communities regarded the Muslim agitation as partly communal and in themselves increased communal feeling.[56]

The above description of post-1931 political developments shows that what happened in Jammu and Kashmir was, in many ways, a repetition of what had already happened in British India.

There Hindu revivalism had provoked a similar revival among the Muslims of British India. There also, fear among the minority (this time Muslims) of majority-community (Hindu) domination had been a major communalizing factor. Finally, socio-economic considerations had been very significant in British India as well—again much with respect to the minority community.

Later Muslim Politics

National Conference

It has been seen that early political activity in Jammu and Kashmir, and to an even greater extent post-1931 politics, were based on religion—religious groupings formed political groupings; the goal of the latter was to promote the interests of the former. But by the end of the decade a new element had entered Kashmiri politics—political groupings based not on religion but on class. This element was introduced by Sheikh Muhammed Abdullah. His decision to move away from communal to non-communal, class politics was based largely on two considerations, one internal, the other external.

The major internal factor has already been considered in some detail, namely Abdullah's growing estrangement from the orthodox Mirwaiz-i-Kashmir, Yusuf Shah. Abdullah knew he could not hope to rival the Mirwaiz as a religious leader, and he therefore adopted a secular approach to politics. By excluding religion from the debate completely, he aimed to undermine the Mirwaiz's influence.

The major external factor was Abdullah's contact with the Indian National Congress, and in particular, with Pandit Nehru. Nehru, as mentioned above, took an especial interest in Jammu and Kashmir as his ancestral homeland. He was keen to draw the State, which he viewed as an integral part of India, into the wider nationalist struggle.[57] Nehru was able to persuade Abdullah that the movement against Hari Singh should not be confined to Muslims, but should include all communities. He helped change Abdullah's view of the Kashmiri struggle—to see it in class terms, as oppressed masses versus their feudal oppressors, instead of the Hindus versus the Muslims.[58] Coupled with Nehru's interest was the growing involvement of the Congress in political developments in the Indian States, largely through the All-India States People's Conference. Abdullah realized that if he was to be involved in and have the support of the subcontinent-wide All-India Conference, he would first have to reform the communal nature of the Muslim Conference.

It is debatable which of the factors—enmity with Mirwaiz Yusuf, the genuine conversion to nationalist politics, or the desire to participate on the all-India stage—exerted the most influence upon Abdullah. In the light of subsequent events, one could plausibly argue that Abdullah's conversion was not ideological at all, but based purely on political considerations. However, this is an issue that will be examined later.

The important point here is that—whatever the motive—by 1938 Sheikh Abdullah had decided to convert the Muslim Conference into a secular, nationalist organization. In his presidential address to the sixth annual session of the party, on 26 March 1938, he articulated his new ideas:

Like us the majority of Hindus and Sikhs have immensely suffered at the hands of the irresponsible government. They are also steeped in deep ignorance, have to pay large taxes and are in debt and are starving. Establishment of responsible government is [as] much a necessity for them as for us.... The main problem therefore now before us is to organise joint action and a united front against the forces that stand in our way in the achievement of our goal. This will require re-christening our organisation as a non-communal political body...[W]e must end communalism by ceasing to think in terms of Muslims and non-Muslims when discussing political problems.... We must open our doors to all such Hindus and Sikhs who like ourselves believe in the freedom of their country from the shackles of a irresponsible rule.[59]

On 28 June, the party's Working Committee passed a resolution, proposed by Abdullah, amending the constitution to allow anyone to become a member. In April 1939, a special session of the General Assembly also passed the resolution, and it was formally adopted at the Muslim Conference's seventh annual session at Anantnag in June 1939. In keeping with the party's new ethos its name was changed to the National Conference.

Whereas the old Muslim Conference had demanded rights for Muslims from the 'Hindu' Government, the National Conference couched its demands in terms of class.[60] It claimed rights on behalf of the masses—both Hindu and Muslim—and called for an end to Hari Singh's 'undemocratic,' 'despotic' (but *not* 'Hindu') rule. Nehru's influence showed clearly in 'New Kashmir,' a document issued by the transformed party, outlining its vision for the State. As well as equality, freedom and democratic rights for all citizens (women specifically), 'New Kashmir' proposed a socialist economic system. Landlordism was to be abolished with proprietary rights transferred to peasants, and all key industries were to be state-owned.[61]

After the formation of the National Conference, Abdullah wasted no time in cementing his links with Nehru, Congress and the All-India States People's Conference. In his presidential address to the States Conference at Ludhiana in 1939, Nehru called for the release of 'popular' leaders imprisoned in Indian States; he specifically demanded that Sheikh Abdullah be set free. The National Conference joined the All-India States People's Conference in 1941. Some time later, Abdullah became its Vice President, and in 1946, President. In transforming the Muslim Conference into the National Conference, he was thus successful in achieving one of his objectives; namely, moving from the small stage of local Kashmir politics, to the much grander national Indian stage.

But Abdullah had far less success in uniting the various religious communities within Jammu and Kashmir. Not only did he fail to win the Hindu community over to his nationalist cause, but he also alienated a significant proportion of the

Muslim community. The latter led to the revival of the communal Muslim Conference—considered below. With respect to the former, Sheikh Abdullah did win the confidence of a handful of prominent Hindus, notably Pandit Prem Nath Bazaz, with whom he had started the newspaper *Hamdard*. But the vast majority of Hindus remained sceptical about his nationalist claims. For them the essential fact was that—in spite of everything Abdullah said about non-communal class politics— his party was predominantly Muslim; in their eyes this rendered his secular credentials highly suspect. Furthermore, as a minority they feared Muslim-majority domination, and felt the best way to protect their interests was to retain their distinct identity, and to support the Hindu Maharaja. [Note how much the situation in Jammu and Kashmir again paralleled that in British India. There the Indian National Congress, a group which also claimed to be secular and nationalist but which had an overwhelming majority of Hindu members, failed in its attempts to assuage the fears of the minority Muslim community and win them over to its cause.]

Revival of the Muslim Conference

Despite their deep divisions, and despite the existence of the semi-official Azad Party (Mirwaiz Yusuf's supporters), the Muslims were still in theory united behind one party: the Muslim Conference which in 1939 had changed its name to the National Conference. However, very soon after the latter was created, a formal split did occur in Muslim politics, and two distinct parties emerged. The National Conference, led by Sheikh Abdullah, and professing to be a secular, nationalist (and socialist) organization and the Muslim Conference, brought back to. life in 1941.

The revival of the Muslim Conference, or at least of a Muslim party, was very much to be expected. The reasons for this are several, the first being the Mirwaiz-i-Kashmir's rigid orthodoxy. We have already seen he could not tolerate even 'Muslim' Qadianis—how could he then support a party that welcomed

Hindus and Sikhs? Referring to Jinnah's departure from Congress and his formation of the Muslim League in British India, the Mirwaiz declared in a speech: 'even when [the Muslims] are in a minority they do not join the Hindus, much less then should the local Muslims of Kashmir do so [when] they are in a majority.'[62] Sheikh Abdullah's attempts to win the confidence of the Hindu community thus served to anger and alienate the Mirwaiz and the significant number of orthodox Muslims who shared his views.[63]

A second reason was the competition for leadership of the Muslim community between Abdullah and Yusuf Shah. As discussed earlier, one of the reasons for the transformation into the National Conference had been Abdullah's desire to suppress his rival. Fully aware that the Mirwaiz derived his authority from being a religious leader, Abdullah calculated the Mirwaiz would have far less influence in a secular organization than in a Muslim one. But the assumption—or hope—that the Mirwaiz-i-Kashmir would then accept defeat and meekly concede leadership of the Muslim community to Abdullah was wrong.

An additional factor that influenced the Muslim Conference's re-emergence, and which was to play an increasing role in Kashmir politics, was the All-India Muslim League. The League was founded in 1906 with the intention of protecting and promoting the interests of Muslims in British India. By 1940, however, its demands had become far more ambitious: it called for a completely separate Muslim State, 'Pakistan'. Muslims from Jammu and Kashmir such as Chaudhri Ghulam Mohammad Abbas, were in regular contact with League leaders in British India, and were undoubtedly influenced by their communal outlook.

A final reason was, of course, that not all Muslims in Jammu and Kashmir supported the idea of non-communal secular politics. They viewed religion and politics as interlinked, inseparable; any political organization that represented the Muslims had to reflect their religious identity. Hence the Jammu and Kashmir Muslim Conference was reborn in 1941. Its main leaders were the Mirwaiz-i-Kashmir Yusuf Shah, and Chaudhri Ghulam Mohammad Abbas.

National Conference-Muslim Conference Interaction

The obvious question which arises from the 'resurrection' of the Muslim Conference is, which party—Muslim or National Conference—enjoyed the most public support? There is no straightforward answer to this question since the level of support for both parties changed over time. Before attempting to assess relative support it would therefore be best to review Jammu and Kashmir politics in the period immediately after 1941. As a preliminary assessment, however, the two parties had definite regional bases of support, with the National Conference being more popular in Kashmir and the Muslim Conference in Jammu.

Relations between the two parties were difficult from the outset. As well as personal rivalries (notably between Abdullah and Yusuf Shah), and diverging approaches to politics in Jammu and Kashmir, conflict arose from a difference in attitude to events in British India.[64] While the National Conference actively supported Congress' 'Quit India' movement,[65] the Muslim Conference backed Jinnah's call for a separate Muslim homeland.[66] This final source of rivalry further demonstrated the strong influence of British Indian politics on developments in Jammu and Kashmir. It was not long before hostility between the two parties erupted into violence. National Conference and Muslim Conference followers clashed initially in October 1942 at Id-ul-Fitr prayers, then again in January of the following year over prayers at the Hazratbal Shrine.[67] Tension between the two parties was further exacerbated by the National Conference receiving support from a somewhat unlikely source—the Jammu and Kashmir Government.

Until 1941, the Government of Jammu and Kashmir had strongly opposed the Muslim/National Conference—opposition testified by Sheikh Abdullah's numerous arrests and long periods of imprisonment. Despite the State's opposition to it, the

National Conference had not as yet denounced Dogra rule but had merely called for a more fair and responsible government. Further, it supported the (predominantly Hindu) Indian Congress and vigorously condemned the Muslim League's call for a separate Muslim homeland. When the new, generally pro-Pakistan, Muslim Conference emerged in 1941, the State Government, taking these two points into consideration, radically revised its approach to Abdullah's party. Seeing it as the 'lesser of two evils,' the Darbar backed the National Conference in its conflict with the Muslim Conference. This backing took various forms, including the appointment of only National Conference members to committees charged with the allocation of rice ration tickets and fuel permits,[68] and the promulgation of an order restricting public meetings which most adversely affected the Muslim Conference,[69] and following inter-Muslim rioting, led to the arrest of mostly Muslim Conference members. The apparent favoured treatment given to the National Conference by the State Government increased Muslim Conference hostility.[70]

Attempts at Unification

In late 1943—early 1944, it seemed possible the two Conferences would unite into a single party. The Muslim Conference was urged to do so by its 'mentor', Mohammad Ali Jinnah. On the National Conference side, moves towards reconciliation appear to have been motivated by a decline in Sheikh Abdullah's popularity. Jinnah paid a long visit to Jammu and Kashmir in 1944, and was given a friendly welcome by both parties. But by the time of his departure, some two months later—having failed in his mission to form a single Muslim party—relations between Jinnah and Abdullah had completely deteriorated.[71] The reasons for Jinnah's failure were twofold. Firstly, he envisaged a single *Muslim* party intended primarily to promote Muslim interests.[72] Its formation would, therefore, have necessitated Sheikh Abdullah abandoning secular nationalist politics in favour of the League's Muslim communalism. Having vigorously backed the former for so long, it would have been very difficult for him to turn back. It would, of course, also have meant cutting off his links with Nehru and the States People's Conference—links from which he derived considerable prestige. But the fact that Abdullah did flirt with the idea of joining the Muslim Conference does suggest that he was not wholly sincere in his professions, and belief, in non-communal politics, and hence that ideology was not the real barrier to party unification.[73] In fact, what ultimately prevented the Muslims of Jammu and Kashmir forming a single political party was the rivalry between Sheikh Abdullah and Mirwaiz Yusuf Shah; neither could accept being led by the other.

A further effort to unite the two Muslim parties, this time without Muslim League involvement, was made in 1946. This second attempt was instigated by the National Conference; again, apparently, motivated by its declining popularity. But as before, all talk of rapprochement stumbled over the obstacle of personal leadership: none of the, by then three, major leaders—Abdullah, Yusuf Shah, or Ghulam Abbas—was prepared to concede his position to someone else.

'Quit Kashmir'

In May 1946, drawing inspiration from the Congress 'Quit India' campaign of 1942, Sheikh Abdullah suddenly launched his own 'Quit Kashmir' movement. Directed against Hari Singh, its main theme was that the Treaty of Amritsar did not legitimize Dogra rule:

> One hundred years ago Kashmir was sold for 75 lakh Nanakshahi rupees to Raja Gulab Singh by a sale deed of 1846 wrongly called the Treaty of Amritsar. Less than 5 lakh pound sterling changed hands and sealed the fate of over 40 lakh men and women and their land of milk and honey. We challenge the political and moral status of this sale deed, this instrument of subjugation, handed by the East

India Company agents to a bunch of Dogras.... A sale deed does not have the status of a treaty. Therefore after the termination of British rule Kashmir has the right to become independent. We Kashmiris want to inscribe our own destiny.[74]

'Quit Kashmir' marked a radical change of direction for Abdullah and this, coupled with its sudden anouncement, meant it caught everyone—the members of the National Conference, Congress, the State Government—by surprise. The British Resident noted in a report 'Sheikh Mohammed Abdullah had, in the booklet "New Kashmir" accepted the continued rule of the Maharaja and it was not until the first half of May 1946 that it was ever suggested that the Maharaja should be ousted from the State. This new policy had neither the formal sanction of the National Conference, though it was immediately accepted by many of the party's adherents, nor of the Congress High Command.'[75] Congress was, in fact, quite embarrassed by it, since at the time it shared the All-India States People's Conference's official position on princely rulers—namely, to retain them as nominal Heads of State. Nehru, however, quickly swung behind Abdullah.

Predictably, 'Quit Kashmir' was greeted with anger by the State Government; Abdullah and most of the National Conference leadership were immediately arrested. Just as predictably, it was greeted with great enthusiasm by the Kashmiri people. Abdullah writes in his autobiography '[t]he people were galvanised. "Quit Kashmir" was on the lips of every Kashmiri.'[76] Support for the movement increased following the detention of Jawaharlal Nehru when he attempted to enter Kashmir to secure Abdullah's release; and even more so after the latter's trial and conviction. '"Quit Kashmir" was spreading in the valley like wildfire. The Muslims were courting arrest by the thousands and many young men were riddled with bullets.'[77]

The desire to increase his public support was in fact the most probable reason why Abdullah suddenly started attacking Dogra rule. Referring to the May 1946 speeches in which Abdullah launched the 'Quit Kashmir' movement the British Resident commented: 'well aware of his declining popularity in Kashmir and of the gradual drift of members of his party towards the Muslim Conference, from this time onwards his speeches became wilder and even less logical than usual...[he] developed an entirely new line of attack on the Kashmir Government.'[78] The interpretation of the 'Quit Kashmir' movement as an attempt by Abdullah to revive his party's flagging popularity was shared by the Muslim Conference leadership, and they, therefore, refused to support it.

Relative Support

We are now in a far better position to assess whether the National Conference or the Muslim Conference enjoyed the most public support, and from what sections of the Jammu and Kashmir population. Considering the Muslim Conference first, we can assess this to be very much a Jammu-based organization. Only one of its main leaders, the Mirwaiz-i-Kashmir, was from the Valley. The rest, including its other leading figure Ghulam Abbas, were from Jammu. The background of the leaders was reflected in the party's support distribution: it was far more popular in Jammu than in Kashmir. As for the leadership factor, another reason was that the Muslims of Jammu formed a much narrower majority than their co-religionists in Kashmir. They, therefore, had more reason to fear Hindu domination, and hence were more sympathetic toward the Muslim Conference's communal politics, and toward its pro-Pakistan tendency. In the initial years after its formation the party's popularity increased, and it did appear to be gaining a foothold in the Valley. But the 'Quit Kashmir' movement very effectively put an end to this. Ultimately, however, the Muslim Conference failed to win over the Muslims of the Kashmir Valley because it did not have a Kashmiri-speaking leader who could match and combat the appeal of Sheikh Abdullah.[79]

Turning to the National Conference, we assess this to be a Kashmir-based organization. There are two principle reasons for this, again related to the question of leadership and the 'Quit Kashmir' movement. Sheikh Abdullah was a native of the Kashmir Valley. Since the early 1930s, he had established his popularity among the Kashmiris—partly because of his moving Quranic and poetry recitation, and partly because of his criticisms of the State Government and his consequent, numerous arrests and periods of detention, and further because of his personal charisma and appeal. When Abdullah shifted from communal to non-communal politics, it would not be unreasonable to assert that the majority of the Muslims who continued to support him and the National Conference did so on the basis of personality, rather than out of a shared conviction in the merits of non-communalism. But personality and charisma alone could not sustain public support indefinitely, as Abdullah discovered within a few years of adopting the non-communal line. Hence his attempts to reunite with the Muslim Conference. On failing, he launched the 'Quit Kashmir' movement which could really be described as the saviour of Abdullah and the National Conference. It struck an immediate chord with the Kashmiri people; its basic theme that they had been sold illegally for 7 paisa per head, was easy to understand and highly effective. With the 'Quit Kashmir' movement, support for Abdullah and the National Conference increased among the Kashmiris—this time based upon shared convictions rather than simply upon personality.

The reasons for Abdullah's great popularity in Kashmir also explain his failure to significantly extend his support into Jammu: Abdullah was perceived as an outsider in Jammu. 'Quit Kashmir' was a protest against the Treaty of Amritsar in which only the Vale had been sold. 'Quit Kashmir', therefore, had little relevance for the people of Jammu. Indeed, it could even have driven them away from Abdullah, for it was the ruler of Jammu who had 'bought' the Valley. An additional factor was the relatively small majority held by the Muslims of Jammu. Further, Abdullah's goal—at least up to the mid-1940s—that Jammu and Kashmir become part of India, aroused considerable apprehension among the Muslims of Jammu. Their fears of Hindu domination were undoubtedly increased by the communal killings in Punjab—and later Jammu itself—that accompanied Partition.

Having assessed the relative support for the Muslim and the National Conference among the Muslims, we may now consider the non-Muslims of Jammu and Kashmir, in particular the Pandits. The Muslim Conference, by definition, did not have Pandit support. The National Conference, however, had the right political ideology; non-communal nationalism; and the right backers, Nehru and the Indian National Congress, to attract the Pandits. However, it was not able to do so.

As described earlier, despite Abdullah's nationalist non-communal rhetoric, the Pandits remained distrustful of Muslim-majority parties and refused to abandon their own Hindu parties. At the annual conference of the Hindu Naujawan Sabha (Jammu and Kashmir Rajya Hindu Sabha) in 1943:

> The President criticised the National Conference Party of Sheikh Mohammed Abdullah, saying that though it sympathised with the National Movement in India and professed itself to be against Pakistan yet its activities were dominated by communal and anti-Hindu feelings. For these latter reasons the Hindus of the State, who [were] also in favour of responsible Government in the State, found it difficult to lend their support to the National Conference in making this demand. He pressed for a strong Hindu front to be formed in the State Praja Sabha to fight for their rights.[80]

1947

Before looking into the events of 1947, it would be useful to review the positions of the three main political groups in Jammu and Kashmir on the question of the State's future.

The non-Muslim (mainly Hindu) community supported continued rule by the Maharaja. The only circumstances under which they said they would oppose Dogra rule would be if further measures were introduced to improve the lot of the Muslims, i.e. if Hindus no longer received preferential treatment. By 1947, however, there seemed little danger of this happening; the earlier 'pro-Muslim' reforms had largely been forced upon Hari Singh by the British, and his close circle of advisers consisted of 'staunch' Hindus—his wife, Maharani Tera Devi, her brother Chand, and a Swami referred to by some as 'the Rasputin of Kashmir'.

The State's Muslim population was divided into those supporting the Muslim Conference and those backing the National Conference. The Muslim Conference Kashmir leader, Mirwaiz Yusuf Shah, was in favour of joining Pakistan, but some of its Jammu leaders—while supporting Jinnah and the Indian Muslims' demand for a separate homeland—preferred independence.[81] All the Muslim Conference leaders agreed, however, that Jammu and Kashmir should become a Muslim state—one in which promotion and protection of Muslim interests would be a priority.

Sheikh Abdullah's National Conference claimed to be a non-religious organization representing members of all communities. In practice, however, it had very few Hindu or Sikh followers— by this stage, even Prem Nath Bazaz had left the party.[82] At the beginning of 1947, the majority of National Conference members opposed the Pakistan idea, and shared the Congress view that Jammu and Kashmir should be part of a united, secular, (socialist) India. Abdullah made his opposition to Pakistan clear in a speech: 'only a unified India can drive away the British usurpers, and liberate the country...on the question of independence all communities should speak with one voice.'[83]

Partition

In 1947, the Indian subcontinent was partitioned in two: Pakistan and India. Obviously this was an event of immense and wide-ranging significance, but this study will confine itself to those aspects of Partition that directly affected Jammu and Kashmir.

These were all related to the division of the Punjab province between the two successor States, based on the recommendations of the Radcliffe Boundary Commission.[84]

The division first unleashed a 'holocaust' of communal killing, as well as mass migrations of Hindus and Sikhs eastward, and Muslims to the west.[85] Some of the Punjabi refugees found their way to Jammu and Kashmir, carrying with them harrowing tales of killings, rape, etc., and the presence of these refugees in the state served to incite and intensify communal violence there. In Jammu Province, to where the majority of Hindus and Sikhs had fled, there was a backlash by their co-religionists against the Muslim inhabitants. Lamb writes that by August 1947:

> the communal situation in Jammu, the one part of the state where there was a large non-Muslim population, had deteriorated rapidly with bands of armed Hindus and Sikhs (including members of the RSS, Hindu extremists, Akali Sikhs and others) attacking Muslim villages and setting in train a mass exodus. It has been estimated that in August, September and October 1947 at least 500,000 Muslims were displaced from Jammu: perhaps as many as 200,000 of them just disappeared.[86]

Many of these then fled to Kashmir and Poonch, adding their tales of woe to those of the Punjabi Muslims who had preceded them. The predictable consequence was another communal backlash, this time by Muslims against Hindus and Sikhs. In Poonch, a rebellion against Dogra rule based essentially on economic (food prices and tax) grievances, was encouraged to take on a 'Muslim vs Hindu' character by the killings in Punjab and Jammu.[87] Further encouragement came from the direction of the North-West Frontier Province; Pathans angered by reports of Muslim deaths, went to Poonch seeking revenge against Hindus and Sikhs.[88]

Looking at the wider picture, the communal violence in Punjab and later in Jammu and Kashmir itself, generally served to harden the prevalent opinions of the three major groups. The state's Hindu community was even more convinced that it had no future under Muslim rule; if the Maharaja could not retain control, they wanted to accede to India. The Muslim Conference supporters, by and large, moved closer to joining Pakistan, though some still favoured an independent Muslim state.

Of the three, only Sheikh Abdullah's position shifted somewhat. He still strongly condemned Pakistan and called for communal tolerance, but he no longer appeared so definite about wanting to be part of India. Addressing a public meeting soon after Partition, Abdullah said, 'We are facing the question of accession to India or Pakistan, or keeping our separate identity.... It is a fact that the Indian National Congress has extended full support to our movement. But the question of accession will be decided in the best interests of the Kashmiri people.'[89] Just as Hari Singh dreamed of being Maharaja of a completely independent Jammu and Kashmir, so it appears Abdullah was having visions of being the democratically-chosen head of just such an entity.

A second aspect of the Punjab division which had a less immediate impact on the internal situation in Jammu and Kashmir, but which was to be of immense significance in determining the state's future, was the positioning of the boundary line separating the Pakistani and Indian sections of the province. The Gurdaspur district of northern Punjab adjoined Jammu. Two of the roads from the Jammu and Kashmir State to British India (Srinagar-Rawalpindi and Jammu-Sialkot) were definitely to fall into Pakistani territory after independence. A third road from Jammu (actually more a dirt track) passed through the Pathankot *tehsil* (subdistrict) of Gurdaspur. If this district also went to Pakistan, the only access from India to the State would be via very difficult mountain terrain in the foothills of the Himalayas, i.e. Indian access to the State would effectively be cut off. In such circumstances, the accession of Jammu and Kashmir to Pakistan would almost be inevitable. Of Gurdaspur's four *tehsils*, Muslims formed the majority in three; only Pathankot had a small Hindu majority. Thus, according to its terms of reference, the Radcliffe Boundary Commisssion could have been expected to award the district to Pakistan. In fact, it divided the district between India and Pakistan such that the former received the three eastern *tehsils*—Pathankot, together with Muslim-majority Batla and Gurdaspur.[90] The historical significance of the Gurdaspur division will be described below.

Accession

Prior to independence in 1947, the Indian subcontinent had consisted of those areas directly administered by Britain (eleven Provinces plus Tribal Areas), and some 562 Indian states. The latter were commonly controlled by the British through paramountcy agreements; basically these entailed the Indian Princes administering their states themselves, but in accordance with British wishes.[91] When the British left in 1947, control of the states, in theory, returned to their princely rulers. In practice, however, they were expected to accede to either India or Pakistan.[92] In most cases their choice was pre-determined by their geographical position, and accession proceeded relatively smoothly. Where a state bordered both new countries, the population's composition was to be taken into consideration. Logically, Muslim-majority states were expected to join Pakistan, and non-Muslim states to India. Problems arose in Junagadh and Hyderabad, both of which had Muslims ruling over predominantly Hindu populations. Junagadh's ruler wished to accede to Pakistan, while the Nizam of Hyderabad favoured complete independence; both eventually joined India.[93]

Jammu and Kashmir presented a similar problem. Geographically it could join either India or Pakistan, and its strategic position made it very important to both. [This was in addition to its emotional significance: Pakistan felt 'incomplete' without the Muslim state; it was Nehru's homeland; through it India could deny the Muslim-Hindu logic of Partition.] In a reversal of the situation in Junagadh and Hyderabad, it had a Hindu ruler but a Muslim majority population. Unlike in those two states where the majority Hindus had clearly wanted to join

India, there was no consensus within Jammu and Kashmir's population about their state's future. We have already seen that the Muslim population was divided into those who favoured joining Pakistan, those preferring India, and an increasing number (perhaps Sheikh Abdullah as well) who wished to be completely independent. Matters were further complicated by the fact that Hari Singh had no desire to hand over his state to either India or Pakistan—with the departure of the British he looked forward to exercising unsupervised power. This was made clear in a press statement issued by his Deputy Prime Minister as late as 12 October 1947: 'Despite constant rumours, we have no intention of joining either India or Pakistan...[t]he Maharaja has told me that his ambition is to make Kashmir the Switzerland of the East—a State that is completely neutral.'[94]

Abdullah-Hari Singh 'Reconciliation'

We have already seen that Sheikh Abdullah enjoyed considerable support among the Muslims of Jammu and Kashmir—particularly of Kashmir. Abdullah's popularity meant that Maharaja Hari Singh had to bring him 'on the side' of whichever country he chose to accede to, and especially if he opted for independence; without Abdullah's cooperation he would not be able to implement his decision.

Hari Singh needed Abdullah's backing for another reason as well. The Poonch uprising had evolved into a complete revolt against Dogra rule; the 'Government of Azad Kashmir' had declared the region independent from the Maharaja.[95] Pathans from the North-West Frontier Province were infiltrating the state in increasing numbers. In the Vale of Kashmir, the atmosphere was very tense. Thus, far from his dream of being sovereign of 'the Switzerland of the East', the Maharaja seemed to be in danger of losing his state to Pakistan (more accurately to pro-Pakistan Muslim elements). If he was to hold on to Jammu and Kashmir he would need Indian military assistance, to prevent further 'Pakistani' encroachments, and to wrest back control of territory already lost. Given Nehru's close friendship with Sheikh Abdullah, and his conviction that the National Conference leader represented the vast majority of Muslim public opinion, such assistance would not come forth without his release (Abdullah had been in prison since his arrest in May 1946) and inclusion in a reformed Government.[96] The situation gained added urgency from the fact that winter was approaching fast; Jammu's road link with India (Pathankot) would then be impassable.

This was the background to the negotiations in September 1947 between the Deputy Prime Minister Batra and Sheikh Abdullah, about terms to secure the latter's backing of Hari Singh. These talks were obviously fruitful for Abdullah was released from jail on 29 September (other Muslim Conference leaders arrested in October 1946 for holding illegal political meetings remained in detention). Soon after being freed, Abdullah went to New Delhi where he stayed as Nehru's guest; he also made it quite clear that he opposed Jammu and Kashmir joining Pakistan—both gestures fuelled speculation that he supported accession to India.

October 1947: Hari Singh Accedes to India

A number of events early in this month gave the impression that Hari Singh had finally bowed to the inevitable—given up all ideas of 'Swiss' independence—and had opted to join India. These events were, the appointment of an Indian, Mehr Chand Mahajan, as Prime Minister of the state,[97] an appeal by the State Government to India for supplies following a blockade imposed by Pakistan—basic commodities were sent to Srinagar from India by lorry,[98] and the arrival of Patiala State troops in Srinagar, again at the Maharaja's request.[99] Moreover, the long-evaded decision was forced upon Hari Singh by developments beyond his control.

Pathan tribesmen had already been supplying arms to, and fighting alongside the rebels in Poonch. In response to the perceived imminent accession of the state to India, they launched a separate offensive around 20 October across the Punjab-Kashmir border in the region of Muzaffarabad. Their aim was to 'save' at least Kashmir Province for Pakistan. The attack almost certainly originated as a spontaneous movement among the tribesmen, but once underway received covert backing (arms plus military personnel) from the Pakistan government.

The plan had been to capture Srinagar by 26 October, in time for Eid celebrations. However, distracted by the temptation to loot and rape, the invaders fell short of this target, getting only as far as Baramulla (though they did manage to cut off power to the Kashmiri capital). Very soon after the tribal offensive began, when it became clear that State troops could not be depended upon to provide much resistance, Hari Singh fled to Jammu. In his absence, Sheikh Abdullah mobilized National Conference supporters into a defence. Meanwhile, Hari Singh sent Mehr Chand Mahajan from Jammu to India to plead for military assistance in combating the attack. The plea was rejected on the grounds that Jammu and Kashmir was not part of Indian territory. Thus, on 26 October 1947, with his back to the wall, Maharaja Hari Singh finally signed the Instrument of Accession to India.[100]

Sheikh Abdullah's cooperation was guaranteed by one of the conditions of accession and Indian military help: that he be appointed head of an interim government.[101] In addition, Abdullah believed that the accession was not completely binding since it was to be ratified by a plebiscite once peaceful conditions were restored. This latter point was made clear when Mountbatten, as Governor-General of India, accepted Hari Singh's request to accede to India:

In the special circumstances mentioned by your Highness, my Government have decided to accept the accession of Kashmir State to the Dominion of India. Consistently with their policy that, in the case of any State where accession should be decided in accordance with the wishes of the people of the State, it is my Government's wish that, as soon as law and order have been restored in Kashmir, and her soil cleared of the invader, the question of accession should be settled by reference to the people.[102]

It seems likely Abdullah felt that 'by reference to the people' independence was still a possibility, with himself instead of Maharaja Hari Singh ruling.

The speed with which the Indian forces and supplies were transported to Srinagar showed that they had been in a state of readiness for some time. The Indian Government had, in fact, premeditated the outcome and already decided to send troops to the State in order to prevent it from falling into Pakistani control, irrespective of Hari Singh's signature.[103] A convincing case has been made to back the assertion that Indian troops went in *before* the Instrument of Accession was signed—in fact, the case even questions whether such a document was signed at all.[104]

1947 Indo-Pak War

Indian troops, replacing National Conference supporters in the defence of Kashmir, succeeded in halting the tribal/Pakistani advance before Srinagar was captured. They also launched a counter-offensive, recapturing Baramulla. Once India had sent her forces into Jammu and Kashmir, Pakistan's Governor-General M. A. Jinnah wanted to send his country's regular troops in as well. But such a move was blocked by the Pakistan Army's acting Commander-in-Chief, General Sir Douglas Gracey, who feared that would spark off a war between the two new states (the two armies were still under the same supreme command). Jinnah still attempted to send help to the pro-Pakistan/'Azad Kashmir' forces, for example encouraging Pakistani regulars 'on leave' to make their way to the State. In May 1948, Gracey reversed his earlier decision, and Pakistan 'officially' sent its troops into Jammu and Kashmir.

A series of offensives and counter-offensives ended with Pakistan controlling Gilgit (which had 'acceded' to that country on 3 November 1947),[105] Baltistan, part of the Vale, most of Poonch, and the Mirpur area of Jammu. Indian forces controlled Ladakh, most of Kashmir and Jammu Provinces, and a small part of Poonch. By the end of 1948, the war, which had so far remained confined to Jammu and Kashmir, threatened to spread to 'proper' India and Pakistan. Such an escalation was avoided by the declaration of a cease-fire—partly the result of United Nations intervention—that took effect on 1 January 1949.[106] The cease-fire line was defined in an agreement between Indian and Pakistani military representatives on 27 July 1949, and remained unchanged until the 1965 Indo-Pak War.

By the time the war ended, the Jammu and Kashmir State had been divided into three separate administrative regions. The first, consisting of Gilgit and Baltistan (the Northern Areas), was controlled directly by Pakistan; these regions had, to all intents and purposes, been integrated with that country. The second region, known as Azad Kashmir, consisted of part of the Kashmir Province, most of Poonch and the Mirpur district of Jammu. This was controlled by a far from united group, that included Poonch Muslims (mostly Sudhans), and former Muslim Conference exiles such as Mirwaiz Yusuf Shah and Ghulam Abbas. In theory, Azad Kashmir was independent, i.e. not part of Pakistani territory. In practice, it had very close links with, and was heavily dependent economically on, Karachi. These links severely restricted its ability to act as a separate entity.

The third part of the State was that held by the Indian troops. In October 1947, in accordance with the terms of accession to India, Maharaja Hari Singh appointed Sheikh Abdullah as the head of an Emergency Government. Though Mehr Chand Mahajan stayed on as Prime Minister, real power lay in the ministry headed by Abdullah. In March 1948, this arrangement was formalized with the return of Mahajan to India, and Hari Singh's announcement that Abdullah would head an Interim Government which was to operate until the State's future constitution could be worked out. In June 1949, the Maharaja was 'persuaded' to appoint his son Karan Singh as Regent, and leave Jammu and Kashmir for what turned out to be permanent exile in India.

Foundations of Conflict

This period of Jammu and Kashmir's history set the foundations for both the international Kashmir dispute between India and Pakistan, and the internal 'ethnic' issue of Kashmir's relationship with India. Evolution of the former is self-explanatory: by hedging on the question of accession, Hari Singh effectively ended up dividing his State between India and Pakistan—but in a manner that did not allow this to be a permanent settlement. Evolution of the latter merits more detailed analysis.

It has been seen that ethno-religious divisions were present in Kashmir from a very early stage. What is noteworthy is that from the very beginning of political mobilization these divisions were also present in the political arena. Taking the Pandits first, group mobilization in this community initially took place to bring about religious reform; later it was directed toward the preservation of Pandit socio-economic privileges. When eventually the Pandits did make political alliances, it was not with the ethnically similar Kashmiri Muslims but with their co-religionists, the Jammu Dogras. The political demands they made also reflected their sense of being a distinct Hindu community: resisting Muslim encroachment into education and state employment, supporting continued Dogra rule and, failing that, accession to India.

The Kashmiri Muslims mobilized initially as a religious community as well, making alliances with the Muslims of Jammu and Poonch. It was to be several years before Sheikh Abdullah presented himself as a non-communal Kashmiri leader and called for Hindu-Muslim unity based on a shared Kashmiri identity. While he was largely successful in winning Muslims from the Valley over to his non-communal politics, his marked failure to attract Pandit converts meant that the ethnicization of

Kashmiri politics apparent in the early stages of mass political mobilization was perpetuated.

Post-1947, Kashmiri Muslims and Pandits with their quite divergent ethnic perceptions and political views, found themselves united under Indian rule (since most of the Valley fell in India's half of the State). The seed of ethnic conflict was thus planted; whether or not this germinated would depend on how Kashmir fitted into the new Indian Union.

NOTES

1. Bazaz writes: 'Even after their conversion to the new faith, the Kashmiris did not altogether abandon the ways of life and mental outlook that their forefathers had cultivated through the thousands of years of their history. A Kashmiri Muslim shares in common with his Hindu compatriot many inhibitions, superstitions, idolatrous practices as well as social liberties and intellectual freedoms which are unknown to Islam.' *Kashmir in Crucible* (New Delhi, Pamposh, 1967), p. 14.

   Walter Lawrence, Settlement Officer in Kashmir from 1889, wrote: 'If a comparison be made between the customs of the Hindus and the Mussalmans, it will be seen that there are many points of resemblance.... Besides the "mehnzrat", or use of the mehndi dye, in both religions there is the "laganchir" or fixing of the marriage day; "phirsal", the visit paid by the bridegroom to the bride's house after marriage; "gullimiut", the giving of money and jewels; the dress and the title of the bridegroom as "Maharaja" and of the bride as "Maharani"; "chudus", the giving of presents, on the fourth day after death, and the "wehrawad" and "wehrawar", the celebration respectively of the birthday and day of death.' *The Valley of Kashmir* (London, Oxford University Press), p. 300, ibid., p. 15.

2. Lawrence wrote that Kashmir Brahmins did things that would horrify the orthodox Hindus. 'They will drink water brought by a Mussalman; they will eat food cooked on a Mussalman boat...remember that eighty years ago Hindus were rigidly orthodox and untouchability at its worst.' Ibid.

3. Gupta, Jyoti Bhusan Das, *Jammu and Kashmir* (Martinus Nuhoff, The Hague, 1968), p. 16.

4. The figure for Sikhs was taken from the previous census; in 1941 it would have been somewhat greater. Source: Bazaz, Prem Nath, *Inside Kashmir* (Mirpur, Verinag Publishers, 1941), p. 305.

5. *The Times*, 5 June 1934, describes the various groups of Hindus: 'the land-owning aristocrats; the pundits of Kashmir; the traders styled "domiciled Hindus"; the Rajputs and Dogras of Jammu; an interesting group of agricultural peasants, reckoned technically among the Depressed Classes; the Meghs, perhaps survivors of an aboriginal race and wholly illiterate; they number some 100,000 of whom one section reckon themselves Hindus and some other prefer to be considered non-Hindu. Finally, there exist the inevitable vocationally depressed classes, leather workers and corpse-carriers.' I.O.L.R., (India Office Library Records L/P&S/13/1263, p. 72.

6. Bazaz writes 'a sort of a Rajput oligarchy began to be formed under his *(Hari Singh's)* shelter. Mediocre Rajputs became Heads of various Departments of the State. The military was exclusively reserved for the Dogras, chiefly Rajputs, and more than sixty per cent of the gazetted appointments went to them.' *Op. cit.* (1941), pp. 87–8.

   'The Rajputs are neither highly educated nor intelligent, yet they are getting the lion's share everywhere.... The total population of the Rajputs in the State is 132,440. A small number of them are Mians, that is, belong to the ruling class. Only 6 per cent of the Rajputs are literate. Yet they dominate the services, both Military and Civil.' Ibid., p. 279.

7. Bazaz, *The History of the Struggle for Freedom in Kashmir* (New Delhi, Pamposh, 1954), pp. 91–2, cited in Bhattacharjea, Ajit, *Kashmir: The Wounded Valley* (New Delhi, UBSPD, 1994), p. 60.

8. At the beginning of the century, the Pandits started campaigning for State employment to be restricted to natives of the state: 'down with the outsiders.' They objected to the State's practice of employing people from outside the state (mostly Punjab) and further, to the replacement of these employees when they retired with their friends or relatives, thereby perpetuating Punjabi domination: 'thus was established a hierarchy in the services with the result that profits and wealth passed into the hands of the outsiders and the indigenous subjects lost enterprise and independence.' Bazaz, *op. cit.*, (1941), p. 80. They achieved success in 1922 when Hari Singh (then Heir Apparent and Senior Member of the State Council of Ministers) issued an order that all departments were to fill vacancies only with state subjects. This, in turn, prompted a precise definition of the term 'State Subject'. Referring to the Pandits' campaign, Bazaz notes that although it was phrased in state-wide terms, in practice it was a movement for greater employment of *Pandits*—since these were the only people in Jammu and Kashmir with the necessary qualifications: 'while they spoke in the name of the people what they demanded was not for the benefit of the masses and the lower strata of the society, but for themselves.' Ibid., p. 97.

9. Bazaz, *op. cit.* (1941), p. 90.

10. *Manchester Guardian*, 17 March 1932; I.O.L.R., L/P&S/13/1261, p. 265.

11. Although the ban on military service applied to the province of Kashmir as a whole, as well as the Northern Areas—in keeping with the Dogras' perception of these as conquered lands—in practice it affected the Muslims, who formed 95 per cent of the Valley population, much more than the Hindus. The ban on arms was retained in the new Arms Act and Rules, 1941. This justified allowing Hindu Rajputs to hold arms without licence 'on the grounds that Dogras worship their arms', Political Dept. note, 29 August 1941, I.O.L.R., L/P&S/13/1264, p. 198.

12. 'Gulab Singh went far beyond his predecessors in the gentle acts of undue taxation and extortion. They had taxed heavily, it is true, but he sucked the very life-blood of the people; they had laid violent hands on a large proportion of the fruits of the earth, the profits of the loom, and the work of men's hands, but he skinned the very flint to fill his coffers.' Lt.-Col. Torrens, *Travels in Ladak, Tartary and Kashmir* (London, Otley, 1865), p. 301, cited in Bhattacharjea, *op. cit.,* p. 56.

13. A memorandum from the Resident in Kashmir compares figures, taken from the Quarterly Civil and Military List issued by the Darbar, for Muslim and non-Muslim gazetted appointments:

   Total Muslim gazetted appointments 134 (64 Army, 6 Police, 64 Other Depts.)

   Total non-Muslim gazetted appointments 484 (207 Army, 30 Police, 247 Other Depts.)

   Memorandum to Political Secretary dated 6 October 1931, I.O.L.R., L/P&S/13/1260, p. 353.

14. The *khutba* was banned on the grounds that it was not part of the religious worship, but rather political. In practice, the *khutba* formed a regular part of Friday prayers in Kashmir; it was only in parts of Jammu that the *khutba* and the calling of the *azan* were restricted. One particular incident in Jammu in the spring of 1931, where a police inspector stopped a *khutba*, caused the 'ban' to be seized on as a grievance by the wider Muslim community. In response to their protests, Hari Singh issued an order on 5 October 1931 that there were to be no restrictions on either the *khutba* or the *azan*.

15. The law relating to apostates ['under law a person who forsakes his religion cannot inherit ancestral property'] was another of those measures which, though applicable to both Muslims and Hindus, had most effect on the former: 'the Mohammedans religion is a great proselytising religion and there are many cases of conversion to that religion, while a case of a Mohammedan becoming a Hindu is not known…there also seems some ground for believing that a change of religion involves not only loss of rights of inheritance, but also loss of property actually held.' Memorandum from Resident in Kashmir to Political Secretary, 6 October 1931, *op. cit.*, p. 352.

16. Ibid.

17. *Times*, 5 December 1931, in I.O.L.R., L/P&S/13/1261, p. 602.

18. Mirza Ghulam Ahmad, an inhabitant of Qadian in Punjab, founded the movement which took his name around 1879. Though some of his other teachings were unorthodox, his claim to be a prophet—thereby challenging the finality of Muhammad's prophethood—was viewed by most conventional Muslims as heretical: the Ahmadiyyas (a.k.a. Ahmadis/ Qadianis) were branded non-believers. Despite this, the Ahmadis were very active in spreading their beliefs. Ghulam Ahmad died in 1908; in 1924 the leader of the community was Mirza Kamalul-Din.

19. Frustrated by the lack of progress after submission of the Sharp report, a group of leading Muslims submitted a memorandum to Lord Reading, then Viceroy of India, when he visited Jammu and Kashmir in 1924. As well as steps to improve Muslim education, they demanded that a larger number of Muslims be employed in the State Services; proprietary rights over land for peasants; and the abolition of the *begar* system.

20. In July 1924, workers at the State Silk Factory in Jammu went on strike. Established in 1907, almost all its approximately 5000 workers were Muslim. In a repetition of previous strikes (1917 and 1920), they demanded better wages—the average pay was just four and a half annas per day. But in 1924 a new demand was added: that Muslims be appointed as officials in place of Hindus. The Government's response was uncompromising; troops including cavalry were used to disperse striking crowds, and the factory was closed until workers agreed to return unconditionally. In the end, the strikers secured only a minute pay increase.

21. '[S]ignatories to the memorandum were hounded by the police. Khwaja Saduddin Shawl was arrested and banished from the State. Khwaja Noor Shah Naqshbandi, son of Khwaja Hasan, was forced to resign from the post of tehsildar. Agha Syed Hussain Jalali was removed from the post of *zaildar* (Territory Officer), exiled from the State, and his jagir forfeited. Mirwaiz's name was removed from the list of durbaries and a strict warning was issued to him. The rest of the signatories, who submitted apologies, were mildly reprimanded.' Sheikh Mohammed Abdullah, *Flames of the Chinar: An Autobiography* (translated Khushwant Singh, New Delhi, Viking, 1993), p. 14.

22. The most influential of these were: Indian National Congress, which on 31 December 1929 had adopted the Resolution of Complete Independence; All-India Muslim League, which in March 1923 had adopted Muhammad Iqbal's (later known as) 'Pakistan Resolution'; All-India States People's Convention. 'Many young men belonging to Kashmir attended these political gatherings and were imbued with fresh ideas and a new spirit. They wanted to do something to put things right at home.' Bazaz, *op. cit.* (1941), p. 104.

23. Abdullah, *op. cit.*, p. 18.

24. 'The government's earlier claim that the scarcity of Muslims in public service was due to lack of education, was no longer acceptable because many educated Muslims had appeared on the scene. Therefore, they had to think up other excuses. First, only non-Muslims were appointed to the Public Service Recruitment Board. Second, Hindi and Sanskrit were offered as options, whereas Urdu, Persian and Arabic were not. Furthermore, the government could recruit 60 per cent of the candidates without referring their applications to the Board. The remaining 40 per cent were required to furnish details about their family background. Finally, the government also had the power to reject candidates without stating any reasons.' Ibid., p. 17.

25. Ibid., p. 21.

26. Bilqees Taseer, whose husband was principal of Sri Pratap College in the early 1940s, cited in Schofield, Victoria, *Kashmir in the Crossfire* (London, I.B. Tauris, 1996), p. 103.

27. In a representation made by the 'Deputation of Muslims of Jammu and Kashmir'on 15 August 1931, the non-Muslim community was accused of interfering in the religious affairs of Muslims: 'and the ball was set rolling by the Government. For example, the prohibition of *Khutba-i-Eid-ul-Azha*, the insult to the Holy Quran, the dismantling of mosques and the stoppage of *Azan* were heart-rending events which grievously wounded the religious feelings and prestige of the peaceful Muslim subjects and they were so impressed by the short-sightedness of the authorities that *they considered Islam to be in danger*' (author's italics). I.O.L.R., L/P&S/13/1260, p. 520.

28. The seven representatives elected to represent Kashmiri Muslims were: Sheikh Mohammed Abdullah, Mirwaiz Yusuf Shah, Mirwaiz Hamadani, Agha Syed Hussain Jalali, Khwaja Ghulam Ahmed Ashai, Munshi Shahabuddin, and Khwaja Saduddin Shawl. Note that at this stage the Muslims—at least politically—were presenting a united front. Representatives for Jammu Muslims were nominated by the Young Men's Muslim Association: Mistri Yaqub Ali, Sardar Gauhar Rehman, Chaudhri Ghulam Abbas, and Sheikh Abdul Hamid.

29. In later incidents, four people were killed at the Jama Masjid on 22 July, and a further nineteen at a demonstration in Islamabad the day after. The Government's response was to promulgate Ordinance 19-L throughout Srinagar. Along the lines of the British Burma Ordinance introduced to put down an organized armed rebellion in that country, it effectively put Srinagar under military control. It gave military and police officers above specified ranks wide powers of arrest without warrant, and control over the movements of suspected people. 'In all cases offences against its provisions or against the rules made under it are tried summarily and punished with imprisonment or flogging or both.' Bazaz, *op. cit.* (1941), p. 150.

30. Report on 'Disturbances in Kashmir', dated 28 September 1931; I.O.L.R., L/P&S/13/1260, p. 331. The Resident's views were echoed by Bazaz: '[T]he driving force behind the mass agitation till the 13th July was the discontent among the rank and file of the Muslims. The attack on the jail was in no way directed against the Hindus, and those who laid down their lives at the jail gate did so fighting against an unsympathetic Government....it was a fight of the tyrannised against their tyrants, of the oppressed against the oppressors.' Bazaz, *op. cit.* (1941), p. 131.

31. Sir Barjor Dalal, Chief Justice, was appointed the Commission's chairman. He was to have been assisted by two Hindu and two Muslim members. But, since the Muslims refused to cooperate with the Enquiry, a purely official committee was set up; it consisted of Dalal and three High Court judges. The Muslims' refusal to cooperate was due to anger at the fact that many of their leaders were imprisoned, and also because they opposed the choice of Dalal for chairman; they mistrusted Dalal and had no confidence of getting 'justice' from a Commission led by him.

32. As well as the shootings outside the jail, the Commission was to look into allegations of State troop involvement in (or at least failure to prevent) revenge anti-Muslim rioting by Hindus in those areas where the latter had been attacked, after State troops had taken control.

33. The Glancy Commission was also to look into the appropriateness of the authorities actions in disturbances subsequent to those covered by the Dalal Commission. The Muslims agreed to cooperate with Glancy's enquiry, so that unlike that of Dalal, it did actually have two Muslims and two Hindus assisting the chairman. The members from Kashmir were Ghulam Ahmed Ashai and Prem Nath Bazaz; for Jammu, Chaudhri Ghulam Abbas and Pandit Lokhnath Sharma. However, the Jammu Hindus later withdrew their representative because they objected to the Commission reviewing the laws relating to apostasy. Thus, when the Commission submitted its report, it consisted of Glancy plus two Muslims and a Hindu.

34. The Glancy Commission did not uphold the Muslims' complaint about converts' loss of property rights, because in Islam also apostates lose their inheritance rights—Islam actually prescribes the death penalty for them. Thus, the Commission concluded, existing State law was based on the religious laws of Hinduism *and* Islam.

35. After the Kashmir Conference on Constitutional Reform recommendation that a legisltive assembly be set up, a Franchise Committee was formed to work out the details with respect to composition of the proposed assembly, qualifications for franchise, etc.... [t]he guidelines laid down by this Committee were: Assembly was to have 75 members of which elected—33, nominated non-officials—30, nominated officials—12; total number of Muslims was to be 32 of which 21 elected and 11 nominated; total non-Muslims 31 of which 12 elected and 19 nominated. By

population Muslims would have got 24/33 elected seats. Weightage in favour of Hindus in these seats, and even more so in the allocation of non-official nominated seats, meant that Muslims and non-Muslims—despite the latter's clear majority in the population—were virtually equally represented in the Assembly.

36. 'It could ask questions, move resolutions, introduce bills and discuss the state budget. But any bill passed by the Praja Sabha could be sent back for reconsideration together with the amendments, if any, proposed by the Maharaja. Should the Praja Sabha refuse to pass a bill proposed by the Council of Ministers of the Maharaja's Government, the Maharaja was empowered to certify such bills be passed in the interest of the State and, on his certification, these would become Acts. The Legislature had no power over the Privy Purse of the Maharaja, the organization and control of the State Army, or the provisions of the Constitution.' Gupta, op. cit., p. 59.

'The use of communal constituencies, a highly restricted electorate (as little as 3% of the total population it has been estimated by some observers), a by no means impartial system of scrutiny of nominations and the presence of nominated and appointed members (who were in a majority in the 1934 Constitution), combined to produce a far from perfectly democratic arrangement.' Alastair Lamb, *Kashmir: A Disputed Legacy 1846–1990* (Hertingfordbury, Roxford, 1991), p. 92.

37. Bazaz, *op. cit.* (1941), p. 178.

38. The following is an example of the organization's attempts to get British intercession in J&K affairs: 'Practical exclusion from the privilege of advising His Highness the Maharaja and from the work of the various departments of the State, coupled with harsh and discriminating laws have kept the Muslims out of even those elementary rights which should belong to them as mere human beings.' Representation by the All-India Kashmir Committee to the Viceroy, requesting him to draw it to the attention of the Kashmiri Durbar, dated 12 April 1932, ibid., p. 632. Calls by the Committee for an enquiry into the background of the 13 July disturbances, probably did contribute to the Government of India 'persuading' Hari Singh to set up the Glancy Commission.

39. The Committee's call to remember those killed in July, on Kashmir Day (14 August), attracted a considerable response—one that extended far beyond the state itself. In British India, meetings were held in major cities like Bombay, Calcutta and Delhi; while in Jammu and Kashmir—despite a ban by the Maharaja—some 50,000 attended a rally outside the Jama Masjid in Srinagar.

40. The *Times*, 6 November 1931, accounts for the Anjuman-i-Islam's interest in Jammu and Kashmir, as an attempt to shake off the group's pro-Congress past: 'The Ahrars are members of a Muslim sect who for some reason cast in their lot with the Congress and became devout followers of

Dr. Ansari (the Congress Moslem leader). Gradually it was forced upon them, not only that they were not standing to gain much in that particular camp but that their allegiance to it was making them highly unpopular with their orthodox brethren. A sudden swing over followed, and they made a public renunciation of the impractical policy of joint electorates. Like most converts, they were regarded with a certain amount of suspicion by their own kind, and the organisaton of this agitation in support of the Kashmir Moslems owed something in the beginning to the zeal of the Ahrars to prove their sincerity and to show that they were prepared to strike a devout blow for Islam.' I.O.L.R., L/P&S/13/1260, p. 248.

41. Sheikh Abdullah wrote that the Anjuman's pro-Congress background, and the acceptance of Government hospitality by one of its delegations to Jammu and Kashmir 'had created doubts about their integrity and credibility in our minds.... They (representatives of Muslims in J&K) considered and rejected the political overtures of the Majlis-i-Ahrar. This offended the Ahrars who dubbed us as Qadianis and circulated the rumour that the President of the Kashmir Committee, Mirza Mahmood Ahmad, who was the grandson of Mirza Ghulam Ahmad, founder of the Ahmadiyya sect, was trying to make Kashmir a centre of his activities.' Abdullah, op. cit., pp. 32–3.

42. 'Two small jathas have left Delhi with the professed intention of proceeding to Jammu within the last twenty-four hours after a dedicatory service held in the Jama Masjid. It is unlikely that the jathas will get far on their way, but the incident is an illustration of the way the agitation is not only being kept alive but spreading in districts which hitherto have not been affected. Indeed the news from Kashmir has been satisfactory to everyone except those who wish to see the crisis continue for their own political ends.' Times, 26 November 1931, I.O.L.R., L/P&S/13/1260, p. 112.

43. In a letter replying to Sheikh Abdullah's invitation to visit Jammu and Kashmir, Nehru wrote: 'It is not necessary for you to invite me to my homeland, for the desire to go back is always present within me. It is 19 years now since I went there and often long to be back'; printed in Hindustan Times, 30 June 1936; quoted in Akbar, M.J., Kashmir, Behind the Vale (New Delhi, Viking, 1991). Abdullah describes Nehru's visit (in 1939): 'At his departure he claimed that he had visited Kashmir, not as a tourist, but as a son of the soil' op. cit., p. 51.

44. At a meeting of the Congress Working Committee held in July–August 1935, the party's position with respect to the Indian states was clarified. The party backed demands for representative government in the states and 'pledged to the States' people its sympathy and support in their legitimate and peaceful struggle for the attainment of full, responsible Government.' But the resolution also made clear this support would be only moral: 'It should be understood, however, that the responsibility and

burden of carrying on the struggle within the States must necessarily fall on the States' people themselves. The Congress can exercise moral and friendly influence upon the States and this it is bound to do wherever possible. The Congress has no other power under existing circumstances.' Akbar, *op. cit.*, p. 81.

45. The Government of India Act, 1935, provided for the British Indian provinces and the states to be integrated in a federal arrangement. Legislative powers would be divided subject-wise between the provinces/states and the centre. The federal arrangement came unstuck when the Princes refused to concede certain subjects to the central assembly—this despite the assembly being heavily weighted in their favour. However, at provincial level the Act was largely implemented; complete responsible government was introduced (i.e. dyarchy was abolished), and the franchise was extended to include a greater proportion of the population.

46. Address delivered on 15 February 1939; Gupta, *op. cit.*, p. 64.

47. 'The non-Hindu peoples in Hindustan must either adopt the Hindu culture and language, must learn to respect and hold in reverence Hindu religion, must entertain no idea but those of the glorification of the Hindu race and culture...in a word must cease to be foreigners, or may stay in this country, wholly subordinated to the Hindu nation, claiming nothing, deserving no privileges, far less any preferential treatment—not even citizens' rights.' Golwalkar, M.S., *We or Our Nationhood Defined* (4th ed., Nadpur, Bharat Prakashan, 1947), pp. 55–6, cited in Baxter, Craig, *The Jana Sangh: A Biography of an Indian Political Party* (Philadelphia, University of Pennsylvania Press, 1969), p. 31.

48. 'The latter party *(of Mirwaiz Yusuf Shah)* known as the Azad Party consider the former known as the Abdullah party as infidel on account of their pro-Kadiani tendencies and their connection with the Mirza of Kadian. Although S. M. Abdullah has denied that he is a Kadiani the State has evidence to show that he is backed by that party.' Report on 'Kashmir Disturbances' from Resident, Kashmir, to Glancy, I.O.L.R., L/P&S/13/1262, p. 95. This evidence included the following letter written by Abdullah to the Mirza of Qadian, in which he refers to the Yusuf Shah faction's plan to hold an 'Azad Conference': 'there is no other alternative to make it impossible except to create a horrible disturbance among the Muslims on the very outbreak of which the state would be obliged to promulgate an ordinance for the protection of peace and thus their conference would be unsuccessful...we have decided to hold a conference "Anjuman Traqai-ul-Ithad" on the very date of the opposite conference.' Quoted in letter from Resident to Glancy dated 1 January 1934, ibid., p. 92.

49. This was certainly the view of the Resident in Kashmir, writing in his fortnightly report for the first half of July 1932: 'The real cause of the antagonism between these parties is the indignation of Mir Waiz

Muhammad Yusuf at the diversion to S. M. Abdullah of offerings formerly made by Muslims to him.' Dated 18 July 1932, ibid., p. 362.

50. The first fighting between followers of the two leaders took place as early as July 1932. Involving stone throwing and the use of *lathis*, it was apparently provoked by Yusuf Shah accusing the Abdullah party of being Mirzais. Further trouble in August prompted the authorities to issue orders confining the Mirwaiz-i-Kashmir and Abdullah-Mirwaiz Hamadani to preaching in separate specified mosques.

51. Bazaz, *op. cit.* (1941), p. 135.

52. Ibid., p. 291.

53. A statement issued by the Sanatan Dharma Youngmen's Association on 8 October 1931, made clear its new priorities. One of its main arguments for the preservation of Pandit employment was that they were not qualified for anything other than State service: 'Solid reforms should continue to be our cry till every evil from which our community is suffering is removed. And the economic and political interests of our community in the State must always engage our attention....More important than anything else is the problem of educated employment among us...we educated ourselves and now we are told that we are Kashmiri Pandits and therefore the doors of Government Service are closed against us. And outside the State Service there are no openings for us'. I.O.L.R., L/P&S/13/1260, p. 57.

54. *Observer*, 29 May 1932, 'Hindu Agitation in Kashmir': 'The Glancy Report recommendation, urging an increased Muslim share in the State services, has aroused the bitterest opposition among the Kashmiri Pandits, who see their traditional places in the services threatened. Both the minority communities also complain of economic grievances.' I.O.L.R., L/P&S/13/1262, p. 534. Earlier, on 2 May, the Sanatan Dharma Youngmen's Association had made a written representation to the Prime Minister, in which they outlined their grievances and demands. These included: 'a) that the recommendations of the Glancy Commission should not be given a practical shape as far as they touched the Kashmir Pandits; b) that a declaration be made by the Government that grants of agricultural land will be made in favour of Kashmir Pandits; c) that the Kashmir Pandits should receive preference as far as the grant of Government contracts are concerned.' Ibid., p. 516. The latter two demands made it clear that, if Pandits had to concede some of their traditional jobs to Muslims, they wanted to be recompensed in other ways.

55. 'The Pandits seem to be adopting an anti-Government attitude. In a speech made yesterday by Pandit Jia Lal Kilam he said that the Hindu Raj was no longer in existence.... He said that unless the Government changed its policy by next Thursday he would start a hunger strike.... The origin of the trouble is somewhat obscure. It appears that the Pandit leaders, chief of whom are Pandit Jia Lal Kilam and Amar Nath Kak, were annoyed by

the fresh distribution of scholarships as between Hindus and Muhammadans. They considered that the Darbar was pro-Muhammadan.' Resident to R. Wingate, Joint Secretary, Foreign and Political Department, Government of India, dated 24 September 1932, ibid., p. 278.

56. I.O.L.R., L/P&S/13/1261, p. 87.

57. In a letter printed in the *Hindustan Times* on 30 June 1936, Nehru made clear he saw Kashmir's future tied to that of British India: 'the bigger problems of India have kept me tied to this part of India. Those problems, as you know, ultimately affect Kashmir also, for the fate of Kashmir is bound up with that of the rest of India. If India is freed Kashmir will participate in that freedom.' Akbar, *op. cit.*, p. 78.

58. Abdullah admitted Nehru's strong influence on him in an interview given much later: 'He (Nehru) suggested opening the Muslim Conference to non-Muslims as well. When I expressed doubt about it, he explained that by opening the membership to all, any campaign against the ruler would gain more strength. Each time we met thereafter our friendship grew stronger.' Bhattacharjea, *op. cit.*, p. 74.

59. Bhattacharjea, *op. cit.*, p. 72 and Akbar, *op. cit.*, p. 76.

60. Abdullah described the class-base of the new party in his autobiography: '[O]ur movement had been thrown open to all religious groups. It became imperative to develop new political and economic rallying points. We had learnt from experience that the real reason for conflict was not religion but a clash of interests between different classes and groups. The primary objective of our movement was to oppose oppression and support the oppressed.' *Op. cit.*, p. 57.

61. The aim of the socialist creed was explained in 'New Kashmir': 'to perfect our union in fullest equality and self-determination, to raise ourselves and our children forever from the abyss of oppression and poverty, degradation and superstition, from medieval darkness and ignorance, into the sunlit valleys of plenty ruled by freedom, science and honest toil.' Akbar, *op. cit.*, p. 84.

62. Resident's fortnightly report for the first half of January 1943, ibid., p. 462.

63. Resident's fortnightly report for the second half of April 1939: 'Ever since the change in the name from the "Muslim" to the "National" Conference, the progressive elements within the Conference have met with serious opposition from the followers of Pir Yusuf Shah Mir Waiz, Maulvi Ghulam Nabi Hamdani, Maulvi Abdullah, Pleader and others. This bloc have expressed their resentment at such aggravating acts as the hoisting of the Congress flag by S. M. Abdullah over a Srinagar masjid and the flirtation of the non-communalists with the Indian National Congress. They fear Congress domination.' Dated 1 May 1939, I.O.L.R., L/P&S/13/1264, p. 402.

64. Developments in British India at the time were: in 1937, following its success in provincial elections, Congress refused to form coalition

governments with the Muslim League—effectively dashing all hopes of Congress-League rapprochement. From this point the enmity between the two became increasingly intense. In 1939, the Congress governments resigned in protest at the Viceroy's taking India into the War without consulting Indians first. The League's reaction was to celebrate a 'Day of Deliverance' and to fill the vacant provincial ministries. In August 1942, Congress (or rather Gandhi) launched the 'Quit India' movement; the Muslim League boycotted this campaign. Rivalry and bitterness between the two parties grew as the Muslim League became more powerful and its dream of 'Pakistan' approached realization. Not surprisingly, this bitterness infected relations between their respective 'daughter' parties in Jammu and Kashmir, the National Conference and Muslim Conference.

65. On 16 August 1942, within a week of Congress launching the 'Quit India' movement, the National Conference issued a statement expressing its support: 'The demand of the Congress is based on just reasons. The Working Committee condemns the reign of terror and repression which the Government of India have launched by declaring the Indian National Congress illegal, by the arrest of the leaders, and by shooting down unarmed people.' Akbar, *op. cit.*, p. 84.

66. 'In several speeches which the Mir Waiz has delivered in Srinagar during the last fortnight he has referred to the alleged disabilities that the State Muslims were suffering and has declared that Pakistan is the only solution of Muslim Problems. In a speech which he made on September 15th he declared that as the British, an alien nation, had taken over the reins of Government in India from the Muslims, they should now return those powers to that community.' Resident's fortnightly report for the second half of September 1942, dated 2 October 1942, I.O.L.R., L/P&S/13/1264, p. 24.

67. Followers of Sheikh Abdullah were already angered by speeches made by the Mirwaiz-i-Kashmir condemning their leader. On the occasion of Eid-ul-Fitr prayers on 12 October 1942, instead of going to the mosque allocated to their party by the Government, they congregated outside the Muslim Conference mosque—predictably leading to clashes between the two groups. In January 1943, there was further trouble over the offering of prayers at the Hazratbal Mosque. Mirwaiz Yusuf was the shrine's *pir*, but its committee and servants were National Conference members. On the ordained prayer day both parties turned up at the shrine. This time, though, physical violence was avoided by the Mirwaiz 'backing down'; he returned to Srinagar without offering prayers. When these were required to be offered again, two and a half weeks later, he did not go at all—again, to avoid clashes with National Conference supporters.

68. By appointing only National Conference members to the committees responsible for allocating rice tickets and fuel permits, the Government gave that party the opportunity—which it took full advantage of—to

assert its authority over Muslim Conference members (principally by withholding tickets).

69. '[A]t the beginning of July Section 144 Cr. P.C. was promulgated in Srinagar banning processions and public meetings for a period of two months, though this was slightly relaxed at the beginning of August...subject to certain conditions. One condition was that no-one who was not a State subject was permitted to attend or speak at any of the meetings....It seems pretty clear that the main purpose of the promulgation of Section 144 Cr. P.C. and of all these restrictions was to prevent the annual session of the Muslim Conference and the Muslim Students Federation (both pro-Muslim League organisations) being addressed and assisted by well-known pro-Pakistan politicians from British India and other Indian States.' Resident's fortnightly report for the second half of August 1943, dated 2 September 1943, I.O.L.R., L/P&S/13/1265, p. 368.

70. Sir Gopalaswami Ayyangar was Prime Minister of Jammu and Kashmir from 1935 to 1943. The Resident described him as 'a strong Hindu and a strong nationalist with not unsympathetic leanings towards the Congress.' ['Appreciation of the Political Situation in Kashmir', ibid., p. 320] In August 1942, Sheikh Abdullah began organizing strikes, processions, etc., in support of the Congress movement in India. Through subordinate officials, Ayyangar advised him not to attack the Maharaja or the British. Heeding this advice Abdullah limited his followers' activities to expressing support for Congress. As a result—unlike in British India— there were no significant arrests in Jammu and Kashmir. In November 1942, Ayyangar held a meeting with Abdullah, the first after several years: 'after which the latter made more protestations of his loyalty to His Highness, and rumours of constitutional reform in Kashmir began to become prevalent.... Shortly afterwards the Kashmir Government entrusted the work of issuing Rice ration tickets and permits for fuel in Srinagar to Committees composed almost entirely of non-officials. The National Conference was represented on these Committees at the instance of the Kashmir Government but no representatives of the Muslim Conference were appointed.' Ibid., p. 321.

71. As the League leader's visit drew to a close, Sheikh Abdullah was threatening him: 'If Jinnah does not give up the habit of interfering in our politics, it will be difficult for him to go back in an honourable manner' [Akbar, *op. cit.*, p. 85]. Jinnah's response was equally strong: 'When I...suggested that the Mussalmans should organise themselves under one flag and on one platform, not only was my advice not acceptable to Sheikh Abdullah but, as is his habit, which has become second nature to him, he indulged in all sorts of language of a most offensive and vituperative character in attacking me.' Bhattacharjea, *op. cit.*, p. 76.

72. Jinnah's arguments were essentially a repetition of those he had used to win over the Muslims of British India: he called on all Muslims to join the Muslim Conference because 'Muslims have one platform, one *Kalma* and one God' [Akbar, *op. cit.*, p. 85].

73. The Resident noted the flexibility of Abdullah's political convictions in his fortnightly report for the second half of January 1944: 'Sheikh Mohammad Abdullah has not yet come to a final decision as to his political future. It has been suggested that he wishes above all to achieve his personal ambition of becoming a Minister in the State. If he succeeds, then there may never be any question of his joining the Muslim League or Muslim Conference. If he fails, he may well throw in his lot with these parties' I.O.L.R., L/P&S/13/1265, p. 280.

74. Abdullah, *op. cit.*, p. 78.

75. 'Disturbances in Kashmir State in May 1946', I.O.L.R., L/P&S/1266, p. 95.

76. Abdullah, *op. cit.*, p. 79.

77. Ibid., p. 82.

78. 'Disturbances in Kashmir State in May 1946', I.O.L.R., L/P&S/13/1266, pp. 188–90.

79. Muhammad Saraf writes 'Quaid-e-Azam realised very early that unless the Party was able to approach Kashmiri speaking Muslims through a leader who could speak to them in their mother tongue, it was not possible to build up the organisation or effectively challenge the leadership of Sheikh Muhammad Abdullah', *Kashmiris Fight for Freedom* (Lahore, 1977), p. 638, as quoted in Schofield, *op. cit.*, p. 113. Schofield goes on 'Attempts to find such a leader, including the suggestion that Ghulam Abbas learn Kashmiri, failed.'

80. Resident's fortnightly report for the first half of May 1943, dated 15 May 1943, I.O.L.R., L/P&S/13/1265, p. 423.

81. Until at least as late as June 1944, the Muslim Conference's Jammu leader Ghulam Abbas opposed Kashmir joining Pakistan—though he supported the idea of Pakistan. In his fortnightly report for the second half of that month, the Resident writes: 'Ghulam Abbas Chaudhri said that...the Muslims of Kashmir State could not unite with the Hindus; at the same time they did not want Pakistan for the State; but would certainly give Mr Jinnah every support in his campaign' [I.O.L.R., L/P&S/13/1265, p. 194]. Elections to the Praja Sabha were held in January 1947. These were boycotted by the National Conference, thus giving the Muslim Conference the majority of Muslim seats in the assembly. On 19 July the Mirwaiz-i-Kashmir passed a resolution advocating Jammu and Kashmir's accession to Pakistan. Party President Ghulam Abbas was in jail at the time, but the resolution was opposed by the Acting President, Chaudhri Hamidullah Khan—like Abbas, he preferred independence.

82. On leaving the National Conference, Premnath Bazaz first joined the new Muslim Conference, and then formed his own Kashmir Socialist Party. At the time of Partition, Bazaz favoured Jammu and Kashmir acceding to Pakistan, on the grounds that both had Muslim-majority populations. Just as he had been the exceptional Hindu in joining Sheikh Abdullah's party, now too he was unique among Hindus in holding these pro-Pakistan views.

83. Abdullah, *op. cit.*, p. 65. In 'A Note on Kashmir' to Viceroy Mountbatten, dated 17 June 1947, Nehru wrote: 'The National Conference has stood for and still stands for Kashmir joining the Constituent Assembly of India' Akbar, *op. cit.*, p. 95. In a later letter (27 September 1947) to Sardar Patel, he reiterated this view: 'Sheikh Abdullah has repeatedly given assurances of wishing to cooperate and of being opposed to Pakistan; also to abide by my advice.' Ibid., p. 104.

84. After it had been agreed in the 3 June 1947 Partition Plan that the subcontinent would be divided (both in the east and the west) to form Pakistan and India, Boundary Commissions were set up to demarcate the boundaries between the two new dominions. In the east, Bengal Province would have to be split up, and in the west, Punjab. Two commissions were appointed, both under a single chairman who held the casting vote; he was assisted in each province by two Congress and two Muslim League nominees. The Muslim League and Congress could not agree on an Indian chairman, so Mountbatten chose an English jurist, Cyril Radcliffe—a man who had never even visited the subcontinent before. The terms of reference for the Commission for the Punjab were: 'to demarcate the boundaries of the two parts of the Punjab on the basis of ascertaining the contiguous majority areas of Muslim and non-Muslim areas. In doing so, it will also take into account other factors' [Lamb, *op. cit.*, p. 104]. Presumably, these 'other factors' were geographical and structural, e.g. rivers, water-works, railways. Radcliffe reached India on 8 July, and had finished his report (mainly relying on maps) within five weeks. Its recommendations were announced on 16 August, after independence.

85. Altogether, some half a million people were killed before the end of 1947. Many more were uprooted: four and a half million Hindus and Sikhs migrated from West Pakistan to India, six million Muslims in the opposite direction. While there was far less killing in Bengal, some one million people were displaced there.

86. Lamb., *op. cit.*, p. 123.

87. Poonch had come under the direct control of Maharaja Hari Singh in 1935/36, but the former *jagir's* population had never reconciled themselves to Dogra rule. Ethnically they had few links with Jammu, and even less with the Vale; they were much closer to the Punjab. The Muslims of Poonch, notably the Sudhen and Satti tribes, had served widely in both the British Indian army, and in the Jammu and Kashmir

forces. In 1947, following the end of the Second World War, some 60,000 ex-servicemen had returned to Poonch. These men possessed both military experience and arms.

In June 1947, a revolt broke out over the State Government's exorbitant taxes, as well as in protest at high food prices. Some 10,000 Poonchis decided to march on Poonch city, but before reaching it clashed with State troops at Bagh. The Government ordered the inhabitants to surrender their weapons; this was largely ignored. The situation was exacerbated on 14 August, when Muslims attempted to celebrate Pakistan Day (also Kashmir Day) in defiance of a Government ban. In addition, the killings in Punjab after Partition and the arrival of large numbers of Muslim refugees in Poonch, pushed the conflict into taking on a communal aspect. By September, the revolt had acquired a degree of organization under Mohammed Ibrahim Khan (the Muslim representative for Poonch in the Praja Sabha and a Muslim Conference member), and had evolved into a secessionist movement. In October 1947, the 'Government of Azad Kashmir' declared the area independent of Dogra rule, and set up its capital in Muzaffarabad.

88. Once underway, the Poonch rebellion received support from a number of sources: defectors from the Jammu and Kashmir forces, former Indian National Army soldiers and Punjabi Muslims especially from Jhelum. But initially the most support came from Pathans of the North-West Frontier Province. The Pakistan Government was at first very reluctant to become involved, e.g. it refused to recognize the Azad Kashmir Government. However, by September, it was providing unofficial aid to the rebels.

89. Abdullah, *op. cit.*, p. 86.

90. Not surprisingly, this decision was much resented by Pakistan. Radcliffe was accused of conspiring with Mountbatten and Congress to ensure Jammu and Kashmir's accession to India remained a possibility. The award has been defended on the grounds that the district included the headworks of canals irrigating East Punjab; these had to be in Indian control (counter-argument: canals from those headworks also supplied West Punjab). Also, that awarding Gurdaspur to Pakistan would have split the Sikh 'heartland'. For a detailed consideration of the 'conspiracy theory', see Wirsing, Robert, *India, Pakistan, and the Kashmir Dispute: On Regional Conflict and its Resolution* (London, Macmillan, 1994), pp. 12–34.

91. The Indian States were constitutionally quite distinct from the provinces and Tribal Areas of British India. But they were part of the British Empire, because they had acknowledged the paramountcy of the British Crown. In practice, relations between the Crown and a particular State, were conducted through the Viceroy (the Crown-Representative in British India) by way of a political adviser or resident. The degree of control a

ruler exerted over his state varied according to its category: a) some 140 major states were 'fully empowered', i.e. had full legislative and jurisdictional powers; b) also around 140 states, which shared administration in various arrangements with the British; c) remaining 300 or so states (usually only a few 100 acres) which had virtually no powers. Jammu and Kashmir fell into the first category.

92. Lamb describes the mechanism of accession as it applied to the first category, 'fully empowered' states, which included Jammu and Kashmir: 'The Ruler of a State...could, if he wished to join, sign an Instrument of Accession in which he transferred to the appropriate Dominion what were deemed the three major powers, those over Defence, External Affairs and Communications.... In the 1947 provisions it was possible for a State, which was deliberating accession or acceding with certain issues unresolved, to sign with one or both of the Dominions what was termed a Standstill Agreement: this would permit the continuation of various essential services even if their constitutional basis was now uncertain' *op. cit.*, p. 5.

93. Junagadh was a small state in western India which, though surrounded by Indian territory, had a sea-link with Pakistan. 80% of its population of 670,719 were Hindus, but the Nawab of Junagadh signed an Instrument of Accession to Pakistan; this was accepted on 13 September. The move led to widespread protests in the state, and pressure on the Nawab (an economic blockade plus military build-up on borders) from the Indian government to reverse his decision in their favour. Eventually, the Nawab fled to Pakistan and Indian troops marched into Junagadh on 9 November. A referendum was held on 20 February 1948, the result of which was overwhelmingly in India's favour.

    Hyderabad was a much larger state in the Deccan. Despite his state's Hindu-majority population, the Muslim Nizam wished to retain his independence. India protested at this move as well. The Nizam signed a standstill agreement with India in November 1947 but talks over a permanent settlement reached a stalemate in June 1948. In September 1948, Indian troops took the state by force. Pakistan protested at Indian actions in both Junagadh and Hyderabad; Islamabad still regards Junagadh legally as part of Pakistan.

94. Quoted in Bhattacharjea, *op. cit.*, p. 120.

95. While the Poonch revolt had long become a secessionist movement, it was not until 24 October that a formal declaration of independence from Hari Singh's rule was made. The new State of Azad Kashmir was headed by 'President' Mohammed Ibrahim Khan; Mirwaiz Yusuf Shah was appointed Minister of Education.

96. Nehru believed that Sheikh Abdullah was the spokesman for Kashmiri public opinion; thus if Hari Singh had Abdullah's support in acceding to India, it could be assumed that he also had the support of the State's

people. In a letter to Sardar Patel, dated 27 September 1947, he wrote: 'It becomes important, therefore, that the Maharaja should make friends with the National Conference so that there might be...popular support against Pakistan.... It seems to me urgently necessary...that the accession to the Indian Union should take place early. It is equally clear to me that this can only take place with some measure of success after there is peace between the Maharaja and the National Conference' Bhattacharjea, *op. cit.*, pp. 117–18.

97. Mahajan had been a member of the Radcliffe Boundary Commission in Punjab. Hari Singh appointed him Prime Minister of Jammu and Kashmir on the recommendation of Sardar Patel. In Alastair Lamb's opinion Mahajan's 'appointed task was to see through accession to India. This impression is confirmed by Mahajan's visit to New Delhi on 11 October 1947, just before formally taking office as Prime Minister, when he called on Sardar Vallabhai Patel, Jawaharlal Nehru and Mahatma Gandhi...V.P. Menon (Sardar Vallabhai Patel's right hand man in matters of the accession to India of states)...advised Mahajan to bring about the accession of the State to India anyhow. Mahajan did not seek an interview with any senior Pakistani politician or official before assuming office.' *Op. cit.*, p. 129.

98. Supply of commodities (petrol, salt, food, cloth) to Jammu and Kashmir, which had previously been transported from Pakistan, certainly decreased from September 1947. The Jammu and Kashmir Government accused Pakistan of trying to apply economic pressure to force it to accede to that country. The Pakistanis denied this, and attributed the fall in supplies to a number of other factors: disruption of the Sialkot-Jammu railway because of shortage of coal, refugees blocking the roads, lorry-drivers afraid to drive through areas of high communal tension. In October, in response to a request by the State Government, India sent supplies of basic commodities to Srinagar by lorry.

99. 'The Government of Jammu and Kashmir during this crucial period was also in contact with the Rulers of a number of Indian States who, despite their own accession to India, may to some extent have been operating independent policies. The Sikh Maharaja of Patiala...in the first two weeks of October 1947 provided his colleague in the State of Jammu and Kashmir with a battalion of infantry and a battery of mountain artillery from his own State Armed Forces.' Ibid., p. 131. Lamb uses the presence of Patiala troops—after accession, theoretically Indian—to back his later argument that Indian troops entered the State before an Instrument of Accession to India had been signed; Patiala gunners were in position at Srinagar airfield by at least 17 October, but Hari Singh did not sign the Accession document until 26 (or 27) October.

100. Maharaja Hari Singh to Mountbatten, Governor-General of India: 'With the conditions obtaining at present in my State, and the great emergency of

the situation as it exists, I have no option but to ask for help from the Indian Dominion. Naturally they cannot send the help asked for by me without my State acceding to the Dominion of India. I have accordingly decided to do so, and I attach the instrument of accession for acceptance by your Government.' Dated 26 October 1947, I.O.L.R., L/P&S/13/1845B, p. 497.

101. 'Mahajan begged for help, but, it would seem, without promising accession, and certainly without committing the State to constitutional reform. Nehru showed reluctance: it was not so easy, he said, to move troops at short notice. Mahajan then gave way. In return for military assistance he agreed to accept a Sheikh Abdullah administration.' Lamb, *op. cit.*, p. 135. At the time (26 October) Sheikh Abdullah was in New Delhi staying with Nehru, in whose residence the talks with Mahajan took place. Lamb implies the Abdullah-administration condition was included to ensure the National Conference leader's support for accession to India.

102. Dated 27 October 1947; I.O.L.R., L/P&S/13/1854B, pp. 497–8.

103. Lamb writes that the Indian Government was making preparations for military intervention long before the Instrument of Accession was signed: 'the first volume of Sardar Vallabhai Patel's correspondence which was published in 1971, makes it clear that both Sardar Vallabhai Patel and Baldev Singh were heavily engaged in the planning of some kind of Indian military intervention in the State of Jammu and Kashmir, if only on a contingency basis, by at least 13 September 1947; and that by the third week of October a substantial foundation for such an operation had been laid', *op. cit.*, p. 130. Much later in March 1951, Nehru admitted in a statement to Parliament that India would have sent her troops into Jammu and Kashmir even if Hari Singh had not signed the Instrument of Accession: 'irrespective of accession we would have had an obligation to protect the people of Kashmir against aggression.' Quoted in Bhattacharjea, *op. cit.*, p. 137.

104. In his 1990 *Kashmir: A Disputed Legacy*, Lamb presents Mahajan's account of his and V.P. Menon's journeys to Jammu and Kashmir in October 1947, to back his claim that the Instrument of Accession could not have been signed before 9.00 a.m. on 27 October, when Indian troops went into the state. From this he draws the conclusion that India had no legal basis to be in Jammu and Kashmir. In a later book, Lamb develops his argument further. He writes there is strong evidence to support the theory that Hari Singh never signed any Instrument of Accession: 'One may well wonder why the Government of India, had it indeed been in possession of a properly signed Instrument, did not publish it as such in the 1948 *White Paper'*, *Birth of a Tragedy: Kashmir 1947* (Karachi, Oxford University Press, 1994), p. 102. The explanation he suggests is that Hari Singh knew, once Indian troops were in the State, they had to

repel the Pathan invaders; he perhaps hoped to retain control of the State—still legally his—once India had rid him of the tribal menace.

105. On 26 March 1935, Maharaja Hari Singh had leased the Gilgit Wazarat north of the Indus and its dependencies, to the British for a period of sixty years. However in April 1947, after just twelve years, Mountbatten decided to hand the area back to direct Jammu and Kashmir control before the subcontinent became independent. This handover took effect on 1 August; Hari Singh's Governor, Brigadier Ghansara Singh, reached Gilgit one day before. The local population, who had not been consulted about the handover, had no desire to return to Dogra rule. The local military force, the Gilgit Scouts, shared these sentiments. Faced with impending mutiny plus a Pathan tribal incursion, the Scouts' British officer, Major Brown, decided the only way to prevent widespread disorder and bloodshed was to put the entire region under Pakistani control. Ghansara Singh was placed under house arrest and, on 3 November 1947, Brown announced Gilgit's accession to Pakistan.

106. India (on Nehru's instigation) first took the Jammu and Kashmir dispute to the United Nations on 1 January 1948. On 15 January, Gopalaswami Ayyangar and Zafrullah Khan presented their respective countries views to the Security Council. During the course of the year various proposals for holding a plebiscite in the disputed region were put forward, but none was acceptable to both India and Pakistan. However, with fighting in the state almost at a stalemate, and war threatening to spread to India and Pakistan themselves, the two sides did agree to a United Nations proposal for a cease-fire.

3

POLITICAL DEVELOPMENTS WITHIN JAMMU AND KASHMIR 1947–1965

Interim Government

The Interim Government came into being on 5 March 1948, replacing the Emergency Government that had been formed the year before in October. The new administration was to govern until a Constituent Assembly could be elected. Sheikh Abdullah took over as Prime Minister from Mehr Chand Mahajan, Bakshi Ghulam Muhammad was appointed Deputy Prime Minister, and other National Conference leaders took over key ministries, e.g. Mirza Afzal Beg headed Revenue and G.M. Sadiq, Development. Two aspects of this Government are worthy of especial consideration: its structure (in terms of democracy) and its socio-economic policies.

Structure of Interim Government

Before considering the nature—democratic or otherwise—of Sheikh Abdullah's government, this is an appropriate moment to describe the fate of Maharaja Hari Singh. One of the main demands in 'New Kashmir' had been for the abolition of Dogra rule. By 1948, Hari Singh had effectively been stripped of all his power. Azad Kashmir had declared itself completely independent of the Dogras, and even in those parts of the former

Jammu and Kashmir where he was still acknowledged Maharaja, all decisions were made by Sheikh Abdullah's National Conference or by India. Any hopes Hari Singh may have nurtured of retaining influence after accession to India were dashed by Nehru's vigorous support for Sheikh Abdullah.

Despite having taken over power, Abdullah was unwilling to retain Hari Singh even as a nominal figurehead; he feared the Maharaja could become a focus for Hindu opposition, especially in Jammu. In June 1949, with Indian support, Abdullah pressurized Hari Singh into handing over what little remained of his powers to his son Yuvraj Karan Singh. Karan Singh took the title Regent; his father, thus the last Dogra Maharaja, moved to India where he died in 1961. In June 1952, the Dogras' hereditary position was abolished completely. It was replaced by a constitutional Head of State, referred to as the Sadar-i-Riyasat, who would be elected by the Constitutional (later Legislative) Assembly for a period of five years. The first Sadar-i-Riyasat of Jammu and Kashmir was Karan Singh. For many of the state's Hindus, the abolition of Dogra rule was yet another example of Muslim discrimination against them.

Turning to the question of democracy the first point to stress is that the only 'legal' basis for Sheikh Abdullah's rule was that the Maharaja had appointed him to the Emergency Government of 1947 and subsequently to the 1948 Interim Government. Hari Singh had been pressurized into doing this by Nehru, who was convinced that the Sheikh enjoyed the support of the majority of the state's Muslims. Nehru's assessment of Abdullah's popularity was not based on any concrete figures. The last elections to the Praja Sabha (in January 1947) could have provided an accurate picture of relative support for the Muslim and National Conferences, but they had been boycotted by the latter. The party with a majority in the legislature was thus actually the Muslim Conference, which had passed a resolution calling for Kashmir's accession to Pakistan. Nehru's decision to overlook the Muslim Conference in favour of Sheikh Abdullah was probably justified with respect to the Valley alone—Abdullah was certainly more popular there than the Muslim Conference. But over the state as a whole, support for Abdullah was less pronounced: most Muslims in Jammu supported the rival Muslim Conference, while Hindus and other non-Muslims opposed both. Hence, one can only conclude that Nehru's decision to hand power to Abdullah was based less on Abdullah's state-wide following as on his non-communal politics.[1]

When Abdullah came to power the only constitutional guidelines in existence, defining the extent of his powers, were those that had applied to the Maharaja in the 1939 Constitution. Sheikh Abdullah did not hesitate to appropriate these constitutional powers for himself. The practical outcome of this was that his government was a virtual one-man dictatorship. Opposition to Abdullah from within the National Conference was suppressed, as Ganguly describes:

> The organizational structure of the National Conference belied its socialist ideology. As a political party it was constructed largely around the personage of Abdullah and his close advisors. Decision-making was concentrated in the hands of the Sheikh. Little internal dissent was permitted.[2]

Political opposition from outside was similarly suppressed. The practise of press censorship established under the Maharaja was maintained. Muslim Conference leaders imprisoned by Hari Singh soon after Sheikh Abdullah's arrest, and who had not been released with him, remained in prison when he came to power. Their numbers were swollen by officials from the previous administration, e.g. the former Governor of Jammu. Since the State High Court had been immobilized, they could expect to stay in jail until Sheikh Abdullah was to decide otherwise—a state of affairs not dissimilar to that prevailing during the Maharaja's rule.

Democratic norms were further compromised by the Abdullah government's corruption. National Conference members did not hesitate to take advantage of their party's position in power for personal advantage, e.g. by selling trade concessions, hiring out State transport and, of course, obtaining official appointments.

Mehr Chand Mahajan was moved to describe Abdullah's Emergency Government as similar to that of Nazi Germany 'run by gangsters without benefit of rule of law'.[3] This was a far cry from the democracy Sheikh Abdullah and Nehru had advocated for so long. Observers in India were disturbed by the Abdullah administration's undemocratic tendencies. However, in the short-term—having declared Abdullah the most popular leader in Kashmir and having on this basis placed him in power—India had little option but to back his regime.

There were also wider considerations. While the Instrument of Accession provided the *legal* justification for India's presence in the State, they needed popular support to give them *moral* justification. This was important in the context of international politics—to refute Pakistani claims that the Kashmiris had really wanted to accede to them and that India was holding the State by force. Finally, Nehru feared that if Abdullah turned against India so too would the people, thereby making India's holding onto the State considerably more difficult.[4] For all these reasons the Indian government turned a blind eye to the corrupt and dictatorial nature of Abdullah's premiership.

Socio-economic Policies

Sheikh Abdullah wasted little time in implementing the policies set out in the 1944 socialist manifesto 'New Kashmir'. Most significant—politically as well as economically—were the land reforms carried out by the new government. Under the Dogras land ownership had been concentrated in the hands of the monarch and a relatively small group of *jagirdars* and *muafidars*. The revenue from land in the State thus benefitted only a small minority of its population. The Abolition of Big Landed Estates Act, passed in 1950, put an end to this concentration of land wealth by putting an upper limit of 182 *kanals* (22.75 acres) on individual land ownership. The 9000-odd landowners who held more than this had their 'surplus' land confiscated by the government. It was either redistributed free among the landless peasantry who traditionally worked it, or converted into State property. The original landowners received no compensation for the often considerable land they lost.

A number of other measures further altered the traditional landlord-tennant relationship in the latter's favour: landlords had to contribute to the cost of tools and seed; tennants were protected from ejection and their share of the crop was increased from one-third to half. Finally, the Distressed Debtors Relief Act (also passed in 1950) effectively abolished peasant debts: if a debtor had repaid one and a half times his original debt this was to be considered cleared. The *jagirdars* were thus deprived not only of their lands but also of the means by which they had traditionally obtained free labour.

Naturally the reforms aroused great resentment among the land-owning classes. As well as the expected class resentment, there was communal resentment. This was pretty much inevitable since most of those who suffered as a result of the reforms—landowners and money-lenders—were Hindu, while most of those who benefitted were Muslim. Hindus viewed the National Conference government's policies not as measures aimed at ending peasant exploitation and creating a more equal society, but as deliberate discrimination against them because of their religion by a Muslim government.

Looking to the longer term, and following the examples of the Soviet Union and the new Indian Dominion, Abdullah's government introduced five-year plans for Jammu and Kashmir. The first Five Year Plan contained programmes for extensive irrigation works and for the construction of a tunnel under the Banihal Pass which would allow year-long access to Jammu Province from Srinagar. There were also plans for greater State involvement in industry.

Constitutional Arrangements

The state of Jammu and Kashmir (this term will now be used to refer to those parts under Indian control) was in a somewhat ambiguous position with respect to its relations with India. On the one hand, Maharaja Hari Singh had signed the Instrument of Accession by which it became part of the Indian Union. On the other hand, the Indian Government had only accepted this on condition that it be ratified by a popular referendum. Thus, until a referendum was carried out, Jammu and Kashmir could not be described as Indian but equally could not be called independent. The ambiguous nature of the State's relationship with India led to a certain amount of ambiguity, and even contradictions, when formulating constitutional arrangements between the two.

Indian Constituent Assembly

Consider first provisions for Jammu and Kashmir in the Indian Constitution. According to the Instrument of Accession, India was to only have control of defence, foreign affairs and communications. All other matters were to remain in the State government's jurisdiction. In the 1950 Indian Constitution, this arrangement was embodied in Article 370. This gave Jammu and Kashmir a special status, notably the right to frame its own constitution. In moving Article 306A (later 370) in the Indian Constituent Assembly, Gopalaswami Ayyangar made clear not only the State's special status, but also the *non*-finality of accession:

> [T]he Government of India have committed themselves to the people of Kashmir in certain respects. They have committed themselves to the position that an opportunity would be given to the people of the state to decide for themselves whether they will remain with the Republic or wish to go out of it. We are also committed to ascertaining this will of the people by means of a plebiscite provided that peaceful and normal conditions are restored and the impartiality of the plebiscite could be guaranteed. We have also agreed that the will of the people, through the instrument of a Constituent Assembly, will determine the Constitution of the State as well as the sphere of Union jurisdiction over the State.[5]

However, it should be noted that the high degree of autonomy granted to the state by Article 370 was intended to be temporary. It was generally assumed that once accession had been ratified greater integration would follow[6] (Article 370 was retained in the 1956 amended Constitution as Article 152).

In apparent contradiction to Article 370—based as just seen on the premise that accession still had to be finalized—Article 1 of the same Constitution described Jammu and Kashmir as an integral part of the Indian Union. In keeping with *this* position the State was allocated four seats in the Indian Constituent Assembly, and subsequently in the Lok Sabha.

The Indian leadership was also divided over the issue of Jammu and Kashmir's accession. Most, including Sardar Vallabhai Patel, felt that the Instrument of Accession was final and not a temporary measure. As far as they were concerned, as soon as Hari Singh had signed it, Jammu and Kashmir had become a permanent part of India, and hence should not be treated any differently from all the other former princely states. Others, notably Nehru and the Governor-General Mountbatten, felt ratification by a popular referendum was important, though their commitment to this would decrease later as circumstances altered.

Jammu and Kashmir Constituent Assembly

Turning to Jammu and Kashmir, there was determination within the state to obtain at least the degree of autonomy guaranteed in the Instrument of Accession. Those who had expected that it would follow in the footsteps of the other former princely states and adopt the Indian Constitution were soon to be disillusioned. In calling for the setting up of a Constituent Assembly, the phrasing 'for the purpose of determining the future shape and affiliations of the State of Jammu and Kashmir' gave a clear indication that the National Conference intended to pursue its own agenda for the State.

Elections for the Constituent Assembly were announced on 30 April 1951, and held in August. Of the Assembly's one hundred seats, only seventy-five were contested, the remainder being allocated to Azad Kashmir (never filled). That the National Conference won all seventy-five seats, and that seventy-three of its candidates were returned unopposed, gives a good indication of the 'fairness' of these elections. In fact, the National Conference ensured victory for itself by strictly controlling both the compilation of electoral rolls, and the nomination of candidates. The Praja Parishad, representing Jammu Hindus and 'the only other tolerably organized party in the State' boycotted the elections after the nominations of all twenty-seven of its candidates were rejected.[7] In addition, only 5 per cent of those eligible to vote actually did so—this alone would have rendered the representativeness of the results highly suspect.

The Constituent Assembly first met on 31 October 1951. In his opening address five days later, Sheikh Abdullah outlined the functions of the Assembly. As well as framing the State's constitution, it would decide on the fate of the Dogra dynasty and on whether former landowners should receive compensation (both of which Abdullah had already reached a decision on), and significantly it was to 'declare its reasoned conclusion regarding accession'. The fact that the Assembly was not going to automatically adopt the Indian Constitution, and that accession was still a debatable issue, undoubtedly aroused some alarm in India. Indian concerns about Abdullah's intentions grew during the course of the following year, and especially after his notorious Ranbisiringhpura speech on 11 April 1952, in which he implied Jammu and Kashmir's accession to India would last only as long as Nehru remained in control.[8]

1952 Delhi Agreement

In order to try and resolve the issue of Jammu and Kashmir's relationship with India, the Indian Government invited leaders from the State to New Delhi for talks. On 17 June 1952, a delegation headed by Mirza Afzal Beg (then Revenue Minister) arrived in the Indian capital. Sheikh Abdullah and other prominent National Conference leaders joined the talks a month later. On 24 July, the two sides reached a consensus in what became known as the Delhi Agreement. According to the terms of this agreement Jammu and Kashmir was part of India, but it would at the same time retain a high degree of autonomy. Thus, for instance while retaining Article 370 and having their Sadar-i-Riyasat chosen by the State Assembly rather than appointed by the Indian President as in other states, Kashmiris would be classified as citizens of India and their flag would take second-place to the Indian tricolour.[9] Approval of the Delhi Agreement by the Jammu and Kashmir Assembly would also have solved Nehru's other problem—his promise of a plebiscite to ratify accession to India. Based on the logic that the public elected the Assembly members, he now felt approval by the latter was an acceptable substitute for a popular referendum—even though this was something that the UN had explicitly rejected.[10]

Having signed the Delhi Agreement, both Abdullah and the Indian government proceeded to abuse it, the former by persisting with calls for independence, the latter by asserting its authority beyond the spheres allocated to it. Consider first Sheikh Abdullah. In his opening address to the Constituent Assembly he had ruled out independence, on the grounds that as a small state Jammu and Kashmir would be vulnerable to outside aggression.[11] (Joining Pakistan was still a total anathema to him.[12]) But his actions subsequent to this made it clear that he still considered it a possibility. In order to overcome the afore-mentioned obstacle to independence, Abdullah attempted to find a powerful 'backer' who could protect an independent Jammu and Kashmir. The main target of his efforts was the United States. In a meeting with Loy Henderson, US Ambassador to India, on 29 September 1950, Sheikh Abdullah made clear not only his own desire for independence, but further claimed that this was what the majority of the State's population wanted, and even that those in Azad Kashmir would join an independent state.[13] However, he acknowleged this could only be possible with US or UN assistance. Abdullah also attempted to win Australian backing when he met Walter Crocker, the High Commissioner for Australia, in 1952.

The Indian Government was not unaware of the nature of Abdullah's discussions with foreign leaders, but after July 1952 they were confident that the independence issue had been buried once and for all.[14] However, in May 1953, less than a year after signing the Delhi Agreement, Abdullah was again discussing independence, this time with Adlai Stevenson, US Presidential candidate.[15] For India this was 'the straw that broke the camel's back'; far from being the loyal ally they had expected when they put him in power, Abdullah had become a liability who had to be removed. In doing so, as will be described below, the Indian Government certainly went far beyond the mandate ascribed to it in the Delhi Agreement. Its subsequent actions increasing Indian influence in the State (see below), further undermined the terms of the Delhi Agreement.

Abused by both parties, the Delhi Agreement failed to live up to its potential to provide a permanent resolution to the question of Jammu and Kashmir's precise relationship with India.

Alienation of Non-Muslim Groups

It had been apparent from before 1947 that Sheikh Abdullah was primarily a Kashmiri leader—he had far less support outside the Valley than within. After taking power in 1947, it also became apparent that Abdullah's primary concern was the interests of the Kashmiris (as in inhabitants of the Vale). He displayed little concern for non-Kashmiris, indeed, he appeared to exploit Jammu and Ladakh for the advantage of Kashmir. Abdullah's attitude was thus almost the mirror image of the former Maharaja—whereas Hari Singh had regarded Jammu as the heartland of the State and the people outside it as 'conquered foreigners', '[f]or Sheikh Abdullah the non-Muslims of Jammu and Ladakh were the colonial subjects of a Kashmiri elite recruited from the ranks of the National Conference.'[16]

The extent of Sheikh Abdullah's disinterest in the regions outside Kashmir became apparent when he expressed his willingness to let those areas separate from the Vale and go their own way: 'If the people sincerely desire to separate and establish an independent "Dogra Desh", I would say with full authority on behalf of Kashmiris that they would not at all mind this separation.'[17] This statement was made in response to demands for a separate Jammu state, but Mahajan reported to Sardar Patel that even before such demands were made Abdullah was considering 'hiving off' those parts of the state that he regarded as non-Kashmiri.[18]

Abdullah's pro-Kashmir attitude and many of the actions of his National Conference government strengthened the regional rift in Jammu and Kashmir politics plus the communal one— both outside the Vale and within it.

Jammu Hindus and Pandits

The opposition of Jammu and Kashmir's Hindus—including Pandits—to Sheikh Abdullah and the National Conference increased greatly after 1947. While Hari Singh remained Maharaja, their opposition had largely been based on a fear of what might happen under National Conference rule. After 1947, opposition was based on what actually did happen under the new regime.

Among Jammu Hindus specifically a major source of grievance were the land reform measures implemented by Abdullah—described earlier as the biggest landowners, they bore the brunt of the losses. Lack of compensation made them even more bitter. A second grievance was the removal of their erstwhile ally Maharaja Hari Singh—replaced by 'Kashmiri' rule—and the subsequent abolition of the Dogra dynasty in favour of an elected constitutional Head of State. There was also resentment in Jammu at the obvious pro-Kashmir bias of the new regime.

Both Jammu Hindus and Pandits suffered in terms of wealth and influence, access to jobs, state contracts, etc., after the National Conference came to power. Whereas under the Dogras they had benefitted from their ethnic and religious closeness to the ruling class, so now they were at a disadvantage because of their differentness. Even though Abdullah's definition of Kashmir included Pandits as an integral part, in practice they received no favourable treatment from his 'Kashmiri' rule. Corruption played a major role in their exclusion. Under Abdullah, basically the only people who prospered were National Conference members, their families and cronies.

Hindus were also disturbed by the regime's markedly undemocratic tendencies. Jammu Hindus were so disillusioned by the government's election-rigging that their party boycotted elections to the Constituent Assembly in 1951. Furthermore, the relative distribution of power between Jammu and Kashmir fell far short of the relative population distribution—Kashmir held a disproportionately large share of power. Thus, even if elections had been fair, Hindus held little hope of attaining a position to bring about change. Finally, something that greatly alarmed all the State's Hindus were Abdullah's continued references to holding a referendum to determine the future of Jammu and Kashmir, and the prospect inherent in this of accession to Muslim-majority Pakistan. Abdullah's own preference for independence—which would result in Kashmiri Muslim domination—was scarcely less alarming for the State's Hindu minority.

The record of Sheikh Abdullah and the National Conference in government thus vindicated the pre-Partition fears of the State's Hindus. Before Partition—failing continued rule by Hari Singh—they had wanted Jammu and Kashmir to accede to India. After Partition and accession they realized that merely joining the Indian Union was not enough to protect them from Kashmiri Muslim domination. They would only be 'safe' if Jammu and Kashmir integrated completely with India, thereby coming under the control of New Delhi and transforming their minority status within the State to part of the India-wide Hindu majority. It is not surpising then, that when the Delhi Agreement was announced in July 1952, they strongly opposed it. If it was implemented, they were convinced they would have no future in the State. So strong was this conviction that it mobilized them into political action.

Hindu Agitation

Small-scale protests against Abdullah's government had been going on for some time in Jammu, mainly through a party formed by Bal Raj Madhok in 1947, the Praja Parishad. After 1952, this movement attracted far greater support and became much more active. Its main demands were for the abrogation of Article 370 and the complete merger of Jammu and Kashmir with India. Opposition to the Delhi Agreement took the form of violent demonstrations, student protests (e.g. against hoisting of the Kashmiri flag in colleges), hunger strikes and pro-Maharaja chants. The Praja Parishad's anti-autonomy views were succintly expressed in a popular slogan:

> Ek desh mein do vidhaan, ek desh mein do nishaan, ek desh mein do pradhaan: nahin chalenge, nahin chalenge. (Two constitutions in one country, two flags, two Heads of State, these will not be accepted.)

In order to reduce the Kashmiri Muslims' domination, the Parishad proposed that Hindu and Sikh migrants from Pakistan be settled in the Vale.

The Praja Parishad movement received strong encouragement from Hindu groups within India, notably the Jana Sangh. Formed by Shyama Prasad Mookerjee in 1951, one of the four points for 'strengthening' Indian unity listed in its first manifesto, was the full integration of Jammu and Kashmir into the Indian Union.[19] In making this demand, the Jana Sangh was motivated not only by concern for fellow Hindus in Jammu, but also by its desire to 'overthrow' the Indian Government's secular policy and have Hinduism be officially acknowledged as the State religion.[20] ('Indian' Hindu interest in Kashmir will be discussed more fully in a later chapter on Indian politics.) As part of its propaganda, the Jana Sangh argued that giving Jammu and Kashmir a special status and a high degree of autonomy, would encourage Muslim separatism and cause it to follow the example of Pakistan. The Sangh also organized demonstrations in India to support those taking place within Jammu.

The Jammu and Kashmir Government responded to the Praja Parishad's agitation with verbal condemnation and later by physically suppressing protests. State troops made *lathi* charges against demonstrators and there were numerous arrests. In November 1952 two of the Praja Parishad's leaders, Prem Nath Dogra and Sham Lal Sharma, were arrested. Hindu anger, already aroused by these arrests, was inflamed by the arrest of Shyama Prasad Mookerjee on 8 May 1953 after he attempted to enter the state, and his subsequent death (of a heart-attack) in detention. What made Mookerjee's death so significant was his position as an all-India leader—Hindus throughout India denounced the Abdullah government, and this put great pressure upon the Indian Government to take some action against him.

Initially, the goals of the Pandits and Jammu Hindus were identical—full integration of Jammu and Kashmir with India. But later, their aims diverged. After the signing of the Delhi Agreement granting Kashmir considerable autonomy, Jammu Hindus decided that their best hope of protecting themselves from Kashmiri Muslim domination lay in their province separating from the Vale, either to become an autonomous state in its own right, or to integrate with Indian Punjab. A 'Quit Jammu' campaign grew. Not surprisingly, any plan to split Jammu from Kashmir was opposed by the Pandits—unless they left the Valley this would make them an even more vulnerable minority.[21]

Removal of Sheikh Abdullah

By 1953 the one-time allies, India (Nehru and Congress) and Abdullah, had drifted far apart. India had been disturbed by the corrupt and undemocratic nature of Abdullah's administration. But this turned into serious alarm when he began calling for independence. Reconciliation seemed possible after the signing of the Delhi Agreement in 1952. But when Abdullah failed to respect the terms of this agreement and made demands that amounted to secession from India, New Delhi began thinking of replacing him with a more reliable ally.[22] Public pressure on the Indian Government mounted after the pro-integration demonstrations in Jammu and Ladakh, and became irresistible after Mookerjee's death in Kashmiri detention. By exploiting a split in the National Conference leadership, New Delhi was able to engineer an internal coup, and thereby avoid what would have been the highly controversial alternative of taking over the State's administration itself.

The split within the National Conference's leadership arose over the autonomy versus integration issue. Sheikh Abdullah and Mirza Afzal Beg wanted the State Government to have at least the powers granted in the Instrument of Accession, but other National Conference ministers (Bakshi Ghulam Muhammad, G.M. Sadiq, D.P. Dhar, S.L. Sharaf) favoured greater integration with India. By July 1953 the rift had become so serious that, according to a report by Dhar to New Delhi, Abdullah was planning to throw the pro-integration Bakshi faction out of the Government and the National Conference. Bakshi Ghulam Muhammad, then Deputy Prime Minister, was therefore receptive to the Indian Government's suggestion that he replace Sheikh Abdullah.

Abdullah's overthrow was planned in a military-style operation, chiefly by B.N. Mullik, Director of the Intelligence Bureau, and one of his officials, D.W. Mehra. Contingency plans had to be made to control the public protests expected in Kashmir after Abdullah's removal. Although the whole operation was supervised by two Cabinet members, Rafi Ahmed

Kidwai and Ajit Prasad Jain, all involved ultimately answered to the Prime Minister himself, Nehru. Mullik's description of 'Operation 9 August' in his memoirs, makes clear Nehru's direct involvement:

> Mehra and I met the Prime Minister at his official residence on July 31, 1953. He talked for about two hours. Explaining the background of the Kashmir problem, the Prime Minister said there was no alternative but to remove Sheikh Abdullah and appoint Bakshi Ghulam Mohammad. The Prime Minister expressed the hope that the transition would be peaceful. He warned us to be prepared for the worst because of Sheikh Sahib's popularity and that the pro-Sheikh elements would be supported by pro-Pakistan elements. Mehra should be prepared to head the Jammu and Kashmir police force and, if necessary, perform the duties of Chief Executive. He would work under the 'Sadar-i-Riyasat'. Never before had we seen Nehru in such a furious mood. It seemed he was bent on destroying that which he had himself nurtured. When Mehra was about to leave, Nehru asked him to keep him briefed about the latest developments, and, if need be, to ring him up even at night.[23]

The Sadar-i-Riyasat was Karan Singh; unlike his father he was strongly committed to Jammu and Kashmir joining India—as an integral part.

Abdullah made things easy for his opponents by providing them with a pretext for his removal. On 6 August 1953 he accused his Health Minister, Sham Lal Sharaf, of corruption and insisted he resign. Encouraged by Karan Singh, Sharaf refused to do so. Together with two other ministers, Bakshi and G.L. Dogra, he then wrote a letter claiming that Abdullah had lost the confidence of the Cabinet and the people. Karan Singh decided this letter provided sufficient justification for Abdullah's dismissal and in his capacity as Sadar-i-Riyasat did so on the evening of 8 August. In fact, according to the Interim Constitution, the issue of Abdullah's support should have been resolved by calling upon the State Assembly.

The so-far smooth operation stumbled somewhat at this point, because Bakshi refused to assume office until Abdullah had been arrested. He was afraid of the public demonstrations the former Prime Minister could organize in the Vale. Around midnight of the night of 8/9 August, Abdullah was duly arrested in Gulmarg, where he had gone for the weekend, and taken to Udhampur, near Jammu. The pretext for his arrest was that he had gone to Gulmarg to meet an emissary of Pakistan—such a meeting 'would constitute a grave danger to the State'. Bakshi was sworn in as Prime Minister by Karan Singh on the morning of 9 August 1953. When news of Sheikh Abdullah's dismissal and arrest became public, there were widespread protests in Kashmir but State and Indian Army troops managed to bring these under control within a couple of weeks (some 60 demonstrators were killed in the process).

Abdullah was accused of the somewhat vague offences of 'inciting communal disharmony' and 'fostering hostile feelings towards India'. He also faced a more specific charge of 'treasonable correspondence with foreign powers', notably Pakistan. In 1957 Abdullah's wife, Afzal Beg and some nine others were charged with conspiring with Pakistan to overthrow the Bakshi Government. Sheikh Abdullah was later also accused of this. Bakshi and the Indian Intelligence Bureau tried for almost five years to obtain strong evidence to prove these various charges. Eventually, in January 1958, Nehru lost patience with them and ordered Abdullah's release. The subsequent popular acclaim he attracted in Kashmir alarmed Bakshi. For its part, the Indian Government was more disturbed by his calls for a plebiscite on the accession issue. The result was his re-arrest on 30 April 1958, again on charges of conspiring with Pakistan to overthrow the State Government. Sheikh Abdullah remained in detention until April 1964, when Nehru again stepped in to bring about his release. But Nehru died soon after, on 27 May 1964, and within a year Abdullah was back in jail. He remained under various forms of detention until 1968.

Before examining events under the new regime one point needs to be stressed: the fact that by removing Abdullah from the Premiership, the Indian Government both abused the terms of the Delhi Agreement and undermined the democratic process in Jammu and Kashmir. Regardless of the fairness or otherwise of the 1951 election results (which at the time New Delhi had been keen to accept), Abdullah was the democratically elected Prime Minister of the State. As such, he could only be removed by popular elections or, failing that, a vote of no-confidence in the State Assembly. The Indian Government had no legal authority to plot and execute his removal. In the short-term it achieved its target of placing a pro-India man in power, but the long-term repercussions for democracy in the State and ethnic identification were more serious. The latter will be discussed at the end of the chapter. With respect to the former, New Delhi's actions set a precedent for future Indian administrations—as will be seen, Nehru's daughter in particular felt little hesitation in interfering with the democratic process in Jammu and Kashmir.

The Bakshi Government

Despite its somewhat inauspicious beginnings, the Bakshi Government actually provided Jammu and Kashmir with one of the longest post-Partition periods of stability it has known. Unlike Abdullah, Bakshi had little popular support. He was totally dependent on the Indian Government to stay in power and therefore had little option but to remain loyal to it. But also unlike Abdullah, Bakshi was a skilled organizer. These talents had earlier been used to promote the National Conference's cause, and were now turned to developing the State.

Both Bakshi and the Indian Government realized that—with their most popular leader behind bars—the only way the people of Kashmir could be kept under control, and convinced of the merits of closer ties with India, was to provide the region with economic prosperity. New Delhi, therefore, gave Bakshi considerable financial assistance to develop the State. Though some of this money was creamed off by the Prime Minister and members of his family, even Abdullah acknowledged that the

Bakshi government did take 'some positive steps' in Jammu and Kashmir:

> For the first time a medical college and a regional engineering college was set up. From primary to university level, education was made free. Bakshi oversaw the construction of a new Secretariat, a tourist reception centre, a stadium, Tagore Hall and some other important buildings in Srinagar. The city of Jammu was extended, its lanes and by-lanes were widened and new roads constructed. In Jammu, as well, a new Secretariat and Assembly Hall were constructed. In rural areas new roads and bridges were made. Preliminary work was started with the intention of converting Kashmir University into a residential institution.[24]

To some extent this strategy worked, in that there was little trouble in the Vale for several years, including 1965 when Pakistan infiltrated the State. However, it failed in that it did not change the people's thinking, something that was to become apparent briefly in 1964 and more persistently in later years.

Turning to the issue of Jammu and Kashmir's relationship with India, with its own man in power in the State, India wasted little time in firstly, finalizing accession, and secondly, expanding New Delhi's authority in Jammu and Kashmir. The legal foundation for this was laid on 5 October 1953 when the State Assembly gave Bakshi a unanimous vote of confidence (pragmatic members were no doubt influenced by the practical reality that Abdullah was in jail and Bakshi Prime Minister). Taking accession first, a Basic Principles Committee and an Advisory Committee on Fundamental Rights and Citizenship were set up on 20 October. The former's recommendations, basically the Delhi Agreement, were accepted by the Constituent Assembly on 6 February 1954, and adopted as law on 15 February. Jammu and Kashmir's accession to India was reconfirmed when its Constitution was finally adopted on 17 November 1956 (taking effect from 26 January 1957). This stated clearly that 'The State of Jammu and Kashmir is and shall be an integral part of the Union of India'. By this stage of course New Delhi had decided that, since ratification of accession by the State Constituent Assembly amounted to approval by the people, there was no need for a plebiscite.[25]

Having finally resolved the issue of accession—at least technically—the Bakshi/New Delhi partnership took steps to bring about the State's greater integration with India. Customs barriers between Jammu and Kashmir and India were lifted on 13 April 1954. On 14 May 1954, certain provisions in the Indian Constitution concerning fundamental rights became applicable in Jammu and Kashmir. The Indian Lok Sabha was also empowered to legislate upon a wider range of subjects than the three listed in Article 370. The 1956 State Constitution recognized the authority of the Indian Supreme Court, and of the Indian Comptroller and Auditor-General. In 1958, further administrative integration was achieved when the Indian Administrative Service and Police were authorized to function in the state—remaining, of course, under Indian rather than State Legislature control.

Elections for the Legislative Assembly were held in Jammu and Kashmir in March 1957, following the adoption of the State's Constitution, and again in 1962. In both cases they were heavily rigged. The extent can be gauged from the fact that, following the 1962 elections in which the National Conference won seventy out of seventy-five seats, Nehru wrote to Bakshi: 'In fact, it would strengthen your position much more if you lost a few seats to bona fide opponents.'[26] But, whilst acknowledging that 'political liberty does not exist there in the same measure as in the rest of India,'[27] he nevertheless found it politically expedient to accept the results. Doing so enabled him to assert that the people of Jammu and Kashmir had expressed their approval for accession, and hence that the plebiscite condition he had attached to accession in 1947 had been fulfilled. In reality, of course, the elections results proved no such thing— something that was to become apparent later.

Bakshi's loyalty to India caused New Delhi to turn a blind eye to the corruption and nepotism in his government. However, by the early-sixties this had grown to such proportions that it could no longer be ignored. The Kamaraj Plan[28] conveniently provided Nehru with Bakshi's resignation on 4 October 1963 and he was replaced by another 'yes-man', the former Revenue Minister Khwaja Shamsuddin. Just before he resigned Bakshi put forward a number of proposals which would have led to Jammu and Kashmir being drawn even further into the Indian Union. They included changing the titles of Sadar-i-Riyasat and Prime Minister to Governor and Chief Minister respectively, the terms used in all other states in India. He also proposed that Jammu and Kashmir's representatives to the Indian Lok Sabha, until then nominated by the State Legislature, be chosen through public elections. This would effectively make Jammu and Kashmir just four more constituencies in the Indian Union.

Bakshi lost power before he could put these proposals into practice, but this did not mean they were dropped. His successors Shamsuddin, G.M. Sadiq and Mir Qasim not only implemented all of them, but also introduced further integrational measures of their own. These included the appointment of the State Governor by the Centre, as in other states, rather than by the State Legislature. More significantly, in January 1965 Articles 356 and 357 of the Indian Constitution became applicable in Jammu and Kashmir. They allowed the Governor to declare President's Rule in the event of a 'constitutional breakdown', *without* consulting the State Legislature. Article 370 has never been dropped, but after the implementation of all these measures there was little to distinguish Jammu and Kashmir from the other states in India, and to justify its title of 'special status'. In practice, if not in theory, Article 370 disappeared.

Internal Political Activity

After Partition and the subsequent division of Jammu and Kashmir into Pakistan—and Indian-held territory, most of the leaders of the Muslim Conference had gone over to Azad Kashmir (the rest following once Sheikh Abdullah released them from jail). By 1948, the only party that could be described as the 'opposition' was the Jammu Hindus' Praja Parishad. But the political activism of this party largely died down after Sheikh Abdullah's removal and the implementation of integrationist policies by his successors. Thus, for a considerable period after 1947, the only political organization active in Jammu and Kashmir was the National Conference.

When opposition did eventually emerge, it came from within the National Conference itself. The first split in the party's leadership, one which India had been able to exploit to its own advantage, had been that between the pro-autonomists (notably Abdullah) and the pro-integrationists (notably Bakshi). After Abdullah's dismissal and arrest, most members joined the pro-integration faction. But in 1955, a significant splinter group re-emerged, the Plebiscite Front, formed by Mirza Afzal Beg on 9 August. As its name suggests, the Front was concerned less with autonomy than with the holding of a plebiscite to decide on accession. Its members argued that without such a popular referendum it was wrong to consider Jammu and Kashmir part of India—ratification by the Jammu and Kashmir Constituent Assembly was not an acceptable substitute.

Sheikh Abdullah lent his support to the Front, but fell short of actually joining it. Perhaps because of this the party failed to attract a mass following. Bakshi and New Delhi, of course, strongly opposed the Plebiscite Front, and they soon took steps to crush it. Charges of conspiracy were made against Beg in 1957—charges which owed less to any conspiracy he might have been involved in than to his own political activities. Similarly, those made against Abdullah when he was re-arrested in 1958, were based more on his support for a Front resolution, dated 7 April 1958, which asserted that accession without plebiscite was null and void, than on hard evidence.

Renewed political competition within Jammu and Kashmir, especially among its Muslims, was really sparked off by the Hazratbal incident at the end of 1963. Maulana Masoodi (one of the founders of the original Muslim Conference and later General Secretary of the National Conference) organized an Action Committee to help recover the missing relic and, once this was done, to verify its authenticity. The Action Committee did not confine itself to the Hazratbal crisis, but also became the voice of opposition to the Bakshi administration and its Indian backers. It was aided in this second role by the fact that it had branches throughout Kashmir.

Initially, both kinds of Muslim 'group' opposed to the State Government's pro-India policy were represented in the Committee, i.e. both those 'secular', 'nationalist' Muslims who wanted the State to be independent or at least have a high degree of autonomy from New Delhi, and those with an Islamic outlook who wanted it to join Pakistan (though some did favour independence). The most important members of the first group were Sheikh Abdullah, Beg and Abdullah's son, Farooq, who was beginning to take an active role in politics. The leader of the second group was the Mirwaiz-i-Kashmir, Maulvi Mohammed Farooq, appointed to the post in 1962 (Yusuf Shah had gone to Azad Kashmir in 1947). The unity between these two groups was a very short-lived affair. In 1964, the Action Committee split in two, with Mirwaiz Farooq's faction taking the name Awami Action Committee.

In many ways the emergence of these two separate Muslim 'parties' marked a return to the pre-1947 political situation of the State's Muslim community. Then the two major parties had been the National Conference and the Muslim Conference; in 1964 their views were represented by the Action Committee (and Plebiscite Front) and the Awami Action Committee. Even the two major protagonists, Sheikh Abdullah and the Mirwaiz-i-Kashmir, were unchanged. Where the situation differed from that of 1947 was in the presence of a third pro-integration-with-India Muslim group. Led by Bakshi Ghulam Muhammad this group initially retained the name National Conference. But in 1965, in a move which reflected Jammu and Kashmir's virtual integration with India, the National Conference was abolished and the Jammu and Kashmir branch of the Indian Congress party established in its place.

It is important to note that while there were three distinct views prevalent within the Muslim community, and while all three were represented by specific organizations, only one of these, the pro-India National Conference/Congress was permitted 'political freedom.' The ability of the other organizations to propagate their views, register their candidates and participate in fair elections was severely restricted. One demonstration of this was the arrest of some 165 Plebiscite Front leaders and supporters in Srinagar in 1965. Between them, the pro-independence and pro-Pakistan groups represented the views of the vast majority of the State's Muslim population. Thus, by denying them political freedom, the State Government (or rather, India) was denying the majority of Muslims in Kashmir the right to express their will in a peaceful and democratic manner. The possible consequences of this were either that the people accepted their loss of rights and remained quiet ('docile'), or that they found alternative, more revolutionary means to express and attain their goals. In fact, as later events will demonstrate, they did both in turn.

Hazratbal 1963/64

The Hazratbal Mosque, overlooking the Dal Lake near Srinagar, contains one of Kashmir's holiest relics—the *Moe-e-Muqaddas*, a hair of the Prophet Muhammad (PBUH). On 27 December 1963, the relic, contained in a glass tube and stored in a wooden cupboard except for the ten ritual occasions on which it was displayed, was found to be missing. The news immediately led to huge public outrage in Kashmir. By that time Bakshi Ghulam Muhammad was extremely unpopular among the public, both because of the widespread corruption in his administration, and because he was perceived as an agent of New Delhi. He and his associates were thus one of the first to be suspected of being behind the theft; a crowd set fire to a hotel and cinema owned by the former Prime Minister. The escalating disorder would probably have gone out of the State Government's control—or required drastic repressive measures—had the *Moe-e-Moqaddas* not mysteriously reappeared in the Hazratbal Mosque on 3 January 1964. Even after its recovery, *hartals* and demonstrations continued by the public which had yet to be convinced of its authenticity. Under pressure from Maulana Masoodi's Action Committee, the Indian Government agreed to the holding of a special *deedar* (verification) ceremony, to be attended by recognized scholars who would determine whether the replaced relic was genuine. This was held on 3 February 1964. Fourteen clerics took part, including Masoodi himself. Fortunately for India they reached the conclusion that it was the genuine *Moe-e-Moqaddas*.

The Hazratbal incident was significant for a number of reasons. One of these has already been mentioned, namely that through the Awami Action Committee it precipitated renewed political activity among the Muslims of Kashmir, particularly among those with an Islamic outlook who still wanted to join Pakistan. Secondly, Hazratbal gave a clear indication of the public mood. Whilst demonstrating at the loss of the *Moe-e-Muqaddas*, the State's Muslims had also expressed their anger against the State Government and India, and demanded the release of Sheikh Abdullah. The 'farce' that because the State Assembly approved accession and integration so too did the people, was exposed as just that. Ironically, just as accession was shown to be far from final in the public mind, the chances of holding a plebiscite on the issue, already very remote, disappeared completely—the risk of Kashmiris rejecting India was too great. In addition, the Indian Government realized that it was not 'safe' to allow political freedom in Jammu and Kashmir; if democracy was restored the first casualty would undoubtedly be the pliant National Conference/Congress government. Hence, restrictions on opposition political activity were maintained.

Thirdly, public anger following the theft shattered the myth that the Kashmiris were a very docile people who would meekly accept anything that was imposed upon them by the State Government and India. This perception had been somewhat eroded during the pre-Partition years (e.g. the 1931 jail incident), but a decade or so of peace under Bakshi (largely the result of economic well-being) had revived it. The fury unleashed on 27 December 1963 showed that the Kashmiris could be provoked into revolt; their quiescence could not be taken for granted.

Fourthly, the nature of the trigger that sparked off public protest at the end of 1963 was very significant. As in 1931, so in 1963 it was a perceived threat to the Kashmiris' religion, Islam. But unlike in 1931, the events of 1963 occurred after a twenty-plus year period during which Sheikh Abdullah and the National Conference had been preaching secularism, or at least secular, non-communal politics. The religious fervour manifested by Kashmiri Muslims during the Hazratbal incident showed what little influence this had had on them.

Release of Sheikh Abdullah; Nehru's Death

The significance of Hazratbal was not lost on the Indian Government. Mullik narrates that at a meeting of the emergency sub-committee of the Central Cabinet:

> The Prime Minister said that after being associated with us for a period of over fifteen years, if Kashmir is so destabilised that an ordinary incident of the theft of a relic provokes the people to the extent of trying to overthrow the government, it is time to adopt a new approach and to bring about a revolutionary change in our viewpoint. He ruefully admitted that even after having done so much for the people of Kashmir, they were not satisfied. The PM stressed that Sheikh Abdullah was still popular, and in the changed situation of Kashmir no political solution was possible without his participation.[29]

A point that became very clear during the *Moe-i-Moqaddas* crisis was that despite the obvious flaws in his administration, the Muslims of Kashmir still regarded Sheikh Abdullah as their leader. Recognizing this, Nehru also realized that the only chance of getting Kashmiris to accept accession and integration with India lay in winning over Abdullah. Hence, on 8 April 1964, Abdullah and fourteen others implicated with him in the conspiracy case, including Beg, were released from prison. After spending three weeks in Kashmir, Abdullah (accompanied by his son, Farooq, and Beg) went at Nehru's invitation to New Delhi, where he stayed as his guest. The two men put aside their differences and resolved to work together to find a lasting solution to the Kashmir problem.[30]

Both Abdullah and Nehru appreciated that, with Pakistan effectively in control of half the former (pre-1947) state of Jammu and Kashmir, the issue of its permanent status could only be resolved with Pakistani cooperation. Abdullah came up with an idea only marginally different from his long-standing dream of independence—that of a confederation of India, Pakistan and Kashmir. Nehru, keen to get the dispute settled before he died, did not rule it out and gave Abdullah the go-ahead to negotiate with Pakistan. Consequently, on 23 May 1964, Sheikh Abdullah travelled to Rawalpindi where he received a warm welcome; his long periods of detention in Indian jails had converted him into a 'hero' in Pakistan. This good-will, however, quickly reverted to sharp criticism (at least in the press) when he made speeches praising India's secularism. In a further setback, Ayub Khan, the Pakistani President, immediately dismissed the idea of a confederation. Despite this rejection, though, the overall atmosphere at the talks remained cordial and chances of a negotiated settlement appeared high.

On 27 May 1964, Nehru died in his sleep. With his death, the situation changed completely. On the international front Ayub Khan and Nehru's successor, Lal Bahadur Shastri, did get together but their meeting produced no concrete results. Shastri was hampered from making concessions by his relatively weak domestic political position. Nehru's death allowed those in India who had always maintained that Jammu and Kashmir's accession was final and should not be open to negotiation, to gain the upper hand. Their political dominance was demonstrated not only in the failure of negotiations with Pakistan, but also by the drive to further integrate the State with India.

New Delhi's relationship with Sheikh Abdullah also declined rapidly after Nehru's death. On the one hand, this was due to the expansion of Indian authority in Jammu and Kashmir; on the other, to 'provocative' actions by Abdullah. On 15 January 1965, at a speech in Hazratbal he hinted at abandoning peaceful agitation against the State Government and India, in favour of a more militant approach. On the 29th of the same month, he criticized all those who had joined the new State Congress Party (formerly the National Conference), and accused Shastri of being a weakling. In March 1965, accompanied by Beg, Abdullah left to perform the *Hajj* in Saudi Arabia. Whilst abroad he made use of Pakistani embassy facilities. He also used the opportunity to canvas international—especially Muslim—support for Kashmiri self-determination. After hearing that 165 leaders and supporters of the Plebiscite Front had been arrested, Abdullah held a press conference in which he refused to condemn Pakistan's relations with China. Coming just three years after China had inflicted a severe military defeat on India, this enraged Indian public opinion. Abdullah's meeting on 31 March with the Chinese Premier, Chou En-Lai, while both were attending an Afro-Asian Conference in Algiers, was the proverbial 'last straw'. India cancelled Abdullah's passport and ordered him to return to New Delhi. Immediately after his arrival there on 8 May, he was arrested and taken to Ootacamund. He was later transferred to Koidakanal in Tamil Nadu, where he was to spend the next three years in detention. In Kashmir, news of Abdullah's re-arrest led to renewed public protests and anti-Government agitation.

Indo-Pakistan Dispute over Kashmir

How was the Indo-Pak dispute over Kashmir developing during this period? The onset of this, at Partition, was described in the previous chapter. After 1947, despite each controlling significant portions of the State, India and Pakistan continued to argue over its status. International bodies became involved in the dispute, attempting to mediate between the two sides, but with little success.

Failure of Negotiations

United Nations Efforts

The 1947/48 Indo-Pak War over Kashmir ended with a ceasefire mediated by the United Nations. This body became involved in the Kashmir dispute when the Indian government appealed to the UN to tell Pakistan to stop meddling in the State—legally Indian territory following Hari Singh's signing of the Instrument of Accession. The Indian complaint was based on Article 35 of the UN Charter whereby any member could 'bring to the attention of the Security Council a situation whose continuance is likely to endanger the maintenance of international peace.'[31] But, instead of condemning Pakistan, the Security Council responded by establishing a Commission on India and Pakistan (UNCIP), which had the dual function of investigating the facts and exercising 'any mediatory influence likely to smooth away difficulties.' Thus, in effect the UN acknowledged that the Kashmir dispute was an international one and not an internal Indian affair. The UNCIP did eventually succeed in implementing a ceasefire, on 1 January 1949, and a UN Military Observer Group (UNMOGIP) was set up to monitor the ceasefire line.

So much for ending hostilities. With respect to permanent resolution of the conflict, the UN's line virtually from day one was to leave it to the Kashmiris themselves—'the future status of the state of Jammu and Kashmir shall be determined in accordance with the will of the people.'[32] Having decided a 'free and impartial plebiscite' was the best way to establish what this was, the UN turned its efforts to creating the conditions for such an exercise to be carried out.

The major stumbling block was demilitarization. In order to guard against 'intimidation and other forms of influence and abuse by which the freedom and fairness of the plebiscite might be imperilled'[33] it was deemed necessary for both Indian and Pakistani troops to withdraw from their respective halves of the State. India—which was already beginning to rue Nehru's referral of the dispute to the UN—was particularly reluctant to withdraw its forces from Kashmir (even though it would be allowed to leave a minimum force). It rejected the demilitarization proposals submitted by General McNaughton, President of the Security Council, in December 1949.

In 1950, the UNCIP—a body whose members often could not agree among themselves—was replaced by a single UN Representative, the first of whom was an Australian, Owen Dixon. Dixon soon concluded that there was little hope of reaching agreement on demilitarization of the entire state.[34] He therefore took a new approach in his report, submitted to the Security Council in 1950—that of holding 'regional plebiscites'... Dixon put forward two main proposals: 1) holding a plebiscite through the entire state, one region at a time, or 2) only holding a plebiscite in regions which were 'doubtful'— those that would definitely vote for accession to India or Pakistan would be allocated to those countries without a vote. The latter plan, in effect, confined a plebiscite to just the Vale of Kashmir. Confident that Sheikh Abdullah could secure the Valley for India, Nehru favoured the second plan; for the same reason Pakistan rejected it (though officially they claimed it was because the State should be considered as a whole; it could not be partitioned). Following Dixon's failure, the UN tried twice more to get India and Pakistan to agree on conditions for holding a plebiscite in Jammu and Kashmir. Frank Graham was appointed UN Representative in 1951—he stayed in the post until 1953—and Gunnar Jarring in 1957. Both were unsuccessful.[35]

After this initial decade of keen involvement in Kashmir, having reached a stalemate, the UN pretty much stepped out of the picture. However, it did leave a very important legacy: the Security Council resolutions declaring the Kashmiri people should decide the future of the State.

Bilateral Efforts

Numerous sets of bilateral Indo-Pak talks were held following the 1949 ceasefire. The first prime ministerial meetings took place in Karachi in July 1953. Further meetings between the prime ministers of India and Pakistan followed: in New Delhi in August 1953 and again in May 1955, and in Karachi in September 1960. None of these meetings produced any concrete results. A renewed effort at direct discussions was launched in December 1960, with the first of six rounds of ministerial talks. However, these too proved unproductive; the joint communiqué issued in May 1963 after the final New Delhi round merely confirmed the two sides' failure to reach agreement on the Kashmir dispute. A last glimmer of hope appeared in 1964, when Nehru sent Sheikh Abdullah as his unofficial emissary to Rawalpindi. This initiative originated almost entirely from Nehru personally (he wanted Kashmir's future settled before he died)— thus it was not surprising that after his death in May 1964 Indian Government support for the initiative died too.

The situation in 1965 then was that on the one hand, neither UN mediation nor bilateral talks had succeeded in peacefully resolving matters. On the other hand, developments within India and Pakistan pushed both parties towards opting for a military solution.

Path to War

In Pakistan, Ayub Khan was facing M. A. Jinnah's sister Fatima in presidential elections. In order to boost their support, both candidates took a hard line on Kashmir while campaigning: the winner, Ayub Khan, found that once aroused, public fervour for action would not easily be subdued. Ayub Khan was also strongly urged to take military action by his foreign minister, Zulfiqar Ali Bhutto.[36] And the international situation appeared to favour such a move: China (following its 1962 war with India) had shifted its position on Kashmir from accepting accession as final to one of supporting Pakistan's call for a plebiscite;[37] 'fence-mending' with the Russians in April 1965 resulted in them being more neutral on the issue (previously they were pro-India); the United States was already pro-Pakistan. Moves by the Indian Government to integrate Jammu and

Kashmir completely within the Indian Union alarmed Azad Kashmir and its Pakistani backers. The agitation within the State following the disappearance of the *Moe-e-Muqaddas* and Sheikh Abdullah's re-arrest, was interpreted by Pakistan as evidence that the Kashmiris were 'ripe for rebellion'; with a little encouragement they would openly revolt against India. This view—accompanied by calls for action—was forcefully echoed in the Pakistani press.[38]

In India, Nehru had been succeeded by the much weaker Lal Bahadur Shastri who—even if he had personally wanted to bring about a peaceful settlement with Pakistan—lacked the political strength to make the concessions this entailed.[39] In the event, Shastri had to bow to pressure from Hindu hardliners in India and Jammu: moves for greater integration were implemented and Sheikh Abdullah re-arrested. Once he became aware of aggressive moves by the Pakistanis, Shastri's position was such that he had no option but to respond in kind. The scenario was thus set for the second Indo-Pak War.

1965 Indo-Pak War

Tensions were already high between Indian and Pakistani forces situated on either side of the ceasefire line in Jammu and Kashmir, following the 'Rann of Kutch affair' in early 1965. The Rann of Kutch was a muddy piece of land, submerged during the monsoons, lying between Sindh in Pakistan and Kutch (part of Gujarat) in India. India claimed the entire territory, while Pakistan argued that the international boundary should run through the middle of the Rann. Limited hostilities took place between India and Pakistan after each side accused the other of crossing what they respectively regarded as the international boundary. The monsoons intervened before the situation became too serious, and both sides accepted a British-mediated ceasefire.[40] It has been suggested that the Rann of Kutch affair was a reconnaissance exercise engaged in by both sides to gain some idea of the other's military strength and resolve.[41] Since by 1965 all attempts at peacefully resolving the Kashmir dispute had failed, this interpretation would certainly correlate with the view that both sides had decided on a military 'solution'.

The Pakistani plan for such a military solution consisted of two stages. Rather than attack India directly, in the first stage Kashmiris themselves would be encouraged to rise against them. This encouragement would come from Pakistanis and Azad Kashmiris who would infiltrate Indian Kashmir territory, incite the locals to revolt, and provide them with arms and assistance for this purpose. In the second stage, with the region already in a state of disorder, regular Pakistani troops would cross over. The success of this plan was dependent on a number of factors: that the Kashmiris would respond favourably to Pakistani incitement; that the Indian army had not recovered from its 1962 defeat at the hands of China; and that India would not extend hostilities outside Jammu and Kashmir into Pakistan 'proper'. In the event, none of these factors worked out as the Pakistanis had predicted.

Bands of trained guerrillas started crossing into Indian Jammu and Kashmir from training camps in Azad Kashmir in early 1965. Most of the 'force'—between 1000 and 3000 in number (the figure varies according to the source!)—crossed over in July. However, instead of welcoming them the local population reacted either with indifference or hostility, even turning infiltrators over to the Indian authorities. Aware by late August 1965 of Pakistani intentions, the Indians launched a counter move aimed at blocking off further entry from Azad Kashmir. Indian troops crossed the ceasefire line on 24 August and occupied certain passes in the Tithwal region. Further passes were occupied in the following days, so that by 10 September the Indians virtually held a line from Uri to Poonch.

Pakistan's response to these essentially defensive measures was to accuse the Indians of invading Azad Kashmir, and to send in its regular troops. The Pakistan army entered in the Chambh district of Jammu, aiming to cut the Pathankot road from Jammu to Srinagar—the main line of communication for the Indian forces. Their advance was quite successful; by 5 September they were within 20 miles of Jammu. But at this point they received their second shock. On 6 September, with Jammu in danger of falling, India launched a counter-offensive across the international Indo-Pak border, towards Lahore. A separate offensive was launched from Jammu into Pakistani Punjab, towards Sialkot. On 8 September, Indian troops crossed the Indo-Pak border in the far south, aiming for Karachi. In addition, the Indian Air Force carried out attacks against airbases in Pakistan. With these offensives the Kashmir conflict escalated into a full-scale war between India and Pakistan.

Neither side was successful in achieving its military objectives. The Indians managed to hold onto Jammu and the vital Pathankot road. The Pakistanis managed to save their major cities—Lahore, Sialkot and Karachi—from falling to the enemy. A stalemate was reached on all fronts. With little to gain from protracted hostilities, and with virtually the entire international community urging cessation,[42] both sides agreed to a UN-mediated ceasefire. This took effect on 23 September 1965. India had captured some 740 square miles of territory, Pakistan 210 square miles.

Tashkent Declaration

By 1965 Russia had changed from its Khruschev-era attitude of being strongly pro-India on the issue of Jammu and Kashmir, to a more neutral (at least in statements; it was still supplying New Delhi with arms) stance under the leadership of Alexei Kosygin.[43] Even before hostilities had started, on 20 August 1965, Kosygin had offered to act as mediator in negotiations between India and Pakistan. At the time both parties had rejected this offer. However, when it was repeated on 17 September with Tashkent suggested as a possible meeting place, Shastri accepted almost immediately, and Ayub Khan some months later (on 25 November). Talks between Kosygin, Shastri and Ayub Khan were scheduled to start in Tashkent on 3 January 1966.

Initially, and indeed until virtually the last moment, there was little hope of the talks generating any kind of agreement—the two parties' positions were simply too far apart. However, both India and Pakistan perhaps realized that failure in Tashkent could result in renewed hostilities, with unpredictable consequences. Hence, on 10 January they did sign an agreement, the Tashkent Declaration. This was less an agreement ending the Kashmir dispute, as one allowing it to be pushed to one side so that the two countries could resume relatively normal relations. Its main point was that both sides' forces would withdraw to the positions they had held before hostilities began (dated 5 August). Other practical points included repatriation of prisoners-of-war and resumption of diplomatic relations. More generally, the Declaration committed both sides to 'settle their disputes through peaceful means,' to 'non-interference in the internal affairs of each other,' and to 'promote the development of friendly relations between the two countries.' Finally, it was agreed bilateral talks would be continued.

The Tashkent Declaration faced domestic opposition in both India and Pakistan. In the former it was felt Pakistani 'aggression' had not been sufficiently condemned. However, the death of Lal Bahadur Shastri just hours after signing the Declaration 'invested (it) with an aura of sanctity' amid muted criticism. The public perception in Pakistan (thanks to army and government propaganda) was that the war had been going well—the 'invaders' had been successfully repulsed from Lahore—and that even agreeing to a ceasefire had been a mistake. Sitting down to negotiations and agreeing terms with an enemy which could have been defeated in battle was, therefore, adding insult to injury! Ayub Khan never recovered from the setback dealt to his popularity by the 1965 War and Tashkent; within a few years he was overthrown in a military coup led by Yahya Khan.

Despite domestic opposition, both sides did respect the terms of the Declaration at least as far as practical measures were concerned. Prisoners-of-war were repatriated and by 25 February 1966 their forces had withdrawn to their pre-5 August positions. However, respecting the 'spirit' of the Declaration (resolving disputes peacefully, promoting friendly relations) proved more difficult.

Significance for Politics within Jammu and Kashmir

The period of Indo-Pak relations up to the signing of the Tashkent Declaration was to prove immensely significant for political developments within (Indian) Jammu and Kashmir. Two aspects were particularly important.

One, the decline in external interest in the State. The UN, as described, had by 1958 reached a stalemate in its efforts to resolve the situation and had effectively left it to India and Pakistan to settle through bilateral negotiations. Meanwhile, Pakistan, which had since 1947 persistently taken a keen interest in Kashmiri affairs, also appeared to bow out after 1965. The Pakistanis had made a military grab for the State and failed; the Kashmiri people themselves had given them a very poor reception; and increasingly Pakistani leaders were distracted by internal power struggles. All these considerations led Pakistan to accept (practically if not formally) the stalemate there.

With external pressure considerably lessened, New Delhi felt far more confident about further integrating Jammu and Kashmir with the rest of India. The decline in external interest also forced political elites within the State, notably Sheikh Abdullah, to re-evaluate their position. Holding a much weaker hand they had little option but to accept the sovereignty of New Delhi, and to strive for the best possible deal *within* India.

The other aspect of this period that was to be significant for future political developments within the State were the UN resolutions stipulating the Kashmiris' right of self-determination. It was one thing for Nehru and Mountbatten to promise a plebiscite and then go back on their word, but quite another for an international body like the UN to do so. Basically, the UN's endorsement ensured that the right of self-determination became enshrined in the Kashmiri psyche—with corresponding consequences for their attitude towards India.

On the one hand, Kashmiri Muslims were growing increasingly frustrated at their lack of democracy and regional autonomy within India. Restricting political opposition, rigging elections, imposing 'puppet' rulers in Srinagar...all caused Kashmiri Muslims to become disillusioned with India. [The lack of democracy cannot solely be blamed on New Delhi: Sheikh Abdullah must also take some responsibility for this. However, in the eyes of Kashmiri Muslims only India was to blame—the Indian Government's removal from power and subsequent detention of Abdullah absolved him of guilt and preserved his status as a popular leader.] The Indian promise to allow Jammu and Kashmir a high degree of regional autonomy was supposedly fulfilled in Article 370. However, though this remained a fixture of the Indian Constitution, successively integrationist legislation effectively rendered it meaningless.

On the other hand, UN involvement in the Indo-Pak Kashmir dispute and the passage of Security Council resolutions calling for Kashmiri self-determination provided a focus for this Kashmiri Muslim anger. As will be seen in later chapters, Muslim frustration at lack of employment, autonomy, etc., was expressed in demands for jobs and the implementation of Article 370, but it was also expressed in demands for the UN resolutions on Kashmir to be carried out. As Muslim disillusionment with India grew, so too did the clamour for the implementation of those resolutions.

The UN resolutions on Kashmir arising from the international Indo-Pak dispute over Jammu and Kashmir, and their impact on Kashmiri Muslim thinking, illustrate the importance of viewing Kashmir the international issue and Kashmir the internal issue in conjunction. Whilst they might appear at times to be quite distinct, this period of Kashmir's history shows that the links between them could be very direct.

NOTES

1. 'The only person who can deliver the goods in Kashmir is Sheikh Abdullah... [T] he real point is that no satisfactory way can be found in Kashmir except through Sheikh Abdullah.' Nehru, quoted in Bhattacharjea, *op. cit.*, p. 166.
2. Ganguly, Sumit, *The Crisis in Kashmir: Portents of War, Hopes of Peace* (Cambridge, Cambridge University Press, 1997), p. 28.
3. Lamb, *op. cit.* (1991), p. 185.
4. 'From our point of view, that is India's, it is of the most vital importance that Kashmir should remain within the Indian Union.... But however much we may want this, it cannot be done ultimately except through the goodwill of the mass of the population. Even if military forces held Kashmir for a while, a later consequence might be a strong reaction against this.' Nehru to Mahajan, 1 Dec. 1947, cited in Schofield, Victoria, *Kashmir: In the Crossfire* (London, I.B. Tauris, 1996), p. 166.
5. Address made on 17 October 1949; Akbar, *op. cit.,* p. 136.
6. At the same time Ayyangar made it clear that the long-term aim was complete integration of Jammu and Kashmir with India: 'This article proposes a special status for Kashmir because of its special circumstances. The State is not in a position to merge with India. We all hope that in future the State of Jammu and Kashmir will get over the hurdles and completely merge with the Union, like the rest of the states'; Abdullah, *op. cit.,* pp. 113–14.
7. Lamb, *op. cit.* (1991), p. 192.
8. After describing full application of the Indian Constitution to Kashmir as 'unrealistic, childish and savouring of lunacy' Abdullah went on: 'Many Kashmiris are apprehensive as to what will happen to them and their position if, for instance, something happens to Pandit Nehru. We do not know. As realists, we, Kashmiris, have to provide for all eventualities'. Akbar, *op. cit.,* p. 148.
9. The main points of the Delhi Agreement were:
- Commitment to Article 370;
- Kashmiris would be citizens of India, but the State Legislature would be empowered to confer the special rights on 'state subjects' won in the struggles of 1927 and 1932;
- The President of India would be the head of State of the whole of India, including Kashmir;
- Kashmir would be allowed its own flag, but not as a rival to the tricolour, which would be supreme;
- The Sadar-i-Riyasat (Governor of the State), although elected by the State Legislature rather than nominated by the Centre, could not assume office without the consent of the President of India;

An internal Emergency could only be applied with the concurrence of the State Legislature'
Akbar, *op. cit.*, pp. 143–4.

10. The UNCIP resolution adopted on 5 January 1949 stated in its first paragraph: 'The question of the accession of the State of Jammu and Kashmir to India or Pakistan will be decided through the democratic method of a free and impartial plebiscite.' It went on to give details of how the plebiscite would be carried out. This resolution was formally accepted by the governments of both India and Pakistan. When in 1950 plans were announced in Indian Jammu and Kashmir for the convening of a Constituent Assembly, the Security Council passed a resolution stating that such an action would not be in accordance with the 5 January 1949 resolution: 'Affirming that the convening of a Constituent Assembly as recommended by the General Council of the "All Jammu and Kashmir National Conference" and any action that Assembly might attempt to take to determine the future shape and affiliation of the entire State or any part thereof would not constitute a disposition of the State in accordance with the above principle.' Cited in Tariq, M. Sharif, *Kashmir in Strangulation* (Mirpur, Tariq, 1991), p. 62.

11. 'We have to consider the alternative of making ourselves an Eastern Switzerland, of keeping aloof from both States [India and Pakistan], but having friendly relations with them. This may seem attractive in that it would appear to pave the way out of the present deadlock. To us as a tourist country, it could also have certain obvious advantages. But in considering independence we must not ignore practical considerations. Firstly, it is not easy to protect sovereignty and independence in a small country which has not sufficient strength to defend itself on our long and difficult frontiers bordering so many countries. Secondly, we do not find powerful guarantors among them to pull together always in assuring us freedom from aggression.' Abdullah cited in Bhattacharjea, *op. cit.*, p. 189.

12. In the same address Abdullah elaborated his reasons for not wishing to join Pakistan: 'This claim of being a Muslim State is of course only a camouflage. It is a screen to dupe the common man, so that he may not see clearly that Pakistan is a feudal State in which a clique is trying...to maintain itself in power. In addition to this, the appeal to religion constitutes a sentimental and a wrong approach to the question.' Ibid.

13. Loy Henderson gave details of his talks with Abdullah in a cable to the State Department: 'In discussion [of the] future of Kashmir, Abdullah was vigorous in restating that in his opinion it should be independent; that overwhelming majority of the population desired their independence; that he had reason to believe that some Azad Kashmir leaders desired independence and would be willing to co-operate with leaders of National Conference if there was reasonable chance such co-operation would result

in independence. Kashmir people could not understand why UN consistently ignored independence as possible solution for Kashmir. Kashmir people had language and cultural background of their own. The Hindus by custom and tradition widely different from Hindus in India, and the background of Muslims quite different from Muslims in Pakistan. Fact was that population of Kashmir was homogeneous in spite of presence of Hindu minority.' Ibid., p. 196.

14. On his return to Kashmir from Delhi on 28 July 1952 Abdullah said, 'Kashmir is part and parcel of India.' Cited in Verma, *Jammu and Kashmir at the Political Crossroads* (New Delhi, Vikas, 1994), p. 41.

15. See Lamb, *op. cit.* (1991), p. 190.

16. Ibid., p. 187.

17. Statement made on 15 August 1949; Verma, *op. cit.,* p. 43.

18. Mahajan to Patel, 24 December 1947; Das (ed.), *Sardar Patel's Correspondance 1945–50: Volume 1: New Light on Kashmir* (Ahmedabad, 1971); cited in Lamb, *op. cit.,* p. 187.

19. The other three points for strengthening Indian unity in the Jana Sangh manifesto were: an educational system based on 'Bharatiya culture', the use of Hindi in schools, and the denial of any special privileges to minorities. See Akbar, *op. cit.,* pp. 142–3.

20. On 27 January 1953, in a letter to the Chief Ministers, Nehru wrote: 'The Jammu agitation…is again a remarkable instance of folly or of mischief. It plays into the hands of Pakistan. It is clear that the objective of these [communal] organisations is not confined to Jammu and that they are aiming at bigger quarry. Their dislike of the Government of India and the secular policy that it pursues is so great that, in order to injure it, they are prepared even to harm our relationship with Jammu and Kashmir State.' Cited in Bhattacharjea, *op. cit.,* p. 195.

21. The majority Buddhists of Ladakh followed a similar path to the Hindus of Jammu. They too were from the beginning reluctant to be administered by a National Conference government. Their opposition to this was increased by the same factors that increased the Hindus opposition to it: its pro-Kashmir bias, corruption, undemocratic practices and land reforms (in Ladakh the major landowner had been the Buddhist 'Church'). Where the Ladakh Buddhists differed, at least initially from Abdullah's opponents in Jammu, was in their demand that Ladakh be allowed to join Tibet. The justification for this claim was that Ladakh had 'joined' the state of Jammu and Kashmir in an agreement with the Dogra ruler Gulab Singh; when Dogra rule ended this agreement had become invalid and they were therefore free to decide their own future. However, after the annexation of Tibet by China, they too called for the integration of their province with India and direct central rule.

22. On 28 June 1953, after Abdullah had declined an invitation to Delhi for talks, Nehru wrote to him: 'It is always painful to part company after

long years of comradeship, but if our conscience so tells us, or in our view an overriding national interest requires, then there is no help for it. Bhattacharjea, *op. cit.*, p. 199.

23. Abdullah, *op. cit.*, p. 120.

24. Ibid., p. 129.

25. In a speech made in Srinagar on 7 July 1955, Union Home Minister Govind Bhallab Pant stated: 'Kashmir's accession was a reality which could not be changed because the people through their representatives in the Constituent Assembly had decided to remain in India. Noorani, A.G., *The Kashmir Question* (Bombay, Manaktalas, 1969), p. 69 cited in Navlakha, G., 'Bharat's Kashmir War', *Economic and Political Weekly* (21 December 1991), p. 2954.

26. Letter dated 4 March 1962; Bhattacharjea, *op. cit.*, p. 213.

27. Letter from Nehru to Prem Nath Bazaz, dated 7 August 1962; ibid.

28. Kamaraj Nadar, leader of the Tamil Nadu Congress Committee, proposed that 'leading Congressmen who are in Government should voluntarily relinquish their ministerial posts and offer themselves for full-time organisational work.' Consequently, all Cabinet and Chief Ministers resigned. Some of these were reappointed by Nehru, but six Chief and six Cabinet Ministers lost their jobs. The former included Bakshi Ghulam Muhammad as well as Kamaraj himself.

29. Abdullah, *op. cit.*, p. 147.

30. Abdullah described their meeting in his autobiography: 'Panditji expressed his deep anguish and sorrow at the past incidents. I also became very emotional and told him that I was glad to have convinced him that I was not disloyal to him personally or to India.' Ibid., p. 152.

31. Schofield, *op. cit.*, pp. 159–160.

32. For full text of 5 January 1949 Resolution see Tariq, *op. cit.*, p. 55.

33. Dixon, quoted in Schofield, *op. cit.*, p. 175.

34. See Lamb, *op. cit.*, p. 171.

35. For details of the efforts made and plans proposed by the various UN representatives, plus Indian and Pakistani Government responses, see ibid., pp. 171–7.

36. Bhutto reassured Ayub Khan that in the event of conflict over Kashmir, 'India's own weakened internal political and economic condition left it 'in no position' to 'risk a general war of unlimited duration' against Pakistan. Zulfi's own 'authoritative sources', moreover, had convinced him of Pakistan's relative military superiority.

'Bhutto bolstered his pro-war arguments by reminding Ayub that the 'morale of our nameless soldier on the front line is high', and the 'justice of our cause is not in doubt.' Time was on India's side: with arms pouring in from both superpowers, within two or three years India's military capability would be such that 'Pakistan would be in no position to resist her.' India's 'ultimate objective' was nothing less than the 'destruction' of Pakistan. Thus, the time to 'hit back hard' was 'now,' to make it virtually impossible for India to embark on a total war against Pakistan for the next decade.' Stanley Wolpert, *Zulfi Bhutto of Pakistan: His Life and Times* (New York, Oxford University Press, 1993), p. 89.

37. Ayub Khan visited China from 2–9 March 1965. The joint statement issued on Kashmir stated: 'the two parties noted with concern that the Kashmir dispute remains unsolved, and consider its continued existence a threat to peace and security in the region. They reaffirmed that this dispute should be resolved in accordance with the wishes of the people of Kashmir as pledged to them by India and Pakistan.' Lamb, *op. cit.,* p. 254. 'China, in other words, was now making as clear a declaration of support for the Pakistani position that a plebiscite should take place, as the Russians had made in 1955 in support of the Indian position, that the matter had already been decided in India's favour.' Ibid.

38. The press campaign for military action rapidly gained momentum after 1 January 1965, when the *Pakistan Times* reported Maulvi Farid Ahmed's statement: 'There is a great fund of goodwill for Kashmir in North Africa and Middle-Eastern countries. Almost everywhere, the question being asked is when Pakistanis or Kashmiris will take up arms for the Valley's liberation.' Some typical press coverage during the early months of 1965 were: 'We are not afraid of war and we will not hesitate to go to war when the time comes' [*Dawn* 11 March]; 'We are sure that President Ayub would teach India a lesson which the Indian rulers would never forget' [*Jang* 18 March]. Kak, *op. cit.,* pp. 80–81.

39. Sheikh Abdullah's assessment of Shastri, after holding talks with the new Prime Minister, was that: 'Shastri was very cordial and it seemed he was keen to complete the work initiated by Jawaharlal Nehru. But he lacked Nehru's popular appeal and did not have the strength to muster his colleagues around to his viewpoint.' Quoted in Bhattacharjea, *op. cit.,* p. 225.

There was also a lot of anti-Pakistan feeling in India at that time: 'In the eyes of self-proclaimed patriots from all parts of the spectrum of Indian political life Pakistan stood doubly damned. On the one hand it was the living symbol of the 'Two Nation' theory, the challenge to Hindu dominance. On the other hand, it had acted of late as the collaborator with China, India's deadly foe. Lal Bahadur Shastri evidently concluded that Indian public hostility towards Pakistan was too great to be ignored.' Lamb, *op.cit.,* p. 251.

40. For details of the Rann of Kutch affair see ibid., pp. 255–7.

41. Lamb speculates 'The real nature of the Rann of Kutch crisis is still obscure. Was Pakistan testing the strength and resolve of the Indian Army here in a kind of dress rehearsal for something contemplated shortly for Kashmir? Was India treating Pakistan to a martial display as a warning against any Kashmiri adventures which might at that time be at the

planning stage? We do not know.' But he goes on 'In the Rann of Kutch affair one has the distinct impression of a reconnaissance in force by both sides, each trying to feel out the other's weakness.' Ibid., p. 256.

42. 'The outside world had watched the mounting crisis between India and Pakistan with ever-increasing alarm. No party in the Cold War stood to benefit at this moment from a major armed conflict in the subcontinent. The United States feared the result would be an increasing alignment of Pakistan with China.... The Soviet Union likewise had no wish to see an increase of Chinese strength in the subcontinent.... The British were much disturbed at the outbreak of war...between two members of the Commonwealth. Even the Chinese...were extremely reluctant to be dragged into a war with India on behalf of their Pakistani friend.' Ibid., pp. 263–4.

43. 'In the era of Khruschev the Soviet Union had publicly declared itself a supporter of the Indian stand on Kashmir. In 1962 a Russian veto had defeated a Security Council resolution on the plebiscite issue. By 1965, and after the fall of the Kruschev regime, Russian attitudes were significantly modified. When President Ayub Khan visited Moscow in early April 1965, Aleksei Kosygin, the Soviet Prime Minister showed himself far more flexible in outlook than Khruschev had ever been. No doubt he was looking for some means to reduce Chinese influence in Rawalpindi.' Ibid., p. 269.

4

POLITICAL DEVELOPMENTS WITHIN JAMMU AND KASHMIR 1965–1989

Elections 1965–1972

Sheikh Abdullah had been arrested for the last time on 8 May 1965, and removed to distant Koidakanal in Tamil Nadu. In October of the same year, several prominent Islamic leaders in the state were also arrested: Mirwaiz Mohammed Farooq on 10 October, and Maulana Mohammed Sayeed Masoodi eleven days later. In the State Government, G.M. Sadiq had replaced Shamsuddin as Prime Minister in 1964. In 1965, he changed the name of the National Conference to Pradesh Congress Party— thereby acknowledging formally that his party was merely an extension of the New Delhi Government party. A greatly reduced National Conference professing loyalty to Sheikh Abdullah did remain in existence, but Abdullah himself became actively involved with Mirza Afzal Beg's Plebiscite Front.

Elections for the State Assembly were held in 1967. These elections were boycotted by the Plebiscite Front as a protest against its leaders' continued detention. Using the by then well-established techniques of vetoing candidates, manipulating electoral rolls, etc., the election results were rigged in the Sadiq Government's favour. The State Congress party emerged the victor with 59 seats; the National Conference won 8; Jana Sangh 3 in Jammu; and 2 seats went to independents.

Soon after the elections Indira Gandhi invited Karan Singh to join her cabinet in New Delhi. He accepted, and therefore had to resign his position as Governor of Jammu and Kashmir. With his resignation all semblance of Dogra rule in Jammu and Kashmir finally came to an end. The State's Chief Justice, J.N. Wazir, took over as Acting Governor, with L.K. Jha eventually becoming Governor.

Having 'won' with such a clear majority, the Sadiq Government/Indira Gandhi felt their position was strong enough to allow the release of their political opponents. Begum Abdullah was allowed to return to Kashmir in April 1967, followed by Afzal Beg in July (though he remained under restrictions until December). Maulana Masoodi was released in December 1967. Sheikh Abdullah himself was the last to be set free. He had been moved to mild house arrest in New Delhi in July 1967, but it was only in January 1968 that he was finally released.

It soon became apparent that Abdullah's thinking had changed little during his incarceration. He continued insisting on the Kashmiris right to self-determination in the form of a plebiscite, i.e. he had still not accepted the finality of accession to India. In October 1968, for instance, he organized a Jammu and Kashmir State People's Convention in Srinagar. One of the speakers, Jayaprakash Narayan, agreed on the State's right to autonomy but ruled out self-determination on the grounds that the 1965 War had taken Pakistan out of the picture. Narayan's argument was refuted by Abdullah, who again called for a plebiscite.[1]

In May 1969, Abdullah announced that the Plebiscite Front would take part in forthcoming elections. The party did well in local (*panchayat*) elections held that August. State Assembly elections were scheduled for March 1971. At the second session of the State People's Convention in June 1970, Abdullah put forward the Plebiscite Front's 'manifesto'. Its main proposal was for a federal government arrangement, consisting of one supreme and several regional bodies. The regions listed include Pakistani-controlled Azad Kashmir and the Northern Areas. The Front envisaged this re-united Jammu and Kashmir either as independent, or else as part of Pakistan: with Abdullah asserting that it had been a mistake to start with, continued accession to India was not an option.

As was to be expected, Abdullah and the Front received the support of the pro-Pakistan Awami Action Committee of Mirwaiz Farooq. Equally to be expected, such statements were not well-received in New Delhi. The government there became very alarmed at the prospect of Abdullah and the Front contesting the 1971 elections on its plebiscite platform and doing well. Rather than take this risk and have to deal with the difficult consequences, the easier course of preventing the Front contesting the elections was chosen. The excuse for a government clampdown against Abdullah and the Front was provided in January 1971 by the Al-Fatah hijacking of an Indian Airlines plane. The Plebiscite Front was accused of associating with Al-Fatah; 'proof' included recent meetings between Abdullah, Beg and the Pakistani High Commissioner in New Delhi—one of 'Al-Fatah's links with Pakistan'. The Indian authorities spent little time verifying the truth of these assertions before taking action. The Ganga was hijacked on 3 January. On 8 January, an externment order was served on Mirza Afzal Beg banning him from Jammu and Kashmir for three months, an action allowed under the Indian Maintenance of Public Order Act. On 9 January, further orders were served against Sheikh Abdullah and his son-in-law, G.M. Shah. In Jammu and Kashmir itself, during the night of 8/9 January, about 350 Plebiscite Front activists were arrested under the Preventative Detention Act. Finally, on 12 January, the Plebiscite Front was declared an unlawful organization.

With its leaders banned from the state, its workers in jail, and itself declared illegal, the Plebiscite Front's non-involvement in the March 1971 elections became automatic. (The externment orders, etc., were appealed, but the special Tribunal of the Jammu and Kashmir High Court convened to investigate the matter did not report its findings until 15 June 1971.) G.M. Sadiq's Congress party duly 'won' these elections, but Sadiq died in office just before the end of the year. He was succeeded by another Indira/New Delhi loyalist, Syed Mir Qasim.

State Assembly elections were held again in March 1972. The various externment orders against Abdullah and his colleagues were still in place, and the Plebiscite Front still illegal. Thus, these elections too were comfortably 'won' by the ruling Congress Party. Of the Assembly's 75 seats, 55 went to Congress, 5 to the Jamaat-i-Islami and 3 in Jammu to the Jana Sangh.

Indo-Pakistan Relations

Before looking at political developments in Jammu and Kashmir after the 1972 elections, concurrent developments in the Indo-Pak dispute over the State will be reviewed. As with the earlier 1947–1965 phase of Indo-Pak relations, these were to have a profound effect on Kashmir's internal politics.

1971 Indo-Pak War

After the signing of the Tashkent Declaration very little attempt was made by either side to permanently resolve the problem of Jammu and Kashmir. An incident in early 1971 involving Kashmir led to a considerable deterioration in Indo-Pak relations.

On 30 January 1971, an Indian Airlines plane (the 'Ganga') flying from Srinagar to Jammu was hijacked by two Kashmiris and forced to land in Lahore. Claiming to be Kashmiri freedom-fighters, the hijackers demanded India release some thirty-six prisoners belonging to a group called the Kashmir National Liberation Front. The hostages were returned to India the next day, but the hijackers destroyed the aeroplane before Pakistan could comply with the Indian demand that it too be handed back. The hijacking received enthusiastic support from the Pakistani public—no doubt delighted by this 'evidence' that the Kashmiris did not want to stay within India after all—and from

Zulfiqar Ali Bhutto.[2] In view of the Pakistani hesitation in returning the plane, their refusal to turn the hijackers over to Indian police (though they did stand trial in Pakistan), and the general support in Pakistan for the hijacking, India accused the Pakistani Government of assisting the hijackers. On 4 February, it banned the overflight of all Pakistani aircraft (civil and military) across Indian Territory.

Various theories have been put forward concerning the hijacking of the 'Ganga'. Pro-Pakistan writers assert it was really all an Indian plot to justify a crackdown against opposition groups in Jammu and Kashmir, prior to the 1971 elections. Bangladeshi and some pro-India writers claim the opposite: that it was a Pakistani plot to divert world attention from troubles in what was then still East Pakistan.[3] Whatever the strategy behind it, it resulted in a marked deterioration in Indo-Pak relations.

Ayub Khan had been overthrown in a military coup in March 1969. His successor, Yahya Khan, had promised to hold free elections to install a civilian government. These elections were duly held—fairly—in 1971. However, problems arose in the next stage: handing power over to the elected victor. Almost all the votes in East Pakistan had gone to Sheikh Mujib-ur-Rehman's Awami League Party. Since the population in the Eastern wing was numerically greater than that in West Pakistan, this result effectively meant that Mujib-ur-Rehman had won in the whole country. However, the West Pakistan establishment and even more so Zulfiqar Ali Bhutto (leader of the Pakistan People's Party which won the most votes in West Pakistan) were unwilling to be ruled by a Bengali government. Predictably, the failure to hand over power to the Awami League led to widespread public protests in East Pakistan. Yahya Khan responded to these protests with a military crackdown, leading in turn to armed resistance by the Bengali Mukti Bahini, a force partly trained and armed by India.

The actual events leading to the creation of Bangladesh are outside the scope of this study. But briefly, as more and more Bengali refugees fled across the border to India, New Delhi sent its forces into East Pakistan to openly assist the Mukti Bahini.

Pakistan responded by invading India from the West on 3 December 1971, and later launched attacks into Indian Jammu and Kashmir. The Indians countered by attacking West Pakistan in Sindh and north Punjab, and by also crossing the cease-fire line in Jammu and Kashmir. The war did not go well for Pakistan, especially in the eastern wing where it faced strong local opposition as well as supply and communications problems (increased by the Indian overflight ban). On 17 December, Pakistani forces in Dhaka surrendered unconditionally to Indian forces, ending the third Indo-Pak war after just fourteen days. [4]

Although this Indo-Pak war had been fought largely outside Jammu and Kashmir, its consequences—aside from the obvious emergence of Bangladesh—were critically felt in that State. These will be considered after the Simla Agreement which rounded off this period of international Indo-Pak relations.

Simla Agreement

The Simla Agreement of 1972 was another attempt to normalize Indo-Pak relations after war. It is significant to note that while the 1971 War had ostensibly been over Bengali separation, Bangladesh—once created—was not an obstacle to friendly Indo-Pak relations. The status of independent Bangladesh was soon recognized by the international community, and even within Pakistan pragmatic elements felt that the loss of the East wing was a blessing in disguise; it would certainly make future nation-building much easier. The real obstacle to harmony in the subcontinent was still Jammu and Kashmir, and thus it was primarily this issue that was addressed in the Simla Agreement. However, like the 1966 Tashkent Declaration, the Simla Agreement did not attempt to permanently resolve the dispute over the status of Jammu and Kashmir; it too took the easier option of putting this 'on hold' so that progress could be made in other aspects of the two countries' dealings.

Lower level negotiations between Indian and Pakistani officials had been underway since April 1972. In early July

Zulfiqar Ali Bhutto—by then Prime Minister of Pakistan—and Indira Gandhi met at Simla for direct negotiations. The two sides went to the negotiating table with very different objectives. India wanted the cease-fire line to become the *de facto* international boundary. It was not particularly interested in gaining control of the entire (original) State, merely of retaining permanent sovereignty over the portion it already held. In addition, despite having initiated UN involvement in Jammu and Kashmir, it now wanted all external bodies excluded—future negotiations should be on a strictly bilateral basis. Pakistan, in contrast, persisted with its claim to the entire State and was, therefore, not prepared to accept the cease-fire line as a permanent boundary. It also opposed ending UN involvement in attempts to resolve the dispute. Coupled with these differences was the desire by both parties—particularly Bhutto—not to be perceived domestically as having 'lost face'. This factor appeared to make compromise yet more difficult.

In 1966, Ayub Khan and Lal Bahadur Shastri had gone to Tashkent as 'equals'; the 1965 War had ended in a stalemate so there was no clear 'winner' and 'loser'. But in 1972, Bhutto and Mrs Gandhi were definitely meeting as 'vanquished' and 'victor'. In addition, India held nearly 94,000 Pakistani prisoners-of-war, and some 5000 square miles of territory in what was formerly West Pakistan. Added together, these gave India a much stronger negotiating position.[5] Despite this, Mrs Gandhi went to Simla in a conciliatory mood, aware of Bhutto's need to placate domestic public opinion, and the agreement which was signed appeared (at least initially) to favour neither side's position. The main points of the Simla Agreement were:

  i) both sides would settle future problems through bilateral negotiations or 'any other peaceful means';
 ii) both sides would respect the cease-fire line, referred to as the line of control; neither would unilaterally seek to alter it;
iii) the UN Charter would govern relations between the two countries;

iv) representatives of the two would meet to discuss normalization of relations including 'a final settlement of Jammu and Kashmir';[6]

Close examination of the terms of this agreement reveals it to actually be much closer to the Pakistani than the Indian position. The inclusion of 'any other peaceful means' certainly did not exclude future UN involvement in Jammu and Kashmir, a point reaffirmed in the reference to the UN Charter. 'Line of control' was not synonymous with international boundary, while the phrase 'future settlement of Jammu and Kashmir' implied Indian sovereignty in the State was far from acknowledged as permanent.

Following the signing of the Simla Agreement, the general Indian view was that Jammu and Kashmir was now a permanent part of the Indian Union, and that the threat to this position from Pakistan had largely disappeared. This thinking, especially in central government circles, profoundly influenced policies towards the State.

Significance for Politics within Jammu and Kashmir

How did the 1971 Indo-Pak War and the subsequent Simla Agreement affect politics and ethnic identification within Kashmir? Basically in the same way as the 1965 War and Tashkent Declaration, six years earlier. As far as Pakistani policy-making was concerned Kashmir was very much pushed onto the backburner. The 1971 defeat in war had shown the Pakistanis that Kashmir could not be won by force from India, and the chances of an internal rebellion handing the State to them appeared remote. Pakistan's effective acceptance of the status quo in turn forced Kashmiri Muslims to accept Indian sovereignty: the 'door' to Pakistan was closed off. Had it not been for the UN resolutions on self-determination, it is possible that all thoughts among Kashmiri Muslims of an alternative to India would have disappeared.

In terms of political developments, Sheikh Abdullah and the National Conference were forced to deal with India: the prime issue became not whether accession was final or not, but what the status of Jammu and Kashmir would be *within* India. From the Indian government's point of view, the main source of external pressure to wrest the State from India had been removed. New Delhi could have taken advantage of the removal of the threat from Pakistan to allow genuine autonomy in the State, and thereby hopefully win the Kashmiris over. Alternatively it could have used its strengthened position to further integrate the State with the rest of India. While the former course would have encouraged the development of a regional non-communal identity, the latter—in view of the Pandits' and Kashmiri Muslims' divergent views on integration—would most likely push them towards communal identification. As will be seen in the rest of this chapter, India chose to follow the latter course. [The reasons for their doing so will be explained in chapter five on Indian domestic politics.]

Post-1972 Kashmir Politics

New Delhi actually started off by relaxing its hold on Jammu and Kashmir. Political freedom within the State was largely restored: about 160 political prisoners, including Maulana Masoodi, were released shortly after the elections. In April, Begum Abdullah was allowed to return to Kashmir, and in June the externment order against Sheikh Abdullah was lifted, quickly followed by those against Beg and G.M. Shah. Sheikh Abdullah returned to Srinagar on 19 June 1972. The ban on the Plebiscite Front was not lifted, but neither was it renewed when it expired on 12 January 1973.

As well as the threat from Pakistan being removed, a major reason why New Delhi loosened its control in Kashmir somewhat was that Congress held power there with a clear majority in the State Assembly. But the party's political power did not necessarily reflect popular support for it. This point was hammered home by a *Moe-i-Moqaddas*-type incident in May 1973.

A book containing a picture of the Prophet Muhammad (PBUH) (something strictly forbidden in Islam) was discovered in a college library in Anantnag, Kashmir, around the middle of May.[7] On the 17th, students carried out demonstrations directed principally against the State Government. The book was banned immediately, but protests continued spreading throughout the Vale—with India and Britain (the author was British) also targets of condemnation. By the time the unrest died down, four people had been killed in clashes with police and some 100 arrested. The significant point about the whole incident was that the book itself could not have aroused such anger. There was probably only one copy in the entire State, it had been sitting in the Anantnag library for decades, and the Government did not hesitate to ban it—not only in Jammu and Kashmir but throughout India. Obviously it provided a pretext for protests whose real cause was dissatisfaction at the political situation.

The May 1973 protests no doubt contributed to New Delhi shifting from its initial liberal approach in Kashmir to a more controlling one. Before looking at how this happened a new feature of Kashmiri Muslim politics should be noted. After Simla for the first time a significant gap developed between Kashmiri political elites and the Kashmiri Muslim public. While the former appeared to accept the reality of Indian sovereignty over Jammu and Kashmir, for the latter an 'exit door' from India— via the UN rather than direct to Pakistan—remained open. This was demonstrated by a series of protests in November 1973, this time obviously political.

In a visit to Muzaffarabad, the capital of Azad Kashmir, on 6 November 1973, Zulfiqar Ali Bhutto condemned India for not allowing a plebiscite in Jammu and Kashmir. The next day there were student riots in Srinagar. On two further occasions (8 and 10 November) Bhutto called for strikes in Indian Kashmir to demand the right of self-determination. The response to these calls was a fortnight of (largely student) protests in Srinagar and other parts of the Vale.

1975 Kashmir Accord

On being allowed to return to Kashmir, Sheikh Abdullah's initial statements appeared to indicate he still had not given up his demand for self-determination, i.e. a plebiscite.[8] However, by the end of 1973 some shift in his position became apparent. He condemned Bhutto for 'meddling in the internal affairs of Jammu and Kashmir', and indicated a willingness to enter into negotiations with the Indian Government on the State's status within India. What prompted this shift can only be speculated at: Pakistan's defeat in 1971 and the 1972 Simla Agreement meant little active help for a secessionist/independence movement could be expected from across the border. Another possible explanation is that having been out of power for almost twenty years, Sheikh Abdullah was eager to grasp at a last chance (in view of his age) to recapture it. The extent of the subsequent compromise made by Abdullah to New Delhi suggests regaining the premiership was the major motivating factor.

Negotiations between the Indian Government and leaders of the Plebiscite Front began early in 1974. There were high profile meetings between Indira Gandhi and Abdullah, but most of the detailed negotiations took place between Mirza Afzal Beg and Mrs Gandhi's special representative, G. Parthasarathi. These two had come up with an agreement by November 1973, which was approved by Abdullah on 12 February, and made public by Indira Gandhi on 24 February 1975. It was known as the Kashmir Accord.

From Sheikh Abdullah's point of view, the major compromise was acknowledgement of the finality of Jammu and Kashmir's accession to India. Article 370 was retained, thereby supposedly allowing the State a high degree of autonomy within the Indian Union. However, closer examination of the Accord revealed Article 370 to be very much in name only: all the post-1953 changes reducing Kashmiri autonomy such as Article 356 (allowing the Centre to assume power) were retained. A further 'green light' for central interference was included: 'Parliament will continue to have power to make laws relating to the prevention of activities directed towards disclaiming, questioning or disrupting the sovereignty and territorial integrity of India.'[9] The only concessions to state autonomy were provisions allowing the State Assembly to legislate on some social and welfare issues (then under Union control)—but even this limited freedom was checked by constitutional procedures effectively requiring the Indian President's approval. The terms Prime Minister and Sadar-i-Riyasat—potent symbols of autonomy— were not to be brought back. In summary, Abdullah compromised both on the issue of self-determination and on that of autonomy.

What did he gain from such a one-sided agreement?

Observers were not kept speculating for long. On 23 February 1975 Syed Mir Qasim had resigned as Chief Minister. On 25 February the State Congress Party elected Sheikh Abdullah as its leader—even though he was not a member of the party—and he was thus sworn in as the new Chief Minister. Beg also received his reward; he was elected a cabinet minister. In subsequent by-elections Abdullah and Beg, standing as independents, won their Assembly seats.

The Kashmir Accord, even during the negotiation stage, attracted some vocal opposition in the Vale of Kashmir. In the first half of 1974 Mirwaiz Farooq accused Abdullah of 'selling out' to India. On 13 July that year, during commemorations for the 1931 Jail 'martyrs', there were clashes between Awami Action Committee and Plebiscite Front supporters—a repeat of numerous similar clashes earlier in Kashmiri history, albeit under different names. Following Mrs Gandhi's official announcement of the Accord, Mirwaiz Farooq repeated his accusations that Abdullah 'had given away his people's right to self-determination'. On the whole, however, public protest in the Vale remained confined to Action Committee supporters; following Abdullah's return to power 'the sharp edge of the ferocity of anti-India groups was blunted with one stroke.'[10] In Jammu, somewhat surprisingly, the Accord attracted condemnation from the Hindu Jana Sangh. Opposed to even the nominal retention of Article 370, the Jana Sangh had wanted it to be abrogated, thereby removing all constitutional distinctions between Jammu and Kashmir and the other states of the Indian Union. Neither the Vale nor Jammu agitation proved a major problem for the Indira Government. The Kashmir Accord was approved by the Indian Parliament on 4 March, and by the Rajya Sabha (Upper House) on 13 March.

1977 Elections

If Indira Gandhi believed that with the Chief Ministership she had brought an end to Sheikh Abdullah's opposition she was soon to be proved wrong. Mrs Gandhi had wanted Abdullah to join the State Congress party, thereby tying him directly to her and hopefully diffusing much of the anti-New Delhi feeling in the Vale. Far from complying, Abdullah suggested that the Congress party be dissolved and merge with the Plebiscite Front to form a new National Conference. When Congress members in Jammu and Kashmir refused this offer, Abdullah went ahead regardless, and the National Conference was revived in July 1975. This produced an unusual division of power: while Congress had a clear majority in the State Assembly, it was the National Conference—with only a handful of seats—that formed the State Government. Sheikh Abdullah wanted this discrepancy removed by dissolving the Assembly and holding fresh elections; he was confident that the National Conference could beat Congress. No doubt for the same reason Mrs Gandhi refused to permit such a move. Relations between her and Abdullah, and between the State Congress party and the National Conference, were thus strained almost from the beginning. A visit by Mrs Gandhi (accompanied by sons and daughters-in-law) to Srinagar in October temporarily healed the rift, but it soon reappeared, widening during the course of 1976 and into 1977.

Crisis point was reached in March 1977 when the State Congress party attempted to remove the 'power-discrepancy' in an alternative way. Congress Assembly members withdrew their support from Sheikh Abdullah's administration and demanded that their leader, Mufti Mohammed Sayeed, be appointed Chief Minister. Had Mrs Gandhi still been in power in New Delhi, they would probably have succeeded. But Mrs Gandhi had just been defeated in national elections by the coalition Janata Party.[11] Thus when Sheikh Abdullah again asked Governor Jha to dissolve the State Assembly and call elections, the prospect of one less Congress state government now raised no alarms in New Delhi (quite the opposite!), and the request was approved.

The Jammu and Kashmir State Assembly elections of June/ July 1977 were—by the standards set in previous state elections—relatively free and fair. Both major national parties, Congress and Janata, joined the traditional local parties— National Conference, Jamaat-i-Islami, Jana Sangh, etc.,—in contesting the elections. Sheikh Abdullah had a mild heart attack three days before voting was due to start, which perhaps helped him achieve a favourable result. Of the total 76 seats being contested, the National Conference won 47 (40 in Kashmir; 7 in Jammu); Janata 13 (2 in Kashmir); Congress 11 (all in Jammu); Jana Sangh 3 (in Jammu); Jamaat-i-Islami 1, and the rest were won by Independents.

Some writers (e.g. M.J. Akbar) have interpreted the results of these elections—the first held after the Kashmir Accord—as indicating public approval for the Accord, i.e. for accession and integration with India.[12] However, such assessments ignore the two years between the signing of the Accord and the elections during which Sheikh Abdullah again demanded Kashmiri autonomy. The National Conference fought the 1977 election on a campaign manifesto of autonomy for Jammu and Kashmir. Thus it was Kashmiri autonomy, and *not* the Kashmir Accord, that received the popular mandate in 1977.

The other noteworthy point about the 1977 election result was the clear correlation between region and political party. National Conference support was largely confined to the Vale of Kashmir. Between them, Janata and Congress—both advocating integration—won only 2 seats in Kashmir. Together with the Hindu Jana Sangh these parties were only successful in

Jammu. The two members elected for Ladakh both ran on a regional, Buddhist, platform.

National Conference Government 1977–1982

Sheikh Abdullah's government had been showing signs of nepotism/corruption and authoritarianism before the 1977 election. However, once Abdullah was established as Chief Minister with a majority in the State Assembly, these traits became far more obvious. Abdullah's closest relatives—his wife, sons and son-in-law—were involved in running the government. The criterion for appointment and promotion in the National Conference administration was loyalty to Sheikh Abdullah. Many well-qualified candidates were overlooked in favour of those who had stood by Abdullah in the past—even though many of these were 'notoriously corrupt'. Money that was not going into the Abdullah family coffers or lining the pockets of his cronies, was wasted on elaborate ceremonies, 'pomp and show'. In the process, economic development was totally neglected.

Criticism of the National Conference administration was curbed by a series of measures introduced in September 1977 that amounted to press censorship. In November 1977, the Jammu and Kashmir Public Safety Ordinance was passed granting the State Government powers of detention for up to two years with no right of appeal. These powers were later incorporated into a new Public Safety Bill passed in March 1978. In September 1978, in an effort to quell the dissenting voices beginning to be heard even within his own party, Abdullah insisted that all cabinet members swear a personal oath of loyalty to him. Mirza Afzal Beg, his associate for the previous forty years, refused and was immediately expelled from the National Conference. In a further move away from democracy towards dictatorship, the Representation of People (Amendment) Bill became law on 29 September 1979. With the passage of this bill any Assembly member who refused to obey the party whip would lose his seat.[13]

Predictably, the National Conference Government's corruption and inertia (with respect to state development), coupled with Sheikh Abdullah's growing authoritarianism, led to widespread public protests. In Kashmir, the protests were largely economic in origin; a huge increase in university graduates had not been matched by an increase in job opportunities. In Poonch City, the riots had the added element of regionalism. Though also predominantly Muslim, Poonch inhabitants felt that their region was being neglected in favour of Sheikh Abdullah's native Vale.

Protests in Jammu, also largely involving unemployed graduates, contained yet another element: communalism. Jammu Hindus felt that they were being discriminated against in State Government policies both because they were not Kashmiri and because they were not Muslim. The riots in Jammu became especially serious in the early months of 1979; eight demonstrators were killed as the police tried to restore order using strong-arm tactics. Abdullah's response to the Poonch and Jammu riots—after liberal use of force had failed to quell them—was to set up commissions of enquiry to look into the demonstrators' complaints, especially those of 'regional imbalances.' This was not a long-term solution to the problem, and within a few months there were renewed protests. By the beginning of 1981 they had spread to Buddhist Ladakh where, as in Jammu, the inhabitants complained that they were the double victims of regional and religious prejudice. Increasingly, in both Ladakh and Jammu the solution to 'regional imbalances' was seen to lie only in the complete integration of those provinces—if necessary without the Vale of Kashmir—into the Indian Union. Sheikh Abdullah who, as late as July 1980, continued to harbour dreams of a reunited, independent Jammu and Kashmir resisted this 'solution'. Indira Gandhi was by then back in power in New Delhi, and in no mood to tolerate such an attitude from Sheikh Abdullah: an Indira-Abdullah clash seemed inevitable.

Before looking into this, a point about the protests against Abdullah should be noted. Those involving Kashmiri Muslims were highly significant. Until then they had pretty much followed Sheikh Abdullah wherever he led them, e.g. resisting Pakistani forces/tribals in 1947 in favour of India, supporting his calls for autonomy/independence, etc. The Kashmiri Muslims' devotion to Abdullah was one of the main reasons (the other being his non-communal politics) why Nehru had 'manoeuvred' him into power in 1947—'get Abdullah on-side and the Kashmiri Muslims will follow.' But the protests against Abdullah at the end of the 1970s showed that Kashmiri Muslims were no longer prepared to follow him blindly. A new generation had emerged that was educated and politically aware—they could think for themselves.

This public-elite divergence had first appeared to a significant extent in 1973, as described earlier. By the end of the 1970s it had become very prominent. Thereafter, the pattern of Kashmiri politics changed very rapidly: from being elite-led with the people following, it became people-driven—elites had to follow a course set by the public. The fact that no leader of Abdullah's charisma and stature appeared after him considerably speeded up this reversal.

Returning to the hostility between Indira Gandhi and Sheikh Abdullah, the long-expected clash between them eventually took place in 1982 over the issue of resettlement of refugees from the pre-Partition state of Jammu and Kashmir, who were then in Pakistan and Azad Kashmir.[14] Sheikh Abdullah saw that if the State Government could control which of these would be allowed back into the State, and which would be granted citizenship, this would amount to a significant measure of autonomy from India.[15] For the same reason, Mrs Gandhi strongly refuted the State Government's right to control the return of refugees. A further reason for her opposition was that Abdullah could use it to increase the Muslim population in the State and hence his own support; and because it would allow the entry of 'undesirable elements' from Azad Kashmir that could stir up anti-India, pro-Pakistan feelings.[16] The Jammu and Kashmir Assembly passed the Resettlement Bill in March 1982, after which it was sent for Governor B.K. Nehru's consideration. He had yet to give his decision when, on 8 September, Sheikh Abdullah died of heart trouble.

Assessment of Sheikh Abdullah

Sheikh Abdullah was a tremendously important figure in Kashmiri history: he played a pivotal role in determining the course of politics and ethnic identification in Kashmir. Before assessing his legacy, two points about Abdullah need to be stressed.

One, he was very much a Kashmiri Muslim leader. His support among non-Muslims was negligible: his non-communal rhetoric stressing that all Kashmiris were one, failed to make any impact on the Pandits. Muslims outside the Vale in Jammu, Poonch, etc., were more inclined to follow their own leaders such as Ghulam Abbas.

Two, while Sheikh Abdullah did want the best for his people, he was also highly ambitious for himself. This became clear very early on when he refused to make common cause with the Mirwaiz-i-Kashmir. During the course of his life his personal ambition came to predominate over his commitment to the public. When in power—aside from the land reforms introduced by his first government—the only people he really helped were his family and National Conference cronies.

Turning to Sheikh Abdullah's relationship with the Kashmiri Muslim public, this is perhaps best understood if viewed as a struggle between opposing forces. On the one hand, Abdullah's towering personality (literally as well as metaphorically!) coupled with his periodic stints in jail for defying the authorities drew them to him. On the other hand, his ambition, his inability to tolerate dissent or opposition and his tendency towards nepotism and 'cronyism' pushed them away. During the early decades of his career the former qualities overcame the latter, but by the end it was not enough. Another factor in finally pushing Kashmiri Muslims away from Abdullah was the public-elite political divergence mentioned earlier. As Kashmiri Muslims became more disillusioned with India, their leader Abdullah appeared to have gone in the opposite direction until finally he came to accept Indian rule. Muslim hostility toward India also became targeted against Abdullah, perceived to be a 'collaborator'. Today it is this perception of Abdullah that predominates, as demonstrated by the fact that Indian forces have to guard his grave from mutilation by Kashmiri Muslims.

With respect to *Kashmiriyat*, Abdullah's role is best summed up as 'failing to fulfil his potential'. Abdullah was in a position to promote *Kashmiriyat*. He started doing this under the Dogras, calling upon all Kashmiris—Muslim and Hindu—to unite, and claiming to represent the interests of all of them. At that stage he failed to make an impression on the Pandits, but had he put rhetoric into practice when he came to power there was a chance he could have done so. As it was, under Abdullah's government the Pandits moved even further away from the Kashmiri Muslims.

Considering ethnic identification among the Muslims only for a moment, while Abdullah failed to promote Hindu-Muslim unity he certainly did not encourage them to see themselves primarily as Muslim. He always stressed they were Kashmiris. Thus, while he constantly shifted between calling for independence and autonomy within India, he never called for accession to Pakistan.

It is no coincidence that it was only after Sheikh Abdullah's death that Kashmiri Muslims really started going down the path of communal identification and rebelling against India. Even during the last decade of his life when protests against him were mounting, Abdullah's influence was still strong enough to prevent public disillusionment with India reaching breaking point. Because of him Kashmiri Muslim opposition was restrained—an observation that has been proved with hindsight. Had it not been for Abdullah, militancy in Kashmir would undoubtedly have broken out much earlier. The calculations of Nehru and later Indira Gandhi, that if they could win Sheikh Abdullah over to India he would win over the Kashmiri Muslims for them, proved partially correct: Abdullah's siding with India was enough to prevent his followers rebelling against Indian rule, but not enough to win their allegiance to New Delhi.

Farooq Abdullah: 1983 Elections

In August 1981, Sheikh Abdullah had appointed his son, Farooq Abdullah, President of the National Conference—thereby effectively making him the 'heir-apparent'. Immediately after Abdullah's death, Farooq was duly sworn in as the new Chief Minister. Like his father, Farooq Abdullah was a strong advocate of Kashmiri autonomy from New Delhi, in accordance with Article 370. However, unlike Sheikh Abdullah, at no point did he question the State's inclusion in the Indian Union; he had no dreams of an independent Jammu and Kashmir, and—with his 'playboy' reputation—he certainly did not wish the State to join Pakistan.

With respect to the Resettlement Bill that he had inherited along with his father's post, Farooq was placed in a somewhat awkward position. Since he owed this post to the fact that he was Sheikh Abdullah's son, he could not abandon the bill; he had to try and push it through the legislature. But he was also aware that such an action would inevitably create problems with New Delhi. In the end, he managed to come up with a face-saving compromise. On 23 September, B. K. Nehru sent the Resettlement Bill back to the Jammu and Kashmir State Assembly for reconsideration. On 4 October, the Assembly, still with a majority of Sheikh Abdullah loyalists, once again passed the bill in its original form. Farooq, however, avoided further conflict with New Delhi by immediately announcing that the re-passed bill would not be implemented until it had been validated by the Supreme Court—a move which effectively put it into 'cold storage'.

The Resettlement Bill experience probably explains Farooq's desire to call early elections: he hoped to win power in his own name and thereby free himself from the restraints associated with ruling as his father's nominated successor. Indira Gandhi, however, was reluctant to hold elections until an alliance could be arranged between Congress and the National Conference. Farooq was willing to field weak candidates in a handful of Vale seats, thereby making the seats easy for Congress to take, but he refused to agree to the two parties openly joining forces.[17] Mrs Gandhi rejected this offer. As a result, in the elections that followed in June 1983, Congress and the National Conference competed against each other for almost all the 76 Assembly seats (Congress left four for its smaller allies). Of the traditional 'regional' parties, the Jamaat-i-Islami boycotted the elections on the grounds that participation would imply acceptance of accession, while in Jammu, Jana Sangh's place was taken by its ideological successor, the Bharatiya Janata Party (BJP).

The failure by Congress to achieve an alliance with the National Conference had a profound effect in determining the major campaign issues. Whereas in the event of an electoral pact the two parties would have downplayed their differences, as rivals these were highlighted. The major difference between them was of course on the question of autonomy versus integration. Farooq Abdullah called for the preservation of Article 370 and the removal of all legislation that undermined it. Indira Gandhi—whose only real chance of electoral success lay in Jammu—promised Hindus there that 'regional imbalances' would be corrected, thereby implying greater integration with India. Campaigning in 1983 was characterized by communalism to a far greater extent than in any previous State election. A large amount of the blame for this must rest on Mrs Gandhi's shoulders: in order to win support in Jammu she played up the threat of Kashmiri Muslim domination, citing the Resettlement Bill as an example. Farooq Abdullah countered by accusing Congress of following Hari Singh in trying to 'enslave' Kashmiris. There was also far more violence in the 1983 elections than in any held before: the Congress office in Srinagar, for instance, was set alight, and there were serious post-electoral riots in which National Conference supporters clashed with opponents.

The results showed that the regional [communal/ethnic] voting behaviour traceable in previous elections had been consolidated in 1983. The National Conference won virtually all the Vale seats, Congress none. Of Jammu's 32 seats, three-quarters went to Congress and eight to Farooq Abdullah's party. Perhaps because both the main parties had virtually abandoned secularism and non-communal politics, the major openly communal party, the BJP, failed to win any seats. Overall the National Conference won 46 seats, giving it a majority in the Assembly. Congress claimed that the elections had been rigged and there was undoubtedly some truth in this assertion.

It should be noted that supporters of G.M. Shah (Gulshah) won a sizeable minority of the National Conference seats in Kashmir. A seasoned politician, Shah had tried for the Chief Ministership after his father-in-law's death. Subsequently excluded from Farooq's cabinet, he had become an outspoken opponent of his brother-in-law. Perhaps bowing to family pressure, or because he still lacked a strong political base, Farooq had included Shah supporters in the list of National Conference candidates. The success of these candidates put Gulshah in a position to undermine Farooq Abdullah's position from inside the Assembly if he wanted. Relations between the brothers-in-law remained acrimonious and they eventually became open political rivals. On 4 October 1983, Farooq had Shah expelled from the National Conference; Shah responded by forming his own party, the Real National Conference, of which his wife (Sheikh Abdullah's daughter) was appointed President. Gulshah went on to play a similar role to that of Bakshi in the dismissal of Sheikh Abdullah in 1953.

1984: Farooq Abdullah's Dismissal

One significant consequence of the Congress failure to enter into an electoral pact with the National Conference (and the two parties' subsequent acrimonious campaigning) was Farooq Abdullah's alliance with other Indian parties also opposed to

Congress. By 1983, a handful of powerful regional opposition parties had emerged: in West Bengal, Tamil Nadu, Andhra Pradesh, and Karnataka. Before long these and other regional parties were drawing together in an unofficial anti-Indira/Centre alliance. Farooq became involved in this 'movement' even before the 1983 elections were over. On 31 May 1983, he attended a conference in Vijayawada arranged by the Andhra Pradesh Chief Minister and Telegu Desam leader, Rama Rao. In total, some fourteen non-Congress leaders took part in this meeting. In early October 1983 (no doubt flushed by his victory over Congress in Kashmir), Farooq arranged an even bigger gathering of opposition leaders—59 representing 17 parties—in Srinagar. At the conference he initiated calls for weaker central government. All these activities undoubtedly angered Mrs Gandhi: already facing violent demands for autonomy in Punjab and Assam, Farooq's encouragement of anti-centre opposition made things even more difficult for her. Ironically, the alliance between Abdullah and other Indian parties was a move indicating *confirmation* of Kashmir's membership of the Indian Union. Indira Gandhi's personal political ambitions, however, prevented her from appreciating this point.

Anger in New Delhi was further aroused by a cricket match between the West Indies and India held in Srinagar on 13 October 1983. During the game a section of the crowd cheered the West Indians, booed the Indian team and waved green Jamaat-i-Islami flags. These had a very similar appearance to the Pakistani national flag. In media coverage of the event the crowd was described as waving Pakistani flags. Mrs Gandhi, looking for excuses to attack Farooq, seized on the incident and accused him of being pro-Pakistan. She made use of another incident in February 1984, the killing of an Indian diplomat in Birmingham by a group called the Jammu and Kashmir Liberation Front (JKLF), to repeat these accusations.

It is difficult to say exactly when Indira Gandhi decided to remove Farooq Abdullah's government. What is clear is that by the end of 1983 the decision had been taken. Soon after the October elections, G.M. Shah's faction in the State Assembly

(13 MLAs) allied itself to the Congress 26 MLAs. With a combined strength of 39 they formed a majority in the Assembly. Offering to demonstrate this majority to Governor Nehru, Shah's supporters asked him to dismiss Farooq Abdullah. He refused on the grounds that constitutionally a majority had to be demonstrated in the Assembly itself—something the Shah group was unwilling to do. B.K. Nehru was not a close supporter of Farooq Abdullah, but he does appear to have been aware of the serious consequences that would follow his dismissal. Mrs Gandhi, however, was guided by other, more personal considerations and ignored his warnings. On 31 December, following her cousin's refusal to co-operate and dismiss Abdullah, she asked Nehru to resign. Later, this demand was revised and he was asked to accept a transfer to Gujarat. Nehru first opted to resign, then to accept the Gujarat offer, but he refused to go until April 1984.

Meanwhile, in February 1984, Farooq Abdullah called a surprise vote of confidence, which he won. This victory apparently lulled him into believing his position was secure—an illusion that was to be shattered by the new Governor of Jammu and Kashmir. Jagmohan Malhotra, Lieutenant Governor of Delhi during the Emergency and thus a proven Indira loyalist, was sworn in as Governor on 26 April 1984. He wasted little time in making arrangements for Abdullah's removal. New Delhi had helped pave the way in January by encouraging Congress supporters in Kashmir to demonstrate against the National Conference Government. This predictably led to clashes between Congress and National Conference supporters, which in turn enabled Mrs Gandhi to accuse Farooq's government of failing to maintain order in the State.

Jagmohan's own arrangements consisted chiefly of bringing extra Indian police into Kashmir to cope with the public protests anticipated after Farooq's dismissal. These arrived in Srinagar from Madhya Pradesh on 2 July 1984. On 28 June 1984, G.M. Shah's supporters in the Assembly had written to the Governor that they had withdrawn their support from the Government and pledged it to Shah. Jagmohan showed this letter to Farooq on 2

July, and he was asked to resign. Abdullah's political naivety was demonstrated by his initial response: he asked Jagmohan to impose Governor's Rule. Only later did he insist that the Assembly be dissolved and fresh elections called. Jagmohan was apparently quite willing to impose Governor's Rule, but by the afternoon he bowed to New Delhi's wishes and swore G.M. Shah in as the new Chief Minister (the 26 Congress MLAs had also submitted a letter to the Governor pledging support for Shah). On 31 July—following the physical removal of the Speaker and a walkout by Farooq's group—Shah was able to demonstrate a majority in the State Assembly.

G.M. Shah had little public support in Kashmir, and his tenure as Chief Minister was notable only for its corruption. On 7 March 1986 he was dismissed for incompetence by Jagmohan, who finally got to run the State himself by imposing Governor's Rule. Following his dismissal, Shah became an open supporter of Pakistan.

1987 Congress–National Conference Alliance

Indira Gandhi was assassinated by her Sikh bodyguards on 31 October 1984. Her son Rajiv Gandhi succeeded her. Initially, Rajiv displayed a completely different approach to government than that of his mother's, particularly on the issue of centre-state relations. While Mrs Gandhi had always stuck to the principle that autonomist/secessionist demands should be met with greater centralization, her son was more accommodating. In Punjab, he was eventually able to reach an accord with the Akali Dal, which paved the way for elections and a return to state government. However, only after being Premier for almost two years did he initiate similar steps in Jammu and Kashmir. By that time it had become obvious that G.M. Shah, though completely subservient to New Delhi, had neither the inclination nor the ability to bring about political stability in the State. Communal violence, in particular, was rapidly escalating out of control.

Rajiv realized that neither replacing Shah with some other 'puppet' nor use of force would stabilize the situation. As in Punjab, the only solution lay in restoring genuinely popular government, i.e. in the return to power of Farooq Abdullah. However, just like his mother, Rajiv was unwilling to relinquish control of the state to an opposition party. The only way to overcome this obstacle would be for the National Conference and Congress to merge or form an alliance. In the ideal scenario such a partnership would ensure public peace, and yet maintain New Delhi's influence in the state—or at least remove the headache of a hostile state government demanding greater autonomy.

In 1983, Farooq Abdullah had rejected Indira Gandhi's offer that their two parties form an alliance. However in 1986— perhaps seeing it as the only way to return to power—he accepted a similar offer from Rajiv. Farooq justified his action by claiming that it would lead to economic development and prosperity for Kashmir—in a subsequent visit to the Valley Rajiv announced a Rs. 10 billion aid package for the region. In September 1986, when the six-month limit for Governor's Rule had expired, President's Rule (still administered by Jagmohan) had been imposed in Jammu and Kashmir. On 7 November 1986, following an agreement between Rajiv Gandhi and Farooq Abdullah, this was lifted and the State Assembly restored. Farooq was again Chief Minister, but this time leading a National Conference-Congress alliance. The Assembly was immediately dissolved and fresh elections called.

The main contestants in the March 1987 elections were somewhat different from those of earlier state elections. Apart from the fact that Congress and the National Conference were campaigning together, a new Islamic group had emerged. The traditional Jamaat-i-Islami had joined forces with other Islamic parties (e.g. the Islamic Student Front) and formed a coalition, the Muslim United Front (MUF). A largely pro-Pakistan group, the MUF received additional support from G.M. Shah's former National Conference faction. Also competing in Jammu was the Hindu BJP.

The standard practices of Jammu and Kashmir elections—
manipulation of candidate and voting lists, arrest of opposition
candidates, ballot box rigging, etc.,—were clearly visible in
1987. The main target was the new MUF coalition, which—
going by attendance at rallies and public meetings—had gained
a significant following, particularly in the Valley. The election
results, however, painted a different picture. Most of the Vale
seats went to the National Conference, which won 38 in all;
Congress took 24 in Jammu, the BJP 2, and the MUF won only
4 seats in Kashmir. On 27 March, Farooq Abdullah was once
more sworn in as Chief Minister of Jammu and Kashmir, head
of a Congress-National Conference coalition government.

The 1987 elections were significant for several reasons.
Firstly, as Farooq was to later appreciate, by allying himself to
Congress he had not won public support for New Delhi, but had
instead lost it from the National Conference. The basis of
popular support for the National Conference—apart from Sheikh
Abdullah's personality—had always been its demand for state
autonomy. The alliance with Congress removed this demand
and hence—irrespective of what the election result suggested—
the party's support.

Farooq's alliance with Congress had effectively put another
New Delhi 'puppet regime' in power. But there was a significant
difference between this 'puppet regime' and that headed by
G.M. Shah. During Shah's rule there had always been an
alternative 'moderate' Kashmiri political party to attract public
support, i.e. Farooq Abdullah's National Conference. 'Moderate'
here refers to the fact that while, for the most part, the National
Conference had always had some grievances against New
Delhi, it had never disputed staying within the Indian Union.
After 1987, with the National Conference effectively
transformed into an extension of Congress, there was no
moderate—as in content to stay part of India—Kashmiri political
party to which a disillusioned public could give their allegiance.
This 'vacuum' in moderate politics was to prove of immense
significance: it was a major factor in pushing Kashmiris into the

arms of groups making far more radical demands in far more radical ways.

While there is little doubt that the 1987 elections were rigged in the government's favour, what is highly disputed is the extent to which the results were manipulated. The MUF, of course, claimed that they would have won an outright majority had the elections been free and fair. Others, such as Hewitt, think it more likely they would have gained around ten seats. But when assessing the significance of the 1987 elections these differing opinions are largely irrelevant. Two points are important. One, that most Kashmiris believed the elections had been heavily rigged. Bearing in mind Kashmir's less than perfect record in conducting elections, the 1987 rigging could be considered the 'straw that broke the camel's back'—it caused people to become totally disillusioned with the electoral process and more so with India. The second important point concerns the MUF itself. This started off as a coalition of political parties and organizations, competing in the political arena. But when, as they felt, they were cheated of victory, many of the members shifted from the political into the militant arena. As Hewitt writes: 'it was the conviction by many MUF candidates that, as they had been prevented from taking power through the democratic process, they could resort to violence as a legitimate means to express their politics.'[18] While acts of violence against Indian rule had been going on sporadically for some time in Kashmir, it was undoubtedly only after the 1987 elections that the process began which led to sustained, organized militancy and the current Kashmir conflict. Had the elections been handled differently it is possible that Kashmir today would still be at peace.

The National Conference-Congress government that took power in March 1987 was not a genuinely popular government. Hence, it was unable to restore peace: public order in Jammu and Kashmir continued on the same downward spiral it had been on during Gulshah's rule. Indeed, with the MUF and the public's faith in the ballot box as a means of bringing about change destroyed, the law and order situation actually deteriorated faster after 1987.

Economic and Social Policies

So far we have only looked at the specifically political aspect of politics in Kashmir, as in party manoeuvring, elections, legislation integrating the State further with India, etc. It is also important to examine other aspects of politics in the State, in particular economic, employment and educational/cultural policies.

Economic Policies

There is a popular perception that Jammu and Kashmir receives preferential financial treatment compared to other Indian states, because New Delhi fears that Kashmiris may secede from India and it hopes to use money (effectively bribery) to keep them within the Union. There is some truth behind this notion. The Bakshi government, for instance, did receive generous funds from Prime Minister Nehru. The per capita aid to Jammu and Kashmir from the Central government is among the highest in India. But this is only a small part of the total picture; when one looks at the whole, Kashmir appears far less pampered.

The first point to stress is that in the past most of the funding Kashmir received from New Delhi was siphoned off into the pockets of the ruling elite. Whether headed by Sheikh Abdullah, Bakshi Ghulam Muhammad, G.M. Shah, etc., the one thing that all Kashmiri administrations have been notorious for is their corruption. As a result, the average Kashmiri has benefited little from Central aid. Secondly, funds promised by Rajiv Gandhi when he reached an accord with Farooq Abdullah prior to the 1987 elections were never delivered. Thirdly, until recently only 30 per cent of the central funding given to Kashmir was in the form of grants; 70 per cent was given as loans that had to be returned with interest. This ratio was vastly different from the 90 per cent grant:10 per cent loan aid given to other states. The high loan percentage meant that receiving central funding actually worsened the State's financial position: 'the bulk of the annually increasing budget deficits is accounted for by the burden of interest payments to the Central Government. Out of the current year's projected deficit of about Rs. 370 crore, almost Rs. 300 crore were interest payments.'[19] Finally, for almost a decade now, the vast bulk of central funding has been spent on maintaining security within Kashmir.

Some reference has already been made to how most of the funds given to Jammu and Kashmir were spent, i.e. on prospering the ruling elite. Of the aid that did find its way to the people very little was spent on developing the State's economy, e.g. on building up industries, that could have made it self-sufficient. G. M. Sadiq complained to Indira Gandhi 'If I were to tell you that the law and order situation requires one more division of the army, you would send it, without the blink of an eye, but if I ask you to set up two factories you will tell me twenty reasons why it cannot be done.'[20]

> Capital investment for industry has been virtually non-existent. The pan-Indian bourgeoisie and Delhi have invested virtually nothing in the field of industry. There are two measly government sector factories—assembly units of the HMT and ITI, with investments of Rs. 5 crore and Rs. 50 lakh repsectively. Wages in Kashmir are quite high—something like Rs. 50 a day for unskilled labour in Srinagar. So, wages are not such as would specially attract the big capitalists to put up plants there.[21]

Not only did India fail to promote industrial development in Jammu and Kashmir but one could say with some justification that it actually made things worse by taking over industrial projects (either already operating or in the pipeline) from the Kashmiris. The National Hydel Power Corporation, for instance, made good use of the periods of 'puppet' (G.M. Shah, etc.) and central (notably under Jagmohan) rule to take over all the key power projects.[22] The NHPC now virtually controls both the power generation and distribution systems in Kashmir.

The only sector of the Kashmir economy which did well was that of handicrafts—the manufacture of shawls, carpets, *papier mache* pieces, etc. By 1989, this had expanded to account for

6 per cent of the GDP. But, by definition, these are very much 'cottage' industries, employing small numbers of people with low turnover and generating little income. The other major source of revenue was tourism, estimated to account for one third of state income in 1983, but with the conflict this has dried up.

Investment by New Delhi in Kashmir was largely confined to improving roads and communications, notably the Jammu-Srinagar highway. The purpose of this was primarily military; to make it easier to transport troops and weapons into the State. A secondary aim was to further trade between India and Kashmir; to facilitate the exchange of goods. Close examination of the trade between India and Kashmir reveals a colonial-type situation where the 'colony', Kashmir, supplies the 'metropolis', Delhi, with raw materials and then becomes the captive market for its manufactures. Consider raw materials first: Kashmir's two main natural resources are timber and water. There has been extensive deforestation with timber sent to India to build railways there. Maqsood notes '[a]part from the widespread adverse ecological impact, a high value resource was sold at virtually a throwaway price which not only did not bring any substantial monetary benefits in terms of current revenues but also eroded the potential for future income and the State's capacity for self-reliance.'[23] With respect to water this has been used to generate power which supplies not Kashmir but India: 'while in the midst of winter Srinagar was without power for three days in the week, power from Salal was being supplied to the northern grid, to meet the needs of Delhi most likely.'[24] Kashmir's other main export, fruit, is sold at auctions in Delhi; growers in Kashmir are estimated to get only 20 per cent of the auction price.

Turning to imports, customs barriers between Jammu and Kashmir and India were lifted after Sheikh Abdullah was replaced by Bakshi Ghulam Muhammad in 1953. The beneficiary of their removal has undoubtedly been India. Imports into Kashmir are some four times greater than exports to India. Almost all items of mass consumption, including food and fuel, come into the State from India.

Overall, then, the economy of Jammu and Kashmir is heavily dependent on New Delhi. What is more, over time, instead of decreasing, its dependence on India has greatly increased. In 1950–51 only 3.71 per cent of revenue came from the national government, 96.28 per cent was generated within the State itself. By 1987–88 the proportions had reversed to a considerable extent: 27.95 per cent from state resources, 72.04 per cent from New Delhi—and since the conflict began this reversal has pretty much become complete.[25] Whether this state of affairs emerged by accident or deliberate design is debatable.

Employment Policies

The issue of employment is worth looking at in detail because it has been a major factor in the current insurgency. Two aspects are particularly relevant: one, graduate unemployment, and two, discrimination against Muslims in government service.

Taking graduate unemployment first, perhaps the one area in which the lot of Kashmiris has significantly improved since accession is in education, particularly higher-level education. The overall literacy rate has improved and the numbers of Kashmiris gaining a high school or college education has increased considerably. Ironically, being better educated has created its own problems. On the one hand, job expectations have been raised—young Kashmiris are not prepared to do the kinds of manual jobs their fathers accepted. But on the other hand, there are insufficient job opportunities to meet this demand. As Farooq Abdullah complained 'What can I do? There are 3,000 engineers looking for jobs even after we gave jobs to 2,000 in the last two years.'[26] Bearing in mind Kashmir's deteriorating economic situation, this gulf between demand and availability is widening rather than narrowing. Schofield writes that prior to the insurgency, unemployment among those with school-leaving qualifications was around 40–50,000. Since the insurgency began the problem has become even more acute: job availability has shrunk to negligible levels.

The problem of graduate unemployment was exacerbated by corruption: the good jobs going to students with contacts in government, or to those who could pay bribes. Bearing in mind the generally corrupt nature of Kashmiri administrations, it was perhaps possible for young Muslim graduates to come to terms with this particular barrier to employment. What was far harder for them to accept was deliberate discrimination against them because of their being Muslim. Favouring Hindus over Muslims when recruiting staff has never been a clearly stated policy of the Indian government, but it is one that has definitely been implemented in practice. Even a cursory examination of employment figures in Kashmir shows this to be the case.

Looking at both State and Central government employment figures, the percentage of Hindus employed (36.59%) is roughly in line with their percentage in the population (32.24%). The figures get somewhat more disproportionate when one looks at the percentage of Hindu gazetted officers (51.18%). But it is when one looks at just Central government figures that the discriminatory recruitment policy becomes really apparent. Of a total of 14,743 Central government employees in Jammu and Kashmir, 11,278 were Hindu, 2007 Muslim; among officers specifically 83.66 per cent were Hindu, 6.89 per cent Muslim.[27] When the Indian Administrative Service was extended into Jammu and Kashmir it was supposed to recruit 50 per cent of its personnel from within the state. However, some twenty years later they were still well short of this target: only 25 per cent were being drawn from Kashmir. Of the 22 secretaries in Kashmir only five were Kashmiri Muslim.[28] Note that it is Muslims only who suffered as a result of the government's recruitment policy: in 1978, 32 per cent of senior civil service officers and nationalized industry managers were Pandits.[29]

It is not surprising, bearing in mind the above figures, that Kashmiri Muslim graduates felt frustrated. If they could not find employment in their own state, if they were being discriminated against in a Muslim-majority region, they certainly had no chance of getting jobs in India. What future then did they have? Putting oneself in the shoes of such young Kashmiris one can perhaps appreciate why militancy was to be so appealing to them: what did they have to lose?

Cultural Policies

India's drive to integrate Jammu and Kashmir fully with the rest of the Union, was not restricted to removing constitutional differences. Since the major factor distinguishing Kashmir from the rest of India was its Muslim-majority status, it was the influence of Islam that New Delhi sought to erode. To some extent this erosion took place automatically. Greater contact with the outside world through the medium of television and satellite dishes, coupled with the Kashmir Valley being an important tourist attraction for north Indians, resulted in many 'unIslamic' activities (drinking alcohol, watching modern films, gambling, free mixing of the sexes, etc.) becoming established there; bars, video parlours, cinemas and night-clubs became a common sight.

But to a considerable extent the erosion was deliberate. Wherever possible the authorities tried to remove Arabic or Persian-based names and introduce Sanskritized names. Terms such as Sadr-i-Riyasat and Wazir-i-Azam were replaced by Rashtrapati and Pradhan Mantri. One of the most important means by which India tried to bring about 'secularization' was through the education curricula. Abdul Majeed Maalik claims that subjects in Kashmiri schools have always been taught from an Indian 'secularist' angle, and that 'it has been done deliberately'.[30] Engineer's description of education in India suggests that the authorities are trying to inculcate not just secular, but Hindu values: 'school textbooks also unfortunately encourage anti-Muslim feelings by teaching and praising the culture and values of the majority community.'[31] Maalik further claims that the authorities have tried to erode *Kashmiriyat* as well, i.e. that they wanted to get rid of the Kashmiri Muslims' sense of distinctiveness not just as Muslims but also as Kashmiris. The evidence he cites to support this is that neither

Kashmiri history nor the Kashmiri language is taught in the State's schools.

Finally, with respect to 'Hinduization', aside from the Sanskritization of names there is little evidence to support the view that India has deliberately pursued such a policy. At most one can say that Kashmiris have been subjected to the same Hindu influences as the other Indians—e.g. television dramas like the Mahabharata.

It will be apparent that the evidence for deliberate identity erosion by India in Kashmir is open to considerable doubt. However, accepting for a moment that India has pursued a deliberate policy of eroding Islam and *Kashmiriyat* in Kashmir, its actions in other ways, e.g., economic policies, have had the opposite effect. Furthermore, with respect to Islam, the process of modernization/secularization in the Valley has been stopped, if not reversed, by the Islamic resurgence—discussed in chapter seven.

Social Changes

Having reviewed political developments in Kashmir up to the present conflict, it would be useful to summarize the social changes that have taken place over the previous forty-odd years. These changes are crucial to understanding the timing of the insurgency—why it broke out at this particular point in Kashmir's history, rather than at any of the previous times when Kashmiris had been oppressed in one form or another.

The most significant change was undoubtedly in education. Indian largesse paid for this to be free from primary to university level. In addition, Srinagar University and numerous colleges of higher education were established. Improving the provision of education in Kashmir certainly produced results: the literacy rate in Jammu and Kashmir more than doubled in the twenty years between 1961 and 1981 (from 11.03% to 26.67%), while enrolment in general colleges shot up from under 3000 in 1951 to 34,000 in 1992.[32]

The impact of this raised level of education has been partially considered above, namely producing a generation of well-educated Kashmiris frustrated at their lack of job opportunities. But its impact actually extended far wider than this. Not only did it raise the Kashmiris' socio-economic expectations, but it also heightened their political consciousness. They were able to appreciate that democracy and political freedom are given in a modern society. They were able to contrast the lack of fair elections in Jammu and Kashmir with the situation in other states in India. They were aware of what was happening in the outside world—the Iranian revolution, the Afghan War, the break-up of the Soviet Union. In brief, they were far better informed about their own situation, about their rights, and about the means by which people in other parts of the world were struggling to achieve their rights.

In terms of material well-being, the Kashmiris were definitely far better off than they had been in 1947. While industrial development in the state had generally been poor, income from tourism and handicrafts, coupled with remittances from workers in the Gulf region and funding from India, had considerably raised the standard of living of most people. If we take television and video-recorder ownership as a reasonable indicator of economic status, it is estimated that by 1992, one in 65 Kashmiris owned a television set with a significant percentage of these also possessing a VCR.[33] [Greater access to information, particularly about events in the outside world, was of course a factor in raising Kashmiri political consciousness.] The rise in living standard was significant because it produced in Kashmir a middle class, one with aspirations for a better life still—modern houses, cars, fridges and microwaves, etc. A backward society with few expectations is relatively easily satisfied but a modernizing society in which people have high expectations becomes discontented when these are not met. The latter was what happened in Kashmir. Since, apart from tourism, there was little economic development in the state, there were no means to sustain a continued rise in the living standard. Frustrated, people directed their anger against those ruling them.

In terms of culture one can identify two opposing trends. On the one hand Kashmiri society, particularly in urban centres like Srinagar, became more 'western' in its tastes and habits. On the other hand, by the 1980s the presence of Islam was being felt more strongly in the Valley. The surge of Islam in Kashmir is something that will be looked at in detail in a later chapter, but for now one can say that it originated externally in the Muslim world-wide Islamic resurgence, and internally in the *madrasas* or religious schools that had been established in Kashmir by the Jamaat-i-Islami. Other factors such as the rise of political Hinduism in India did, of course, also influence it. The important point to note here is that by the end of the decade the trend towards Islam was predominant.

Evolution of Ethnic Conflict

Before summing up how ethnic mobilization progressed during the period 1965–1989, the major influences on this process will be assessed. Externally, these were political and militant Islam, and political Hinduism—the former originating throughout the Muslim world but particularly in Afghanistan and Iran, the latter in India. Both these influences will be assessed in detail in later chapters, but it should be borne in mind that as well as the developments described in this chapter they too were highly significant with respect to ethnic identification in Kashmir.

Of the internal (within Kashmir) factors, ethnic mobilization among Kashmiri Muslims was most influenced by the lags between one, mass mobilization and the development of political institutions, and two, socio-economic expectations and economic development. Consider the lag between political awareness and political participation first. On the one hand, the education revolution in Kashmir, coupled with greater contact with and access to information from the outside world, produced a generation of Kashmiri Muslims that was highly politically conscious. They knew what they could expect as citizens of the state—free and fair elections, the right to elect their rulers through democratic means, and the right to express their political views. On the other hand, they found themselves in a state where election results were regularly 'manipulated', rulers were more concerned with furthering their own interests than those of their electorate, and political expression was highly restricted. The stark discrepancy between the desire for political participation and the state's inability to allow such participation inevitably generated tension—tension which found expression in heightened ethnic consciousness, both of being Kashmiri and of being Muslim. (The latter was, of course, also due to the rise of political Hinduism and the resurgence of Islam.)

The 1987 elections can be considered as the breaking point—when the gap between political consciousness and political institutions became too great to sustain. After the National Conference-Congress 'victory', the Kashmiri Muslims lost faith in the political system altogether: they stopped seeing democracy and the ballot box as the means to bring about change. Thus, while it was to be some years before the secessionist movement in Kashmir got underway, by the end of 1987 it had definitely taken root.

Turning to the lag between socio-economic expectations and what the State was actually able to deliver. While the Kashmiris were now better educated, and thanks to their greater contact with the outside world, expected to enjoy a more comfortable standard of living, opportunities for them to get good jobs and attain the kind of lifestyle they desired were highly limited. This too led to frustration, enhanced by the perception that economic opportunities were deliberately being denied to them, and it too was manifested in heightened ethnic consciousness.

Both these factors fit in well with the theory discussed in the introduction of economic and/or political discrimination (or the perception of this) leading to stronger ethnic consciousness.

Having outlined the major factors influencing ethnic identification during this time, we may consider now how this developed. The first point to make is that this period of Kashmiri history represented perhaps the last real chance for Kashmiri Muslims and Pandits to develop a shared identity: even as late as the mid-1980s separate communal identification was not inevitable. What made it come about was the failure of both State and central government leaders to counteract the divisive forces of political Hinduism and Islam. Indeed, by restricting political participation and failing to develop the State's economy, they actually fuelled those divisive tendencies. In doing so, the State leaders were largely motivated by greed, Indian leaders by the desire to centralize power and by unwillingness to tolerate opposition-controlled state governments. [These latter reasons will be assessed further in the chapter on India's domestic politics.]

Among Pandits then, distrust of Muslim-majority rule coupled with bitter experience of successive corrupt National Conference governments, pushed them away from Kashmiri Muslims, while the rise of political Hinduism in India drew them to other Hindus. The result: Pandits increasingly identified themselves in terms of their religion.

Among Kashmiri Muslims, the picture is somewhat more complex. Certainly lack of autonomy, democracy and economic development alienated them from India—and hence also from the Pandits. But in terms of ethnic identification they had a choice: to stress being Kashmiri (irrespective of whether the Pandits joined them) or to stress being Muslim. Which of these they opted for depended on various, largely external, factors: the situation in Pakistan, the contemporary Islamic resurgence, and the signals they received from their leaders in Kashmir. The first two of these will be assessed in later chapters. With respect to the third, it has been seen that up to 1987 the message Kashmiri Muslims were getting from the National Conference (first under Sheikh Abdullah, later under Farooq) was: 'you are Kashmiri; based on this you have the right to autonomy/ independence.' But when in 1987, Farooq allied himself with the Indian Congress he lost the support of the Kashmiri Muslims. No other leader was there to take his place and tell them that they were Kashmiri. The only other political activists were members of the MUF—who told Kashmiri Muslims to see themselves as Muslim. In the absence of any counteracting message, this is what many of them did.

With Pandits becoming more consciously Hindu, and Kashmiri Muslims more consciously Muslim, and with their self-perceptions being manifested in divergent political demands (for integration and autonomy/secession respectively), it is no surprise that the result was ethnic conflict.

NOTES

1. At the Convention J.P. Narayan argued that 'after 1965 conflict, no Government of India can accept a solution that places Kashmir outside Union of India', and hence the right of self-determination needed to be interpreted afresh. Sheikh Abdullah's response to this was: 'no world power, no army and no threats can browbeat us from demanding grant of right of self-determination to the people of Kashmir.' B.L. Kak, *Kashmir: Problems and Politics* (Delhi, Seema, 1981), p. 91.
2. See Lamb, *op. cit.*, p. 289.
3. Ibid., pp. 290–93.
4. Ibid., pp. 259–63.
5. A Government of Pakistan *White Paper*, published later in 1977, admitted as much: 'Pakistan had suffered a disaster…. The disparity between its military strength and India's was far wider than ever before…. Politically, Pakistan was isolated…. Pakistan was economically shattered and psychologically bruised while India was feeling the euphoria of triumph.' Cited in ibid, p. 296.
6. The most significant paragraphs of the actual text were as follows: 'That the principles and purposes of the Charter of the United Nations shall govern the relations between the two countries'…'That the two countries are resolved to settle their differences by peaceful means through bilateral negotiations or by any other peaceful means mutually agreed upon between them. Pending the final settlement of any of the problems between the two countries, neither side shall unilaterally alter the situation and both shall prevent the organisation, assistance and encouragement of any acts detrimental to the maintenance of peaceful and harmonious relations'…'In Jammu and Kashmir, the Line of Control resulting from the ceasefire of December 17, 1971 shall be respected by both sides without prejudice to the recognised position of either side. Neither side shall seek to alter it unilaterally irrespective of mutual differences and legal interpretations. Both sides further undertake to refrain from threat

or the use of force in violation of this Line'; for complete text, see Tariq, *op. cit.*, pp. 121–2.

7. The book by Arthur Mee was entitled *Book of Knowledge—Children's Encyclopaedia*. It contained a picture of the angel Gabriel reciting verses of the Quran to the Prophet (PBUH).

8. Soon after his release, addressing a meeting in Sopore, Abdullah said, 'the final arbiters of the destiny of the State are its people, and not India or Pakistan. We will not permit others to divide our home. We are its rightful owners.' Akbar, *op. cit.*, p. 185.

9. The complete text continued 'or bringing about cession of a part of the territory of India or secession of part of the territory of India from the Union or causing insult to the Indian national flag, the Indian anthem and the constitution.' Bhattacharjea, *op. cit.*, p. 235.

10. Kak, *op. cit.*, p. 107; he adds 'Abdullah and his associates had proved beyond any doubt that their aim was to secure political power.'

11. On 18 January 1977, Indira Gandhi announced that elections would be held in March. Confident of victory, she relaxed some of the Emergency's restrictions, e.g. allowing public meetings. Contrary to her expectations, the numerous opposition parties were able to (temporarily) set aside their differences and wage a united campaign against her. The main opposition party, Janata, was a coalition of four parties: Congress (O), Jana Sangh, the Socialist party, and the Bharatiya Lok Dal (BLD). Mrs Gandhi suffered a massive defeat; Janata and its allies took 330 out of 548 Lok Sabha seats. Congress dropped 198 seats, ending up with just 154. Moraji Desai, leader of the Congress (O), became the new Prime Minister.

12. 'Sheikh Abdullah symbolised Kashmiriyat: a spirit of independence and secularism *joined by free will to a larger comity....* The National Conference won an overwhelming victory.... Kashmir in 1977 suddenly seemed safe, Indian democracy triumphant, and Indian nationalism vindicated.' Akbar, *op. cit.*, p. 192.

13. So disgusted was Prem Nath Bazaz with the Abdullah administration that he wrote a book about it entitled *Democracy Through Intimidation and Terror: The Untold Story of Kashmir Politics* (New Delhi, 1978).

14. Sheikh Abdullah justified the Resettlement Bill: 'It deals with those of the State subjects, who in March 1947, in harassment left the State for Pakistan or who owing to misunderstanding could not return to the State. Now, under certain conditions they are entitled to return...one of the conditions necessary to its completion is the grant of a visa from Government of India. Under Delhi Agreement of 1951 we are obliged to fulfil it. These evacuees do not belong to the Pakistan occupied Kashmir but simply reside in Pakistan...in accordance with law, they continue to be citizens of Kashmir.' *Daily Aftab*, Srinagar, 9 May 1982, cited in Abdul Jabbar Ganai, *Kashmir National Conference and Politics 1975–1980* (Srinagar, Gulshan, 1984), p. 105.

15. Referring to the subsequent Resettlement Bill passed by the State Assembly, Lamb writes: 'In its way it was as near to a formal declaration of the virtual independence of the State of Jammu and Kashmir as Sheikh Abdullah ever got since Maharaja Hari Singh let him out of prison in late September 1947.' *Op. cit.*, p. 320.

16. Inder Malhotra voiced New Delhi's objections to the Bill: 'The profoundly disturbing political and psychological fall out of the Bill is already in evidence. But a bigger disaster is bound to follow if the Bill is allowed to become law. For under it, not only will countless Pakistanis be able to come and settle in Kashmir (or elsewhere in India) but a floodgate will have been opened for Pakistani spies, saboteurs, disruptors and trouble makers to operate with impunity in the country's most sensitive State.' *Times of India*, 3 June 1982, cited in ibid., pp. 105–6.

17. In his book, *My Dismissal* (New Delhi, Vikas, 1985), Farooq Abdullah explained this refusal: 'The decision that was made by our party was consistent with the views of Sheikh Abdullah who had always wanted that the National Conference should stand on its own and retain its identity. This would have been seriously jeopardised if we had gone in for an electoral alliance on the lines suggested by the Congress.' Akbar, *op. cit.*, p. 200.

18. Hewitt, *op. cit.*, p. 152.

19. Maqsood, Arshad, 'New Delhi and Kashmir: Integration or Alienation?' in *The Kashmir Dossier* (February 1991), p. 10, cited in 'Kashmir and India', *Economic and Political Weekly*, 24 August 1991, p. 1959.

20. Cited in Schofield, *op. cit.*, p. 208.

21. 'Kashmir and India', *op. cit.*, p. 1961.

22. 'The 400 kv transmission line was handed over to NHPC during the period of G. M. Shah, while Jagmohan's two spells of governor's rule were very beneficial in extending Delhi's control—the Sawalkot and Baghlihar projects on the Chenab were handed over to NHPC during his first spell in 1986, and in 1990 the 200 kv line project was handed over to NHPC.' Ibid.

23. Maqsood, *op. cit.*, p. 11, cited in ibid., p. 1959.

24. Ibid., p. 1961.

25. Ganguly, Sumit, *The Crisis in Kashmir: Potents of war, hopes of peace* (Cambridge, C.U.P., 1997), p. 74.

26. Cited in Schofield, *op. cit.*, p. 239.

27. All employment figures as on 1 July 1987. 'India's Kashmir War', *Economic and Political Weekly,* 31 March 1990, pp. 660–61.

28. In the nationalized banks in Kashmir only 1.5% of the officers were Kashmiri Muslims. Ibid.

29. Hewitt, *op. cit.*, p. 148.

30. Chairman of Human Rights Division of the Kashmir Bar Association; interview with author; London 1998.

31. Engineer, Ali Asghar (ed.), *Communal Riots in Post-Independence India* (London, Sangam Books, 1991), p. 59, cited in Akbar Ahmed, *Jinnah, Pakistan and Islamic Identity: The Search for Saladin* (London and New York, Routledge, 1997), p. 230.
32. Ganguly, *op. cit.*, pp. 32–3.
33. Ibid., pp. 35–6.

5

INDIA AND KASHMIR

Several factors have been identified repeatedly in previous chapters as leading to heightened ethnic consciousness among Kashmiri Muslims and Pandits. Among the Muslims, the major factor has been the Indian State: more specifically its failure to allow Kashmir autonomy; its interference in the political process there and imposition of pliant rulers; some Central Governments' intolerance of opposition-controlled State Governments; the repeated failure to make political concessions to Kashmiri Muslim demands; and most recently, the massive use of force in the Valley (discussed in Chapter Eight). In the context of Pandit ethnic identification, the rise of Hinduism in India, both a social and political force, has also been mentioned.

We have seen how the actions of the Indian State in Kashmir and the rise of Hinduism in India have contributed to Kashmiri Muslims and Pandits evolving distinct communal identities, to the extent that—as will be seen in Chapter Eight—their traditional plural society has broken down. This chapter proposes to explore the background to these various 'ethnic catalysts'. Why have successive Indian administrations sought greater control over Kashmir? Why have some Indian prime ministers been intolerant of opposition chief ministers? Why have leaders in New Delhi often found themselves unable to adopt a moderate approach in Kashmir? What has led to the erosion of Indian secularism? How has Hinduism become such a powerful political force?

This covers India's role in Kashmir vis-à-vis the internal ethnic issue. But of course India is also one of the parties in the international dispute over Kashmir. While the two roles are closely inter-linked, there are nonetheless important distinctions between them. The factors driving Indian policy on Kashmir as a constituent state are not always the same as those dictating its international policy. This chapter will, therefore, begin by examining the latter: why is Jammu and Kashmir so important to India?

India and Kashmir: The International Dimension

India's stand on Kashmir in the international arena has changed little in fifty years: Hari Singh signed the Instrument of Accession making Jammu and Kashmir an Indian State; Pakistan is illegally occupying a large part of the State; there can be no discussion on the sovereignty of Kashmir—it is Indian. The only shift in this otherwise very rigid position has been dropping the initial commitment to hold a plebiscite to determine the will of the people—ratification of accession by the State Assembly has been presented as an acceptable substitute for this.

Indian determination to implement this policy in practice has been demonstrated repeatedly: sending troops in to the State in 1947 to prevent it being taken over by Pakistani tribals; going to war with Pakistan proper in 1965 when it looked as if Kashmir could be lost; using massive force to suppress the current secessionist movement. Apart from Nehru's initial error (as it is now viewed in India) of taking the Kashmir dispute to the UN, India has persistently maintained that whatever happens in Kashmir is its own internal affair, it totally refuses to concede there could be any question mark over Kashmiri sovereignty, and therefore rejects the involvement of outside bodies like the United Nations.

What determines this rigid international stand? Why is it so important to India that it hold onto Jammu and Kashmir? The answer is not one but several factors, some symbolic and some practical.

Looking at the former first, in 1947 the Indian subcontinent was partitioned on the grounds of religion with Muslim-majority regions combining together in a new country, Pakistan. The notion that Hindus and Muslims formed separate nations and hence should have separate states, Jinnah's two-nation theory, was strongly rejected by Nehru and the Indian National Congress leadership. Jammu and Kashmir was a Muslim-majority state. The Indians wanted to hold onto it in order to disprove Jinnah's two-nation theory. By showing that a Muslim state could flourish in Hindu-majority India, Congress intended to refute the need for a separate Muslim homeland, Pakistan.

Jammu and Kashmir's Muslim-majority status was, and is still, also important in the context of Indian secularism. There is no other Muslim-majority state in the Union. It, therefore, provides an important bulwark against calls for India to abandon its official ideology of secularism and become a Hindu state. However, it must be stressed that it can only do so if its Muslims stay within India voluntarily. As Jayaprakash Narayan explained:

> What is meant by Kashmir being an example of Indian secularism? It means, I believe, that the people of India have given such proof of their non-communal outlook that the Muslims of Kashmir, even though they are in a majority there, have freely decided to live with India which is a Hindu-majority but secular country, rather than with Pakistan which is a Muslim-majority but an Islamic state. But suppose we had to keep the Muslims of Kashmir within India by force: would that also be an example of our secularism? The very question exposes its absurdity.[1]

More practically, the treatment of non-Kashmiri Indian Muslims is intimately tied to the fate of Kashmir—a point discussed more fully below.

The third symbolic significance of Kashmir lies in the fact that it was Nehru's ancestral homeland. As leader of the Indian National Congress and the country's first Prime Minister, he used his influence to ensure India's commitment to retaining the state. Chadda writes:

> There can be no doubt that Nehru desperately wanted Kashmir to join India. When Mountbatten sternly rebuked him on July 27,

1947, for wanting to go up to Srinagar against the Maharajah's explicit wishes...and risk being himself thrown in prison just eleven days before he became prime minister of free India, Nehru broke down during a stormy meeting with Gandhi and Patel and said that Kashmir was more important to him than 'anything else.'[2]

Finally, a symbolic reason put forward by successive Indian governments and numerous Indian writers for Indian determination to hold onto Jammu and Kashmir, one that in fact applies to all the Union's states, is that its secession could set a dangerous precedent for other states disillusioned with New Delhi. Since independence in 1947, India has faced numerous secessionist challenges from its peripheral states. So far it has managed to contain them all, but if Jammu and Kashmir were to break away it would become immensely more difficult for it to do so in future.

Turning to practical reasons for Jammu and Kashmir's significance to India, these can be divided into security and economic needs. Tucked in the extreme north-west of the Indian subcontinent, the strategic importance of Kashmir's position was acknowledged even by the British, for whom it was a vital buffer between India and Russia. This 'buffer' function remained important to independent India. In a cable to Attlee, Nehru stressed that:

> Kashmir's northern frontiers...run in common with those of three countries, Afghanistan, the USSR and China. Security of Kashmir...is vital to security of India, especially since part of southern boundary of Kashmir and India are common.[3]

Post-1947 Kashmir's strategic importance grew because of the creation of 'hostile' Pakistan: 'India and Pakistan had one another to contend with' as well as threats from outside the subcontinent. Kashmir's location was such that whichever country controlled it would be in a strong military position to attack the other. Economically, as a timber-rich state with the headwaters of three major rivers, Kashmir could be very useful to India [even though in 1947 Kashmir's economic links with Pakistan were far greater].

In conclusion then, there are numerous very solid reasons for Indian determination not to lose Jammu and Kashmir. Added to these over the past fifty years there have been domestic political pressures for it not to do so.

India and Kashmir: The Internal Dimension

The growing Indian control over Jammu and Kashmir since 1947, and the integration agenda pursued by successive central administrations, could be explained in the context of the State's immense significance to India. India had to bring the State firmly within the Union to prevent it ever leaving. However, this is not a sufficient explanation. As seen earlier, had New Delhi allowed the State autonomy and had it exerted a little less control, Kashmir would now probably be securely 'Indian' rather than the site of a violent secessionist movement. Indian leaders in 1947 recognized this when they wrote Article 370 into the Indian Constitution. In order to explain the change in approach to Kashmir since then one must look at the development of the Indian State.

Crisis of Governability

This term was coined by Atul Kohli to describe the effect produced, on the one hand, by weakened ruling institutions, and on the other, by increased struggles for power.[4] These have combined to reduce the ability of New Delhi to take decisions and implement policies in the national interest. Consider the various reasons for this.

One, is the personalization of power and rise of populist politics. These can be traced to Indira Gandhi. Yogendra Malik notes that under her leadership 'the Congress party simply became an instrument of personal power.'[5] Governmental and party appointments were controlled by Mrs Gandhi herself, with the criterion for posting being loyalty to her personally rather than ability or party following. Internal Congress elections were postponed indefinitely, leading to the party's organizational decline. In order to win elections, the party became increasingly dependent on Indira's charismatic leadership and her populist appeals. The first of these, *'Gharibi hatao'*, won Mrs Gandhi a huge electoral victory in 1971. Thereafter, it became the norm in Indian politics for elections to be fought over such slogans (*'Indira hatao,'* *'Ram Rajya,'* etc.), rather than on the basis of ideology and programmes of action.

Mrs Gandhi's example of personalizing power was followed by her son, Rajiv. Riding to electoral victory in 1984 on a wave of sympathy generated by his mother's assassination, he too favoured personal control over power-sharing in a representative Congress and government. The corresponding decline of the Congress party—as an organization—was clearly demonstrated by the appeals to Sonia Gandhi, Rajiv's Italian-born, Roman Catholic wife, to lead the party after Rajiv was killed: it was feared that without a member of the Nehru-Gandhi dynasty at the helm, victory at the ballot box would be difficult. The effects of the Gandhis' personalized, populist approach to politics and government have been far-reaching.

While Indira, and later Rajiv, certainly succeeded in concentrating greater power in their own hands, Kohli claims that such power was in fact illusory—or rather, that New Delhi's power decreased instead of increasing. He argues that power won through personalized, populist politics cannot be used to solve socio-economic problems[6]—a strong party organization would be required for that. The consequent policy failures lead to greater dependence on populist appeals and charismatic leadership, leading to further weakness in party organization,[7] and hence to further erosion of the capacity to govern. A vicious cycle of increasing political de-institutionalization is in operation.

Another factor making effective government difficult is the rapid erosion of the moral authority of the state. A major cause of this was the seemingly endless series of corruption scandals that hit successive governments: Sanjay Gandhi and Maruti, Rajiv Gandhi and Bofors, Narasimha Rao and the Harshad Mehta affair, Yadev and the 'invisible' cows... Chadda writes that such scandals had a disastrous effect on public confidence: 'by the early 1980s, after more than a decade of blatant corruption, the political system as a whole...had been severely delegitimized.'[8]

The government's growing incapacity to implement policies has been accompanied by a rise in the demands being made on it. Political mobilization has led to an increased number of players in the political arena, particularly from the formerly quiescent backward castes, all demanding their share of power. Diverse political interests had originally been accommodated in what Rajni Kothari described as the 'Congress system'.[9] But as the party suffered an organizational decline—and no new national party emerged to take over its mediating role—it became harder and harder to satisfy competing demands. Within the political process, governments found themselves effectively immobilized by the fact that policies to appease one group would anger many others. Outside it, mass mobilization produced conflict: 'caste, class and ethnic interests were pursued militantly and through extra-constitutional channels.'[10]

It should be noted that the state governments' ability to govern has been affected by factors similar to those eroding the national government's, i.e. increased mobilization leading to competition and conflict; populist as opposed to ideological politics; poor party organization, etc. While state governments have not always been rendered as ineffective as New Delhi, P.K. Das's comment that 'the octopus of "non-governance"... seems to have gripped all centres of power, whether in Delhi or the state capitals'[11] is in general a valid one.

Centralization of Power

The constant undermining of state governments by New Delhi to ensure that only parties or leaders who toed the central line held power was not confined to Jammu and Kashmir but instead was something of a nation-wide phenomenon. As with the personalization of politics, much of the responsibility for the massive centralization of power (or attempt to) rests with Indira Gandhi. Chadda offers one explanation: 'Lacking the base of a unified and dominant Congress, an advantage Nehru had that his successors did not, Mrs Gandhi reacted with greater anxiety to the demands for regional autonomy.'[12] Her 'authoritarian personality' was, of course, another factor.

The undermining of opposition state governments actually dates back to 1959 when the Congress Central Government toppled the Kerala State Government, but it was Janata that took it up on a larger scale in the late 1970s and Mrs Gandhi who, on her return to power in 1979, made it an established practice. She dismissed nine non-Congress governments on the same grounds Janata had used to dismiss Congress ones, i.e. that Lok Sabha Congress victories in those states had invalidated their mandate. Commenting on the initial 1959 toppling, Baxter writes:

> Thereafter it became common practice that a central government, whether Congress or Janata, would seize on any sign of weakness to displace elected state governments headed by rival parties or coalitions... Only a few opposition-led state governments have been able to survive.[13]

Liberal use of President's Rule through pliant governors was a common feature of many state government removals. With respect to the latter, Rao comments that under Indira 'the office of the governor of the state became the agent of the party in power at the centre,'[14] e.g. Jagmohan in Jammu and Kashmir, Ram Lal in Andhra Pradesh, and S. D. Sharma in West Bengal.[15] President's Rule was imposed only six times in the fourteen years between inauguration of the Constitution (1950) and

Nehru's death (1964); in contrast, between 1966, when Indira first became Prime Minister, and 1984 when she was killed, it was imposed fifty-five times.[16] Rao claims that after the 1967 elections New Delhi basically treated it as 'an instrument for interfering with inconvenient non-Congress governments in the states.'[17]

Even with Congress-controlled governments, Mrs Gandhi did not hesitate to assert her authority. Fearful of challenges from within the party, she deliberately appointed chief ministers with little following in the states; dependent on her for their position, their loyalty was thus assured.[18] Not surprisingly, this practice led to further organizational decline in the Congress, with the result that more and more states came to be dominated by regional parties. And since by definition such parties have little hope of winning power at the national level, tensions between New Delhi and the states correspondingly increased. Furthermore, such tensions were increasingly manifested in political violence.

The centre's response to growing rebellion in the states was to increase both the extent and use of its coercive powers. The former came about through the passage of new legislation allowing the suspension of fundamental rights, e.g. the 59th constitutional amendment,[19] and 1984 TADA (see chapter on Kashmir conflict). With respect to the latter, Mathur points out 'the increasing reliance on police and other such organizations for effective governance.'[20] The number of armed police battalions and paramilitary forces has grown, as has the strength of the Central Reserve Police Force (CRPF—from 66 battalions in 1981/82 to 83, just 6 years later).[21] Furthermore in 1967, a new unit, the Border Security Force (BSF) was set up; it has quadrupled in size since its creation. Malik and Vajpeyi note that Indira Gandhi called the CRPF out on 227 occasions in less than two years 'to deal with popular unrest resulting from her intervention in state affairs.'[22] However, this growing 'recourse to covert authoritarianism' has tended to exacerbate rather than solve the problem of deteriorating order.[23]

In summary, then, New Delhi's attempts to centralize power actually produced the opposite effect—in real terms its control over the states decreased.[24] More importantly—bearing in mind the often blatant wielding of central authority and abuse of constitutional powers—in many states they generated a backlash of regional movements demanding (as a minimum) greater autonomy from the centre.

Rise of Hinduism as a Social and Political Force

Hinduism in India has, for some years now, been witnessing a rise in its influence, both as a religion (in everyday life) and as a political force. As the former, Hinduism has actually always had a great impact on life in the subcontinent—determining food, dress, social dealings, etc.,—but its latter role in politics is a completely new phenomenon. Smith explains the traditional absence of Hinduism from government and politics: 'The ultimate philosophical and religious values of Hinduism do not require a Hindu state or any particular kind of political structure for that matter.'[25] In the most recent Lok Sabha elections, however, it was the Hindu nationalist party, the Bharatiya Janata Party (BJP), that emerged with the largest number of seats.

Growth in the social (religious) and political influence of Hinduism are strongly inter-related. Both have been fuelled by generally the same causes and hence will be considered together. These causes can be divided into two broad categories: factors eroding Indian secularism, and factors increasing religious consciousness. Obviously there will be a degree of overlap between the two. Consider the erosion of Indian secularism first.

Erosion of Indian Secularism

The erosion of secularism in India arises both from the tendency of recent governments to abandon it under Hindu pressure and from the Constitution's somewhat half-hearted approach to it— seen for example by the fact that only with the Forty-fourth

Amendment in 1976, was the term 'secular state' included in its Preamble.

Constitutional weaknesses are of two sorts: one, violation of secular principles in the Constitution itself, and two, failure to implement secular measures that are in it. The former were included mainly because of Nehru's concern that the Muslims left in India after Partition should be made to feel at home.[26] Violations include the failure to completely separate state from religion, to maintain equality before the law and non-discrimination, and to treat all religions identically. In order to bring about social welfare and reform, the state is allowed to interfere in Hindu religious institutions (article 25.2b), while article 290A makes provision for state maintenance of Hindu temples and shrines. Articles 15.1 and 16.4 make provisions for the advancement of the Scheduled Castes. Turning to the failure to maintain religious neutrality, unlike Hinduism the Constitution makes no provision for the state to reform Muslim religious practice. More seriously, it is unclear in the case of Muslims whether civil law is supreme over the *Sharia*, or vice versa.

The early failure to implement the secular provisions that were included in the Constitution, can be blamed in large measure on the strong Hindu influence within Congress.[27] It is important to bear in mind that few Congressmen were as deeply convinced about and committed to the idea of a secular state as Nehru; most were aware that their support came from the Hindu majority.[28] Mitra sums up their dilemma: 'How could a state use the power that it received from accommodating prevailing social interests to destroy at least some of those interests in fulfilling the requirements of its modernizing agenda?'[29]

A more fundamental explanation for the erosion of Indian secularism is that the whole attempt to exclude religion, i.e. to make India a secular state, was misplaced. Proponents of this view argue that secularism emerged from the specific historical context of the conflict between church and state in the West. Its two basic conditions—separation of sacred from secular, and restriction of religion to private worship—are empirically impossible to fulfil in India. On the first, Nandy comments 'to the faithful...religion is precisely what it is because it provides an overall theory of life,'[30] while Oommen highlights the difficulty of implementing the second: 'the practise of religion assumes a community of believers and their common presence and conjoint action at least on selected occasions.'[31] Madan sums up the state-society contradiction in India: 'In an open society the state will reflect the character of society. Secularism therefore is a social myth.'[32]

If this view is accepted, then the rise of religion in politics could be interpreted as rejection of the Western-imported secular state model, and the development of an indigenous state tradition. The generally extremist tone of religious politics can be seen as a consequence of its initial exclusion: 'it is the marginalisation of religion which is what secularisation is, that permits the perversion of religion. There are no fundamentalists or revivalists in traditional society.'[33]

So much for the erosion of secularism because of fundamental flaws in the Constitution and weaknesses in implementation. Moving on to more recent times, secularism has been eroded because one, governments have lacked the power and/or moral authority to defend it and two, because they have been tempted to follow the communalist path being trodden by the 'Hindu' parties—because they have lacked the will to defend it.

Taking lack of power and/or moral authority first, the causes of this were described above. Two examples of its impact on secularism are provided by the Shah Bano case, and by the destruction of the Babri Masjid (mosque) at Ayodhya. The former involved Rajiv Gandhi's Congress government. An elderly divorced Muslim woman took her husband to court claiming maintenance. The court upheld her claim and ordered her husband to pay her. This civil law judgement clashed with the Islamic *Sharia* injunction that in the case of divorce, a man has no obligation to support his ex-wife. Sections of the Indian Muslim community protested loudly at the Supreme Court ruling. Rajiv Gandhi, instead of standing firm and upholding the secular principle that the law applied to all citizens equally, passed the

Muslim Women (Protection of Rights on Divorce) Bill. This Bill effectively encompassed the *Sharia* in Indian law.

The second example involved Rajiv's Congress successor, Narasimha Rao. His government's first act of weakness was its failure to prevent the destruction of the Babri Masjid by Hindu militants. After the mosque was destroyed, it did try to take a strong stand, dismissing not just the Uttar Pradesh BJP administration but all four BJP state governments, and promising to rebuild the mosque. However, when faced with 'widespread pro-Hindutva sentiments among Hindus, Rao backed down: no move was made towards reconstruction, either by him or his successors. As Vanaik puts it: 'The politics of expediency and cowardice were of greater consequence than any politics of principles.'[34] As the trend toward minority, coalition government in India continues, the chances of Indian leaders having the ability to defend secularism in the face of such attacks become more remote.

Turning to lack of will to defend secularism, this is even more alarming than the lack of authority to do so. Evidence of traditionally non-communal secular parties abandoning this in favour of communal politics is abundant. Once again Indira Gandhi's name is at the fore. Under her leadership Congress embarked on the communal path, even before the emergence of the BJP. Achin Vanaik writes:

> After the 1971 War, Mrs Gandhi was widely acclaimed as 'Durga,' the Hindu mother goddess of destruction. She and her Congress party did not hesitate to make use of and encourage the Hindu image. After this victory Mrs Gandhi began to make use of Hindu symbols and rituals, to make well-publicised visits to temples...and so on.[35]

Vanaik notes that after her return to power in January 1980, the switch in the Congress populist rhetoric from socialism to Hinduism was even more obvious. Rajiv Gandhi followed his mother's example in this as in much else. Among his first acts after being elected in 1984 was to hold a Ramayana recitation at

Ayodhya. Chadda claims that in those elections 'a large number of RSS cadres had worked...for Rajiv Gandhi.'[36] During the 1989 elections his campaign promise at Faizabad was 'only Congress can give you Ram Rajya.'[37] Vanaik concludes 'there is little doubt that the Congress, to its shame, has pursued a perspective that is accurately described as "pale saffron", saffron being the emblematic colour of political Hindutva.'[38] Once overtly Hindu parties such as the BJP entered the political arena and were seen to be making huge electoral gains, the incentive for non-communal parties to follow their example was even greater: few resisted.

Increased Religious Consciousness

This has numerous causes:

1)   'Religion in Danger'

This feeling has arisen partly in reaction to modernization. As people have become more educated and prosperous, and their lifestyle more westernized, they have experienced a sense of cultural insecurity, an identity crisis. The response among many has been to cling more firmly to their 'roots', particularly their religious beliefs and practices. This phenomenon is, by definition, largely confined to urban Hindus[39] but a more widely-perceived threat comes from India's Muslims. Hindus fear that Indian Muslims will follow the fundamentalist path taken by Iran, and to a lesser extent, Pakistan and Bangladesh, and with the backing of petro-dollars from the Gulf states, they will try and convert Hindus to Islam. Just how real these fears could be was demonstrated in 1981, when 100 Harijans in the Tamil Nadu village of Meenakshipuram converted en masse to Islam: the issue was taken up and grossly exaggerated by the Indian press as endangering India's Hindu majority. Secondly, it is feared that with their supposed higher birth-rate Muslims will eventually succeed in outnumbering the Hindu population.[40] No matter how irrational such fears might seem, they have struck a chord among many ordinary Hindus. As Engineer points out 'it is the perception of reality rather than reality itself which is more important as far as human behaviour is concerned.'[41]

2) Minority Complex

This is found among many Hindus, despite the fact that they form over 80 per cent of the population. There is a growing feeling that in the effort to safeguard Muslim and other minority interests, Hindu interests have been neglected. Such feelings have arisen largely because, while minority laws and customs are protected in the Constitution, Hindu laws have been radically reformed by the state. Examples include polygamy, which is allowed in Hinduism, being made illegal, and divorce, which Hindu law strictly forbids, being legalized. The Shah Bano case and its aftermath exemplified for many Hindus minority pampering by the government. Hindus were infuriated both by the government backing down under Muslim pressure, and by the protection of Muslim religious laws while their own were constantly challenged.

The 'minority complex' also has its origins in Indian history, and the perception of Muslims as conquerors. Before the British Raj (northern) India was ruled for centuries by the Mughals, last of a series of Muslim rulers. The current assertion of Hinduism is partly aimed at redressing this historical 'wrong', putting the minorities in their 'proper place'—subjugated to the Hindu majority. As neo-Hindu politicians put it: 'For centuries the injustice to the Hindu community by Babur's hordes cannot be allowed to perpetuate.'[42] The Muslims' historical ruling position in the north helps explain why communalism and support for neo-Hindu parties is far greater there than in the south, where Muslims went mostly as mystics and preachers.

3) Social and Economic Factors

These contribute to religion entering politics in two ways. One, as competition for jobs and resources has increased, communities that lag behind others tend to attribute their backwardness to religious discrimination.[43] Second, social and economic backwardness produces a frustrated, discontented class receptive to communal propaganda. Religion offers a legitimate reason to vent frustrations violently, and provides a visible target.[44]

4) Ideological Vacuum in Politics

Centrist-left politics in India is suffering from an ideological vacuum. If any ideology could be said to exist 'power at any price' probably best describes it. Certainly there is no message being presented with the forcefulness and coherence of the *Hindutva* call. Religious political parties have also been assisted by the decline in the moral authority of the state.[45] This has had the effect of driving disgusted voters to look for a 'cleaner' alternative: the BJP (until very recently) shrewdly portrayed itself as the party of incorrupt government.

5) Ramayana/Mahabharata

Lloyd Rudolph claims that television serializations of Hindu epics, the Ramayana and Mahabharata have, by replacing a large variety of local and regional versions of these with a uniform national one, played 'a leading role in creating a national Hindu identity, a form of group consciousness that has not hitherto existed.'[46]

Bharatiya Janata Party (BJP)

The growth of political Hinduism has been manifested in the phenomenal rise to power of the Bharatiya Janata Party. This was formed in 1980. In the 1984 national elections it won just two of the 545 seats in the Lok Sabha. By 1989 this figure had shot up to 85, 119 in 1991, and in the 1996 elections passed the 180 mark (with allies). The party briefly formed the national government after those elections. Then again in early 1998 the party repeated that stunt. At the time of writing (June 2001) it was back in power in New Delhi. The BJP has thus, in the space of just fifteen years, replaced Congress as India's largest party.

Aside from the general factors described above leading to the rise of Hindu consciousness and hence the BJP's popularity—the decline in Congress party's organization, cultural insecurity, growing economic competition, etc.,—one issue in particular has greatly enhanced the party's appeal: its call for the building of a temple on the site of the Babri Masjid in Ayodhya.

The Ram-Janmabhoomi campaign was actually launched by the hard-line Vishwa Hindu Parishad (VHP) in the mid-1980s, but it was the BJP that reaped huge political benefit from it. Claiming that the Babri Masjid had been built after destroying a temple that marked the site of the Hindu god Ram's birth, the BJP successfully focused Hindu grievances on the issue. Redress of previous Muslim injustices against Hindus, Congress pampering of minorities, the need to replace secularism with *Hindutva* as the basis of Indian nationhood—the temple-mosque controversy was used to highlight all these BJP views. Party leader, Lal K. Advani's 'pilgrimage' across India in a vehicle made up to resemble Ram's chariot, and the call for Hindus throughout the country to send bricks to build the temple, were both—in PR terms—strokes of genius.

Following the destruction of the Babri Masjid by Hindu militants in December 1992, the party appeared to have run out of steam. Removing the mosque to make way for the temple had, after all, been the party's main demand until then. In the 1993 state assembly elections (precipitated by the 'rubble-making in Ayodha'), the BJP suffered serious setbacks in the northern Hindi-speaking belt—previously its main source of support. However, these losses proved to be just a blip in its upward popularity curve—not the peak some observers had predicted. As mentioned above, with its allies it went on to form the national government in 1996, and again in 1998 and 2001.

The BJP's coming to power in spite of the fact that it has not yet come up with an issue to match the potent appeal of

Ayodhya, indicates that the party's success is due as much to voter disillusionment with Congress (and the National Front), as with mass support for *Hindutva*. Repeated corruption scandals, factional infighting, hardships brought on by economic liberalization rather than simply religious rhetoric have fuelled the BJP's rise. The party itself seems to recognize this because it has consciously tried to moderate its Hindu chauvinist image and portray itself as a responsible party that can govern effectively. Thus, it has been distancing itself—at least publicly—from its more militant allies, the RSS and VHP, and anti-Muslim rhetoric has been far less noticeable. Instead, more attention has been given to economic policy—this has been outlined in detail, and the initial stance of discouraging foreign investment has been dropped. The appointment of Atal Bihar Vajpayee, a moderate, as party leader symbolized the BJP's new approach.

Consider now what the BJP actually stands for—calling it a 'Hindu fundamentalist' party is after all a very broad description. The party itself actually refutes this image. It does acknowledge its desire to change India from an officially secular state into an officially Hindu one, but claims that 'Hindu' refers to culture and not religion. Such Hindu nationalism, according to BJP logic, could therefore incorporate the country's non-Hindu minorities—Sikhs, Buddhists, Jains and even Muslims.

In terms of specific policies, the party would like to see all minority 'privileges' removed, e.g. it would like *Sharia* law to be abolished and a uniform civil code introduced, and the Minorities Commission to be replaced by a general Human Rights Commission. Other policies include the expulsion of illegal Muslim immigrants from Bangladesh (though not Hindu ones), a ban on cow slaughter, and the development of the country's nuclear weapons programme. It could be described as generally hostile to western culture; the BJP's initial policy of opposition to multinational firms entering the Indian market was based not only on their being seen as a threat to Indian businesses, but also 'to the country's culture'.[47]

When analyzing BJP policy it is important to bear in mind the internal party division between moderates and extremists. While the party manifesto portrays the views of the former, the latter's views probably more accurately reflect those of the majority of BJP supporters. Thus, for instance, while official party policy called for the shifting of the Babri Masjid to make way for a temple, it was BJP supporters who joined with RSS and VHP activists in completely demolishing the mosque. It is a debatable question whether the party's moderate leadership can maintain control over its more extreme rank and file.

Summary

Before looking at Kashmir in the context of Indian politics it would be useful to give a summary of the contemporary state and politics in India. Congress, the party that has dominated Indian politics and government since independence, is now in serious—perhaps irreversible—decline. Many of the factors that have contributed to its fall, especially the rise of populist politics and increased pressure to deliver benefits to supporters, also conspire against the emergence of a new national party. Diverse regional parties have for a long time dominated state-level politics in India. National-level politics are increasingly following the same path, i.e. shifting away from one-party dominance, to a multi-party system in which no single party can exert overall power. The consequence of this is minority, coalition government, in which policy-making is by definition constrained by the need to satisfy all partners. The phenomenal rise of the Hindu nationalist BJP also imposes restraints on New Delhi; policy-makers are wary of provoking a mass Hindu backlash. Indeed, far from condemning Hindu communalism, the 'secular' parties not infrequently appear tempted to jump on to the Hindu band-wagon themselves.

Indian Domestic Politics and Kashmir

Most of the effects of domestic Indian politics—the desire for centralization of power, the rise of populist politics, the 'crisis of governability'—upon Kashmir have already been described in previous chapters reviewing developments in the State: the removal of elected leaders/governments, the failure to allow regional autonomy, alienation of Kashmiri Muslims, etc. These effects will not be described here again. Instead, this section will look at the effects of the rise of Hindu consciousness, and particularly political Hinduism, on politics and ethnic identification in Kashmir.

BJP Policy on Kashmir

Basic BJP policy on Jammu and Kashmir is that it is a permanent and integral part of the Indian Union. Stemming from this basic position is the belief that there should be no further question of holding a plebiscite in the State to ratify accession, and that the Kashmir dispute should be withdrawn from the UN. Also stemming from it is the view that nothing should distinguish Jammu and Kashmir from the other states of the Indian Union. This means, of course, the abrogation of Article 370 which grants the state special autonomy (now more in theory than practice).

The BJP would also like the ban on non-Kashmiris owning property within the State to be lifted. The ban is in place to prevent mass migration of non-Kashmiri Hindus overwhelming the local Muslim community. Since the State's total population is around 7 million, with about two-thirds Muslim, only 'a modest migration by Indian standards would produce a Hindu majority. The BJP sees this as a highly desirable result that would keep the State firmly within India's embrace and out of Pakistan's.'[48] Finally, the BJP views Pakistani-controlled Azad Kashmir as rightfully belonging to India.

Influence of Growing Hindu Consciousness

A point which has come up again and again in previous chapters is the rise in Hindu consciousness among Pandits. While this arose in part because of developments within Kashmir—perceived discrimination by National Conference governments, for instance—it should also be viewed in the wider Indian context. Just as the various factors described earlier led to a rise in Hindu consciousness among Indian Hindus, so too did they among Pandits.

Looking at political Hinduism specifically this has been instrumental in raising religious consciousness—both Hindu and Muslim—in Kashmir (promoting Hindu identification among Pandits will obviously have the reactionary effect of promoting Islamic identification among Muslims). How have parties like the BJP done this? It was seen above that 'Muslim/minority bashing' has been a very important weapon in the BJP's campaign arsenal. The situation in Kashmir offers numerous examples for the party to draw on in its 'Muslim bashing'. Article 370 has, of course, been the obvious target: the only Muslim-majorty state in the Union being guaranteed autonomy in the Constitution constitutes, perhaps, the greatest proof of minority pampering.

A more emotive issue, and one that has had a greater impact on people within Kashmir, has been the BJP's taking up the cause of the Pandits as a beleaguered Hindu minority. During periods of National Conference rule in the State it complained of Hindus being discriminated against (e.g. in jobs) by a Muslim government; of a Hindu minority being persecuted and living in fear of a Muslim majority population. Since the conflict in Kashmir started, the BJP has taken up this line even more forcefully: Hindus killed by Muslims; Hindus forced to flee their homes by Muslim terrorists; Hindus living in poverty because of a Muslim insurgency. It has become apparent that the BJP views the situation in Kashmir as one of Muslims versus Hindus. The notion of a shared *Kashmiriyat* is never entertained. And this is what it encourages the Pandits of Kashmir to think:

to see themselves as Hindus and the majority community as Muslims—as the 'other' rather than fellow Kashmiris.

Aside from reactionary religious consciousness, the rise of political Hinduism in India has had a direct impact on Kashmiri Muslims. This is in the context of Indian secularism. As India becomes a more overtly Hindu state (in the official sense) and as the BJP becomes a more regular holder of power in New Delhi, the notion of India as a secular state grows ever more distant. This is tremendously significant for Kashmiri Muslims: there is a fundamental contradiction in a Muslim-majority region being part of a Hindu state. The 'de-secularization' of India would arguably alone be enough to alienate Kashmiri Muslims from India and make them determined to secede. Political columnist Kemal Verma writes:

> Kashmiri Muslims opted to join India in the belief that this country would remain secular. They acceded to Gandhi's India, Nehru's India, not to Golwalkar's India...[w]hen India is...turning communal that trust is betrayed. Only a secular India can keep Kashmir within it democratically. A communalised India can keep Kashmir only by force.[49]

The Kashmir Conflict

How has the domestic Indian political situation affected the handling of the Kashmiri insurgency? In brief, it has contributed to the conflict being exacerbated and made resolution very difficult. Two factors are of particular significance: weak government and the growing might of political Hinduism.

Taking weak government first, this has been largely responsible for New Delhi's virtually standard approach of dealing with the insurgency by force, described in detail in chapter eight. As the situation in Kashmir has deteriorated, ever greater numbers of security forces have been drafted into the region to restore order. A hefty chunk of India's defence budget is now allocated for Kashmir. That this approach has failed will be seen clearly in the chapter on the Kashmir conflict: far from 'restoring order' it has alienated Kashmiri Muslims, perhaps permanently, from India and fuelled greater militancy.

The palpable failure of the use of force to curb the insurgency suggests an alternative, more moderate, approach be taken. There are undoubtedly politicians in India who recognize this—hence, for example, the release of former 'militants' Shabir Shah and Yasin Malik. However, their hands are tied when it comes to greater implementation by: one, the growing trend in India towards minority, coalition government—in which, compared to a single party administration, it is obviously far harder to reach unanimity on policy; two, the general decline in authority of the state; and three, the pressure of political Hinduism.

The BJP's position on the Kashmir insurgency is very hard-line: curb the insurgency by force, no negotiations with militants, no concessions to Pakistan. This is the stance it has taken when in office; out of office its political strength is sufficient to ensure that all other governments take it too. The party made clear its determination to hold on to Kashmir in its 1991/92 *Ekta Yatra* (Unity March). Starting in Kanyakumar, at the southernmost tip of India, this was planned to end on Republic Day (26 January) with the raising of the Indian tricolour in Lal Chowk, Srinagar. The cry throughout the 1400-km journey was '*Chalo Kashmir! Karpom Kashmir!*' (Forward to Kashmir! Save Kashmir!) BJP President Manohar Joshi declared the *Yatra* 'a challenge to terrorism and secession'. Austin and Lyon add that '[t]he raising of the national flag at Srinagar was also intended to assert the unity of India against the mutinous defiance of the one state within the Union with a Muslim majority.'[50]

The BJP interest in the Kashmir conflict has also, as indicated above, been a major contributor to this being seen as one of Muslims versus Hindus. Rita Manchanda points out that the BJP and its ally, the RSS, have 'by politically appropriating the issue of the Kashmir Hindu refugees—transformed an agitation against the central government into one of Muslim fundamentalists against a Hindu state.'[51] This portrayal obviously makes it even harder for any concession to be made to Kashmiri Muslim demands: the rest of India would probably tolerate concessions to linguistic or cultural regional movements, but never to religious ones—and particularly never to Muslim ones. It is also worth noting that just as Kashmir has come to be seen by many within India as a communal conflict, so the outside world sees it in the same light. One obvious consequence of this is the interest and, in some cases, active participation of Muslims from other parts of the Islamic world in the Kashmir 'jihad'.

Indian Muslims and Kashmir

The significance of India's Muslim population (outside of Jammu and Kashmir) to the ethnic conflict in the State can be viewed from two different perspectives: one, the role of these Muslims in the conflict (moral support, active participation, condemnation, etc.); two, the linkage—largely by others—of the Kashmir problem to the wider Indian Muslim question. In order to understand both these perspectives, a brief review of the position of Indian Muslims since Partition would be helpful.

After India gained independence from the British in 1947, its Muslim inhabitants found their circumstances hugely altered. In the first place, with Muslim-majority provinces lost to Pakistan, their numbers shrank from 40 per cent to just 14 per cent of India's population. Secondly, relations with the country's Hindu majority became even more strained. Muslims were widely regarded by Hindus as being sympathetic to Pakistan. In addition, there was hostility produced by the communal massacres and upheavals that accompanied Partition.

The Muslims responded to their new situation by becoming politically very quiescent, and even apologetic. Omar Khalidi writes that '[t]hroughout the 1950s and 1960s, a demoralized Muslim leadership reeling under the accusation of having partitioned the country, publicly proclaimed loyalty to India.'[52] Having abandoned communal politics, i.e. separate Muslim parties, India's Muslims now flocked to support Congress. Under Nehru's leadership, Muslims saw the party as their best hope for safeguarding their interests in Hindu-majority India. But by the mid-70s Muslim thinking began to change. There were a number of reasons for this. Firstly, the break-up of Pakistan in 1971, largely put an end to the option of migrating to that country: 'Pakistan was no longer seen as a bulwark, a hope, as a protector.'[53] In its place came the realization that the only way to improve their position would be to struggle within India, and hence a stronger commitment to that country. Secondly, by the 1970s a new generation of Muslims was reaching maturity; a generation born after 1947, and thus free of guilt about Partition. This new generation was much more assertive than the previous one. Changed thinking became apparent first in changed voting patterns. Up to and including the 1972 general election (with the exception of 1967) they had voted en masse for Congress. However, after 1972, Brass notes that Muslim voting behaviour differed little from that of the general population.[54] [One negative consequence of this was the Congress shift—since it could no longer count on Muslim bloc votes—to appeal to the Hindu majority, i.e. to pursue communalist politics.] As of yet, Muslim communal politics of the pre-independence era, have not re-emerged. In other words, Muslims still look to mainstream national parties to represent their interests. With the 'Hindu-ization' of Congress, some have turned to the Janata Dal-National Front. And since the rise of the BJP, Muslims tend to vote for whoever has the best chance of keeping that party out of power.

Turning now to the position of Indian Muslims on the Kashmir issue. This has changed in accordance with the changing position of Muslims within India. Thus, in the years immediately after Partition, when India and Pakistan were fighting for control of the State, Indian Muslims loudly voiced their support for India and condemned 'Pakistan's interference in India's internal affairs.'[55] However, Omar Khalidi claims that '[p]rivately...most of the Muslim elite and masses were sympathetic to Pakistan'.[56] In other words, Muslim support for Indian claims to the State reflected their own vulnerable position rather than what they actually felt. But with the post-70s growing assertiveness of Muslims, some have openly begun to question Indian claims. While few would go so far as to support Kashmiri secession, many call for the state's autonomy within India to be restored. Even among those in favour of integration, there is condemnation of central government policy, and especially human rights abuses by the security forces. However, unlike Muslims from other parts of the Islamic world, Indian Muslims have generally refrained from active participation in the Kashmir conflict.

The direct role of Indian Muslims in the Kashmir conflict is thus relatively insignificant. However, their 'indirect' involvement is far greater. Secularists and Hindu communalists have both linked the Kashmir issue to the status of Indian Muslims generally. The former argue that India must retain Kashmir in order to safeguard Indian secularism. Justice V. M. Tarkunde predicts that were Kashmir to separate from the rest of India '[a]nti-Muslim feeling on the part of Hindu communalists would increase manifold...increasing the danger of India becoming a non-secular Hindu state.'[57] The linkage of Kashmir's fate to that of Indian secularism is something the country's Muslims are beginning to question forcefully—'[t]he logic that the only security of Indian Muslims is our secular structure and Kashmir being its central column is wrong... Kashmir is just one of our 25 states and 10 Union Territories, while secularism is a state ideal yet to be achieved'[58]—but as yet have failed to break.

Hindu communalists make even more dire predictions, threatening not just official secularism but the Muslim community itself. BJP leader A. B. Vajpayee was quoted in a Delhi newspaper warning Pakistan that 'if it is asking for 4 million Kashmiri Muslims, it should be ready to receive 120 million Indian Muslims in case Kashmir secedes from India.'[59] Holding all Indian Muslims responsible for what their co-religionists in Jammu and Kashmir do is, of course, a repetition of what happened after Partition in 1947. But today's Muslims are less ready to take on the burden of guilt. As Sayyid Abdullah Bukhari says 'we cannot be asked to do or say anymore than is expected of other Indians. Asking Indian Muslims to say or do above and beyond the normal call of duty is a back-handed tribute to Quaid-i-Azam's assertion that Hindus and Muslims are two separate nations.'[60]

At the end of the day, regardless of what India's newly assertive Muslims say, many Hindus *do* link Kashmir to the entire Muslim community, and this in turn gives an added incentive for India to hold on to the state: its loss could well lead to a communal bloodbath.

NOTES

1. 'The Need to Re-Think', *The Hindustan Times*, 15 May 1964, cited in Varshney, Ashutosh, 'Three Compromised Nationalisms: Why Kashmir has been a Problem' in Thomas (ed.), *op. cit.*, p. 202.
2. Chadda, Maya, *Ethnicity, Security and Separatism in India* (New York, Columbia University Press, 1997), p. 43.
3. Cable from Nehru to Prime Minister Attlee, 25 October 1947; cited in Wirsing, *op.cit.*, p. 86.
4. See 'Introduction' in Kohli, Atul, *Democracy and Discontent: India's Growing Crisis of Governability* (Cambridge, Cambridge University Press, 1990).
5. Malik, Y., and Vajpeyi, D.K., 'Indira Gandhi: Personality, Political Power and Party Politics', *Journal of Asian and African Studies* (XXII:3–4, 1987), p. 150.
6. Kohli, *op. cit.*, p. 377.
7. 'Once in power, populist leaders have neither the capacity, nor the incentive to build party organisations. They rule by theatrics, rather than by the painstaking, mundane tasks of building party cells.' Ibid., p. 191.
8. Chadda, *op. cit.*, p. 106.
9. See Rajni Kothari, 'The Congress System in India' in *Asian Survey* (1964), p. 1170. J. Manor describes it as 'A huge hierarchically structured party, broadly rooted throughout the countryside, apparently provided the mechanism whereby a plurality of elites, sub-elites and groups could both voice their claims and attempt to realise them. At the same time, Congress could adequately mediate and settle these multiple and often conflicting claims.' 'Party Decay and Political Crisis in India', *Washington Quarterly* (Summer 1981), p. 26, cited in Achin Vanaik, *The Painful Transition: Bourgeois Democracy in India* (London and New York, Verso), p. 77.

10. Mohammed Ayoob, 'Dateline India: The Deepening Crisis', *Foreign Policy* (85, Winter 91/92), p. 175.

11. Das, P.K., 'The Changing Political Scene in India: A Comment', *Asian Affairs* (25 February 1994), p. 24.

12. Chadda, *op. cit.*, p. 103.

13. Baxter, C., 'Democracy and Authoritarianism in South Asia', p. 309.

14. Rao, Chandrasekhara, 'Mrs Indira Gandhi and India's Constitutional Structures: An Era of Erosion', *Journal of Asian and African Studies* (XXII:3–4, 1987), p. 165.

15. See Dua, B.D., 'Federalism or Patrimonialism: The Making and Unmaking of Chief Ministers in India', *Asian Survey* (25:8, August 1985), p. 802.

16. Jeffrey, Robin, *What's happening to India?* p. 181.

17. Rao, *op. cit.*, p. 164.

18. B. D. Dua claims that 'Mrs Gandhi simply was not interested in surrounding herself with durable and secure chief ministers for fear they would hegemonise the centre and paralyse her dynastic ambitions.' *Op. cit.*, p. 795.

19. See Mathur, K., 'The State and the Use of Coercive Power in India', *Asian Survey* (32:4 April 1992), pp. 342–3.

20. Ibid., p. 344.

21. Ibid., p. 345.

22. Malik and Vajpeyi, *op. cit.*, p. 139.

23. Jalal, Ayesha, *Democracy and Authoritarianism in South Asia: A comparative and historical perspective* (Cambridge, Cambridge University Press, 1995), p. 10.

24. Distinguishing between centralization of power and quantum of power— 'the latter refers to a state's ability to resolve conflict without violence and move ahead with its modernisation agenda...[*the former to*] concentration of administrative power at the top'—Chadda concludes: 'Mrs Gandhi's attempts to centralise power had led to a corresponding decline in the quantum of power enjoyed by the government in its dealings with the state'; *op. cit.*, pp. 104–6.

25. Smith, D. (ed.), *South Asian Religions and Politics* (Princeton, Princeton University Press, 1966), p. 6.

26. See Rudolph, L. and Rudolph, S.H., 'Confessional Politics, Secularism and Centrism in India' in Bjorkman, J.W., (ed.), *Fundamentalists, Revivalists and Violence in South Asia* (New Delhi, Manohar, 1988), p. 79.

27. See Smith, D., *India as a Secular State* (Princeton, Princeton University Press, 1963), pp. 479–80.

28. Congressmen were also influenced by the massive shift in the communal balance following Partition. The Muslim percentage of the population had fallen from 40% to 14%.

29. Mitra, S.K., 'Desecularising the State: Religion and Politics in India after Independence', *Comparative Studies in Society and History* (October 1991), p. 767.
30. Nandy, Ashis, 'The Politics of Secularism and Recovery of Religious Tolerance' in Das, Veena (ed.), *Mirrors of Violence: Communities, Riots and Survivors in South Asia* (Delhi, Oxford University Press, 1992), p. 80.
31. Oommen, T., *State and Society in India: Studies in Nation-building* (New Delhi, Sage, 1990), p. 118.
32. Madan, T., 'Secularism in its Place,' *Journal of Asian Studies* (46:4, November 1987), pp. 748–9.
33. Ibid., p. 749.
34. Vanaik, *op. cit.*, p. 303.
35. Vanaik, *op.cit.*, p. 259.
36. Chadda, *op. cit.*, p. 120.
37. Nugent, N., 'Rajiv Gandhi and the Congress Party—The Road to Defeat' in Chiryankandath and Mitra (ed.), *Electoral Politics in India: A Changing Landscape* (New Delhi, Segment Books, 1992), p. 45.
38. Vanaik, *op. cit.*, p. 302.
39. Ainslee Embree notes that: 'The Hindu radical right does not appeal to the peasants, whose religious beliefs and practices have been scarcely touched by the modern world, but appeals to those, particularly in the urban areas, who are most conscious of the pressures of change,' *Utopias in Conflict: Religion and Nationalism in Modern India* (California, University of California Press, 1990), p. 46.
40. See 'India's Numbers game' *Economist*, 7 November 1992, p. 95.
41. Engineer, A. A., 'Hindu-Muslim Relations Before and After 1947' in Gopal, S. (ed.), *Anatomy of a Confrontation: The Rise of Communal Politics in India* (Penguin Books India, 1991), p. 190.
42. Rajmata Scindia quoted in Bhattacharya, N., 'Myth, History and Politics of Ramjanmabhumi' in Gopal (ed.), *op. cit.*, p. 128. Akbar Ahmed writes: 'The contemporary slogan throughout India is '*Babar ki aulad—ya qabristan ya Pakistan*': the choice for the descendants of Babar is either the grave or Pakistan, that is they must expect to be killed or else migrate to Pakistan and leave the land of Mother India. It sums up an entire political philosophy, which implies that Muslims are invaders, descendants of Babar now seen as the symbol of Muslim barbarism, invasion and aggression.' *Jinnah, Pakistan and Islamic Identity: The Search for Saladin* (London and New York, Routledge, 1997), p. 221.
43. For example, riots in Moradabad, Uttar Pradesh, in the 1980s arose because of the growing prosperity of Muslim groups being resented by Hindus. Similarly, economic and social changes that accompanied the Green Revolution in Punjab were a contributory factor in the Sikh rebellion there. Technological advancements in agriculture led to the

emergence of a new class of 'capitalist farmers', mostly Sikh Jats. When their interests came into conflict with the mainly Hindu merchant sector of the cities, they saw the obstacles they faced as arising from religious bias, rather than being purely economic in origin.

44. For example, during the riots in New Delhi following the assassination of Indira Gandhi, in which almost two thousand Sikhs were killed, both killers and victims generally came from the most deprived, slum-dwelling classes.

45. The Hindu upsurge 'feeds on...the decay of the state.... Hindu militancy is a symptom of the state's dangerous sickness, not the sickness itself' *Economist*, 6 February 1993, 'The Hindu Upsurge: The road to Ayodhya,' p. 23.

46. Rudolph, L., 'The Media and Cultural Politics' in Nugent, *op. cit.*, p. 45.

47. See Andersen, W.K., 'India in 1994' *Asian Survey* (35:2, February 1995), p. 136.

48. 'The Hindu Charioteers', *Economist*, 14 December 1991, p. 70.

49. 'Facts and propaganda', *Far Eastern Economic Review*, 19 July 1990, p. 25.

50. Austin, D., and Lyon, P., 'The Bharatiya Janata party of India' in *Government and Opposition* (28:1 Winter 1993), p. 37.

51. 'Playing with Fire: Emphasizing Hindu unity could provoke a backlash' *Far Eastern Economic Review*, 26 September 1990, p. 34.

52. Khalidi, Omar, 'Kashmir and Muslim Politics in India' in Thomas (ed.), *op. cit.*, p. 280.

53. Syed Shahabuddin, Lok Sabha member, ibid., pp. 280–81.

54. Brass, Paul, *Politics of India Since Independence* (Cambridge, Cambridge University Press, 1990), p. 199.

55. Khalidi, *op. cit.*, p. 280.

56. Ibid.

57. Turkande writing in an editorial of *The Radical Humanist* (March 1990), ibid., p. 277.

58. *Radiance*, 13 April 1990, ibid., p. 282.

59. *Afkar-i-Milli*, 4 February 1990, cited in ibid., p. 277.

60. Quoted in ibid., pp. 281–2.

6

PAKISTAN AND KASHMIR

India is, of course, the major 'external' player involved in Kashmir—both as the country of which Jammu and Kashmir is a constituent state, and as a party to the international dispute over its sovereignty. The second major player is Pakistan. It provides the main challenge to Indian sovereignty of Kashmir. And while its role in Kashmir's internal politics is far less direct than that of India, it is nonetheless significant. Pakistan, like India, is thus involved in both Kashmir issues, internal and international.

Pakistan's involvement in Kashmir viz. the international issue is relatively straightforward. For various reasons—again some practical, some symbolic—it has always laid claim to Jammu and Kashmir. However, its involvement in Kashmir's internal politics is more complex. It is perhaps best viewed as a two-way relationship: Kashmir has a profound impact on Pakistan's domestic situation, which, in turn, dictates Pakistan's direct role in Kashmir. Pakistan also has an indirect role in Kashmir serving as a potential alternative homeland for Kashmiri Muslims. Both, its attraction in this respect, and the reasons why Kashmir is so important to Pakistan domestically, stem from the country's fifty-year history.

Pakistan's relationship with Indian Kashmir is further complicated by the fact that it controls Azad Kashmir. As will be seen, this restricts Pakistan's international policy on Kashmir, and gives Kashmiri Muslims something else to consider when weighing up the merits and demerits of joining that country.

Significance of Jammu and Kashmir to Pakistan

The original significance of Jammu and Kashmir to Pakistan lay in the two-nation theory upon which Jinnah based his demand for a separate Muslim homeland: namely, that Hindus and Muslims are two separate nations who cannot ever live together in harmony. Consistent with this view, Muslims believed that the Muslim-majority parts of the subcontinent should have been joined to form Pakistan, and non-Muslim areas, the new India (the only justifiable exceptions being where geographical divisions were too great to make this practical). Thus, when the Muslim-majority state of Jammu and Kashmir—right on the border of Pakistan—went to India, that, in Muslim eyes, blatantly contravened the principles on which Partition was supposed to have been implemented.

Since Pakistan was formed on the basis of the two-nation theory it can never—even fifty years after Partition—concede sovereignty of the state to India. To do so would imply that Muslims and Hindus *can* live together, i.e., it would negate the validity of the two-nation theory, and hence the creation of Pakistan itself.

As well as this symbolic reason, Jammu and Kashmir was important to Pakistan for practical—strategic and economic—reasons too. The strategic significance of Kashmir, for Pakistan, was the same as seen in the previous chapter for India. In a cable to Nehru, on 16 December 1947, Prime Minister Liaquat Ali Khan observed that 'the security of Pakistan is bound up with that of Kashmir.'[1] The Pakistanis too were as much concerned about the implications of losing Kashmir for threats were present from within the subcontinent (i.e. India) as well as from outside (Russia, etc.). Liaquat made this clear in a 1951 interview: 'the very position of Kashmir—the strategic position of Kashmir—is such that without it Pakistan cannot defend itself against an unscrupulous government that might come in India.'[2]

The economic importance of Kashmir for Pakistan was greater than for India. Mahnaz Ispahani explains why:

Kashmir…had numerous links to Pakistani territory: its partition had meant economic disruption, since its waters were essential to the irrigation and power supplies of (Pakistani) west Punjab; its timber resources were rafted down west Punjab's rivers; its willow and resin were used in Pakistani industry;[3]

Kashmir's river links with Pakistan were particularly vital. The waters of the Indus, Jhelum and Chenab rivers all flowed through the State before reaching Pakistan. The agriculture of the Punjab as well as Sindh was dependent on them. If Jammu and Kashmir became Indian territory, Pakistan would face the permanent threat of having its water supply 'switched off', as pointed out by Pakistan's Foreign Minister Zafarullah Khan: 'If Kashmir should accede to India, Pakistan might as well, from both the economic and strategic points of view, become a feudatory of India or cease to exist as an independent sovereign state.'[4]

Whilst retaining their original significance to Pakistan, Jammu and Kashmir have become important to it for a number of additional reasons. Virtually all of these have their origin in the country's domestic political scene, and hence will be considered later in the chapter.

Review of Pakistan's History

Laying the Foundations

When Pakistan was formed in 1947, its founder Mohammad Ali Jinnah faced a number of problems—a virtually non-existent administrative structure, shortage of funds, ethnic divisions, two 'wings' separated by India, differing views on whether Pakistan was created merely to be a safe-haven from Hindu domination, or to be an Islamic state, and, before long, a war with India over Kashmir. Faced with such a litany of problems, and aware that his Muslim League party's main support base had been left behind in India, the prescription Jinnah came up with had three main ingredients: bureaucratization, centralization and homogenization.

Pakistani bureaucrats had been accustomed to wielding considerable power under the British. Motivated by the urgency of developing an effective administrative structure; as well as by the Muslim League's lack of strong, grass roots support within Pakistan[5] and his own preference for constitutional, as opposed to mass, politics, Jinnah ensured that the trend of bureaucratic rule continued. He depended on bureaucrats, not politicians, for running the country. In doing so, he quashed political participation and the democratic process.

Jinnah believed that the best way to ensure the survival of the new state was through a unitary, central government. Central domination was established early. Jinnah dismissed the NWFP provincial government within a fortnight of Pakistan's creation, and the Sindh government of M.A. Khuhro, seven months later. In January 1949, after his death, the most powerful provincial government, that of the Punjab, was also dismissed—this, despite the fact that it still commanded a majority in the provincial legislature. As provincial governments were weakened, the bureaucracy was strengthened. Sayeed writes that civil servants 'effectively controlled the entire administration in the provinces and the politicians there were kept in power subject to their willingness to obey central government directives.'[6]

The major obstacles to national integration in Pakistan were ethno-linguistic divisions, and differing perceptions of the role of Islam in the new state. To replace ethnic identities, Jinnah sought to forge a national Pakistani identity, based upon loyalty to the state, Urdu and Islam. Urdu was chosen as the national language because it was a legacy of India's last Muslim rulers, the Mughals, and thus the medium of 'high' Muslim culture and literature. The fact that most of the powerful bureaucracy consisted of native Urdu-speakers, was also an incentive. Opposition to Urdu was particularly vocal in East Pakistan but Jinnah dismissed this by telling the Bengalis '[w]ithout one

State language, no Nation can remain tied up solidly together and function.'[7]

Islam, or rather the cry 'Islam in Danger!' had been the principal force behind the Pakistan Movement. While this succeeded in achieving a consensus among the subcontinent's Muslims in favour of Pakistan, the same could not be said about the precise role that Islam would play in the dreamed-of homeland. Opinion fell into two broad camps: those like the founder of the Jamaat-i-Islami, Maulana Maudoodi, who wanted Pakistan to implement Islamic government (his argument was that if Pakistan was going to be secular, why could not it have remained in a united India?); and 'secularists', who wanted religion to be confined to personal worship, and the state to follow liberal, Western models of government. In 1947, the ruling League-bureaucratic (military) elite largely fell into the latter camp. Consequently, it was their interpretation of a Muslim state that prevailed. Jinnah's inaugural address to the Constituent Assembly replaced the religious nationalism of the independence struggle, with a territorial-political nationalism, based on citizenship of the new state.[8]

Islam was retained, however, in the new national identity. Apart from acting as a unifying element, this was necessary to avoid embarrassing questions about the *raison d'etre* of Pakistan (*a la* Maudoodi). The contradiction between Islamic identity and a secular state was resolved by 'paying lip-service' to Islam in the Objectives Resolution (a statement of intent about the future Constitution), and later in the 1956 Constitution itself. While acknowledging Allah's sovereignty, and asserting that all laws should conform to the Quran and *Sunna*, no mechanism was established to actually ensure this.[9] Abbas Rashid notes that the Resolution and the subsequent Constitution reflected 'on the one hand, the need to project an Islamic orientation and, on the other, the intent to deny it substance.'[10] Ignorance on the part of the masses about what an Islamic state actually entailed, helped the ruling elite overcome objections by the religious parties.

Pakistan's rejection of an Islamic government was highly significant in the context of its relations with India. Since Pakistan was not created to be an Islamic state, the only possible explanation for its splitting away from India was that Muslims would not have been safe under Hindu-majority rule.[11] And in order to justify its continued existence—at least until a measure of national integration could be achieved—Pakistan's leaders had to keep evoking the Indian bogeyman. The dispute over Jammu and Kashmir, and disagreements about the division of assets, together set the tone for a hostile attitude towards India.

Jinnah survived barely long enough to see his creation through its first year, but that was sufficient time to lay the foundations of its future development. Apart from a shift in the balance of power between the bureaucracy and the military, the initial characteristics of the Pakistani state—lack of democracy and provincial autonomy, suppression of regional identities, paying lip-service to Islam, hostility toward India—have persisted remarkably unchanged for almost fifty years.

1949–1988

During these forty years Pakistan experienced four different forms of government: bureaucratic, secular-military, civilian and Islamic-military. However, all followed the blueprint laid out by Jinnah. Centralization was continued. Indeed, under the bureaucrats and Ayub Khan, the four provinces of the then West Pakistan were even amalgamated into One Unit. Democracy and the establishment of political institutions was discouraged.[12] The bureaucrats ordered a military coup rather than hold elections, while Ayub Khan came up with a novel scheme of being elected by a college of Basic Democrats—nominated by the regime—to legitimize his rule. He too chose to relinquish power to the military, to Yahya Khan, rather than the politicians. Yahya did hold elections in 1970, but his refusal to allow the victorious Awami League to form the government led to civil war and the eventual secession of East Pakistan, to form

Bangladesh. Bhutto became Prime Minister, the first democratically elected one, in 1971. But, once in power, he too proved to be a stalwart opponent of democracy and the political process.

Two major changes that occurred during this period were a shift in the focus of power from the bureaucracy to the army, and the consolidation of Punjabi (and to a lesser extent Pathan) domination in the ruling circles. The former was, to a large extent, a consequence of the lack of democracy. Without a popular mandate to rule, Pakistan's leaders depended on the military to keep power. The latter, not surprisingly, led to resentment in the smaller provinces.[13] Bhutto's dismissal of the provincial government in Balochistan on the pretext that it had been plotting to secede from Pakistan,[14] led the Balochis to attempt to follow the example of East Pakistan. They waged a five-year insurgency against Islamabad in the 1970s, but the lack of external support allowed the army to eventually quell it. Of the two options for the basis of Pakistani nationhood, the Islamic state or fear of Hindu domination, until Zia's seizing power in 1977, the latter was pre-eminent, manifested in a recurrent anti-India theme. In 1965, Ayub Khan invaded Indian-held Jammu and Kashmir in the hope of gaining control of the entire state. The war was very popular in the West, and would undoubtedly have boosted Ayub's domestic position had the Pakistan army not accepted a cease-fire. The public perception that Ayub had halted the army's advance when victory was within reach, meant the 1965 war proved a major factor in his downfall.

Post-1971 the issue of nationhood really came to the fore as Pakistan was beset by doubts about its existence. The secession of the East Wing appeared to disprove the viability of Islam as a basis for nationhood. While Islamists countered that it was failure to implement Islam properly that had led to Bangladesh,[15] other Pakistanis had no option but to cling more firmly to the 'threat' from 'Hindu' India to justify their State's independence. Indian involvement in the 1971 War lent credence to this explanation.

Bhutto, throughout his political career, made liberal use of the India card. He condemned Ayub for calling a halt to the 1965 War, claiming that Pakistan had been in a winning position.[16] One day before Pakistan surrendered to India, in the 1971 War, he had stormed out of the UN Security Council chamber promising a 'thousand years war' with India—a move which won him huge acclaim at home.[17] The dismissal of Balochistan's NAP-JUI coalition government was justified using highly dubious evidence to show that the administration was plotting with external powers to secede from Pakistan. At Simla in 1972, Ayesha Jalal claims that Bhutto's only aim was to secure the release of Pakistani POWs; 'as a politician whose domestic fortunes soared in proportion to his anti-India rhetoric…[he] had no intention of trying to build friendlier relations with India.'[18] Quite the opposite, Bhutto took the Cold War with India to new heights by launching Pakistan's nuclear weapons programme.

Ziaul Haq seized power in a military coup in July 1977. Unlike previous rulers Zia stressed that the purpose of Pakistan's creation was not simply to provide a safe haven from Hindu oppression—it was to be a state where true Islamic government would be implemented. Zia saw Islam as a better means of achieving national integration than evoking the Indian bogeyman; he was also motivated by the need to legitimize his rule and by his deep personal faith.[19] But the piecemeal measures he implemented, whilst going a lot further than any of his predecessors, fell far short of the Islamic parties expectations. Perhaps because he implemented only partial Islam, he failed to achieve national integration; for, as Punjabi domination increased, so too did the resentment of the smaller provinces. In Sindh a new mohajir ethnic identity emerged, represented by the Mohajir Qaumi Movement (MQM).[20] Its clashes in Karachi with other ethnic groups, including native Sindhis,[21] and the authorities, claimed thousands of lives. Zia proved an extremely reluctant democrat. After eight years of procrastination he finally installed a limited-democracy civilian government led by Muhammad Khan Junejo, but the moment it attempted to assert its authority, it was dismissed and martial law re-imposed. It was really only Zia's sudden death in 1988 that paved the way for rule by elected politicians in Pakistan.

Contemporary Democracy

In the decade after General Zia's death, Pakistan was, in theory, ruled by democratically elected governments, but in practice power remained firmly in the hands of the army and the President.[22] The fact that elected governments were dismissed by the President four times and a new Prime Minister sworn in over fifteen times in the past ten years (including interim governments), clearly shows the fragility of elected institutions.

What is to blame for the chronic weakness of Pakistan's political system?

On the surface the answer would appear to be the Eighth Amendment that granted the President the right to dissolve elected assemblies.[23] But a closer examination reveals the real cause to be a lack of party organization and lack of ideology. Zia, not surprisingly, had been opposed to political parties, and had done his best to eradicate them. For the first eight-year period of martial law political parties were completely banned. The first elections to be held in 1985 were of local bodies in which voters were swayed by promises of local patronage rather than party affiliation. The National and Provincial Assembly elections that followed, were party-less. Jalal comments 'under the rules of Zia's non-party political system individual candidates had no reason to forge any kind of vertical ties.'[24] A measure of party organization did emerge among members of the new National Assembly, but martial law was re-imposed before it could be consolidated. It was only Zia's sudden death that made it possible for party politics to re-emerge. But after such a long period of suppression, many parties found themselves having to contest elections with their grass roots organizations virtually non-existent.

The two main national parties are the Pakistan People's Party (PPP) and Nawaz Sharif's Pakistan Muslim League (PML: previously part of a coalition known as the Islami Jamhoori Ittehad, IJI). Despite considerable rhetoric, neither has shown commitment to a specific ideology. Benazir Bhutto's PPP might be expected to be the more left-leaning of the two. But, in fact, apart from its name, her party has little in common with the socialist party founded by Zulfiqar Ali Bhutto (her father). Nationalization has been abandoned; support is sought from the 'propertied classes' rather than the masses; and many party stalwarts from the Zulfiqar era have abandoned his daughter. The PML, particularly its leader Nawaz Sharif, is widely regarded as coming from the Zia mould. But, he too has demonstrated little enthusiasm for his supposed mentor's policies. While in office Sharif's priority was economic reform rather than Islamization. Both the Benazir and the Sharif governments proved to be incredibly corrupt.

Lack of ideology has produced two almost identical parties: identical in terms of policies—economic reform, hardline on India and the bomb, not keen on genuine Islamization (though strong on rhetoric); and identical in terms of popular support— there has been little difference in the two parties' share of votes in recent elections, or in the kinds of groups that support them. Benazir is more popular in rural Sindh, Sharif among middle-class Punjabis, but the rest of the population can be swayed by either.

Lack of organization and lack of ideology have resulted in endemic patronage politics and political horse-trading. Parties depend, for a large measure of their popular support, on holders of large vote-banks who give their votes in return for financial or other favours—to be delivered when the party is in office. The PPP, for instance, courted the big landlords and once in power found itself unable to impose an agricultural tax on their vast income. Just as parties win votes on the basis of what they can 'pay', so members elected on a particular party ticket stay with that party just as long as the material rewards are greater than those being offered by opposition parties. In other words, governments are vulnerable because their members can be bought off by the opposition.

In summary, the pressures of 'paying back' vote-bank holders, preventing members defecting to other parties, and lining their own pockets (which, in Pakistan, appears to be the whole purpose of winning office), combine to prevent elected governments forming strong, stable administrations. Since governments are so weak they cannot address the country's pressing internal problems—upwardly-spiralling ethnic and sectarian violence; poor economic development and a widening rich-poor gap; an endemic 'drug and Kalashnikov' culture (a legacy of the Afghan War); and a general breakdown of law and order. Curbing the power of the army remains an even more distant dream.

Pakistan and Azad Kashmir

After Partition in 1947, and the first Indo-Pak War, those areas collectively known as the Northern Areas (Gilgit, Baltistan/ Skardu, Hunza) came under direct Pakistani administration, while the other parts of the state, controlled by Pakistan, formed the 'independent' entity of Azad Kashmir. Comprising of parts of the Vale of Kashmir, Poonch and Jammu, the population of Azad Kashmir is made up largely of Punjabi-speakers, ethnically distinct from the Vale Kashmiris. Political life in the new 'State' was initially dominated by the Muslim Conference, whose leaders included Ghulam Abbas, Mirwaiz Yusuf Shah, and Muhammed Ibrahim.

The fifty year relationship between Pakistan and Azad Kashmir can perhaps best be summed up as 'uneasy'. The main reason for this has been the two sides differing interests and objectives. Consider, first, the Pakistani perspective:

Pakistan's position with respect to the whole of Jammu and Kashmir is that it is disputed territory, whose fate can only be decided after a plebiscite. On the basis of this position, Pakistan has consistently condemned moves to integrate Indian-held

Jammu and Kashmir into the Indian Union. But also because of the very same position, it cannot itself integrate Azad Kashmir into Pakistan: to do so would amount to accepting the LoC as a permanent boundary, and hence demolish its claims to the Indian-held parts of the State. Pakistan has, therefore, been careful to maintain the 'independence' of Azad Kashmir (at least on paper). It enjoys all the trappings of a separate state: its own constitution, prime minister, president, legislative assembly, national flag, judicial system, capital, etc.

In reality, however, Azad Kashmir is far from autonomous. As far as the state's economy and armed forces are concerned, this is perhaps to be expected. Its small size and population, plus geographical location, render autonomy in these areas impractical. Large-scale migrations out of the state have reduced its already low tax income, thereby making it even more financially dependent on Pakistan. In 1989, for example, over 80 per cent of state expenditure on education, agriculture and infra-structural development came from the Pakistani central government.[25] Less understandable is the degree of decision-making power exercised by Islamabad: for instance about half of the 1989 money went to specific projects approved by Pakistan Ministry of Finance and Development.

Breaches of the state's political autonomy have been more serious. In varying guises, the federal government has always played a role in the running of the state, e.g. through the 1952 Ministry for Kashmir Affairs. At present, Azad Kashmir has a 48-member legislative assembly, of whom forty are elected and eight nominated; and a State Council, half of whose fourteen members are appointed by the President of Pakistan, who himself is the Chairman of the Council. Azad Kashmir's lack of political autonomy becomes more obvious when one sees how similar political development in the state has been to that in the rest of Pakistan. During Ayub Khan's period in office, for instance, the new Basic Democracy system was implemented in both Pakistan and Azad Kashmir. Similarly, under Zia, martial law regulations were applied equally in the state, albeit under separate presidential ordinances.

As well as formal arrangements, successive Pakistani administrations have sought to ensure control of Azad Kashmir by manipulating the choice of state government. When Zia seized power in July 1977, Muhammed Ibrahim, leader of the Azad Kashmir Muslim Conference and an ally of Zulfiqar Ali Bhutto, was President of Azad Kashmir. Zia first pressurized him into resigning, then held fresh elections in October. But when these returned Ibrahim to power, he dismissed him and appointed Brigadier Muhammed Hayat Khan as President.

Before considering the period since Zia's death, it should be mentioned that, in order to maintain Azad Kashmir's (theoretical) autonomy, Pakistan's national parties have refrained from opening branches in Muzzafarabad. Instead, they work through 'surrogate' parties, e.g. 'the All Jammu and Kashmir Muslim Conference functions as the Azad Kashmir branch of the Muslim League.' The only exception is the PPP, which since 1974 has had an official organization in the state.

Post-Zia, then, democratically elected governments in Islamabad have proved as unwilling as he was, to tolerate Azad Kashmir governments controlled by opposition parties. In 1990, for instance, following the dismissal of the first Benazir administration, the PPP government in Azad Kashmir led by Raja Mumtaz Rathore came under tremendous pressure from both the new Islamic Democratic Alliance (IDA) federal government and Sardar Qayyum Khan, President of Azad Kashmir, and an IDA ally. Eventually, Rathore resigned, and fresh elections were held that brought the Muslim Conference to power.[26] In the July 1996 state elections the positions were reversed: Qayyum Khan accused Bhutto of using federal government powers to ensure the election of PPP candidates.[27]

While Islamabad has been careful to preserve Azad Kashmir as a separate political unit, it has had few qualms about integrating the Northern Areas into Pakistan. Administration of the Northern Areas, originally, fell to Pakistan because, in 1947, this was beyond the capability of the newly established Azad Kashmir government. However, Muzaffarabad always believed that the transfer of control to Pakistan was a temporary measure, to be reversed when the Azad Kashmir administration was more firmly established.[28] This reversal has not happened. Instead, Pakistan has pursued a policy of gradual integration. In 1972, Zulfiqar Bhutto brought Gilgit and Baltistan formally under direct federal administration, followed in 1974 by the incorporation of Hunza into the Northern Territories. Bhutto's successor Ziaul Haq continued the political integration of the Northern Areas into Pakistan: in 1977 they were included in Martial Zone E; in April 1982 three members of the federal Majlis-e-Shura were drawn from the Northern Areas, and in July, Zia declared that the northern regions of Gilgit, Hunza and Skardu were 'an integral part of Pakistan'. Hewitt notes that: '[h]aving clarified the separation of the Northern Territories (including Hunza) from Azad Kashmir, Pakistan had gone a long way towards integrating about 25% of the former Dogra kingdom into the Republic.'[29]

Turning to the Azad Kashmir perspective: Pakistan's actions, in relation to Azad Kashmir, have aroused anger within the state. There is resentment at the region's 'bogus' independence—a 'constitutional fiction', and at central interference in state politics. Perhaps, most anger has been aroused by what is effectively 'the permanent alienation of the Northern Areas from Azad Kashmir.'[30] Muzaffarabad regards these areas, part of the pre-Partition state of Jammu and Kashmir, as being an integral part of Azad Kashmir; hence it sees their incorporation into Pakistan as illegal. In 1992, the Muzaffarabad High Court ruled that Gilgit, Skardu and Hunza were integral to Azad Kashmir and that their political rights were inseparable. The ruling 'meant that Pakistani administration of the area was unlawful.'[31] Although the Pakistan Government successfully challenged the ruling in the Supreme Court, the case demonstrated that Azad Kashmir is still far from a passive puppet of Islamabad.

Almost as great a source of anger is the perceived economic exploitation of the region by Pakistan. Ballard notes that 'the level of expenditure on rural development has...long been a good deal lower in Azad Kashmir than in the rest of Pakistan.'[32]

The only real exception has been the Mangla dam project. But far from mollifying Azad Kashmiris, this enraged them even more; while it was their lands and villages that disappeared under the water, and their infrastructure—particularly roads—that was badly disrupted, the benefits of Mangla's power are being enjoyed in Lahore and other parts of Pakistan. Islamabad's failure to repair the infrastructural damage, indeed its apparent lack of concern over the issue (which caused a marriage party of fifty to drown) severely damaged its standing in Mirpur.[33] Many Azad Kashmiris are settled abroad, mostly in Britain. Their foreign currency remittances are very important to Pakistan's economy, but they themselves—in view of the fact that little of that money goes to economic development in Azad Kashmir—are questioning what they gain from it.

Azad Kashmiri leaders have been constrained in expressing their anger at Islamabad by the reality of their situation, i.e. their heavy economic-military dependence on Pakistan. But pragmatism has not always prevailed. On several occasions, Azad Kashmiri politicians have embarrassed Pakistan by trying to cross the LoC; the aim being to convey the message that Azad Kashmir and Indian Jammu and Kashmir are part of the same entity (implying that Azad Kashmir should not be seen as just another part of Pakistan), and to put pressure on Islamabad to take a more vigorous role in the Kashmir insurgency. Some have gone so far as to issue statements to the effect that their ultimate goal is the re-unification of the entire state of Jammu and Kashmir, not as part of Pakistan, but as an independent entity.[34]

Do most Azad Kashmiris wish to stay within Pakistan, or have an independent Kashmiri state? Field research in the region suggests that while there is support for both options, staying with Pakistan is still favoured in most of the region, and only in Mirpur is the general mood pro-independence. With respect to the former it should be stressed that a desire to stay within Pakistan by no means implies satisfaction with Pakistan's actions—even staunch pro-Pakistanis voice criticism of these actions and demand greater autonomy. Commenting on the latter, pro-independence Mirpuris, Ballard writes:

they have adopted this position not so much as a result of a clear and positive commitment to the cultural distinctiveness of the Kashmir region as a whole, but rather as a consequence of their strong sense of disillusionment about the way in which Pakistan has treated them.[35]

In summary, there is considerable 'similarity in the way Islamabad and New Delhi have treated their respective Kashmirs ever since the State was split between them.'[36] The major difference between the two is that New Delhi has, to a large extent, formalized integration, while Islamabad has tried to disguise the process with 'constitutional fictions.' There is little doubt, however, that were it not held back by its desire to gain control of the Indian-held half of the State, Pakistan would have long ago made Azad Kashmir its fifth province. The second important difference between Pakistani-held Kashmir and Indian-held Kashmir is that the former's population is not, at least as yet, angry enough to launch a violent insurgency against Islamabad. But it would be a mistake to conclude from their docility that they are content with their position in Pakistan, or that they do not entertain hopes of independence. Following Azad Kashmir PPP leader Rathore's arrest in 1991, Benazir Bhutto claimed as much: 'Pakistan had arrested the Prime Minister of Azad Kashmir, rigged the state election, and alienated the Kashmiris to such an extent that they want an independent Kashmir.'[37]

Determinants of Pakistan's Kashmir Policy

The main features of Pakistan's domestic political scene that emerge from the above review of the country's first fifty years are as follows: a strong, very influential army, weak government, poor national integration, and a resurgence of Islam in social and political life. All these features influence Pakistan's policy on Kashmir. Hence, before considering what this is exactly, the interest of these various forces in Kashmir will be assessed.

The Army

> The army is perceived as the ultimate arbiter of Pakistan's destiny.[38]
> The permanent militarisation of society requires a permanent
> enemy.[39]

The two statements, above, pretty much sum up the army's
influence on Pakistan's Kashmir policy. As unofficial head of
the country's ruling troika between 1988 and 1999 (the other
members being the Prime Minister and President), was the Chief
of Army Staff (COAS), who was powerful enough to ensure
that the military's views prevailed in foreign policy decisions.
These views are shaped by a number of considerations:

Military Expenditure

During the 1980s, high levels of military expenditure were
justified by Pakistan's role as a 'front-line state' in the Afghan
War. Helped by copious amounts of foreign aid, mostly from
the United States, the army both expanded and modernized. But
after the Soviet Union's withdrawal from Afghanistan, and the
former's subsequent break-up, this 'excuse' was no longer
viable. Understandably reluctant to have its budget cut, the army
has looked around for a 'replacement enemy'—and who better
than the old foe, India? It is in the army's interest to portray
India as a constant threat; to claim that any Indian military
build-up (new weapons, military exercises, etc.) is intended for
use against Pakistan. They are helped in this by the fact that, as
Ahmed Rashid notes: 'no other issue makes Pakistanis feel more
vulnerable than the perceived threat of an "Indian hegemony"
over the subcontinent.'[40]

The State of Jammu and Kashmir is a vital element of the
'Indian threat' strategy to justify 'militarization'. India and
Pakistan have already fought three wars over the State. Hence,
it is the most likely trigger for future Indo-Pak hostilities. As
long as the dispute over its sovereignty remains unresolved, the
threat of a fourth war will '(hang) like a stationary cloud over

the subcontinent.'[41] The current Kashmiri insurgency makes the chances of resolution more remote. The longer it goes on and the more intense it becomes, the less likely it is that India and Pakistan will end their mutual hostility. In other words, the army will be able to go on warning of the danger from India. It is important to stress here that the military does not want actual war with India; what it wants is the possibility of war to remain high—thereby necessitating massive defence expenditure.

The Bomb

Pakistan's nuclear weapons programme was launched by Zulfiqar Ali Bhutto in the early 1970s, as a defence against 'Indian hegemony' ('proved' by the 1971 War), and in response to India's peaceful explosion of a nuclear device in May 1974. Today the same threat is used to maintain the nuclear programme. The army argues that India's conventional military superiority is too great for Pakistan to ever equal. Hence, the only way to ensure that India does not attack Pakistan, is to have a nuclear deterrent. Some observers do actually support this argument, albeit a modified version: that the threat of nuclear war has prevented Indo-Pak hostilities over Kashmir escalating into full-scale war as in the past.[42] Putting aside the issue of which version (if any) is correct, what is clear is that the army has to keep the Kashmir conflict alive—and thus the 'Indian threat'—in order to justify its nuclear capability.

Islam

There is a significant fundamentalist element within the Pakistan army.[43] Under Zia, of course, they had the upper hand—seen, for example, in the ISI's promotion of hard-line Islamic factions in the Afghan resistance. Though not as dominant now, they do still exert an influence on the army's thinking.[44] This is particularly true in the context of India and Kashmir. To Islamic fundamentalists within the army (and elsewhere), India is the enemy because it is 'Hindu'; the Kashmir insurgency must be supported because it is a struggle being waged by Muslims against non-Muslims, i.e. because it is a *jihad*.

In summary, all the above-mentioned factors combine to produce the army policy of maintaining a hard-line position in relations with India, and opposing any compromise on Pakistan's original demands in Jammu and Kashmir. As explained earlier, army policy becomes foreign policy in Pakistan, a lesson that Benazir, as Prime Minister, learnt the hard way. One reason for her disagreements with the army in 1990, and hence her dismissal, was her perceived soft stance on India and Kashmir. While she 'did not want to heighten the conflict on the ground', the army was 'keen to go further in arming and financing Kashmiri separatists.'[45] Second-time around she was careful not to make the same 'mistake'.

Weak Government

The weak position of elected governments affected policy on Kashmir in two ways: one, it made any compromise to try and end the Kashmir conflict very difficult; two, it increased the temptation to take an even harder line on the issue, i.e. to aggravate the conflict.

The first obstacle faced by any democratically elected Pakistani government attempting reconciliation with India and a resolution of the Kashmir conflict, is domestic opposition. Any softening towards India immediately prompts opposition accusations of lack of patriotism, and selling out Pakistan's interests. Benazir experienced this reaction during her first Premiership, and consequently took a traditional, hard-line position in her second term. This still failed to prevent opposition attacks over the issue, demonstrated, for example, when a proposed UN resolution condemning human rights abuses in Indian Jammu and Kashmir, was withdrawn by the Bhutto government. The resolution had no chance of being passed, but the IJI still used its withdrawal to accuse Bhutto of betraying the Kashmiris. As the *Sunday Times* comments: 'Kashmir is not a cause, it is a shoe with which to beat the opponent over the head.'[46]

As well as opposition attacks, the government is trapped by decades of anti-India rhetoric that has sunk deep into the national psyche. The Pakistani public firmly believe what their politicians have been saying virtually non-stop since Partition: namely, that Jammu and Kashmir rightfully belongs to Pakistan, and that India is the enemy. Any stepping down from this position, would, therefore, unleash a huge popular backlash—one that any government knows it could not survive, and hence, is careful not to provoke.

Another important factor is that, while there are powerful forces ever-ready to voice their opposition to any pro-India moves, there are none raised to encourage them. Put more bluntly, being reconciliatory wins no votes at home. Being hard-line and nationalistic, on the other hand, definitely does. In the 1991 election campaign, for instance, one of the promises made by the IDA, which helped secure its victory, was the liberation of Indian Jammu and Kashmir within three months of taking power.[47]

Kashmir's importance in domestic politics is greatly enhanced by the fact that there is little to distinguish between the two main parties (alliances), Nawaz Sharif's IJI and Bhutto's PPP. With similar policies, and both equally vulnerable to charges of corruption, the Kashmir conflict is one of the few issues on which genuine inter-party political debate can take place. Unfortunately, since it is such a potential vote-winner, the 'debate' tends to be little more than a competition in nationalist rhetoric. A final point: successive governments have found expressing support for the Kashmir insurgency a wonderful ploy for diverting public attention away from their own failures and unpopular policies. Bearing in mind that these are far from inconsiderable, there appears little likelihood of democratic governments toning down their pro-Kashmir rhetoric.

In conclusion, while Pakistan's military rulers take a 'strongman' posture, on India and Kashmir, in order to try and compensate for their regimes' lack of legitimacy, democrats—

despite ruling legitimately—are forced by numerous other pressures to adopt the same stance. Indeed, as Devin Hagerty comments 'democratic practice...[has] exacerbated rather than dampened tendencies towards conflict.'[48]

Poor National Integration

Pakistan has completed half a century as an independent entity. One would have expected that during such a period, a country, even one starting life with so many divisions, would have achieved some measure of national integration. As we have seen, in Pakistan's case, a tradition of undemocratic, centralized, and Punjabi-dominated government has prevented this from happening. Furthermore, the Kashmir conflict is also an important factor in the context of national integration for two reasons.

One, the failure to become a nation means, that in order to remain united, Pakistanis constantly need to refer back to the original reason for their being members of the same state, i.e. to the two-nation theory. As explained in the introduction above, without Kashmir, that theory remains incomplete. By reiterating Pakistani claims to the whole of the State, and highlighting Indian 'oppression' of the Muslims there, Pakistan's leaders reaffirm the creation of Pakistan—the need for a separate Muslim homeland in the subcontinent. In Sohail Inayatullah's words: 'Pakistan's self-image was and continues to be defined in its otherness to India. India is the enemy that gives unity.'[49]

Second, Kashmir (coupled with the nuclear bomb)—or rather, the rightfulness of Pakistan's claim to the State—is just about the only issue on which there is a nation-wide consensus. Zia's Islamization programme showed that even belief in Islam—the one thing nearly all (over 95 per cent) Pakistanis share in common—can turn into a divisive issue. Attempts to define Islam precisely (a preliminary to Islamic government) resulted in the exacerbation of sectarian differences. Thus, Pakistan's support for the Kashmir insurgency is important as a unifying force within Pakistan itself. As Wirsing writes, Kashmir has always 'stood as a symbol of collective national injury suffered at the hands of the Indians and as a spur to patriotism.'[50]

Islamic Resurgence

Pakistan, like most other countries in the Muslim world, is experiencing a resurgence of Islam as both faith and political ideology. Many of the reasons for this are common to most Muslim countries: a reaction to modernity, socio-economic problems, the influence of the Iranian Revolution, etc. But some are specific to Pakistan, e.g. Zia's Islamization programme, and, more recently, Western opposition to the country's nuclear bomb capability (seen in Pakistan as motivated by anti-Muslim sentiments, rather than by the desire for non-proliferation).[51] Overall 'the country is slowly drifting into a pro-Islam, anti-West mood.'[52] The Islamic lobby in Pakistan has negligible representation in the legislative assemblies, yet it had constituted a very powerful force[53]—one that governments are wary not to annoy. Its strength was seen, for instance, when the second Benazir Bhutto administration was forced to abandon its attempts to liberalize Pakistan's strict blasphemy laws.[54]

The resurgence of Islam has influenced attitudes to the Kashmir conflict in several ways. Firstly, it has increased public hostility towards India, a 'Hindu' country. Thus, it has become even harder for any democratic Pakistani government to resolve differences with India through negotiation—any such move would provoke accusations of being 'un-Islamic'. Indeed, since Islam is so much more prominent in Pakistani society, politicians stand to benefit by taking the opposite approach, i.e. increasing their own Islamic rhetoric, particularly with respect to India and the Kashmir conflict. This is something they have proved far from reluctant to do.

Perhaps the most significant effect of the Islamic resurgence, in the Kashmir context, has been on Pakistani perceptions of the conflict. While nationalist interests remain paramount, increasingly it is also being seen in terms of Islam: as a struggle being waged by Muslims against non-Muslims, i.e. a *jihad*. Paula Neuberg comments that: 'for Pakistan it has become an emblem of Muslim politics in a world hostile to Islam.'[55] This, in turn, has greatly enhanced its emotive impact on Pakistanis. Practically, this perception of the Kashmir conflict as a *jihad* has led many Pakistanis to join the conflict as '*mujahideen*'.

In summary, the resurgence of Islam in Pakistan has strengthened traditional feelings of hostility towards India, and, with it, popular support for the Kashmiri insurgency.

Pakistan's Kashmir Policy

From the above, we see that Pakistan is forced to take a hardline stance on India and the Kashmir issue by the interests of various powerful groups at home, most notably the army, which needs an enemy to strengthen itself against, and politicians who have found nationalism a useful vote-winner and a distraction from other problems. In addition, the Pakistani public has been psyched up to such an extent about Kashmir that any softening on the issue would meet fierce resistance.

What then is Pakistan's Kashmir policy? Basically, refusal to compromise on its claims to Indian-controlled Jammu and Kashmir. In international fora this claim tends to be expressed in the following manner: the whole of Jammu and Kashmir is disputed territory and, in accordance with UN resolutions, a plebiscite should be held to determine whether the people of the State wish to join India or Pakistan.[56] In other words, rather than openly demanding the whole State for itself, Islamabad presses for the right of self-determination for the Kashmiris— confident that most would then volunteer to join Pakistan. At the same time, Pakistani leaders condemn India's integration of its part of the State into the Indian Union, and voice their support for the Kashmir insurgency.

It is important to note that Pakistan (and India for that matter) does not acknowledge a third option for Jammu and Kashmir—

that of independence. There are several reasons for this. Firstly, this position is a hang-over from Partition thinking, when the subcontinent was to be divided into just two new political units, India and Pakistan, and all the princely states had to join one or the other. Secondly, a Kashmiri struggle for independence, rather than to join Pakistan, would lose much of its political value at home. Thirdly, and perhaps most importantly, if Pakistan were to agree to independence for Jammu and Kashmir, it would have to give up those parts of the State currently under its control: Azad Kashmir and the Northern Areas. The loss of these regions would be a massive blow, both to Pakistan's economy and its strategic interests (cutting it off from China, for instance), not to mention national pride (after almost thirty years still smarting from the secession of East Pakistan). Referring particularly to the economic cost to Pakistan of allowing an independent Kashmir, Ballard writes:

> [A] major portion of Pakistan's current hydel capacity, and the principal reservoir for the entire canal system in West Punjab would be contained within the boundaries of such a state.... It is for this reason that there is no prospect whatsoever of Pakistan being prepared to allow all of Punjab's immediate submontane tracts to fall under the control of an independent state, whatever the opinions of the local population may be and however much they may hanker for the creation of a truly Azad Kashmir.[57]

Pakistan's opposition to Kashmiri independence has influenced its role in the insurgency. Islamabad has been highly selective in its support of militant groups, encouraging groups that are fighting for Kashmir's accession to Pakistan, and discouraging those fighting for independence. Since militant groups in Kashmir cannot survive without outside backing, this has resulted in the insurgency being dominated by pro-Pakistan groups.

The other point to note, about Pakistan's involvement in the Kashmir conflict, is that its support has been much less than it could have been. Providing overt support to the Kashmiri militants would obviously place Pakistan in a difficult position internationally, but covertly through the Azad Kashmir administration, or agencies like the ISI, it could give them a lot more practical assistance. By not doing so, it reflects the motives of Pakistani policy-makers: as seen above their support for the Kashmir insurgency arises more from self-interest (justifying arms expenditure, to win popular support, etc.) than genuine concern for Kashmiri Muslims. [The Pakistani public should not be included in this assessment; they see the Kashmiri militants struggle as both a pro-Pakistan movement and a *jihad*, and hence, genuinely support it.]

Pakistan's Impact on Kashmir

The numerous ways in which Kashmir has come to feature in Pakistan's domestic politics have been described, as have the ways in which these, in turn, determine Pakistan's policy on Kashmir. How has Pakistan affected Kashmiri politics? As indicated at the beginning of this chapter, Pakistan's role in Kashmiri affairs has been both indirect and direct. The former is, as a potential homeland for Kashmiri Muslims, and the latter is, in its promotion and support of secessionist elements. Consider Pakistan's indirect impact first:

Kashmiri Muslim attitudes to Pakistan have been most influenced by three aspects of the country's domestic politics. One, the role of Islam in Pakistan. Two, Pakistan's record with respect to democracy and regional autonomy. And three, Pakistan's treatment of Azad Kashmir. The first of these is important because one of the main reasons why Kashmiri Muslims might consider joining Pakistan would be their belief in Jinnah's two-nation theory. Pakistan was formed as a homeland for the Muslims of the Indian subcontinent: Kashmiris belong in it because they too are Muslim. It is obvious that this argument can only hold if Pakistan remains true to its Islamic nationhood. If Pakistan were to become a secular state today why should Kashmiri Muslims join it? Apart from Islam, they have little in common with other Pakistanis.

Pakistan's record on democracy and regional autonomy is important because, as seen in previous chapters, a major reason for Kashmiri Muslim alienation from India has been New Delhi's persistent refusal to allow them political participation and autonomy. Kashmiri Muslims are not likely to be drawn toward Pakistan if they are to be denied these rights here as well.

Pakistan's treatment of Azad Kashmir is significant for the same reason. It gives Kashmiri Muslims in India an indication of the kind of treatment they can expect if they join Pakistan. Plus, being the other half of the pre-1947 state of Jammu and Kashmir, it allows for easy comparison between Pakistani and Indian rule.

Taking Islam first, it was seen in the above review of Pakistan's history that over the last fifty years it has made very little progress on the path towards becoming an 'Islamic' state. What progress it has made has largely been cosmetic and has been motivated by political ambition rather than a genuine desire to implement Islamic government. Pakistan has not even succeeded in persuading its citizens to see themselves primarily in terms of their religion and to unite on this basis; proof of this lies in the country's limited success in bringing about national integration and in the escalating ethnic and sectarian tensions. A Kashmiri Muslim looking to move from secular (Hindu) India to an Islamic country—as in one run in accordance with the Quran and *Sunna*—would, therefore, find much in the Pakistan State that contravened Islamic principles.

On the other hand, a Kashmiri Muslim looking to move to a Muslim country—as in one where the majority of inhabitants are Muslim—would feel totally at home in Pakistan. For such a Kashmiri, other factors such as Pakistan's democratic credentials and its record on regional autonomy would be significant. Pakistan's record on democracy can at best be described as dismal vis-á-vis changed circumstances. For most of its first forty years it has been run by the bureaucracy or the military; popular governments were dismissed over the last decade and, finally, on 12 October 1999 military rule was directly established. However, the damage done to the political process by four decades of undemocratic rule was so great that even though democracy was restored for a time, it hardly proved a great success in dealing with the country's problems. By 1999 Pakistan was back under military rule. Pakistan's treatment of its various constituent groups has, and continues to be, very poor. Power in the country has increasingly been dominated by a Punjabi (and to a lesser extent Pathan) elite. The other population groups—Bengalis (pre-1971), Sindhis and Balochis—have been given little opportunity to share power in the centre or to exercise this in the form of regional autonomy. Bearing this poor record in mind, as Hewitt says: 'It is a fair question to ask whether Indian Kashmiris would ever opt to live in a Pakistani State still effectively run by an ethnically exclusive elite from which they would almost certainly be excluded.'[58]

Turning to the third factor likely to influence Kashmiri Muslim attitudes to joining Pakistan: its treatment of Azad Kashmir. As seen earlier, this has not differed greatly from India's treatment of its Kashmir. Lack of autonomy, intolerance of opposition-led state governments, and (in the case of the Northern Areas) escalating integration have been common elements of both. As such, Indian Kashmiris would have little to gain from exchanging New Delhi's control for Islamabad's.

The above would suggest that Kashmiri Muslims would not be interested in joining Pakistan. However, when assessing Kashmiri Muslim views on Pakistan, a number of other points need to be borne in mind. One, that while the major political developments in Pakistan, e.g. the secession of the East Wing to form Bangladesh, changes in government, etc., are reported in the Valley, events such as ethnic and sectarian clashes, anti-government protests, load-shedding, price hikes, etc., are not. This is significant, because it is the latter which give a better indication of public feeling—of how content ordinary Pakistanis are with the state of affairs in their country. In general, it would be correct to say that the Valley Muslims are not fully aware of what is going on in Pakistan; they are ignorant of many of the problems faced by people there. The consequence of this is that most Kashmiri Muslims have a somewhat rose-tinted picture of Pakistan—their perceptions of it correlate more with the ideal of what it was meant to be, than with the reality of what it actually is.

Second, since the conflict in Indian Kashmir started with its accompanying security clampdown (including human rights abuses) by the authorities, Azad Kashmir and Pakistan undoubtedly appear in a more favourable light to the Valley Muslims. For people living in fear of their sons being dragged off to torture centres, their women raped, or their houses burnt down, the grievances of native Azad Kashmiris will seem insignificant. From their perspective, the most important point will be that Azad Kashmir and Pakistan are places where Muslims are safe.

This combination of lack of detailed information about what is happening in Pakistan and its being seen as a far more secure place for Muslims than India, counteracts the negative feelings that Kashmiri Muslims are likely to host towards Pakistan, because of its far from perfect fifty-year record and its treatment of Azad Kashmir.

Consider now, Pakistan's direct impact on Kashmir. Kashmiri Muslims have been prompted to view Pakistan as an alternative homeland (not simply because it is there: Pakistan has deliberately encouraged them to think like this). It has kept the Kashmir issue alive in the UN and international community generally. It has persistently claimed that Jammu and Kashmir is not an integral part of India but disputed territory, and it has persistently pressed for the UN resolutions on Kashmiri self-determination to be implemented. The effect of this persistent questioning of Jammu and Kashmir's membership of the Indian Union on Kashmiris themselves, has, not surprisingly, been to keep the 'exit door' from India open. And as Kashmiri Muslims have become more alienated from India because of the various State policies described in earlier chapters, the Pakistan factor has gained significance.

Pakistan has periodically, most notably in 1965, tried to actually incite rebellion in Indian Kashmir—generally without success. As will be seen in Chapter Eight, the current Kashmir insurgency was not the result of Pakistani instigation. Once underway, however, Pakistan became a vital source of moral and practical support to the Kashmiri Muslims in their struggle to secede from India. Without active Pakistani support, India would probably have crushed the secessionist movement long ago. Pakistan's involvement in the Kashmir conflict will be looked at more fully in Chapter Eight.

The Siachen Glacier Dispute

The Siachen Glacier covers an area of about 1000 square miles in the north of Jammu and Kashmir, adjacent to China. It begins from map co-ordinate NJ9842. This is the point at which both the 1949 Cease-fire Line (CFL) and the 1972 Line of Control (LoC) ended. Since the glacier was completely uninhabited and since it was useless militarily (the harsh conditions made it impossible for Pakistan to attack India via the glacier, or vice versa), it was considered unnecessary to define precisely how much of it was under Pakistani control, and how much under Indian control.

Since 1984, India and Pakistan have been fighting a very low-key 'war' for control of the glacier. It is unclear precisely how the fighting began, but it was most probably initiated by India. The designation of the region in recently published international atlases as being under Pakistani control, coupled with the fact that mountaineering parties sought Islamabad's rather than New Delhi's permission to climb there, appears to have raised alarms in India that the glacier was evolving into internationally acknowledged Pakistani territory. To prevent this, and to re-establish New Delhi's claims to the area, Indian forces were sent to the glacier in the spring of 1984. Pakistan's army was slow to respond to the challenge, only managing to retain control of one of the three passes through the Saltoro range, leading to Siachen—India seized the other two. This situation had been reached by December 1985. Since then there has been a stalemate in the fighting.

Soldiers from both sides continue to be killed at the Siachen Glacier, though the cause is more likely to be extreme cold rather than the opposing troops. Both countries are spending huge amounts of money maintaining their forces in the incredibly hostile conditions. Indian costs in 1992/93, for example, were approximately Rs 50 million (US$1.94 million) per day, working out at more than 10 per cent of the total annual defence budget.[59] To the outside observer it would appear to be in the interest of both sides to reach a settlement and be able to withdraw their forces—particularly since the region has no military or other (e.g. mineral) value. Why is it then, that despite several rounds of talks between Indian and Pakistani officials, the situation remains essentially unaltered from that of 1985?

> ...whatever salience [*the Siachen Glacier*]...has in the political outlook of either India or Pakistan...[*arises*] solely from its connection with the parent Kashmir conflict; [*by itself*] the area has no political life.[60]

Hence, it is no surprise that the main stumbling-block in negotiations (Pakistan's refusal to agree to any kind of formal division of the Siachen Glacier between the two countries, i.e. to an extension of the LoC northwards) is derived from that preventing resolution of the wider Kashmir dispute. Pakistan's position is that the State of Jammu and Kashmir remains disputed territory, and hence the LoC is not, and never can be, a formal boundary. The fear is that any extension of the LoC could imply acceptance of it, and hence of the permanent division of Jammu and Kashmir between India and Pakistan. As seen earlier, there are strong domestic pressures blocking any kind of compromise on Pakistan's claim to the entire State. Consider the main factors shaping politics in Pakistan in the specific context of the Siachen Glacier.

First, the army. Were Pakistan to concede any part of the glacier to India, this would reflect very badly on the army. The popular perception would be that not only had the army failed to gain control of Indian-held territory, it had even failed to retain control of areas already held by Pakistan.

Second, the government. Any government that signed an agreement with India formalizing the LoC in the Siachen Glacier, would come under attack from political opponents, the Islamic lobby and the public in general—variously accusing it of betraying the Kashmiris, Pakistan's interests and Islam. In other words, it would be committing political suicide. Conversely, continuing hostilities with India (provided the costs are played down) is a vote-winning policy. Division of the glacier is thus not an option.

With respect to national integration, as with Kashmir, Pakistan's claim to the Siachen Glacier and the imperative of not letting it fall into India's hands, is something upon which all Pakistanis—regardless of ethnic or sectarian background—are united. Finally, a significant element of Pakistan's Islamic resurgence is opposition to 'Hindu' India—it therefore goes without saying that the Islamist lobby wants Pakistan to hold onto the glacier. In the context of public opinion, it should be stressed that the cost of Pakistan's Siachen forces is not something that most people are aware of; politicians, of course, never mention it, but neither is it discussed—let alone questioned—in the media.

The only solution to end the fighting that would be acceptable in Pakistan would be for India to withdraw its forces completely from the glacier and acknowledge Pakistani control of the region. But since any Indian government that did so would also be sealing its own fate, this is not about to happen. Hence this seemingly pointless, high altitude 'war' drags on.

NOTES

1. Wirsing, *op. cit.*, p. 86.
2. Interview with David Lilienthal, 1951; ibid.
3. Ibid., p. 87.

4. Brecher, Michael, *The Struggle for Kashmir* (Toronto, Reyson Press, 1953), p. 48, cited in Amin, Tahir, *The Tashkent Declaration—Case Study—Third Party's Role in Resolution of the Conflict* (Islamabad, Institute of Strategic Studies, 1980), p. 13.

5. The League's own constituency had largely been confined to the Muslims of North-Central India. It was only by allying itself with regional parties in the Muslim-majority provinces that the League had secured significant popular support for the Pakistan Movement. Post-independence it was those provincial parties and not the Muslim League that enjoyed a mass support base.

6. Sayeed, K. B., *Pakistan: The Formative Phase* (Oxford University Press, 1968), p. 329.

7. This was actually Jinnah's last major public address, delivered in Dhaka on 21 March 1948. *Quaid-e-Azam Speaks: Speeches of Quaid-e-Azam Muhammad Ali Jinnah* (Karachi, Ministry of Information and Broadcasting, 1950), pp. 133–6, cited in Wolpert, S., *Jinnah of Pakistan* (New York and Oxford, Oxford University Press, 1984), p. 359.

8. 'You are free to go to your temples, you are free to go to your mosques or to any other place of worship in this state of Pakistan. You may belong to any religion or caste or creed; that has nothing to do with the fundamental principle that we are all citizens and equal citizens of one state... [Y]ou will find in the course of time, Hindus will cease to be Hindus, and Muslims will cease to be Muslims, not in the religious sense because that is a personal faith of each individual, but in the political sense as citizens of the State', Ahmed, J. (ed.), *Speeches and Writings of Mr Jinnah, Vol. II* (Lahore, Ashraf, 1960), pp. 403–4, cited in Harris, Nigel, *National Liberation* (London, Penguin, 1990), p. 199.

9. 'This Resolution, though grandiloquent in words, phrases and clauses, is nothing but a hoax...not only does it not contain even the semblance of the embryo of an Islamic state but its provisions, particularly those relating to fundamental rights, are directly opposed to the principles of an Islamic state', *Munir Report* (Government of Pakistan), p. 203, cited in Noman, O., *Pakistan: Political and Economic History since 1947* (updated edition, London, Kegan Paul, 1990), p. 7. In a speech delivered at the White House, the Prime Minister, Liaquat Ali Khan, reaffirmed that the Objectives Resolution did not imply an Islamic state.

10. Rashid, A., 'Pakistan: The Ideological Dimension' in Khan, Asghar (ed.), *Islam, Politics and the State* (London, Zed Books, 1985), p. 86.

11. Ayub Khan set out this argument in his autobiography: 'The end of British domination should not become for the Muslims the beginning of Hindu domination. They were not seeking to change masters. They knew through past experience that the Hindus would not agree to live with them on equal terms within the same political framework...losing their identity...is what would have inevitably happened if they had been

compelled to accept the political domination of the Hindus.' *Friends Not Masters: A Political Autobiography* (London, Oxford University Press, 1967), p. 200.

12. 'Pakistan needed a strong government capable of taking decisions which might not be popular but which were necessary for the safety, integrity and...development of the country. We could not afford the luxury of a system which would make the existence of the government subservient to the whims and operations of pressure-groups.' Ibid., p. 213.

13. Balochistan was Pakistan's poorest province, and the economic and development policies of successive Pakistani governments ensured it stayed that way. Though rich in natural gas and mineral resources the region received little benefit from them: most of the revenue went to other provinces, particularly Punjab. Even extraction was controlled by the central government in collaboration with foreign companies; Balochis themselves did little more than provide unskilled labour.

14. Reports appeared in the government-controlled press of a 'London Plan'. Wali Khan, chairman of the Balochi NAP, was alleged to have met Sheikh Mujib, by then President of Bangladesh, in London to plan a secessionist uprising. Ataullah Mengal, another NAP leader and Chief Minister of Balochistan, was implicated with him. An arms cache found in the Iraqi Embassy in Islamabad, was linked by the regime to the London Plan, and amid accusations of plotting with Iraq and the USSR to break up Pakistan, the NAP administration in Balochistan was dismissed. Ghaus Bux Bizenjo, Governor of the province, Khair Bux Marri, Baloch NAP President, and Mengal were all arrested. The NWFP's NAP-JUI government resigned in protest at the dismissal and arrests.

15. 'The Islamic groups were quick to seize upon the opportunity and point out that East Pakistan was lost only because the people had not been good Muslims in their personal as well as collective behaviour. They also accused the rulers of neglecting Islam as a source of public policy, a fact which, in their view, had led to the emergence of a wide variety of anti-national forces in the country. According to this formulation, the secession of East Pakistan was, therefore, not a failure of Islam but of un-Islamic parties and conduct of the rulers.' Ahmed, Mumtaz, 'Islamic Revival in Pakistan', in Bjorkman, James (ed.), *Fundamentalists, Revivalists and Violence in South Asia* (New Delhi, Manohar, 1988), p. 99.

16. Ayesha Jalal writes that Bhutto's criticisms of Ayub Khan's handling of the 1965 War and the Tashkent Agreement 'accusing his old patron of bartering away Pakistan's chance to wrench Kashmir out of New Delhi's control...was an immensely popular stance and one that added to Bhutto's fame and notoriety.' Jalal, A., *Democracy and Authoritarianism in South Asia: A Comparative and Historical Perspective* (Cambridge, Cambridge University Press, 1995), p. 78.

17. As Foreign Minister in the Yahya government, Bhutto had gone to America to address the UN Security Council. He stormed out after tearing up a resolution offered by Poland to end the fighting. 'This extraordinary scene, viewed by millions of people on television in Pakistan, was to burnish in their minds an image of a remarkable patriot refusing to submit even as his own forces were about to surrender to an invading army. This performance won Zulfiqar Ali Bhutto the support even of those who had not voted for him in the election of December 1970. It also won him the support of young army officers who had felt humiliated by the conduct of the generals', Burki, *Pakistan: The Continuing Search for Nationhood* (2nd edition, Boulder, Colorado; Westview, 1991), p. 61.

18. Jalal, *op. cit.*, p. 81.

19. '[T]he creation of a theocracy was an attempt to fill the political vacuum created by Zia's renegation on his promise to hold elections. Islamisation provided an objective for utilising state power, which the military had refused to transfer to civilians.' Noman, *op. cit.*, p. 151. Wirsing quotes a Pakistani academic with close links to the Jamaat-i-Islami: '[Zia] was not a fundamentalist but a secularist and pragmatist.... In 1977 he recognised the political utility of Islam and coopted it. Always, however, his first concern was his own political survival, not the propagation of Islam', *op. cit.* (1991), p. 58.

20. Mohajir alienation was due in large measure to the decline of the bureaucracy. The rise of the army, dominated by Punjabis and Pathans, opened up greater opportunities for these ethnic groups—in employment, business, land allocation. The Mohajirs felt discriminated against. They also resented the influx of large numbers of Punjabis and Pathans into big cities like Karachi; their presence made it even harder for the Mohajirs to compete for jobs, do well in business, etc. The MQM started in 1984 as a student movement, but within two years became the voice of the wider Mohajir community. It wants the Mohajirs recognized as Pakistan's fifth nationality, and allocated a 20% quota of jobs, etc, in the centre, and 50–60% in Sindh. It also wants quotas in Sindh reserved exclusively for Mohajirs and native Sindhis, i.e., Punjabis and Pathans resident in Sindh excluded. See Hamish McDonald, 'A new ethnic flexes its muscles', *Far Eastern Economic Review* (1 December 1988), p. 14.

21. Native Sindhi alienation from Islamabad increased considerably after Zia came to power. The reasons for this alienation included: the replacement of Zulfiqar Ali Bhutto's central government—the first ever to be led by a Sindhi—by a Punjabi-Pathan dominated military regime; removal of PPP appointees (many of them Sindhis) and replacement by Punjabi officials; land allocation of newly irrigated areas of north Sindh to retired army and civil service personnel; stress on Urdu rather than Sindhi in schools. See Rakisits, C. P., 'Centre-Province Relations in Pakistan Under

President Zia: The Government's and the Opposition's Approaches' in *Pacific Affairs* (61: Spring 1988), p. 80.

22. Before being appointed Prime Minister in 1988, Benazir Bhutto had to agree that the Inter-Services Intelligence (ISI) would continue to direct policy on Afghanistan; to retain Sahabzada Yaqub Khan—a Zia appointee—as Foreign Minister; not to cut the army's 34% share of government spending; and to support Ishaq Khan's bid for re-election in December's presidential elections.

23. According to the 8th amendment, the country's executive authority is vested in the President, and is exercised by him either directly or through subordinates. The role of the prime minister and cabinet is advisory. Powers granted to the president include: the right to order the Prime Minister to seek a vote of confidence in parliament; to dissolve parliament and appoint a caretaker cabinet; to make important appointments including military chiefs, provincial governors, the Chief Justice. For more details see Salamat Ali, 'Zia's Legacy' in *Far Eastern Economic Review* (18 March 1993), p. 18.

24. Jalal, *op. cit.*, p. 105.

25. Hewitt, *op. cit.*, p. 119.

26. Ali, Salamat, 'Remote control' in *Far Eastern Economic Review* (15 August 1991), p. 27.

27. 'Qayyum Alleges Rigging' in *Dawn* (Pakistan), 2 July 1996.

28. See Wirsing (1991), *op. cit.*, p. 152.

29. Hewitt, *op. cit.*, p. 117.

30. Wirsing (1991), *op. cit.*, p. 152.

31. Hewitt, *op. cit.*, p. 120.

32. Ballard, *op. cit.*, p. 513.

33. Ibid., pp. 514–15.

34. For example, Muhammed Ibrahim in the 1950s formed the Kashmir Liberation Movement, committed to a 'united and independent' Kashmir; Abdur Rehman, who became President of Azad Kashmir in October 1969 made clear in his public statements that Azad Kashmir was committed to '[i]ndependence, friendship with Pakistan without being part of it.' See Hewitt, *op. cit.*, pp. 113–15.

35. Ballard, *op. cit.*, p. 513.

36. Ali (15/8/91), *op. cit.*,

37. Cited in Hewitt, *op. cit.*, p. 119.

38. Ali, Salamat and Clad, James 'Democracy on Trial: Political uncertainty likely to follow army-backed polls' in *Far Eastern Economic Review* (4 October 1990), p. 28.

39. Hoodbhoy, P., and Nayyar, A., 'Rewriting the History of Pakistan' in Khan, Asghar (ed.), *op. cit.*, p. 175.

40. 'Delhi-bashing: Pakistani politics keeps Indian bogey alive' in *Far Eastern Economic Review* (11 April 1996), p. 26.

41. Burke, S.M., and Ziring, L., *Pakistan's Foreign Policy: An Historical Analysis* (2nd edition, Karachi, Oxford University Press, 1990), p. 469.

42. See Hagerty, Devin, 'Nuclear Deterrence in 'South Asia: The 1990 Indo-Pakistani Crisis' in *International Affairs* (20:3, Winter 1995), and Rashid, A., 'War talk as Bhutto goes' in *Far Eastern Economic Review* (11 August 1990), p. 52.

43. Ahmed Rashid notes that 'Increasingly the officer corps, which was once recruited from elite schools and the families of the landed gentry, is now being filled with less privileged young men whose vision is far more Islamic than their predecessors. Many have been inspired by the "jihads" in Afghanistan and Kashmir, and are virulently anti-American.' 'Fundamental Problem: Islamic officers' coup plot shocks country' in *Far Eastern Economic Review* (26 October 1995), p. 18.

44. The Islamic element within the Pakistan army has periodically made its presence felt. For example, Mirza Aslam Beg, Chief of Army Staff under Nawaz Sharif, opposed the sending of Pakistani troops to Saudi Arabia, to participate in the alliance against Iraq. He was said to have described Iraq's armed forces as 'a source of strength which could help save the international Islamic community from destruction' [*Far Eastern Economic Review*, 12 December 1990, p. 13]. More recently, a coup plot involving 10 officers, 26 enlisted men and several civilians, was uncovered. The conspirators 'planned to eliminate the army's high command and top politicians in Islamabad, declare martial law, and impose *sharia*, or Islamic law, in the country' [*Far Eastern Economic Review*, 26 October 1995, p. 18].

45. 'A coup in Mufti' *Economist* (11 August 1990), p. 51.

46. Cited in Rashid, A., 'Losing Streak: Foreign Policy Failures dog Islamabad' in *Far Eastern Economic Review* (25 August 1994), p. 27.

47. Ali, Salamat, 'No, Prime Minister: Nawaz Sharif runs into constraints' in *Far Eastern Economic Review* (15 August 1991), p. 20.

48. Hagerty, *op. cit.*, p. 112.

49. 'Images of Pakistan's Future' in *Futures* (24 November 1992), pp. 870–71.

50. Wirsing (1991), *op. cit.*, p. 175.

51. Pakistan's nuclear weapons programme has come in for considerable criticism in the West, particularly the United States. According to the Symler and Pressler amendments, the US President has to certify that Pakistan's nuclear programme is peaceful before Congress can authorize aid to the country. During the Afghan-Soviet War, Pakistan's strategic role allowed successive US Presidents to ignore its nuclear capability. But with the end of that war, non-proliferation concerns have again taken precedence. In 1990, President Bush Sr. refused to issue the necessary certification to Congress. Hence military, and eventually economic, aid to Pakistan was cut off. The move led to wide-spread anti-American feeling in Pakistan. The popular perception there was that if the US was

sincere about non-proliferation it would also target other nuclear powers like India and Israel; since it was not doing so, its condemnation of Pakistan must be based on its being a Muslim country.

52. 'Pakistan's mighty Khan' in *Economist* (7 January 1995), p. 54.

53. In the 1993 elections, Islamist parties suffered a 'virtually complete rout'; e.g. Jamaat-i-Islami fielded 80 candidates, but won only 3 seats. Rasul Baksh Rais estimates the Islamist parties combined voter base to be 6% maximum. 'Pakistan: Hope Amidst Turmoil' in *Journal of Democracy* (5 April 1995), p. 139. But as Abbas Rashid notes, 'the political philosophy of the Jama'at seems to have gained more political ground than the party itself,' and that its significance 'is reflected not in the heights of political success which...[*it*] could manage to scale but in the extent to which it relocated the ideological centre of gravity.' 'Pakistan: The Ideological Dimension' in Khan, Asghar (ed.), *op. cit.*, pp. 84–90.

54. See 'Pakistan: The Retailer's Revolt' in *Economist* (16 July 1994), p. 63.

55. Newberg, Paula, 'Dateline Pakistan: Bhutto's Back' in *Foreign Policy* (95: Summer 1994), p. 169.

56. 'No discussion about any compromise formula about the Kashmir issue is to be held. We are very clear. It is on the basis of the UN Resolution', Pakistani Foreign Minister, Sardar Assef Ali, referring to talks scheduled for January 1994 between India and Pakistan. 'Out of the Shadow: Pakistan pleased with global attention on Kashmir' in *Far Eastern Economic Review* (23 December 1993), p. 23.

57. Ballard, Roger, 'Kashmir Crisis: View from Mirpur' in *Economic and Political Weekly* (2–9 March 1991), p. 517.

58. Ibid., p. 123.

59. Manchanda, Rita, 'Frozen Waste: Mountain campaign shows little sign of ending' in *Far Eastern Economic Review* (26 November 1992), pp. 28–30.

60. Wirsing (1991), *op. cit.*, p. 170.

7

THE ISLAMIC RESURGENCE:
INFLUENCE ON KASHMIR

The rise of Islamic consciousness among Kashmiri Muslims has already been referred to in previous chapters. While this partly arose in reaction to internal developments (within the State and in India) it should also be viewed as part of a Muslim world-wide Islamic resurgence.

The Muslim world has, for some years now, been witnessing an Islamic resurgence: in private worship, culture, education, economics and politics. While these different aspects are closely inter-related, it is the political aspect of the Islamic resurgence that is particularly relevant to this study. This chapter will begin by looking at the relationship—both theoretical (ideal) and historical—between religion and politics in Islam. After a general description of the current revival of political Islam throughout the Muslim world, it will examine the causes of this revival.

It will then assess the influence of the Islamic resurgence on the Muslims of Kashmir: Which causes of the Islamic resurgence are applicable to Kashmir? How marked has the rise in Islamic consciousness been among Kashmiri Muslims? How has it been manifested? How has raised Islamic consciousness among Kashmiri Muslims affected their relations with the Pandit community, and their political goals?

Islam and Politics

In order to understand the relationship between politics and Islam, one must first appreciate that the latter does not recognize any separation into 'secular' and 'religious': everything comes under the mandate of religion. Hence, as well as providing guidance for personal worship and salvation, Islam also has detailed rules governing social relations, law, economics and politics. The Islamic state (i.e. Islamic government) is perhaps the most important practical component of the Islamic world-view. This is because through the agency of state government Islam can determine all other aspects of the life of the *ummah*, or Muslim community: social and criminal laws, finance and banking, foreign policy, etc. Sayyid Qutb, leader of Egypt's Muslim Brotherhood, summed up its significance:

> If Islam is to be effective, it is inevitable that it must rule…. It has come that it may govern life and administer it and mould society according to its total image of life, not by preaching or guidance alone but also by setting of laws and regulations.[1]

The ideal Islamic government differs markedly from traditional concepts of government, in that its role is not to formulate or determine policies, but merely to implement in practice what has already been laid down in the Quran, *Sunna* (sayings and practice of the Prophet Muhammad PBUH), and *Sharia* (Islamic law). The first Islamic state, regarded by most Muslims as the ideal or model state, was set up by the Prophet Muhammad (PBUH) in seventh century Madina. Following the death of the Prophet, the state expanded rapidly into an empire, governed until AD 661 by his successors, the four 'rightly guided' caliphs. It was at this point, with the establishment of the hereditary Ummayyad dynasty, that the drift away from the 'ideal' began. The Ummayyads were followed by the Abbasids, also hereditary rulers. By the end of the Abbasid period the caliphate had become a token institution, stripped of any real power. It was formally ended in the thirteenth century. In its place a number of regional ruling dynasties emerged, e.g. the Mughals in the Indian Subcontinent, the Saffavids in Persia, and the Ottomans in Turkey (who actually retained the title of Caliph). The splitting of the *ummah* marked a further drift away from the Madinan ideal.

But it would be a mistake to conclude that the Islamic state ended with the death of the fourth caliph, Ali. Certainly the 'ideal' Islamic state ended. But, apart from the introduction of hereditary succession in place of rule by the 'most pious', the Umayyads and Abbasids retained most aspects of the original Islamic state. Their legal, judicial and educational systems, for example, continued to be run according to Islamic guidelines. Thus the essential unity of state and religion was maintained, and—by and large—this was also true of the various dynasties that succeeded them. 'Thus, from Muhammad's (PBUH) seventh-century Arabia to the dawn of European colonialism in the sixteenth century, Islam was an ascendant and expansionist religio-political movement in which religion was part and parcel of both private and public life.'[2] As Esposito indicates, it was only with colonization, and the introduction of Western concepts of law, justice and education, that religion was formally separated from the state and confined to the sphere of private worship.

In summary, Islam envisages an integral relationship between religion and politics. In practice, the 'ideal' Islamic state (that of the Prophet and first four caliphs) was a relatively short-lived affair. But, for many centuries after it, Islam continued to play a major role in public life in the Muslim world.

Twentieth Century Political Islam

As Western legal, judicial, educational, economic and political systems became established in the Muslim colonies, the role of Islam was increasingly limited to personal faith and worship; it was no longer seen as relevant to public life. Initially, this process was carried out by the ruling Western powers, but, as Muslims acquired Western education, a new class of native

Westernized elites emerged who colluded in the restriction of Islam to private worship. Providing a modern education did, however, also 'back-fire' on the colonial powers, because their newly-educated subjects then began demanding for themselves the self-determination, freedom and democracy they had been taught were enjoyed elsewhere in the world. Educated elites were at the forefront of independence movements throughout the Muslim world.

Many of the Muslim independence movements were based on nationalist ideologies imported from the West: nationhood on the grounds of territory, language, shared (myth of) descent and history, etc. But some also made use of a common religion, i.e. Islam. The use of Islam in anti-colonial independence movements marked the first significant reappearance of political Islam in the twentieth century. The most obvious example that springs to mind is, of course, that of the Pakistan Movement in the Indian subcontinent. Here the claim to nationhood by Indian Muslims was based solely on their shared belief in Islam. Jinnah argued that this was enough to make them incompatible with the majority Hindu population, and to justify their own, separate homeland. Elsewhere, although the role of Islam was not as primary, it did help promote separate identities on which claims for independence were then based, e.g. in Morocco, Tunisia and Algeria.

After the shake-off of colonial rule, it was generally the educated, Westernized elites who acquired power in the new nation-states of the Muslim world. As indicated above, they had no desire to create Islamic states, or even to involve Islam in public life. Indeed the new rulers 'judged Islam as either the cause of Muslim decline or as incapable of meeting the new demands of modern life.'[3] Rapid modernization, westernization and secularization were seen as the key to 'catching up' with the West. Even in those countries where Islam had played a significant role in independence movements, it was generally excluded from post-colonial public life. One can only conclude from this that Islam had merely been used by leaders as a mobilizational tool to drum up popular support for independence, and as a unifying force—something that could overcome divisive regional and linguistic differences.

Islam made a return to public life in the 1950s and 60s. But again it was used merely as a political tool, this time to legitimize the rule of those in power. Nasser of Egypt exemplified this trend. When Nasser took power in 1952, he continued with the Western, secular approach to the state adopted by his predecessors. However, challenges at home from Hassan al-Banna's Muslim Brotherhood, plus a desire to win wider Arab support, caused Nasser to draw Islam into politics. His shift towards Islam was also acknowledgement of Islam's continued huge influence over the majority of Egypt's population: 'Islam remained the widest and most effective basis for consensus despite all efforts to promote nationalism, patriotism, secularism and socialism.'[4] Nasser's successor, Anwar Sadat, initially appealed to Islam as well in order to 'enhance his own political legitimacy', though he later abandoned it in favour of autocratic rule when the demands by Muslim groups for genuine implementation of Islamic law (as opposed to mere rhetoric) became too persistent. Colonel Gaddafi of Libya seized power in a military coup in 1969. He, too, 'turned to Islam for popular support and legitimation', e.g. banning alcohol and gambling, and introducing *zakat* and Islamic criminal laws (though implementation was highly limited). In the 1970s, Zulfikar Ali Bhutto's rule in Pakistan followed a similar pattern to that of Nasser's. As opposition from the Jamaat-i-Islami mounted, Bhutto toned down his socialist rhetoric and promoted Islam, e.g. announcing the banning of alcohol, and closing of nightclubs.

The general picture which emerges is of Muslim rulers recognizing that attempts at westernization and secularization imposed from above had not succeeded in altering the Islamic outlook of the vast majority of their populations.[5] This in turn led them, when they felt their power threatened, to draw on Islam as a means of legitimizing their rule and gaining popular support. Esposito sums up the trend: 'It was a partial retreat by political leaders in a number of countries from a secular, political path as they selectively appealed to Islam for legitimation and support.'[6]

Contemporary Islamic Resurgence

The reassertion of religio-cultural identity in public as well as personal life has become a major factor in contemporary Muslim life and politics at the national and international levels.[7]

[I]t is hard to think that a movement of this kind has ever been simultaneously so intense and widespread as is the case today.[8]

As explained in the introduction to this chapter, this study is largely concerned with the resurgence of political Islam, and its consequences. So, is it true to say that the Muslim world is witnessing a resurgence of political Islam, one that genuinely desires Islamic government, as opposed to the rhetorical use of Islam in the 1950s/60s? Consider the evidence.

Looking at North Africa first, in Algeria the Islamic Salvation Front (FIS) won the regional elections held in June 1989; with 49 per cent of the vote in the first round of national elections in December 1991, it appeared headed for victory. However, the government cancelled the second round, and in February 1992 the military took power and banned the party. Since then the FIS has been waging a violent campaign against the military regime. Members of the Islamic Jihad assassinated Egypt's Anwar Sadat in 1981. In elections held there in 1987, the Muslim Brotherhood (with its coalition partners) formed the largest opposition group. Islamic militants have for some years been waging an FIS-style campaign against the government (also targeting foreign tourists), which has responded with harsh repression. Sudan, following a military coup in 1989, moved increasingly towards an Islamic government guided by Hassan al-Turabi, leader of Sudan's Muslim Brotherhood. Sudan has also established much closer links with Iran.

The Islamic resurgence has also been felt in Europe. In Turkey, attempts by Kemal Ataturk in the first half of the twentieth century to secularize the country largely failed. While political and legal institutions are still run on Western lines, Islamic consciousness in the population is rising. The Islamically-oriented Welfare Party until recently formed the government. In Bosnia, religious consciousness has increased hugely among the previously very Westernized Muslims there. Bosnian Muslims have far more contact with other parts of the Muslim world; they received financial, medical and most probably military aid from Muslim countries during the war.

Turning to the Arab world, Islam was the main trigger behind the Palestinian *intifada* in the late 1980s. Militant Islamic groups, notably Hamas and Islamic Jihad, have attracted great support, particularly among the young. This has prompted the previously secular PLO to adopt a more Islamic stance. Though ruled by a monarchy, Saudi Arabia has, for decades, been a fundamentalist Islamic state, carrying out Islamic punishments for example, and enforcing *purdah* in public. However, the regime is increasingly coming under attack from Islamic groups that want to see greater implementation of Islam, even challenging the monarchy itself. The government's response has largely been to repress such opposition.

Finally, in Asia the Shah of Iran was overthrown in 1979 by an Islamic Revolution, headed by Ayatollah Khomeini. Secular and moderate Islamic elements, also opposed to the Shah, were harshly repressed by the conservative Shia government that succeeded him. The Iranian government's declared aim is to 'export the Revolution'; it is an active supporter of Islamic militant groups (Shia, but recently Sunni as well) in other Muslim countries. Pakistan, under General Zia's martial law regime, embarked on an Islamization programme (although implementation has been piecemeal). All political parties in the current parliamentary democracy use Islamic rhetoric, but the main advocate of Islamic government is still the Jamaat-i-Islami, founded by Maulana Maudoodi in the early 1940s. In Afghanistan, opposition to the communist regime that took power in 1978, and its Soviet backers, who invaded soon after, was characterized as a *jihad*, or holy war. Following the defeat of the Soviets, fundamentalist Islamic groups engaged in a bitter civil war; the ultra-conservative student movement, Taliban, was until recently in control of most of the country, including Kabul.

The answer to the question posed above must therefore be: yes, political Islam is undergoing a resurgence in the Muslim world. Two aspects of this resurgence are noteworthy: one, its geographical range, stretching from North Africa, through the Middle East and into South and Central Asia—even penetrating Europe; and, two, its intensity—often manifesting itself as violent conflict. A further point to stress is that contemporary political Islam is not a monolithic phenomenon. The brief descriptions given above show the extent to which it varies from one context to the next.

Causes of Contemporary Islamic Resurgence

Numerous theories have been presented to explain the rise of political Islam in the Muslim world today. The most plausible ones are considered below:

Search for Identity

The Muslim world is facing an identity crisis. On the one hand, identities imposed from above by ruling elites, generally based on secular, territorial nationalism, have failed to make a deep impression on Muslim populations. The fact that many of the new Muslim states had no pre-colonial history, i.e. that they only acquired their present form (borders) as a result of colonization, is probably a major reason for this. On the other hand, Muslims are facing an increasing challenge from Western culture and values. Modernization, increased global communications, the wide availability of television, video and satellite dishes, and migration from rural to urban settings, all have increased their exposure to the non-Muslim world. The result, many Muslims feel, has been detrimental to their own culture and values.

Islam offers a solution to both these aspects of the identity crisis.

With respect to national identity, Islam firstly represents an authentic, indigenous identity; not one imported from abroad. Further, it is an identity rooted deep in the past, and, because of the former Islamic empire, is a source of pride and self-respect for Muslims. Secondly, within Muslim states, Islam is often the single, common, unifying factor in otherwise ethnically/ linguistically diverse populations.[9] The success of the FIS in Algeria, for example, has been attributed to the fact that 'only... Islam—the religion of virtually all Algerians—has succeeded in obscuring the cultural divisions evoked by other parties.'[10]

With respect to the challenge of Western civilization, the recent Islamic resurgence 'is a response to the confusion and anxiety of modernity.'[11] It is important to bear in mind that, accompanying the rise of political Islam, there has been an increase in religious observance manifested, for example, in greater attendance at mosques and observation of Ramadan, increased mosque-building, more women opting for *purdah*, spread of Islamic literature, etc. All of these could be interpreted as attempts by Muslims to preserve their own values and culture, and prevent the erosion of their traditional family and social life by modernization.

In summary, then, the recent resurgence of Islam is, in the words of Vatikiotis, the 'assertion', of an Islamic cultural-political identity that wishes to distinguish, separate itself from, and challenge another internationally dominant imprint of world modernity, based on Western industrial (Christian) civilization.'[12]

Socio-Economic Problems

Many parts of the Muslim world are facing serious socio-economic problems: rapidly increasing populations, unemployment, urban overcrowding, and a growing rich-poor gap.[13] The modernization agenda adopted by many post-independence Muslim leaders, while raising popular expectations, has exacerbated rather than alleviated these problems. As a result western models of development (both capitalism and socialism) are now widely perceived as having been inappropriate for Muslim countries.[14] In their place, the appeal of Islamic government as the solution to socio-economic problems, is growing.[15]

This socio-economic explanation for the resurgence of Islam is borne out by two observations. One, that the Islamist alternative attracts greater support in those countries where the government's socio-economic failures are most pronounced.[16] Two, that within any population it is the socio-economically backward sectors that are most receptive to Islamic ideology.

The appeal of political Islam as an economic panacea is enhanced by the fact that many Islamic groups (e.g. Egypt's Gema'a al-Islamiyya and Hezbollah in Lebanon) run their own networks of schools, clinics, and hospitals. They are thus seen in a favourable light compared to governments that have failed to provide such facilities. Also, the majority of Islamists active in the contemporary resurgence have made a clear distinction between modern science and technology, which they support, and westernization and secularization, which they reject. By making this distinction, they present a vision of the future in which modernization is possible without loss of traditional values.

Political Failures: Lack of Democracy

The lack of democracy in most Muslim countries, or at least its presence in highly limited forms, is cited as a major factor in the rise of political Islam.[17] Press censorship, banning of political parties, suppression of opposition, and human rights abuses are commonplace in much of the Muslim world. In such circumstances, especially where there is no 'secular' opposition, the only outlets for public anger against the government are religious groups and institutions.

Muslim governments, as a rule, are unwilling to come down visibly hard on religious leaders and mosques for fear of provoking a backlash among their highly religious populations. Even where they do try to curb Islamic groups, their measures tend only to restrict the more moderate ones. If anything, such an approach makes it easier for militant, fundamentalist groups to attract support. William Dalrymple claims that this is what has caused the rise of the Muslim Brotherhood and, more recently, the militant Gema'a al-Islamiyya in Egypt: 'because there is thus no real secular opposition and the popular religious parties are all banned, the extremist groups attract an inordinate number of adherents for the lack of any more reasonable way to oppose the regime.'[18] The same could be said of most Muslim countries. In the words of the *Economist*:

> If the government of a Muslim country clings doggedly to power, growing more corrupt and inept by the year and allowing no safety-valve for opposition, the steam will escape through the mosques...most Arab regimes have no time for a free vote, and not much for free expression. This gives Islamic preachers the field to themselves in voicing opposition, and Islamic militants a spur to violence.[19]

In summary, then, political Islam derives its support from the fact that it fills an 'opposition-vacuum'—one created, ironically, by the very regimes it opposes.

Triggered by Specific Events

According to this view, the current wave of political Islam was triggered by specific events in the seventies, with subsequent developments acting as catalysts for its growth.

The 1967 Arab-Israeli War is considered significant, because the defeat of the Arabs effectively finished Arab nationalism (pan-Arabism) as a viable political ideology and source of identity for Arab Muslims. In addition, its main proponent,

Nasser, died in 1970. But it is 1973 that is generally regarded as the year the resurgence 'began'. Two related events in that year, the Arab-Israeli War and the oil embargo imposed by Muslim states, were seen to have restored Muslim pride and dignity. Egypt achieved significant initial victories against Israel in the 1973 War; the eventual defeat of the Arab forces was widely attributed to American assistance of the Jewish state, and hence did not detract from the early successes. Sadat used Islamic terminology during the war, thereby ensuring it was not seen as a nationalist struggle but as a Muslim versus non-Muslim one— as a *jihad*. This, in turn, won him the support of the entire Muslim world, and allowed all Muslims—not just Egyptians, or Arabs—to feel pride in his achievements. While the '73 War restored military pride, the '73 oil embargo was seen as restoring Muslim political and economic power after centuries of Western colonial (and post-colonial) domination.

Perhaps the single most important contributory event took place six years later: the Iranian Revolution of 1979. It marked the first real return to power of Islam,[20] demonstrating that Islam was still a 'vital, political and spiritual force.'[21] It raised the level of debate about Islam and politics/state, from the level of hypothetical theorizing to that of practical implementation. However, its greatest significance lay in its huge impact on thinking throughout the Muslim world:

> Even Muslims who were non-political, or had no definite political affiliation, felt renewed confidence in the political relevance of Islam, in the capacity of the Muslim world to regain its economic and cultural as well as political independence and to assert itself as a force in world affairs.[22]

The pro-Islam shift in Muslim populations, inspired by the Iranian revolution, forced their leaders to also take a more Islamic stance, at least in their rhetoric: 'they were liable to feel that a greater emphasis on Islam (however interpreted) in their own policies would be a useful prophylactic. No one would want to repeat the Shah's mistake of underrating Islam as a political factor.'[23]

The Iranian revolution has also had a far more direct impact on other Muslim countries. From its inception, the Islamic Iranian government has actively pursued its goal to 'export the Revolution internationally.' This has generally taken the form of training and of financing indigenous militant groups, e.g. the Hezbollah in Lebanon.

[Note: despite its undoubted huge impact on the Muslim world, the Iranian Revolution would perhaps have been even more significant, had it not been based on Shia Islam (most Muslims are Sunnis), and had the government not implemented Khomeini's very conservative interpretation of Islam.]

A second event, beginning in 1979, was the Afghan war. Directed against the ruling communists and their Soviet backers, this was always regarded—both by the Afghans, and by Muslims elsewhere—as a holy war, or *jihad*. 'The resistance of the Afghan mujahideen is essentially by definition motivated by a commitment to defend Islam.'[24] The aim of the *mujahideen* was not just to free their country from the Soviets, but also to establish an Islamic government in Afghanistan.[25] Overall, the Soviet invasion served to radicalize Islam in Afghanistan, a process encouraged by the Zia government's patronage of fundamentalist *mujahideen*, in preference to the more moderate resistance groups.

Like the Iranian revolution, the Afghan resistance helped Muslims to once again see Islam as a political ideology—not just as a religion. But its greatest impact was undoubtedly on militant (activist, violent) Islam. The Soviet retreat from Afghanistan and the subsequent break-up of the USSR—perceived by many Muslims as a consequence of the former—demonstrated the military power of Islam; the potency of war waged in the name of Islam as opposed to secular ideologies like nationalism.[26] If Islam could defeat a superpower, could it not also topple un-Islamic regimes? On a more practical level, the Afghan war—which attracted considerable numbers of '*mujahideen*' from other parts of the Muslim world—helped produce an international force of trained, experienced and often armed militant Muslims. On returning to their various homelands, they made use of their experience in Afghanistan to promote militant Islam in those countries.[27] Furthermore, once the Soviets had gone and the Afghan resistance had degenerated into a civil war, many redundant fighters—having acquired a taste for *jihad*—actively sought new arenas to continue it, e.g. Bosnia.

During the 1990s, two developments fuelled the Islamic resurgence: the Gulf War and the conflict in Bosnia.

The significance of the Gulf War lay not in Iraq's invasion of Kuwait, but in the nature of the offensive mounted in retaliation throughout the Muslim world:

> Religious concerns—the deployment of non-Muslim troops in the land of the Holy Places for the first time since the time of the Prophet—were combined with nationalist ones as the involvement of the West awakened deep-seated antipathy towards 'imperialist' intentions for the region.[28]

Muslim resentment was directed both against the West, and against those Muslim regimes that had invited Western involvement, notably the Saudi government. The West, as well as exploiting the situation to its own advantage, was seen by Muslims as having double standards: where the principle of freedom coincided with Western interests (in this case, oil) it was upheld, but where there was no such coincidence, or where it conflicted with other interests (notably in the Palestinian struggle against Israel), it was ignored. The major Muslim participants in the anti-Iraq alliance, Saudi Arabia and Kuwait, were condemned for having sacrificed their countries' economic and political integrity in order to preserve their own hold on power.[29] Inevitably, both strands of resentment took an Islamic orientation.

In contrast to Western 'interference' in the Gulf War, it was the West's perceived inaction over the conflict in Bosnia that boosted political (and militant) Islam. The failure of Western powers to actively support the Bosnian Muslims (e.g. refusing to lift the arms embargo) was interpreted in the Muslim world:

a) as further proof of Western double standards with respect to defending freedom, and b) as evidence of anti-Muslim feeling in the West: 'that the US fears the possibility of even a secular-Islamic mini-state within Europe's boundaries.'[30] The result has been, a heightening of Islamic consciousness among Bosnian Muslims,[31] and in the Muslim world, generally, a further shift towards seeing Islam as a political force.

Disillusionment with the West

This can be summed up as the conviction among Muslims that the West is not sincere towards them (even its dealings with 'allies' like Saudi Arabia are actually based on self-interest), and that it actively opposes their gaining power. Disillusionment with the West has helped generate the contemporary Islamic resurgence.

The conviction that the West is anti-Muslim is based, in part, on specific events alluded to above: namely, the Gulf War and the conflict in Bosnia. But it is also based on more general, and more long-term factors. The general factor is the West's perceived double standard on democracy: while generally upholding the principle of democratic rule, where its own interests are at stake, or where it fears democracy would bring in an Islamic government, the West condones undemocratic regimes. Mushahid Hussain forcibly makes this point:

> Simply because an Islamic party was winning, Algeria declared a state of emergency after the recent elections; and the West acquiesced. In contrast, the West's continued support for Saudi King Fahd despite his refusal to allow free elections in the kingdom underlines the West's preference for authoritarian regimes over popularly elected Islamic democracy.[32]

The *Economist* acknowledges that there is some truth in this argument: 'There is now a growing danger of the West falling into the dreary cold-war trap of keeping tinpot dictators in power because of the service they do in keeping undesirables down.'[33]

The long-term factor provoking anti-Western sentiments among Muslims is its—and especially the United States'—sustained support for the state of Israel. Not surprisingly, the creation of a Jewish state in the heart of the Arab world, in the process depriving the Palestinians of their homeland, arouses strong Muslim sentiments. Muslim leaders are beginning to show political pragmatism by acknowledging that Israel will not go away and hence striving to make peace with it. But among their populations' resentment toward the Jewish state and its American backers remains high. Zionism, and Western support for it, has been a major contributory factor in the rise of political Islam.

The extent to which accusations are justified, that the West is anti-Muslim, is a matter for the reader's own judgement. However, following the collapse of communism as a major world power, there definitely appears to be a trend towards portraying Islam as the next threat ('bogey-adversary') to the West. This is especially evident in media coverage of the Muslim world.[34] It could be argued that such presentation, firstly, influences Western governments to respond to the 'challenge' posed by Islam, and to try to curb it, and secondly, becomes self-fulfilling in provoking radical forms of Islam even where not found previously.[35]

Islamic Reform Movements

Throughout Islamic history reform movements have periodically emerged to revitalize the Muslim *ummah*. The word 'reform' is used here to include both revivalist movements that sought a return to the Islam of the Prophet's time, and those movements that actually tried to change Islam—or to be more accurate, its practical implementation—so that it was better suited to contemporary conditions. Both types have contributed to the Islamic modernist movements that are having a huge impact on the current Islamic resurgence.

Revivalist movements date back to pre-colonial times, and were a response to the 'internal decay' (i.e. un-Islamic practices) of the Muslim community. These included Muhammad ibn Abd al-Wahab's 'puritan' movement in Arabia; Shah Wali Ullah's in post-Aurangzeb Mughal India; and the various Mahdist movements in North Africa. Besides being directed against 'corrupt' rulers, these also aimed to rid Islamic worship of accretions acquired from non-Muslims, notably the practice of venerating saints and their tombs, and the trend towards mysticism. Revivalist movements were important because they reasserted the primary role of religion and stressed that the 'socio-moral revival of Islamic society required political action.'[36]

Modernist movements emerged largely in response to Western colonialism. They called for the reassertion of Muslim identity and unification of the *ummah* to face 'European imperialism.' However, they did not reject the West completely; Muslims were urged to take advantage of modern science and technology. This approach—a blend of revivalism and modernism—was first propagated by Jamal al-Din al-Afghani, in the nineteenth century, and later by his disciples, Muhammad Abduh and Rashid Rida. In India, Sir Sayed Ahmed Khan, founder of the Aligarh College for Muslims, and Muhammad Iqbal, deviated somewhat from Afghani's pan-Islamist ideology by endorsing nationalism.[37] Apart from their acceptance of Western science, the main difference between Afghani, Sayed Ahmed Khan, Iqbal, and revivalists like Abd al-Wahab, lay in the former's calls for socio-legal reform. Without contradicting the Quran and *Sunna*, they urged changes in the laws that had been derived from these sources by religious scholars of previous times, so that these could be applied more suitably to their own, changed societies. Esposito sums up the significance of modernists like Afghani and Iqbal:

[they] paved the way for contemporary Islamic activism by alerting the Islamic community to the dangers of Western domination and arguing for a modernity grounded in Islam...[t]hey rekindled an

awareness of the totality of Islam, the integral relationship of religion to all areas of life—politics, law and society. They restored pride in Islamic history and civilisation and, by extension, acceptance of reason, philosophy, modern science and technology.[38]

Turning to the twentieth century, the ideology and organization underpinning the current mainstream Islamic resurgence can be attributed largely to three thinkers and the movements they founded. The thinkers were Hassan al-Banna and Sayyid Qutb, both of Egypt, and Maulana Maudoodi of Pakistan; the movements being, Ikhwan al-Muslimeen (Muslim Brotherhood) and Jamaat-i-Islami.

Hassan al-Banna regarded Westernization as a threat both to Islam and to Egypt. The solution he proposed to combat it was a return to 'pure' Islam (i.e. the Quran and *Sunna*) as faith and as the basis of the state. To implement his ideas, he formed the Muslim Brotherhood in 1928. This was more than just an ideological organization; it was also a socio-welfare organization with its own social clubs, schools, clinics and hospitals. It thus reflected Hassan al-Banna's belief in the relevance of religion to all aspects of life, and his philosophy of achieving an Islamic state by changing society (the outlook of the masses), rather than through revolution carried out by a minority—i.e. from the bottom up, rather than top down. The Muslim Brotherhood was banned by the Egyptian government in 1948, and (apart from brief periods of freedom) has remained so to the present day, members operating either underground or from exile. Hassan al-Banna was himself exiled to England in 1949, where he died soon after (Egypt's secret police were widely held responsible for his death).

Perhaps even more influential than al-Banna was another Muslim Brotherhood leader, Sayyid Qutb. Qutb held far more militant views than al-Banna, advocating *jihad* to achieve Islamic rule. In 1964, the Egyptian government executed him, but his influence persists through his numerous writings.

Maulana Maudoodi probably resembled al-Banna more than Qutb in his thinking. The most prolific writer of the three, he was also the most specific among them in outlining exactly what Islamic rule entailed, e.g. the form of government, constitution, economic system, law. In order to achieve his vision of an Islamic society, Maudoodi founded the Jamaat-i-Islami in India in 1941, moving to Pakistan in 1947. Membership of the Jamaat was based strictly on religious integrity and an understanding of Islam. The Jamaat does provide some social services, mainly educational, but it is primarily an ideological organization and a political party, actively participating in Pakistani politics. As yet it has only achieved limited electoral success. However, in its other role, as propagator of Maudoodi's ideology, it has made some impact on Pakistani society. This appears likely to increase in future because of the work of the Jamaat's student organization, the Jamiat-i-Tulaba. Favouring a more revolutionary approach than the Jamaat, the Jamiat has been successful in student politics. More significantly, it has acquired a firm ideological following among Pakistani students. These are the bureaucrats, businessmen, military officers, doctors, etc., of tomorrow; it is highly likely that this influential group will then seek to implement Maudoodi's ideas. In the words of Sayyed Nasr: 'They have become the vehicles for a gradual, yet fundamental, process of cultural engineering—the crux of Maudoodi's original programme—which has far greater social and ultimately political ramifications than the immediate gains of Jamiat.'[39]

The widespread availability of Islamic literature means that, although all three are now dead, the influence of al-Banna, Qutb and Maudoodi not only persists, but in fact extends far beyond their native lands. With respect to organization, the Muslim Brotherhood and the Jamaat-i-Islami have served as models for Islamic groups in other Muslim countries. The former, in particular, has inspired Brotherhoods elsewhere (e.g. Hassan al-Turabi's in Sudan) and has promoted transnational links between Islamic organizations. Dekmejian notes that 'more than any other factor or organization, the Brotherhood and its affiliates have contributed to Islamic reawakening at the mass level throughout the Arab world...the Brotherhood has created a massive constituency of politically conscious Muslims.'[40]

Neighbours: Pakistan, Afghanistan, Iran

The role of Islam in these three countries has already been discussed at various points, but since these are Jammu and Kashmir's closest Muslim neighbours it would be useful to take a closer look.

Pakistan

The official drive for Islamization was initiated by Ziaul Haq after he ousted Prime Minister Zulfiqar Ali Bhutto in a military coup in July 1977. More than any previous ruler Zia pushed Pakistan in the direction of an Islamic state. Initially, he received the backing of religious parties such as the Jamaat-i-Islami. However, the limited nature of Zia's Islamization agenda— excluding the issue of government completely—and its only partial implementation, eventually alienated these groups.

Zia was killed in 1988, but by then the reforms initiated by him had become established and they persist to the present day. Two aspects of Zia's 'legacy' are particularly significant. One, the increased emphasis on religious education—seen both within mainstream state and private schools, and in the huge numbers of new *madrasas* (religious schools). Some of the latter emphasize Islamic as well as modern knowledge.[41] Thus, as with the Jamiat-i-Tulaba at university level, they are moulding a new generation of educated Pakistanis committed to Islamic rule. Two, the Islamization of politics. No political party in Pakistan today can afford to ignore Islam; none would dare to present itself as 'secular'. Indeed, most actually make liberal use of Islamic rhetoric, aware that the majority of Pakistanis are still highly religious.

A disturbing consequence of the rise of political Islam in Pakistan has been the increase in sectarian violence. Though largely Shia-Sunni, there have also been clashes between various Sunni factions.[42] Outside factors have contributed to this development: the main Shia party, Tehrik-i-Fiqah Jafria, receives support from Iran, and the Sunni Sipah-e-Sahaba Pakistan from Saudi Arabia. Finally, the Afghan War, a *jihad*, waged just across the border, had a tremendous impact on Pakistani society. Ideologically, it raised Islamic consciousness; practically, it encouraged Islamic militancy.

Afghanistan

As mentioned previously, the struggle against the Soviets served to radicalize Islam—already very conservative—in Afghanistan. Secular and moderate Islamic voices have been almost completely silenced. The victorious *mujahideen* engaged in civil war after the Soviets' departure, were not fighting over ideology—all agreed with Islamic rule—but for the right to implement that ideology, i.e. for power. The student movement, known as the Taliban, that controlled much of the country from the mid-1990s including the capital Kabul, was the most fundamentalist of all the groups. The *Guardian* reported that 'the Taliban brand of Islam is puritanical and regressive. Women in areas under their control have been told to stay indoors. Men have been told to grow beards. Even non-Muslim foreigners are obliged to join their prayer sessions five times a day.'[43]

Iran

Since the revolution in 1979 that toppled the Shah, Iran has been run by a conservative, Shia version of Islamic government. Condemnation of the West, particularly the United States, and of un-Islamic rulers in the Muslim world is a hallmark of the regime. One of its oft-stated ambitions is replication of the

Islamic Revolution in other Muslim countries. To this end, Iran actively supports a wide range of Islamic militant groups; from Lebanon's Hezbollah, and the Palestinian group Hamas, to Pakistan's Tehrik-i-Fiqah Jafria. In spite of the Iranian government's professed unselfish motives in helping other Muslims, it would perhaps be more accurate to describe its efforts as part of its struggle with Wahabiist (puritan, Sunni) Saudi Arabia for domination of the Muslim world. Since the death of Ayatollah Khomeini, the Iranian government has extended its support to Sunni groups, for example co-operating closely with the Muslim Brotherhood in Sudan.

In summary then, of Jammu and Kashmir's three closest Muslim neighbours, one has already achieved Islamic government through revolution, a second was until recently under very extreme Islamic rule, and the third is experiencing a resurgence of political Islam. These regional developments are, of course, taking place against the backdrop of political Islamic resurgence throughout the Muslim world.

The Islamic Resurgence in Kashmir

Causes of the Contemporary Islamic Resurgence Applicable to Kashmir

The various causes of the contemporary resurgence of Islam, in particular, political Islam, throughout the Muslim world have been described. These will now be reviewed in the context of Kashmir to see which are relevant there.

Consider, first, the search for identity. Kashmiris have not been immune to the influence of Western culture—music, films, alcohol, gambling, free inter-mixing of the sexes, etc. Returning to Islam is thus a way for them to preserve their traditional values from erosion. With respect to identity, being Muslim is one of the most significant things differentiating them from India's Hindu majority. Disillusionment with India, and a desire to cut off links with India, would therefore, almost automatically, lead them to stress the Islamic part of their identity. [In the converse scenario of their wishing to draw closer to India, Kashmiris would stress those aspects of their culture that they shared with other Indians.]

It could, of course, be argued that, as well as Islam, there are other things differentiating Kashmiris from other Indians—language and culture, for instance—and that they could just as likely stress this '*Kashmiriyat*' to highlight their distinctiveness. The counter-argument to this would be that, firstly, *Kashmiriyat* is something only the Valley Muslims can properly identify with—but disillusionment with India is felt by the state's other Muslims as well. The only thing, apart from shared history, that can unite all Jammu and Kashmir's Muslims is Islam. Secondly, as will be seen below, there are several other factors pushing Kashmiris down the Islamic rather than the *Kashmiriyat* route.

Turning to socio-economic problems, as seen in the last chapter, Kashmir's economy is in serious trouble. It is heavily dependent on India: there has been very little industrial development within the state, there are large numbers of unemployed graduates with little prospect of getting good jobs, and a middle class has emerged with high expectations. In some other Muslim societies, people became receptive to Islamic economic ideas, after having tried both 'Western' economic ideologies, capitalism and socialism, and seen them fail to deliver results. The situation in Kashmir is somewhat different in that, with the exception of some of Sheikh Abdullah's early socialist reforms, Kashmiri administrations have generally been too busy lining their own pockets to seriously implement either capitalist or socialist economic agendas. Thus, for Kashmiris, turning to Islam represents not so much conviction in the Islamic economic system, as frustration at socio-economic conditions. This frustration causes them to look for ways to express opposition to the government, and one way is, through Islam.

Lack of democracy has been a major factor in the Islamic resurgence in Kashmir. As seen in other Muslim countries, when democracy is weak and political opposition suppressed, the mosque becomes an important venue for venting anger at rulers.

'Lack of democracy' in Kashmir is a general term referring to the persistent rigging of elections (with the exception of 1977), the banning of political parties, detention of opposition leaders, curbs on press freedom, etc. But there are two specific factors, both to do with the electoral process, that have been particularly important in causing Kashmiris to express their opposition to India in Islamic terms.

The first, not strictly undemocratic, was the National Conference's alliance with Congress in 1987. Until it formed that alliance, the National Conference had represented—in theory, if not in practice—the non-communal aspects of Kashmiri identity (as opposed to the Islamic). By allying itself with Congress, it effectively removed itself from the political scene, and consequently left Kashmiris wishing to oppose New Delhi with no non-communal Kashmiri party to support. A vacuum emerged in Kashmiri opposition politics, which was filled by Islam-oriented parties, such as Jamaat-i-Islami.

The second factor was the rigging of the 1987 elections, depriving the Muslim United Front of seats (and possibly outright victory). Until then, the Islamic opposition to India that had emerged in Kashmir had operated within the political arena. After 1987, it shifted to the militant arena. In this sense what happened in Kashmir was a repetition of what had already happened in, for instance, Egypt. By cutting off all other avenues of opposition, the Indian authorities could be said to have left Kashmiris with no option, but to go down the militant Islam route.

In brief, then, of the two specific factors described above, the first paved the way for political Islamic opposition, the second for this to be transformed into militant Islamic opposition.

A further element, not generally found in other Muslim societies, was lack of state autonomy. Kashmir had been guaranteed a high degree of autonomy from the centre in Article 370. In practice, however, not only did New Delhi fail to respect Article 370 but it also introduced a great deal of integrationist legislation that effectively rendered it meaningless. Though having no direct link with the autonomy question, Islam entered the picture because India's actions, with respect to Article 370, caused Kashmiris to be further alienated from India. Their opposition to India increased, and it was through Islam that it found expression. Furthermore, and this applies to both lack of democracy and lack of autonomy, New Delhi's actions caused Kashmiris to ask themselves whether the reason they were being denied these rights was because they were Muslim? Discrimination based on religion (or any trait for that matter) automatically leads to greater identification with that religion or trait.

How influential have events elsewhere in the world, particularly in the Muslim world, been on thinking in Kashmir? The first point to stress is that Kashmiris have, for many years now, been well aware of what is going on in the outside world. On the one hand, the availability of information—through radio, television, satellite dishes, newspapers and journals—has greatly increased. On the other hand, a far larger section of the population is educated and able to take in and appreciate the significance of outside events. Both these developments have combined to make Kashmiris much more politically conscious. Thus, for example, when they hear about an Islamic revolution in Iran, they are able to ask themselves if the same thing would be possible in Kashmir? Akbar criticizes the freedom of the press for this very reason:

In Delhi, Doordarshan, still excited about its pyrrhic post-Congress flexibility, went overboard with live coverage of the mass movements against authoritarianism in East Europe and Central Asia, inanely oblivious of the tremendous impact each visual of a woman kissing the Quran and taunting a soldier was having on Kashmir.[44]

One transnational event that triggered a huge knock-on reaction in Kashmir was the Afghan War. This was perhaps to be expected, since, unlike the Palestinian *intifada*, for instance, in the remote Middle East, this was something taking place on Kashmir's doorstep. But aside from geographical proximity there are several reasons why the Afghan War had such resonance in Kashmir. Firstly, the relative status of the Afghan *mujahideen* and the Soviet Union was comparable to that of Kashmiri Muslims and India, i.e. weak minority versus strong majority. Secondly, the *mujahideen* waged a struggle and, against the odds, succeeded in forcing the Soviet troops to leave their country. The Afghans thus showed that even though the opposing force might be larger, stronger and better armed, all this did not make it invincible. Thirdly—in the view of many in the Muslim world—it was the actions of the *mujahideen* that eventually led to the break-up of the Soviet Union. If one of the world's two superpowers could be 'destroyed' by a band of guerrillas, why could not the same be done against India? It is not difficult to see how Kashmiri Muslims could be inspired by the Afghan resistance to wage an insurgency against Indian rule:

> A small nation with a small population, with limited resources and weapons rose in revolt against the Soviet onslaught in Afghanistan, to the extent that the Soviet Union ultimately disintegrated into fragments. Out of that five Muslim states emerged as independent states. So we got inspired, if they could offer tough resistance to a superpower in the east, we too could fight India.[45]

The other lesson that many Kashmiri Muslims learnt from Afghanistan, was the importance of waging any struggle in the name of Islam, i.e. a *jihad*. Throughout the Muslim world the Afghan resistance was acknowledged as being more than just a nationalist struggle; it was a struggle of the forces of Islam against those of the unbeliever. And the reason why the Afghans were successful was—in Muslim eyes—because they were fighting for Islam; this ensured they received help from Allah. Similarly, if the Kashmiris wanted 'Allah's help' to win, they would have to fight in Allah's name.

The war in Afghanistan did, of course, also have a direct impact on Kashmir, in that many *mujahideen* left redundant after the departure of the Soviets turned to the Valley as their next *jihad*. It also flooded the whole North-west of the Indian subcontinent with arms, and it created a 'gun culture', which made it far easier to actually become a militant.

Ganguly claims that besides Afghanistan, the Palestinian *intifada* influenced Kashmiri Muslims to adopt a more fundamentalist—and militant—Islam. The reason for this was that a considerable number of Palestinian students studied at the Kashmir University during the 1970s and 1980s. 'These Palestinian students became an important conduit for information about the success of the *intifada* against Israel. Their struggle against the Israeli armed forces in the occupied territories animated many university students in Kashmir.'[46] In his book, *My Frozen Turbulence*, Jagmohan cites a newspaper interview with a militant commander which makes clear the influence of the Afghan and Palestinian struggles:

> The strongest weapon of the Muslim is his faith—Islam. The examples of the people of Afghanistan and Palestine are before us. If the hearts of the Kashmiri Muslims were warmed by the light of Islam, I am confident that we would soon be free.[47]

Wani also highlights the importance of external events in making Kashmiri Muslims more Islam-conscious. He writes that 'although failure of the democratic and secular forces' *(within India)*:

> [have] paved the way for the emergence of Islam as an alternative source of inspiration for the masses, it was only after the consolidation of Zia's regime in Pakistan and Islamic revolutionary struggles...in Iran and Afghanistan that Kashmir also witnessed Islamic resurgence.[48]

Consider next the influence of Islamic reform/revivalist movements. Of the two major (socio-)political Islamic organizations operating in the latter half of the twentieth century, Ikhwan-ul-Muslimeen and Jamaat-i-Islami, it is the second that has undoubtedly been most influential in Kashmir. Wani writes: 'It is Jamaat-i-Islami of Kashmir which became a bridge connecting Kashmir with the overall Islamic resurgence.'[49] Jamaat-i-Islami, of course, originated in India, and a branch of the organization has been operating for many years in Jammu and Kashmir. Unlike Ikhwan, which functions almost as much as a social welfare group as an Islamic propagation one, the stress of the Jamaat has always been on education; on firmly instilling in people the ideology of Islam. This is particularly true of the Jamaat in Kashmir.

While the organization in the state takes a vocal part in local politics, and has regularly fielded candidates to stand in elections, its most important work—and where it has achieved the most success—has been in education. Apart from the fact that propagating Islamic education is standard Jamaat policy, in Kashmir it was prompted to do so by the secularization (some would say Hinduization) drive of the Indian authorities in state schools and colleges. Fearing that as a result of such policies young Kashmiris would emerge with scant knowledge of Islam and what it means to be Muslim, the Jamaat set up its own schools. Some 17,000 students were enrolled in 125 Jamaat schools.[50] In these *madrasas* (religious schools) Islamic and modern knowledge was taught side by side. Furthermore, the Islamic knowledge that was taught was not limited merely to learning the Quran and *Sunna*, but included the application of Islamic teachings to society. This produced a whole generation of young Kashmiris for whom Islam was not just a personal faith consisting of some rituals and regulations, but a way of life—something to be implemented as much in collective, public life (including government) as in private. [The role of the Jamaat in the insurgency—its 'militant' activities—will be considered in the chapter dealing with the conflict.] Furthermore, the 'brand' of Islam that they learnt was quite militant. Rajesh Kadian writes:

> Senior Indian officials began to notice the increasing number of Maulavis [Muslim religious leaders] from U.P. and Bihar in the local mosques and madrasas. These new maulavis did not share the gentle Sufism of their indigenous Kashmiri brethren for most of

them were young and educated in the Deoband region of western U.P. They taught of pride in militant Islam and branded Muslim children going to secular schools as Kafirs. Their teachings struck a ready chord in a population already stimulated by Islamic revolution in neighbouring Iran.[51]

An additional factor that has been very significant in prompting the rise of political Islam in Kashmir, has been the rise of political Hinduism in India. Looking specifically at its influence on Muslims, Vanaik explains that the aim of *Hindutva* advocates is 'the self-conscious unity of Hindus as a religio-cultural grouping,' but since India's Hindus are so diverse the best way to achieve this is to stress:

> not...what they are supposed to share but what they oppose, even to the point of hostility. Indeed, the more strongly emotional the common opposition to the external 'other' or 'enemy,' the stronger is the desired unity likely to be. The only feasible candidate for this status as the hostile 'other' to Hindus, given India's history, are Muslims and Islam.[52]

The rise of Muslim consciousness in response to political Hinduism is, therefore, hardly surprising. The major developments associated with growing Hindu consciousness were described in the chapter on Indian domestic politics. However, one development should be mentioned here because it had a direct impact on Kashmiri Muslim thinking: the Nellie massacre of 1983. Most of the Muslims of this village in Assam were killed by Hindus, leading other Muslims to flee the area. The significance of the events in Nellie lies in the fact that many of the migrants settled in Kashmir. They chose it in the hope that—being a Muslim-majority state—they would be safe from Hindu persecution there. The arrival of these migrants, and the tales of killings they brought with them, would have made Kashmiris more wary of India, in particular of their prospects—as Muslims—of receiving a fair deal from it. Furthermore, Ganguly writes that, because many of the Bengali migrants were religious scholars/teachers (maulvis) who found employment in Kashmir's mosques and *madrasas*, they helped promote Islam in the Valley.[53]

Manifestations of Greater Islamic Consciousness in Kashmir

How has the rise in Islamic consciousness, particularly political Islam, been manifested in Kashmir?

With respect to general Islamic consciousness this is manifested in the absence (closure) of places like bars, cinemas and nightclubs, and by the more common sight of young men with beards, women in *purdah*, bigger congregations at mosques, etc. Of course, to some extent the former can be attributed to force being applied by fundamentalist militant groups. But not wholly. There has been a definite drawing away from Western culture among ordinary Kashmiris. Left to their own devices they might not have retreated as far as they have done, but the overall trend is undeniable. Of the various factors contributing to the rise in Islamic consciousness discussed above, the one that has played the major role specifically in bringing about this cultural sea-change is the Jamaat's *madrasas*.

Turning to political Islam, the obvious way to assess its rise in Kashmir would be to look at the electoral fortunes of the Islamic parties, notably the Jamaat-i-Islami. This reveals that prior to 1987 the party never won more than 5 seats in an election, a figure which would appear to indicate negligible public support. However, in the words of former Governor Jagmohan 'it had always more strength beneath the surface than above it. And its electoral performances of the past are no indication of its real hold on the people.'[54] Its poor electoral showing was partly due to the generally widespread rigging of Kashmiri elections; partly to the fact that for a long time the Jamaat's stress was on promoting Islamic education rather than winning elections; and partly to the presence of non-communal anti-centre parties. The proliferation of Islamic parties in the late 1980s (Mahaz-e-Azadi, Islamic Student's League, Anjuman-

e-Ittehad-e-Musalmeen, Islamic Study Circle, etc.) indicated that
Islam was making inroads into Kashmiri politics. But the 1987
elections, in which these parties took a very active part, were so
heavily rigged that the results cannot be taken as an accurate
reflection of popular support. For almost a decade after 1987
the electoral process in Kashmir was suspended, thereby
rendering it completely impossible to use the ballot box to assess
the strength of political Islam. One must, therefore, look for
other indicators of its strength.

Perhaps the most visible sign of the rise of political Islam in
Kashmir are the mosques. For many years now these have
functioned as the voice of opposition to India. Describing the
aftermath of the Gowkadal massacre in January 1990, Akbar
writes:

> In Srinagar, each mosque became a citadel of fervour; the khutba
> became a sermon in secession, the loudspeakers played tapes that
> echoed against each other from the minarets, or picked up a dying
> chant and threw it further: 'Hum kya chahte hain? Aazaadi...
> Aazaadi... Allah-o-Akbar!'[55]

Visiting the Valley in 1993, Andrew Whitehead found the
mosques playing the same role:

> At Friday prayers in Srinagar's main mosque, the chief priest leads
> the thousands of worshippers in chants of 'Aazaadi,' the freedom
> cry of the Kashmir Valley. No-one thinks it the least amiss when a
> leader of a local Mujahideen guerrilla group then takes the
> microphone. The loudspeakers stationed outside Srinagar's mosques
> are routinely used to abuse the security forces and broadcast anti-
> India slogans.[56]

The reason why the mosques have become so prominent in
articulating opposition is, of course, because there is no other
avenue for political discourse. But in carrying out this role,
Pasha notes that 'the cultural and political dimensions of
religious life have not only been united, but energized'[57] —
(whether this was the case at the outset or not) by having the

mosque as its mouthpiece Kashmiri politics has become Islamized, religion politicized. Islamic slogans such as '*Allah-ho-Akbar*' generally feature prominently in the Kashmir insurgency [something which the *Economic and Political Weekly* notes 'hardly provides any space for the non-Muslim resident of the Valley'[58]]. Another indication of strong political Islam is the revitalized role of the Mirwaiz-i-Kashmir. From relative obscurity this position has returned to the political limelight; the current Mirwaiz Omar Farooq until recently headed the All Parties Hurriyat Conference, the coalition of parties opposed to Indian rule; he has been succeeded by Jamaat leader Ali Gilani.

One aspect of political Islam that has often featured prominently in other Muslim countries, but is only now beginning to make an appearance in Kashmir is anti-Westernism. Disdain for Western culture (cinemas, nightclubs, etc.) has, of course, been apparent for many years, but dislike for Western governments such as the United States has emerged more recently. Schofield attributes the anti-West feelings among Kashmiri Muslims to the West's failure to intervene in the Kashmir conflict, and in particular its failure to persuade/pressurize India to hold a plebiscite in the state.[59]

The role of Islam in the current conflict, e.g. the various militant Islamic groups, will be considered in the chapter dealing with the conflict. But here, in the context of Islam in Kashmir, it is important to stress that fundamentalist militant Islam and greater Islamic consciousness among Kashmiri Muslims cannot be viewed as the same phenomenon. While it is true that their causal factors do partially overlap, e.g. both draw inspiration from the Afghan *jihad*, it is also the case that they have quite separate causal factors. The same can be said of the way these two phenomena are manifested; while this is sometimes in an identical fashion, e.g. liberal use of the term 'Allah-ho-Akbar', quite often takes different forms. The issue of *purdah* illustrates this divergence. Greater Islamic consciousness among Kashmiri Muslims has made them less tolerant of immodestly dressed women, but they still resist efforts by the fundamentalists to make women cover themselves up completely. In brief, Islamic awareness among Kashmiris—though linked to the militant fundamentalists—is relatively autonomous of them.[60]

Consequences of Greater Islamic Consciousness in Kashmir

The obvious consequences of greater Islamic consciousness, namely the more visible presence of Islam in everyday life (dress, observance of rituals like prayer, giving up un-Islamic practices, etc.), have already been described.

How has it affected relations between Kashmiri Muslims and Pandits? Obviously as Kashmiri Muslims have become more conscious of being Muslim, and as their observance of Islamic practices has increased, the differences between them and Pandits have become more acute. When coupled with the growth in Hindu consciousness among Pandits, this has led to a massive widening of the gap between the two communities.

One point that should be stressed here is that, while increased Islamic awareness among Kashmiri Muslims has contributed to the gap between them and the Pandits being widened, it has not really generated great hostility towards the Pandits. Towards India certainly but, contrary to what one might expect, Kashmiri Muslims have not expressed their new Islamic consciousness by abusing or attacking Pandits. [Note: 'Kashmiri Muslims' here refers to the general population rather than fundamentalist militants.]

The question that remains to be answered is how has greater awareness of Islam, and in particular the rise of political Islam in Kashmir, affected political goals there? Has it irreversibly alienated Kashmiri Muslims from India? Has it caused them to desire an Islamic form of government? Has it caused them to draw closer to Muslim-majority Pakistan? These questions cannot be considered in isolation from other factors like what kind of state Pakistan is, developments in India's domestic politics, Indo-Pak relations, etc. Hence the effect of Islam on Kashmiri political goals will be assessed in conjunction with the influence of these other factors in the concluding chapter.

NOTES

1. Cited in Haddad, Y.Y., 'Sayyid Qutb: Ideologue of the Islamic Revival' in Esposito, John (ed.), *Voices of Resurgent Islam* (New York, Oxford University Press, 1983), p. 70.

2. Esposito, 'Islam in Asia: An Introduction' in Esposito (ed.), *Islam in Asia: Religion, Politics and Society* (New York, Oxford University Press, 1987), p. 15.

3. Esposito, *Islam and Politics* (New York, Syracuse University Press, 1984), p. 66.

4. Ibid., p. 127.

5. 'Modernisation for the Muslim world has not necessarily followed the general wisdom of Western political theories by resulting in the progressive secularisation of state and society. While a minority elite class accepted and implemented a Western secular worldview along with its ideologies and values, the majority of the Muslim population has not truly accepted and internalised a secular outlook.' Ibid., p. 212.

6. Esposito (ed.), *op. cit.* (1983), p. 10.

7. Esposito, *op. cit. (1984)*, p. 211.

8. Humphreys, R.S., 'The Contemporary Resurgence in the Context of Modern Islam' in Dessouki (ed.), *Islamic Resurgence in the Arab World* (New York, Praeger, 1982), p. 67; cited in Choudhry, G.W., *Islam and the Contemporary World* (London, Indus Thames, 1990), p. 196.

9. 'The recent emergence of Islamist ideology can be traced in part to the abortive search for workable ideologies of nation-building', Dekmejian, R.H., *Islam in Revolution* (New York, Syracuse University Press, 1985), p. 26.

10. Spencer, Claire, 'Algeria in Crisis' in *Survival*, Volume 16: No. 2 (Summer 1994), p. 158.

11. Hadar, Leon, 'What Green Peril?' in *Foreign Affairs*, 72 (Spring 1993), p. 35. This view is echoed by *The Times*: 'The strength of fundamentalism is its discipline, coherence, and appeal to a gnawing sense that the Islamic way of life is being destroyed by the permissiveness and all-conquering materialism of the West...[t]hey *(fundamentalists)* reaffirm traditional values', 'Islam against the state', 25 May 1993.

12. Vatikiotis, P. J., 'Islam on the move? The Will to Power' in *Encounter*, 73 (November 1989), p. 47.

13. Referring to the Middle East, Sir Allan Ramsay, recently retired as Britain's Ambassador to Morocco, is quoted in *The Times*, 4 April 1996: 'too much of the best of all that is available is concentrated in too few hands.' In her article 'Islam moves into the gap as sanctions impoverish Iraq', Christina Lamb quotes Mohammed Vejjari, head of the UN development programme in Iraq: 'The middle class has practically

disappeared in economic terms. All that remains is a large number of poor and a few rich', and she comments: 'One result is an increasing number of people turning to religion, particularly the hard-hit salaried classes and the young', *The Times*, 30 October 1994.

14. Referring to Iran and Turkey 'two classic models of failure of Westernisation models', Khurshid Ahmed writes: '[w]hether we judge on the basis of the material results these experiments have produced or the moral havoc, the social ills and the psychological shock that have come in their wake, it is the profound feeling of the Muslim people that the Westernisation experiment has decisively failed. Both its variants, the capitalistic as well as the socialistic, have been tried and found wanting.' Ahmed, 'The Nature of Islamic Resurgence' in Esposito (ed.), *op. cit.* (1983), p. 224. Esposito comments that: 'Western models of development had been abruptly transplanted; they were adopted, not adapted to their new environments. Institutions and codes that were the product of the West's historical/cultural experience, spanning several centuries of development, were often uncritically and suddenly applied to people with a different historical tradition, experience and values'. Ibid., p. 7.

15. Hadar asserts that 'the political clout that the Islamists have now is due not to the desire of Arabs and others to live under strict Islamic rule, but to the perceived failure of Western models of political and economic order, including nationalism and socialism, to solve the Middle East's problems...[t]he mosque...has become an important centre for expressing the discontent of the unemployed', *op. cit.*, p. 35.

16. Emmanuel Sivan writes that the Islamic resurgence and state [government] performance are inversely proportional: 'the worse the state's record in gratifying economic needs, in creating and transmitting a nation-state mystique, the better the chances of the resurgence.' Sivan, 'The Islamic Resurgence: Civil Society Strikes Back' in *Journal of Contemporary History*, 25 (1990), p. 358.

17. 'The enemies they [*Muslim radicals*] seek to overthrow are not attractive. Most of the regimes they are fighting are oligarchic, corrupt and dictatorial. Muslim states are vulnerable to Islamism because they lack democracy' in *The Sunday Times*, 1 January 1995. 'Sir Allan Ramsay, Britain's Ambassador to Morocco until his retirement this week, said that military-backed rulers throughout the Arab world must choose between an end to their autocratic rule or face an increasingly bitter battle with Islamic fundamentalists', *The Times*, 4 April 1996.

18. Dalrymple, William, 'Islamic Fundamentalism in Egypt' in *The Sunday Times Magazine*, 24 April 1994.

19. 'Steam from the Mosque', *The Economist*, 329:6 November 1993, p. 15.

20. Edward Mortimer writes: 'For the first time since Nasser in 1956 a Muslim nation successfully defied, humiliated and inflicted material

damage on the interests of a major Western power.' Mortimer, *The Politics of Islam* (London, Faber & Faber, 1982), p. 355.

21. Beeman, W.O., 'The Ayatollah has set Forces in Motion', *The Sun* (Baltimore, USA), 11 June 1989, cited in Choudhry, *op. cit.*, p. 215.

22. Mortimer, *op. cit.*, p. 356.

23. Ibid., p. 358.

24. Newell, R.S., 'Islam and the Struggle for Afghan National Liberation' in Pullapilly, C.K. (ed.), *Islam in the Contemporary World* (Cross Road Books), p. 252, cited in Choudhry, *op. cit.*, p. 220.

25. 'The fundamentalists, in theory, see their task to be that of bringing about an Islamic revolution in the Muslim world. In this vision, the struggle against the Soviets in Afghanistan is an important but subordinate task of the larger task of restructuring society', Ghani, Ashraf, 'Afghanistan: Islam and Counter-Revolutionary Movements' in Esposito (ed.), *op. cit.* (1987), p. 92.

26. Ali Mazrui notes that, up to 1989/1990, Afghanistan was 'the only successful case of satellite resistance to Soviet power.' Mazrui, 'The Resurgence of Islam and the Decline of Communism: What is the Connection?' *Futures*, 23 (April 1991). 'The war in Afghanistan (1979–1989)…provided inspiration for a whole generation of Islamists. Young men from Sudan, Egypt, Algeria and other parts of the Islamic world fought in the war. They later returned to their home countries with stories of how *Islam had defeated a modern superpower*', *Guardian*, 28 February 1995.

27. 'Once praised as heroes, they are now denounced as villains. Young Muslims from all over the Middle East were inspired by their preachers to join Afghanistan's glorious war against the communist infidels. Now, not so long after the rebels won, their war has been ignominiously recast in official Arab circles as a training school for religious terrorists.

    Security officials in Algeria, Tunisia, Jordan and Egypt blame the 'Afghanis' as the Arab veterans of the war are called, for importing military discipline and expertise about weapons into their own countries' Islamic fundamentalist movements', *The Economist*, 327: 5 June 1993, p. 63.

28. Azzam, Maha, 'The Gulf Crisis: Perceptions in the Muslim World', *International Affairs*, 67 (July 1991), pp. 478–9.

29. For example, in a declaration by the London-based Islamic Council, published in several Arab countries. See ibid., p. 480.

30. Ranstorp, Magnus, and Xhudo, G., 'A Threat to Europe? Middle East Ties with the Balkans and Their Impact upon Terrorist Activity throughout the Region', *Terrorism and Political Violence* 6:2 (Summer 1994), p. 208.

31. '[T]he Muslims of Bosnia have been thoroughly disenchanted with the West since the outbreak of conflict. By allowing for the destruction of most of their state, the killing of thousands of Muslims and the forced

removal from their homes, many Muslims have drawn parallels between themselves and the Palestinians. These 'angry and dispossessed' people have realised that the West has abandoned them to their fate when vital interests were not at stake. This feeling has gained an increased following among Bosnia's Muslims. Even moderates are suspecting the West of never intending to allow for the exertion of power by Muslims.' Ibid., p. 207. Such feelings have pushed Bosnian Muslims towards Islam: 'Harsh conditions create new national psychologies and retroactive myths... Bosnian Muslims are probably in the process of acquiring a Muslim identity that was only weakly present in the past.' Fuller, Graham, 'A Bosnian "Palestine"? Iran Muddies the Waters', *International Herald Tribune*, 16 May 1994, ibid., p. 210.

32. Hussain, M., 'Cold War Against Islam', *Far Eastern Economic Review*, 155:22 (2 July 1992), p. 22.

33. 'Living with Islam', *The Economist*, 323: 4 April 1992, p. 13.

34. *The Economist*, for example, begins an article entitled 'Islam resumes its march' with the sentence: 'One *anti-westernism* is growing stronger' and goes on to ask 'Is it right to be scared?' Ibid., p. 73. In her article, 'The Challenge of Radical Islam' [*Foreign Affairs*, 72 (Spring 1993), pp. 43–56], Judith Miller argues against allowing Islamic groups to gain power through the ballot box; she claims that once in power they would turn their backs on democracy and implement theocracies/autocracies. Leon Hadar describes the new trend: 'with communism's death, America must prepare for a new global threat—radical Islam. This spectre is symbolised by the Middle Eastern Muslim fundamentalist, a Khomeini-like creature armed with a radical ideology and nuclear weapons, intent on launching a jihad against Western civilisation.... Like the red menace of the Cold War era, the Green Peril—green being the colour of Islam—is described as a cancer spreading around the globe, undermining the legitimacy of Western values and threatening the national security of the United States', Hadar, *op. cit.*, pp. 27–9. Mazrui goes so far as to say: 'Muslims may be among the major casualties of the end of the cold war', *op. cit.*

35. Charles Krauthammer writing in the *International Herald Tribune* ['Iran as a Source of Militant Spread of Fundamentalism', 4 January 1993], stresses the need for the US to take 'swift', 'proactive' measures against states like Iran and Sudan: 'As with Soviet communism, this new messianic creed must be contained. That means aid—material and political—to those fighting to contain Iran and its emanations...[t]he new threat is as evil as the old evil empire. Fortunately, it is still in a primitive state. We must keep it primitive.' Cited in Ranstorp and Xhudo, *op. cit.*, p. 199.

36. Esposito, *op. cit.* (1984), p. 39.

37. Choudhry quotes Iqbal: 'by accepting nationalism, the Muslim states cannot cease to be Islamic because so long as the Muslims believe in

Tawhid (Unity of God) and prophethood of Muhammad (PBUH), they do not step out of the fold of Islam...many nations can belong to a community of faith', *op. cit.*, p. 159.

38. Esposito, *op. cit.* (1984), p. 219.
39. Nasr, Sayyed Vali Reza, 'Students, Islam and Politics: Islami Jami'at-i-Tulaba in Pakistan', *Middle East Journal*, 46 (Winter 1992), p. 76.
40. Dekmejian, *op. cit.*, p. 167.
41. Ahmed Rashid notes that: 'In the nearly 30 years from Pakistan's independence in 1947 to 1975, about 870 new madrasas were set up. But between 1976 and 1990—half the earlier period—the increase was 1,700. Most of the new schools were established during the Zia years, 1977–88. Besides ensuring the Islamic schools were well-funded, Zia raised their academic status. From being on the social periphery, Islamic education came into the mainstream of Pakistani education.' 'Schools for Soldiers', *Far Eastern Economic Review*, 158: 9 March 1995, p. 25.
42. See Rashid, A., 'The Great Divide: Shias and Sunnis battle it out in Pakistan', ibid., p. 24.
43. 'New Warriors of Islam advance in Afghanistan', *Guardian*, 5 December 1994.
44. Akbar, *op. cit.*, p. 219.
45. Azam Inquilabi, Srinagar teacher, cited in Schofield, *op. cit.*, p. 220.
46. Ganguly, *op. cit.*, p. 42.
47. Interview with Hilal Ahmed Baig, Area Commander of Kashmir Students Liberation Front, published in *Sada-i-Huriyat*, 9 February 1990; Jagmohan, *My Frozen Turbulence in Kashmir* (New Delhi, 1994), p. 398.
48. Cited in Chadda, *op. cit.*, p. 69.
49. Ibid.
50. According to Gull Mohammed Wani, cited in Chadda, *op. cit.*, p. 69.
51. Kadian, Rajesh, *The Kashmir Tangle: Issues and Options* (New Delhi, Vision Books, 1992), p. 13, cited in Chadda, *op. cit.*, p. 69.
52. Vanaik, *op. cit.*, p. 308.
53. Ganguly, *op. cit.*, p. 32 and p. 76.
54. Jagmohan, *op. cit.*, p. 180.
55. Akbar, *op. cit.*, p. 219.
56. Whitehead, Andrew, 'Killing time in Kashmir', *New Statesman and Society*, 3 September 1993, p. 23.
57. Pasha, Mustafa Kamal, 'Beyond the Two-Nation Divide: Kashmir and Resurgent Islam' in Thomas (ed.), *op. cit.*, p. 377.
58. 'India's Kashmir War', *EPW.*, *op. cit.*, p. 656.
59. Schofield, *op. cit.*, p. 288.
60. See Pasha, *op. cit.*, pp. 381–2.

8

THE KASHMIR CONFLICT

In earlier chapters we have seen how various developments within Jammu and Kashmir—most notably the revolution in education and rising socio-economic expectations—when coupled with Indian policy towards the State that effectively suppressed democracy and eroded regional autonomy, led Kashmiri Muslims to become disillusioned with India. This process was further encouraged by the rise of political Hinduism in India, and by the resurgence of Islam throughout the Muslim world—making Kashmiris more aware of their Muslim identity—this naturally pushed them away from Hindu-majority India. There has been a mirror effect on Kashmiri Pandits: as they have become more conscious of their Hindu identity, the gulf between them and Kashmiri Muslims has widened and their determination to remain 'Indian' increased.

On the international front, Indian and Pakistani determination to win Jammu and Kashmir has been explained. So, too, has the growing encroachment of Kashmir in both countries' domestic politics. Chapters Five and Six have shown how different elements in India and Pakistan ensure that both governments persistently adopt a hard-line on Kashmir: furthermore, as the international Kashmir dispute has dragged on past its fiftieth anniversary, the chances of it being resolved and permanently settled peacefully have become correspondingly less.

This chapter on the current Kashmir conflict brings these two issues, internal and international, together.

The Kashmir conflict can be divided into two distinct phases. The first of these dating from 1987–89 can be considered as the period of 'build-up to insurgency'. The second from 1989 to the present day is the period of 'actual/full-scale insurgency'. Obviously, the major difference between these two periods is, one, the intensity of public alienation from India, and two, militant activity in Kashmir: both have been much greater in the latter period. It is useful to consider these two periods separately since, aside from the intensity of protest, one can also detect differences between them in the responses of the public and the Indian authorities. One could argue that recently a third phase has started—internationalization of the Kashmir conflict. This phase involves the escalation of hostilities from Indian Kashmir—between Kashmiri Muslims and Indian forces—to direct conflict between India and Pakistan.

Build-up to Insurgency

Militant Activity

Kashmir today is a state in conflict. It has been so since 1989. However, militant activity in Kashmir actually predates the current conflict by many years—though obviously on nothing like the current scale. There is some evidence to suggest that a handful of groups started operating in the 1960s, e.g. Al-Fatah[1] and, somewhat later, the Jammu and Kashmir Liberation Front (JKLF).[2] These groups presented an alternative form of opposition to growing Indian control in Kashmir to that of the Plebiscite Front, carrying out acts of sabotage, small-scale assaults on the police authorities, etc.

But probably the first significant act of militancy involving Kashmir was the hijacking of an Indian airliner by the Kashmir National Liberation Front early in 1971 (see Chapter Four). The second major incident that attracted international attention was the kidnapping in February 1984 of a senior Indian diplomat in England, Ravindra Mahtre. The group responsible was the Kashmir Liberation Army (KLA), thought to be closely linked to (and possibly even part of) the JKLF. In exchange for letting Mahtre go, the KLA demanded the release of Maqbool Butt, one of the JKLF's leaders, and several other prisoners being held in Indian jails, as well as a ransom of £1 million. At the time of Ravindra Mahtre's kidnapping, Maqbool Butt had already been tried for involvement in the killing of a judge and sentenced to death by an Indian court.[3] The Indian authorities had yet to give their final reply to the kidnappers' demands when, on 6 February, Mahtre was discovered killed. Subsequently, on 11 February, the execution order on Maqbool Butt was carried out.

Two events in 1986/87 caused this highly sporadic militant activity to shift up a gear. One was the arrival in Azad Kashmir of Amanullah Khan, along with Butt, one of the leading figures in the JKLF. He was in England when Mahtre was kidnapped, and though suspected of involvement in his death, was actually charged and tried for possession of illegal weapons. He was released because the jury failed to reach a verdict, but Douglas Hurd, the then Home Secretary, still ordered his deportation to Pakistan. This took place in 1986. According to Victoria Schofield, in Azad Kashmir, Khan proceeded to recruit four Kashmiris to participate in a militant movement: Yasin Malik, Ashfaq Majid Wani, Sheikh Abdul Hamid and Javed Ahmed Mir—collectively known as the 'HAJY' group.[4] The Indian authorities have also linked Amanullah Khan's deportation to the spate of terrorist attacks in Indian Kashmir that followed soon after it. But while his group certainly had a hand in these attacks, it is unlikely that they alone were responsible for all of them.

The second much more significant event was the 'victory' of the National Conference-Congress alliance in the 1987 elections. Public anger at the result, in particular at the way it was achieved, was what really marked the beginning of the shift from political activity to militancy as the means of protesting against State and Central Governments and bringing about change in Kashmir. This shift did not start overnight: the process of change from political opposition to insurgency actually took some two years (1987–1989). It was marked by one, increasing public protests, and two, increased militant activity. Consider the former first.

11 February, the anniversary of Maqbool Butt's execution, had already become an annual occasion for demonstrations against India. But after the 1987, elections and the 'installation' of Farooq Abdullah's Congress-National Conference alliance government, these shifted up several gears, with even relatively minor issues becoming the pretext for widespread public protests. In October 1987, Abdullah's decision to end the annual migration of government staff in winter from Srinagar to Jammu, and subsequent reversal of that decision under pressure from Jammu, led to protests in Srinagar. The following year, the raising of electricity tariffs—even though Abdullah claimed this would only have affected some 10 per cent of the population—produced the same effect. A good indication of the public mood comes from the fact that in 1989 there was a *hartal* (strike) on almost one third of the total working days. While some of these strikes were undoubtedly carried out under duress, the majority can be taken as reflecting genuine public anger at the State and Central governments.

It is interesting to note that at the same time as protesting more vigorously against India and the National Conference, Kashmiri Muslims expressed greater support for Pakistan (recall that both in 1947 and 1965 when they had the opportunity to side with their Muslim neighbour they did not do so). The death of Pakistan's General Zia in August 1988 was followed by pro-Pakistan demonstrations in the Valley. A few days earlier Pakistan's national day (14 August) had been celebrated in the Valley, while India's on the 15th had been designated 'a black day.' Schofield gives another example of the Kashmiris' 'reinterpretation' of history: 27 October, the anniversary of the 1947 airlift of Indian troops into Kashmir, in previous years considered a liberation, in 1988 was marked as 'occupation day'.[5]

Turning to the increased militant activity, among the earliest (unsuccessful) targets of militant activity was Chief Minister Farooq Abdullah; in May 1987 his motorcade was attacked on the way to a mosque. The following summer saw the first bomb blasts in the Kashmir Valley: one missed the Central Telegraph Office in Srinagar while another was directed against the Television Station. The Director General of Police, Ali Mohammed Watali, survived an attack in September 1988. National Conference leader, Mohammed Yusuf Halwai was not so lucky; he was killed by the JKLF in August 1989. Schofield claims his assassination was actually part of a wider strategy: 'to intimidate National Conference activists in order to oblige them to disassociate themselves from the party, ultimately leading to a complete breakdown of the political process.'[6] Members of the authorities were not the only targets of militant wrath: Halwai's killing was followed by a series of assassinations of leading Hindus. BJP leader, Tikka Lal Tapoo, was killed on 13 September, and Neel Kanth Ganjoo, the judge who had sentenced Maqbool Butt to death, on 4 November 1989.

Public protests and militant activity increased steadily after 1987, but the event that pushed these disjointed attacks into a sustained, full-scale insurgency against Indian rule was an incident in December 1989. The JKLF kidnapped Rubaiyya Sayeed, daughter of the Home Minister, Mufti Mohammed Sayeed, and demanded the release of five JKLF activists being held in Indian prisons. Public opinion did not support the kidnapping of a young unmarried woman. Chief Minister Farooq Abdullah warned Union ministers not to surrender to the demands of the kidnappers. He argued that surrender would lead to a flood of similar incidents, and he probably also calculated that the rising tide of public opposition to the JKLF's action would force them to release their hostage unconditionally. However, the V.P. Singh government in New Delhi ignored Farooq's warnings and authorized making a deal with the JKLF.

By conceding to the kidnappers' demands and releasing the five imprisoned militants, the Indian Government firstly, reversed public disapproval of the militants' action into approval and secondly, ushered in the next stage of militancy—full-scale insurgency. Farooq's prediction that the exchange of militants for Rubaiyya Sayeed 'would open the floodgate for the future and provide a boost to anti-national actions of trying to separate Kashmir from India'[7] proved correct. Ganguly explains why: 'Insurgent groups throughout the Valley saw that the government lacked the necessary discipline to stand firm when confronted by an act of terror.'[8] Four months later the JKLF took three more hostages—H.L. Khera, Manager of the Kashmir Machine Tools Factory, Professor Mushir-ul-Haq, Vice-Chancellor of Kashmir University, and Abdul Ghani, his secretary—and made similar demands. This time the government did take a hard-line stand and refused to comply (consequently all three hostages were killed). However, by then the damage had been done: the Kashmir insurgency was underway.

Indian Government Response to Build-up

The response of the Indian government to the rising levels of public unrest and militant activity following the 1987 elections was highly significant. There was still a chance then that political concessions by New Delhi could have nipped the insurgency in the bud. Even at that eleventh hour the right gestures could have prevented Kashmiri Muslims giving up on India altogether. But the Indian government decided that, rather than try and win the Kashmiris over by persuasion, it would crush the budding insurgency before it could take off. As is apparent from the current situation in Kashmir this strategy failed. Indeed, it will be seen below that Indian actions could actually be said to have served as a catalyst in hastening the onset of the Kashmir insurgency: if in 1987 there was a chance that conflict could have been prevented, by 1990 Indian policies had made it a certainty.

Up to 1989, Rajiv Gandhi's Congress party formed the government in New Delhi. It tried initially to calm things down in Kashmir by restoring a popular government in the State— this would remove one of the main causes of public anger, rule by New Delhi. However, the caveat that this 'popular' government should still be controlled by the Congress administration in New Delhi made the plan backfire. As seen above, the situation in Kashmir actually deteriorated more rapidly after the National Conference-Congress alliance came to power. Rajiv then proceeded to restore order by drafting in large numbers of police and paramilitaries from other parts of India, notably units of the Central Reserve Police Force and the Border Security Force. Often making very liberal use of force in their attempts to impose law and order, the increased police/paramilitary presence also failed to control public unrest.

V.P. Singh's Janata coalition displaced Congress in New Delhi just before the Sayeed kidnapping and the new government's capitulation to the JKLF paved the way for full-scale insurgency in Kashmir. In India its action—its 'surrender'—was strongly criticized. One of the most influential voices of criticism was that of Janata's coalition partner, the BJP. The government responded to its critics by resolving to take a much tougher approach in dealing with militancy. An immediate sign of this was the reappointment of Malhotra Jagmohan as Governor of Jammu and Kashmir on 18 January 1990 (after a five-year tenure he had been replaced in July 1989 by Krishna Rao). Farooq Abdullah resigned in protest at the appointment, thereby passing responsibility for the State's administration over to Jagmohan. Theoretically, then, the Central Government was again in charge of the State and the duality of authority (State and Centre) that could, as in the Sayeed kidnapping, have prevented concerted action by the various official bodies in Kashmir had been removed.

In practice, however, Jagmohan showed a tendency from the outset to think and act independently of New Delhi. He wasted no time in implementing his own interpretation of a 'tough approach': a two-pronged strategy that consisted of repressive measures to prevent militancy, and a firm response when it did occur. On the night of 18/19 January, Jagmohan ordered paramilitary units to carry out intensive house searches in the Gowkadal area of Srinagar. No doubt influenced by the 'get tough' attitude of the new Governor, the paramilitaries killed more than fifty people. Predictably, the killings inflamed public anger and encouraged greater militancy. Jagmohan responded with more house searches, curfews, arrests of suspects...which led to greater public alienation, greater militancy and so on, in a vicious cycle of escalating violence.

In February 1990, Jagmohan demonstrated his determination to continue with this hard line approach, as well as his disregard for the government in New Delhi. Using powers in the Kashmir Constitution intended for an elected Sadar-i-Riyasat, and without informing Prime Minister Singh, he dissolved the State Assembly and imposed Governor's Rule. His justification for this action was that without it 'there was no moral legitimacy for the use of force on an extensive scale.'[9] Jagmohan's arrival in Kashmir also coincided with the mass migration of Pandits from the Valley—something in which he was widely suspected of having a hand.

In New Delhi, Jagmohan's tough approach raised concerns about human rights abuses, and—in view of its singular failure to control militancy in the State—doubts about its effectiveness. But at the same time, images of Pandit refugees and attacks on security forces seemed (for some) to justify Jagmohan's actions. V.P. Singh responded to these opposing forces with a compromise that he hoped would satisfy both moderates and hard-liners. Whilst retaining Jagmohan as Governor he appointed George Fernandes, Union Minister for Railways and a known human rights activist, as Minister for Kashmir Affairs. This was in March. By May 1990, however, Singh had once again bowed to pressure from the hard line BJP and abandoned moderacy: just as the new minister was beginning to explore avenues for talks and reconciliation, he was withdrawn from Kashmir.

An incident in the same month led to the removal, or more accurately the forced resignation, of Jagmohan. Mirwaiz Maulvi Farooq, one of the most influential Islamic leaders in the State, was assassinated on 21 May. His killers were probably militants angered by Farooq holding talks with Fernandes. At the Mirwaiz funeral, crowds of mourners clashed with paramilitary forces and in the ensuing firing about twenty-four were killed; two bullets struck the coffin. Public anger that had been directed against the militants for allegedly killing the Mirwaiz was—ironically—diverted by this incident towards the Indian authorities. For the V.P. Singh administration this was the last straw: Jagmohan was summoned to New Delhi where on 25 May 1990 he resigned as Governor of Jammu and Kashmir. Girish Saxena replaced him.

In summary, under Rajiv Gandhi's pre-1989 Congress government the rising level of public unrest and the relatively few incidents of militant activity were tackled by simply increasing the numbers of security forces in the region. There were some indications that the Janata Government—whose rise to power coincided with the major onset of militancy in Jammu and Kashmir—was willing to try a more conciliatory approach to the problem. However, its precarious political position, in particular its dependence on the goodwill of the BJP, forced it to adopt a Congress-like hard line policy. Appointed to implement this tough approach, Malhotra Jagmohan went far beyond the scope of his brief and effectively carried out a policy of repression and punitive reprisals. By the time he resigned public alienation in the Vale had increased dramatically, as had the intensity of militant activity.

Public Response to Build-up

How did the Kashmiri Muslim public respond to the rising militancy? The fact that protests against the State/Central Government continued to increase in frequency and intensity during the late eighties suggests that the public at least shared the views of the militants. An indication that they also approved of their tactics was given by the fact that 11 February, the date in 1984 on which JKLF leader Maqbool Butt had been executed in New Delhi, was commemorated every year with public demonstrations. But the Sayeed kidnapping in 1989 showed that there could be a distinction between public attitudes to the militants' ideas and to their tactics.

In the days immediately after Rubaiyya's capture it became apparent that there was little popular support for the JKLF's action. What was also apparent, however, was that opposition arose solely from the choice of hostage—a young, unmarried Muslim woman—and not from disapproval of the JKLF itself. Thus, when the Singh government accepted the JKLF's demands and the hostage was released unharmed, there was loud support for the group. Early disapproval because of the means used by the JKLF changed into approval when its 'ends' were achieved.

The Sayeed incident showed that, up to a point, the Kashmiri Muslim public supported militancy—particularly when it was seen to produce results. The return of Jagmohan to Kashmir in 1990, and the subsequent clampdown which affected the public at least as much—if not more—than the militants, undoubtedly increased this support. Aside from resentment at Jagmohan's strong-arm tactics, his dissolution of the State Assembly and imposition of Governor's Rule made Kashmiri Muslims despair even more of the political process as a means to bring about change. The only alternative to this that they could see was militancy.

It should be stressed here that the observation that the Kashmiri Muslim public largely supported the militants applies only to the initial build-up and outbreak of the insurgency. Public mood is dynamic: it should not be assumed to have stayed constant since then.

Turning to the other ethnic group in Kashmir, the Pandits: how did they view the rising militancy? Not surprisingly, with great alarm. Even if the militants' attacks been confined to the Indian authorities it is likely that the Pandits—because of their own strong pro-India leanings—would still have felt alarmed. However, a number of leading Hindus were also assassinated and, according to the All India Kashmir Pandit Conference, thirty-two Pandits were killed in the seven months from September 1989. The fact that Pandits were targeted along with the authorities meant that they really feared for their lives. So great were their fears that by the beginning of 1990 a mass migration of Pandits, mostly to Jammu was underway. As the *Economic and Political Weekly* reported at the time:

> The exodus of Hindu refugees...is due to the tremendous fear created by large rallies and angry demonstrations against the government by the majority community. The Muslims claim and the refugees agree that there were no communal incidents or burning and looting of houses, misbehaviour with women, etc. The refugees say that they left their houses because they feared that something of this kind would happen soon.[10]

There was possibly also another reason for the Pandits fleeing the Valley: it has been alleged that Governor Jagmohan encouraged them to migrate because, in Akbar's words, he was 'convinced that their refugee status would generate support for the whip-hand tactics which appealed to his temperament.'[11] Schofield suggests his motives were more communal:

> There was and still is...a widespread feeling that the departure of the Hindus was not necessary and that Jagmohan, who had a reputation for being anti-Muslim dating back to the days of the Emergency, attempted to give the Kashmiri problem a communal profile by facilitating their departure in government transport.[12]

Evidence cited to back these allegations includes, as Schofield mentions, that Jagmohan provided the fleeing Pandits with government transport, and that he reassured them that their salaries (many were government employees) would still be paid in Jammu.[13] An Indian team visiting Kashmir in March 1990 raised these allegations with R. K. Takkar, Chief Secretary of Jammu and Kashmir:

> When confronted with evidence *(of government transport being provided to Hindu families to leave the Valley)* he claimed that it could have been done by individual government officials but it was not the policy of the state government. He claimed that according to state government sources, till March 15, about thirteen thousand non-Muslims, mostly Hindus and Sikhs, had left the Valley. He

also admitted that of these about 11,500 families were Kashmiri Pandits. We asked him why the government was encouraging this exodus by paying salaries to these people in Jammu. He said that to refrain from doing so would be inhuman. When we pointed out that due to closure of the treasury and banks for the last two and a half months all the government employees *(Muslims)* in the Valley were going without salary, he had no comments to offer except that no one left their hearth and home for fun. He told us that at a rough estimate about eighty per cent of the Hindu migrants were employees of the state government. When we asked how many of these people were under real threat he told us that according to the state intelligence only twelve of these migrants were under real threat from the militants and the government was going to provide security to these people.[14]

The contrast between the Pandits' great apprehensions about the militants and the Kashmiri Muslims' vocal support of them, showed how much the two groups' political views—never close—had diverged by 1989. The Pandits' migration from the Valley was highly significant because it added geographical distance to the numerous other factors already dividing them from Kashmiri Muslims. Indeed, it could be said to have put the final nail in the coffin of *Kashmiriyat*. Thereafter, the question in Kashmir was not 'Can *Kashmiriyat* evolve?' but, 'How far would communal identification by Muslims and Pandits drive the two apart: would it ever be possible for them to live together again?'

Full-Scale Insurgency

Militant Activity

In separatist movements in other parts of the world it is often possible to identify one militant group as the 'main player'— ETA in the Basque region of Spain, and the Tamil Tigers in northern Sri Lanka, for instance. In Kashmir, however, it is impossible to pinpoint one—or even a few—groups as being behind the armed struggle. There are numerous militant groups involved in the Kashmir conflict. They differ in size, ideology, popular support, military strength, tactics employed and durability. While some groups have gained in strength since the conflict began, others have declined or even disappeared from the scene completely. Of the few dozen groups currently operating in the Valley, only about a dozen could be described as 'major players'. Many of these are closely associated with particular political parties. All the major groups will be considered individually below.

Group Differences

Generally speaking, the most fundamental division between militant groups is ideological: those favouring independence and those favouring accession to Pakistan. The former—of which there is actually only one significant group, the JKLF—were dominant in the early years of the conflict but more recently their influence has waned. Pro-Pakistan groups are now the most significant participants in the conflict. Whether this shift from pro-independence to pro-Pakistan militants reflects a similar shift in public opinion is debatable.

Relations between the various militant groups—even among those with the same political objectives—have tended to be difficult. Aside from differences in ideology, military strategy and tactics, etc., personality clashes have prevented separatist forces in Jammu and Kashmir from waging a concerted campaign against Indian rule. At times, relations between opposing groups have deteriorated to the extent that they fight among themselves rather than against the security forces. Certainly, at least some of the assassinations of political leaders in Jammu and Kashmir were carried out by militants. On 21 May 1990 Mirwaiz Maulvi Farooq was shot dead in his home; the killing was widely perceived as the action of militants opposed to his recent talks with the government. Similarly, the shooting of a known JKLF sympathizer, Dr Abdul Ahad Guru, in March 1993 was believed to have been carried out by members of the pro-Pakistan Hizbul-Mujahideen. Note that in both instances the authorities dispelled public revulsion at the killings by themselves killing numerous people at the funerals of Maulvi Farooq and Dr Guru.

In recent times, infighting between the militants has decreased. This is probably a consequence of the State's political organizations achieving a measure of unity, as well as no doubt to an awareness of the damage such 'bickering' was doing to the separatist movement as a whole. But while 'loose co-ordination of militant group activities is reported...no central command for the formal integration of military operations appears to exist.'[15]

Strength

How many militants are there? What kind of military capability do they have? What tactics have they employed in Kashmir? It is very difficult to give a precise figure as to the number of militants active in the Kashmir conflict. Apart from the obvious problem of the militant groups being far from open organizations, an additional complication arises from the fact that their membership can fluctuate widely. Militants are captured or killed; there is also a trend to fight for several months/years, and then to drop out—perhaps to take up arms again after a respite. The closest figure that can be given is of several thousand (not more than ten) hard core insurgents. Most of these are young men from the Kashmir Valley and Azad Kashmir. However, since the insurgency became established it has also attracted a significant number of 'foreigners'—Pakistanis, Afghans, Iranians, Arabs from different parts of the Arab-speaking world, even Bosnians. The influence of these 'foreign *mujahideen*' will be considered below.

Turning to the military capability of the militants in Kashmir, this can best be summed up as being sufficient to keep Indian security forces tied up in the Valley, but not enough to inflict an outright military defeat on them. Two major factors explain the weakness of the separatist movement. One, the divisions among the militant groups that prevent them waging a concerted campaign and utilizing their men and resources in the most effective manner. Two, while they have access to an almost endless supply of light arms (guns, rifles, grenades, etc.), thanks largely to the Afghan war which flooded the north-west of the Indian subcontinent with weapons, they do not yet appear able to get their hands on larger, more powerful weapons such as long-range missiles. This obviously imposes a limit on the kinds of attacks they can launch. Wirsing writes:

> the Kashmiri militants are armed and equipped in large part for hit-and-run missions against lightly protected targets; for raids on isolated army or police outposts; for ambushes; for mining of roads and sabotage of power, communications and transport facilities...but—so far at least—not for head-on clashes with India's regular or paramilitary forces.[16]

With respect to strategy, since the conflict began the militants have become more selective in targeting the security forces.[17] This shift came after numerous civilians were killed or injured by indiscriminate attacks such as bombs planted in public places. Not surprisingly such killings alienated the public without whose support the separatist movement—waged as it is in such a small, often urban, area—would not be able to survive for long.

Backing

Who supports the various militant groups? Where do they get their training and arms?

Training for the militants—apart from those coming 'blooded' from the Afghan War—has been provided in Azad Kashmir. This is not disputed. What is disputed is who provides the training? The Pakistan government? The Azad Kashmir 'government'? Non-governmental organizations? Depending on who one talks to one can easily reach the conclusion that all three are responsible. The Indian government naturally blames Pakistan, whose government—equally naturally—denies providing anything more than moral and diplomatic support to the Kashmiri separatists. Most commentators agree that the truth lies somewhere between these two extremes: while Pakistan did not instigate the Kashmiri insurgency, once it started it certainly did get involved.

Muhammad Saraf eloquently argues in favour of Pakistani non-instigation: 'You don't give people money and weapons and they just start dying. The question you have to ask is what made them prepared to start dying?'[18] Even if instigation is ruled out, two major arguments can still be put forward for Pakistani involvement in the Kashmir conflict. One, the fact that the pro-independence JKLF has been displaced in the field by the pro-Pakistan Hizbul-Mujahideen and similar-thinking groups. The JKLF claims that this is due to Pakistan only supporting those groups working for its interests, i.e. the accession of Jammu and Kashmir to Pakistan. Wirsing backs this view: 'Pakistan's support of the uprising, in terms of militant organizations financed, trained and equipped...has gradually been focussed to reflect its own political interests.'[19] The second argument in favour of Pakistan's involvement in the Kashmir conflict is based on the ISI's recent experience of training and arming *mujahideen* groups engaged in the Afghan resistance. It would have been very easy to transfer the same set-up to Kashmiri insurgents, particularly after the withdrawal of Soviet troops from Afghanistan reduced the need for external assistance there.

The Pakistani authorities' reply to such arguments is that they do not officially provide military assistance of any kind to the Kashmiris, but that they cannot prevent non-governmental organizations or non-serving military personnel from doing so. They also claim that the supply of weapons and the LoC are impossible for them to control. While there is some truth to these assertions, Wirsing notes:

> When all is said and done...there is very little likelihood that many infiltrators have made their way across the LoC into Indian Kashmir without the knowledge and active co-operation of the Pakistan army,

of the Afghan-seasoned ISI, and, indeed, of key elements in the civil bureaucracies of Pakistan and Azad Kashmir.[20]

Official Pakistani support for the Kashmiri separatists is very much linked to political thinking in Islamabad, and hence has shown considerable fluctuation as the government there has changed. Benazir Bhutto, for instance, was far less committed to arming the militants than her predecessor Nawaz Sharif. During her period in office, the army/ISI-run camps were largely shut down. Even regimes such as Sharif's that were very vocal in their support of the insurgency, did not always translate their words into actions; a frequent criticism made against Pakistan's rulers is that their backing is limited to rhetoric. The Pakistan government's role in the Kashmir conflict, and particularly the factors influencing this role, was discussed in Chapter Six.

The Azad Kashmir government, as discussed in the same chapter, is only nominally independent; in practice it is firmly controlled by Islamabad. Hence, with respect to supporting the Kashmir insurgency its actions have been largely the same. The only difference between Muzzaffarabad's approach to the insurgency and Islamabad's is that the former has been less inhibited in publicly acknowledging its role in the Kashmir conflict; the Azad Kashmiris can claim that they are helping their fellow countrymen across the LoC. Note that Azad Kashmir governments have also been criticized for not being sincere in their expressions of support for the militants; they have been seen as more concerned with lining their own pockets.

The third source of support for the militants is non-governmental organizations and foreign (non-Pakistani) Islamic governments. Considering the latter first, there is little evidence that any of the traditional sponsors of insurgency ('terrorism'), such as Libya and Iran or even Saudi Arabia (which does back militant Sunni groups within Pakistan), have taken great interest in the Kashmir conflict. This perhaps explains why the Kashmiris are less well-armed than the Afghans were in their struggle against the Soviets. What aid Islamic governments, and indeed non-official organizations in these countries, do provide is more likely to be humanitarian [clothing, medicine, schoolbooks, etc.], directed at the civilian population.

However, non-governmental organizations within Pakistan, while also trying to improve the conditions of civilians, have in addition been very active in their support of the militants. By far the most significant of these is the Jamaat-i-Islami. The Jamaat sponsors Hizbul-Mujahideen, which thanks to its backing as well as that of the Pakistani authorities, is now the largest, best-armed and most effective militant group operating in the Kashmir Valley. Like the Pakistan government, organizations such as the Jamaat are highly selective in which militants they support: basically those that share their Islamic ideology and have the same aspirations for Kashmir.

With respect to backing for the militant groups one final point to stress is that backers have been at least as influential—if not more—than the groups they sponsor in determining the course of the insurgency. This is because no militant group can operate for long without outside funding, training and arms. Hence, by backing certain groups and sidelining others, 'external' groups like the Jamaat are able to 'decide' who participates in the Kashmir conflict as well as dictate their strategy and activities. It should also be stressed that it is by no means certain that the aspirations of such backers and the groups they sponsor are also shared by the majority of Kashmiris.

Criminal and Foreign Elements

Public support or lack of it for the militants will be assessed below, but one can say now that by the early 1990s (1993–94) this had waned considerably. One reason, also considered later in this chapter, was the impact prolonged conflict was having on the lives of the civilians. But there were two other reasons, both specifically attributable to the militants.

The first of these was the criminilization and commercialization of the separatist movement. With many militants uneducated and having received little or no military training, and with no central body to exert discipline on the numerous groups, it is perhaps not surprising that for a significant number the insurgency became an opportunity for personal profit. The separatist movement became an excuse to extort money out of the civilian population, while the atmosphere of violence and conflict made it easier to get away with criminal acts. Even where funds collected by force were used to fight the security forces, the method of their extraction cannot have endeared the militants to the public. Far more alienating than the forced collection of money, were the acts of violence—including rape and murder—carried out by militants on civilians. Supporters of the Kashmir insurgency claim that such criminal elements have since been filtered out and that the militants now enjoy public support.[21]

A second reason for public alienation was the arrival of foreign '*mujahideen*' in the Valley. Motivated by a desire for *jihad*, or merely at a loose end after the withdrawal of Soviet troops from Afghanistan, several hundred Arabs, Iranians, Afghans and Muslims from other parts of the Islamic world, made their way to Kashmir to participate in the conflict there. Their arrival was viewed with mixed emotions. While those who saw the Kashmir insurgency as a *jihad* welcomed the help of their Muslim brothers, others for whom it was a nationalist struggle resented the foreigners' presence.

But more than ideological differences, it was the actions of the foreign '*mujahideen*' that provoked resentment among the civilian population. Firstly, they tended to be very 'fundamentalist/orthodox' in their practice of Islam, and—more disturbingly—insisted that the Kashmiris follow their example. For a while it became unsafe for women to walk out with their faces uncovered because the *mujahideen* enforced the Islamic dress code, *purdah*, by spraying acid on exposed women. Secondly, for the same reason and because they came from other parts of the world, the foreigners did not share the Kashmiris' reverence of local saints and shrines, and hence were prepared to violate such 'holy' places. In March 1995, the Charar-i-Sharif shrine of the saint Nand Rishi was occupied by foreign militants and, in disputed circumstances, was eventually destroyed by fire.[22] Its destruction provoked great ill-feeling among Kashmiris towards the foreigners fighting in their name.

Thirdly, militants from abroad have shown a tendency to be very single-minded in their struggle to 'liberate' Kashmir, and hence more willing than native militants to use ruthless tactics. In 1995, five Westerners were taken hostage by an Afghan group called Al-Faran; one of the hostages was later discovered decapitated, and it is generally assumed that the remainder have also been killed (though their bodies have never been found). The kidnapping and execution of innocent bystanders was condemned by Kashmiri civilians and militants alike. The Kashmiris' worry is that by carrying out such acts, that arouse revulsion within the international community, the foreigners give the entire struggle a bad name.

Major Militant Groups

1) Jammu and Kashmir Liberation Front (JKLF)

The goal of this group is an independent Jammu and Kashmir with the borders of the pre-1947 state, i.e. including both Indian Jammu and Kashmir, and Pakistan-controlled Azad Kashmir as well as the Northern Areas.[23] The JKLF claims such a state would be secular—though it would not contradict any of the principles of the Quran and *Sunna*—and hence they welcome all Kashmiris, Hindu as well as Muslim, in their movement. In practice, they have had little success in winning non-Muslims to their cause. But most commentators agree that among Muslims in the Valley, the JKLF enjoys considerable popular support. However, as a military force it has been virtually eclipsed by pro-Pakistan groups like the Hizbul-Mujahideen. Recently, the JKLF split into two factions led respectively by Amanullah Khan and Yasin Malik. This split emerged partly out of personality differences, but mostly over divergent attitudes to militancy. On his release from jail by the Indian authorities in 1994, Malik announced that he was renouncing violence and would in future be seeking a resolution of the conflict through peaceful means; Amanullah Khan, however, remained committed to the armed struggle.

2) Hizbul-Mujahideen (HUM)

HUM could be described as the complete opposite of the JKLF: HUM wants Indian Jammu and Kashmir to accede to Pakistan, and the resulting state to be run on Islamic lines. They thus see the insurgency in Kashmir not as a nationalist struggle but a *jihad*, and non-Muslims like Pandits as the 'other'—to be treated well but nonetheless as outsiders. HUM is openly sponsored by Pakistan's Jamaat-i-Islami, and probably covertly by the ISI. HUM appeared on the scene in 1990, well after the JKLF, but it is now the best-financed and best-armed militant group operating in the Valley—and hence the most effective force in the field. Membership is estimated at 4000 and is drawn largely from the Valley, Azad Kashmir, Pakistan, and Afghanistan.

3) Harkat-ul-Ansar

Consisting largely of Afghans, this group joined the Kashmir conflict from the war in Afghanistan It was formed in 1993. Like HUM they want Indian Jammu and Kashmir to accede to Pakistan, but are far more extreme than HUM. Hewitt writes:

> Harkat is linked to some of the more unstable and dangerous elements within the Islamic world, sustained mainly by contacts made during the Afghan war with organisations like Iranian-backed groups working throughout the Middle East (Hamas... Palestinian Hezbul). If any of the groups active in the field...merits the label 'Islamic fundamentalism' it is the Harkat.[24]

Harkat-ul-Ansar were responsible for the kidnapping of two British holidaymakers, Kim Housego and David Mackie, in the summer of 1994 and of four more Westerners that October; the former were released unharmed while the latter were rescued by police. Harkat are also believed to have been holed up in the Charar-i-Sharif shrine prior to its destruction in May 1995.

4) Al-Faran

Closely associated with Harkat-ul-Ansar, this group achieved notoriety in 1995 when it kidnapped several Westerners. One was later found beheaded and the others are also believed to have been killed.

5) Lashkar-e-Tayyeba (LT)

A pro-independence but strongly Islamic group, LT gained prominence in the late 1990s because of its use of suicide missions and a number of high profile attacks. It was blamed for the massacre of 35 Sikhs in Jammu and Kashmir in March 2000. Later, it launched attacks on Srinagar airport and the Red Fort in Delhi. On 1 October 2001, a bomb attack and firing on the Srinagar Legislative Assembly killed thirty-eight people. LT initially claimed responsibility, but later denied it. India holds the group responsible for the 13 December 2001 attack on the Lok Sabha. In December 2001, the US placed it on its list of terrorist groups.

6) Jaish-e-Muhammad (JM)

JM was formed in January 2000 by Maulana Azhar Masood. Masood was originally a member of Harkat-ul-Mujahideen, but was captured by Indian security forces in Srinagar in 1994 and jailed. He was released following the hijacking of an Indian Airlines plane by Kashmiri militants in December 1999. The plane was flown to Kandahar in Afghanistan, and the hostages released after the Indians set Masood free. JM is based in Pakistan.

7) Smaller groups

These are numerous. They include:
Al-Barq – the militant wing of the People's Conference led by Abdul Ghani Lone, pro-independence;

Al-Fateh and Al-Jihad – the militant wings of the two factions of the People's League, both pro-independence;

Allah Tigers – an extremely fundamentalist group responsible for the forced closure of video shops, cinemas, beauty parlours and other 'un-Islamic' institutions;

Operation Balakot – originally known as Mahaz-i-Azadi (Independence Front) led by Azam Inquilabi, wants Kashmiris to have the right of self-determination, including the option of independence.

Indian Response: Security Forces

'By 1991, the Indian government had abandoned any political approach to the state of Jammu and Kashmir, and had adopted a military framework for dealing with the crisis.'[25] This description by Hewitt of the Valley at the beginning of the decade can pretty much be applied to the current situation—the only modifications being that recently some efforts have been made to restart the political process, and—somewhat ironically—that the Indian government's dependence on military force has increased.

The state police (mostly Muslim in the Valley) were considered insufficient in both number and training to deal with the militant threat. Many were also 'widely suspected of harbouring ambivalent feelings about, if not actively sympathizing with, the Kashmiri militants.'[26] Hence, the majority of security forces tackling the insurgency in Jammu and Kashmir have been drawn from other parts of the country. There are two main kinds: paramilitaries and army personnel. The former are drawn largely from the Border Security Force (BSF) and Central Reserve Police Force (CRPF), and in lesser numbers from the Indo-Tibetan Border Police (ITBF) and Rashtriya National Rifles (RR). The latter consist of various infantry and mountain divisions. Both the paramilitaries and soldiers are predominantly Hindu.

The number of security forces deployed in Jammu and Kashmir is disputed: while opponents of Indian rule claim there are 700,000–800,000 men from various forces stationed in the Valley, the Indian authorities strongly refute this figure as a huge exaggeration. Wirsing put the number of Indian forces between 300,000 and 400,000 in 1993;[27] it has undoubtedly gone up since then. Somewhere between 600,000–700,000 is probably the most accurate estimate.

The operational procedures of the security forces consist of: sealing up the LoC to prevent the crossing of militants and weapons; mounting cordon and search operations to find militants and weapons; and holding large numbers of suspected militants in custody. These are in addition to the usual security procedures followed in such a conflict situation such as a heavy security presence around government and other important personnel and buildings, the setting up of numerous checkpoints and frequent verification of identity papers. Consider these operational procedures in more detail.

The Indian authorities have for the large part persistently refused to acknowledge that there could be domestic reasons for unrest in the Valley; they put the blame squarely on Pakistan for formenting and sustaining the insurgency. For this reason sealing off the LoC dividing Indian and Pakistani-held territory has been a major part of their counter-insurgency strategy. The use of better fencing, searchlights, tripwire, etc, as well as more intense patrolling have certainly made the LoC less porous than it was when the insurgency began. Militants in Azad Kashmir acknowledge that it is now harder to get into the Valley—harder, but not impossible; 'determined infiltrators...[*can*] penetrate Indian defences.'[28] The Indian failure to completely seal the border is due, firstly, to the physical difficulties in undertaking this task along a stretch of hilly/mountainous territory 450 miles long, and secondly, to the lack of corresponding measures on the Pakistani side. Schofield quotes Sardar Abdul Qayyum Khan, on-off Prime Minister of Azad Kashmir 'We don't mind the boys coming in and going back.'[29]

A second major part of Indian strategy has, therefore, been the mounting of cordon-and-search operations in civilian areas to try and find militants and/or weapons that have made it into the Valley. Wirsing describes the usual procedure:

> the targeted area is generally surrounded by troops in the predawn; all persons within the area—whatever their age or gender—are commanded to vacate their dwellings or business establishments and to assemble in a designated area, where they are held under guard; a meticulous house-to-house search, often requiring four to six hours to carry out, is then conducted; and in the meanwhile a so-called parade of the inhabitants, following segregation of women, small children, and aged males[ ] from teenage and adult males, is held, in which hooded informers are invited to identify suspects. Suspects, if any, are then led away for interrogation and possible detention.[30]

The effect of such operations on the public, as well as the possible abuse of human rights during them, will be considered below. The third major element of Indian counter-insurgency is the detention and questioning of suspected militants. As with many other aspects of the Kashmir conflict, it is impossible to get accurate figures for the number of Kashmiris currently being held in custody. Indian government statistics put the number around 5000, while its opponents claim ten times that figure. The truth lies somewhere between these two extremes but 'until Indian arrest, detention and penal procedures achieve vastly greater transparency than they now have…the Kashmiri Muslim prison population must remain a matter largely of conjecture.'[31] The treatment of Kashmiris held in Indian custody will be considered below. Describing the atmosphere of heightened security in the Valley, Andrew Whitehead writes:

> The security clampdown in Srinagar is ferocious. Thousands of soldiers and paramilitary troops—hardly any of them Kashmiri speakers—line the streets. Sandbagged bunkers, sheathed in anti-grenade netting, have been constructed at street corners. In the words of one foreign diplomat, it has the feel of a city under occupation.[32]

The security forces are helped in their counter-insurgency operations by a formidable legislative arsenal. In a hangover from the days of colonial rule, Indian statute books contain a number of provisions allowing preventive detention in an emergency. When Jammu and Kashmir was declared a disturbed area and placed under emergency rule by Girish Saxena on 5 July 1990, these statutes came into force in the State:

1) Terrorism and Disruptive Actions (Prevention) Act 1987 (TADA)—originally passed to contain Sikh militancy in the Punjab, this act allows anyone suspected of involvement in terrorist or 'disruptive' activities to be held in custody for up to one year, without being charged or tried. In order to qualify for bail, those detained must first prove their innocence and a judge must guarantee that after being released they will not commit an offence—'a guarantee that few judges are likely to make.'[33] The term 'disruptive' merits further attention; it is defined as:

> any action, whether by act or by speech or through any other media or in any other manner, which questions, disrupts...the sovereignty or territorial integrity of India, or which is intended to bring about or supports any claim for the cession of any part of India or the secession of any part of India from the Union.[34]

It will be apparent that with such a definition TADA can be used to restrict legitimate political activity as well as militancy.

2) Jammu and Kashmir Public Safety Act 1978—passed by the Jammu and Kashmir Assembly, this act goes even further than TADA, allowing suspects to be held in detention for up to two years without trial. PSA detainees are also worse off than their TADA counterparts because while the latter must by law be held within Jammu and Kashmir, the former can be held anywhere in the Indian Union. 'The cumulative effect of such legislation is that the government has been able to act with relative impunity in the State of Jammu and Kashmir.'[35] It is not uncommon for someone held under TADA for one year to

be released at the end of that period, only to be immediately rearrested under the PSA and incarcerated for a further two years—or vice versa.

3) Jammu and Kashmir Disturbed Areas Act 1990—promulgated in all six districts of the Valley, this act forbade the assembly of more than five people; authorized relatively low-ranking personnel to shoot anyone they suspected of disturbing public order; and permitted the destruction of any building thought to be an arms dump or providing shelter to militants.

4) Armed Forces (Jammu and Kashmir) Special Powers Act 1990—this act basically handed control of 'disturbed areas' over to the army. Officers were entitled to fire upon anyone contravening any law or order in force, in the disturbed areas; destroy any structure thought to be an arms dump, militant shelter or training camp; arrest people without warrant if suspected of having committed or being about to commit an offence; enter and search any premises without a warrant; and stop and search any vehicle suspected of carrying 'offenders' or arms.

These last two acts effectively gave the security forces a free hand to use lethal force. Commenting on them and the wide powers of detention available to the authorities in Jammu and Kashmir, Wirsing writes: 'it is the quite legal, judicial punishments that may have had the greatest negative impact on Kashmiri Muslim attitudes both toward the security forces and toward India.'[36]

Human Rights Abuses

Both parties in the Kashmir conflict—militants and security forces—have been accused of abusing human rights. Accusations against the latter are far greater and hence will be considered first.

Human rights abuses allegedly committed by the security forces in Kashmir include: rape and sexual molestation; torture and killing of people held in custody; assaults on and execution of civilians; arson and destruction of property; and theft. All sides in the Kashmir conflict—including the Indian government—acknowledge that such abuses do take place. What they disagree over is their frequency, and 'the earnestness of government efforts to stop them and to punish the guilty.'[37] Consider the alleged abuses in turn.

Rape and Sexual Molestation

Acts of rape have been commonplace in times of conflict and war since time immemorial; there is nothing new in this. What is new, however, is the deliberate and systematic use of rape as a weapon or strategy to weaken the enemy. This practice was seen in the Bosnian conflict and is allegedly being repeated by the Indians in Kashmir. A report published in 1993 jointly by Asia Watch and Physicians for Human Rights, a US-based human rights group, stated that: 'rape is used as a means of targetting women whom the security forces accuse of being militant sympathizers; in raping them, the security forces are attempting to punish and humiliate the entire community.'[38] Most assaults on women take place during house searches—men are either separated or, presumably to maximize the psychological impact, forced to watch. In other cases, women are assaulted while out, or are abducted and taken to military camps. Hundreds of individual acts of rape are alleged to have been committed by the Indian forces. Among the most notorious was the gang-rape of a bride—seized during her wedding—in Anantnag in April 1990, and the rape of some fifty-three women at the small town of Kunan Poshpura during a cordon-and-search operation, by soldiers of the 4th Rajput Rifles. The latter incident was disputed; the Indians claimed the whole thing was a massive hoax designed to discredit them, but human rights observers concluded that 'while mass rape at Kunan Poshpura may not have been proved beyond doubt, there are very substantial grounds for believing that it took place.'[39] As in Kunan Poshpura, so in the Valley as a whole the figures given by Kashmiri sympathizers are likely to have been exaggerated. A point to note, however, is that in the case of rape the nature of abuse is such that many Kashmiris would feel ashamed to speak of it, and hence incidents of rape might actually be far more frequent than alleged. Whatever the exact figure, the fact that sexual assaults by the security forces do take place on a large scale is beyond dispute.

Torture and Custodial Killings

The 1994 report on human rights violations in Kashmir by the International Commission of Jurists noted that:

> [t]orture is virtually a matter of routine in interrogation. The forms of torture range from electric shocks to beatings, other forms of violence and sexual abuse.... The situation is aggravated by the fact that...forced confessions are admissible in trials.[40]

Amnesty International has commented 'the brutality of torture in Jammu and Kashmir defies belief.'[41]

The various security forces maintain their own interrogation centres; there are several dozen throughout the State, with around thirty in Srinagar alone including the notorious Hari Nawas—formerly a palace used by the Maharaja of Kashmir. The use of torture in these centres has been extensively chronicled. Not surprisingly, many detainees are killed while in custody—precise figures are impossible to ascertain, but numbers run at least into the many hundreds, and most likely thousands. One correspondent, writing in an Indian newspaper, reported:

> Very few of them *(young Kashmiri men)* get released after having been severely tortured in investigation centres which are torture chambers...but one does hear from time to time that mutilated bodies were seen floating in the River Jhelum, or on the road. Death in custody is a common practice in Kashmir.[42]

Abdul Majeed Maalik, Chairman of the Human Rights Division of the Kashmir Bar Association, claims that the situation with respect to deaths in custody is now so bad that Kashmiris released after being tortured are considered fortunate and are congratulated—they have at least made it back to their families alive![43] It is also a common practice in Kashmir for people to 'disappear.' Known as 'missing persons,' their disappearance is widely attributed by Kashmiris to the security forces. Ashok Jaitley, a senior IAS officer brought into the State to help cope with the crisis, failed in his attempts to locate the whereabouts of 81 'missing persons;' he subsequently requested to be transferred elsewhere.

Extra-judicial Killings

These are also common in Kashmir. The authorities' usual justification is that there was an encounter in which the suspects were killed or, in the case of civilians, that they were 'accidentally' shot in cross-fire.[44] Wirsing cites an Indian civil servant who speculated that such killings,

> were part of a deliberate strategy learned from the experience of the security forces in the Punjab. There, he said, faked encounters had been used by the security forces to conduct summary executions of hardcore Sikh militants...[t]he model, he guessed, had been imported into Kashmir as a strategy for curbing attacks upon and abductions of BSF personnel and their families by Kashmiri militants.

A civil rights activist suggested another motive: 'extra-judicial killing of suspects was the most efficient—in fact the only efficient—means of contending with the insurgency. Public trials in India, after all, were notoriously slow, costly, and of very uncertain outcome.'[45]

A third reason for the killing of civilians by members of the security forces is to avenge attacks by militants; unable to always get their hands on those directly responsible, angry soldiers vent their anger on the civilian population. The Asia Watch report described the usual procedure:

> Often within hours of coming under gunfire or grenade attack by militants, the security forces cordon off the neighbourhood from *(sic)* which they believe the attack was launched and conduct house to house searches. Civilians suspected of supporting the militants are routinely beaten and in many cases either arrested or shot dead.[46]

Incidents of troops firing indiscriminately in crowded bazaars have been recorded, the worst being that of 6 January 1993 in Sopore when it is estimated 100 people died, either as a result of being shot or burnt. Amnesty's report on the Sopore incident stated: 'The soldiers were out of control. They were firing in every direction.'[47]

Arson and Destruction/Theft of Property

Acts of widescale arson have been carried out by the security forces in Kashmir, both to avenge attacks by militants and to 'suppress' the civilian population and deter them from backing the insurgency. A *Newsweek* correspondent reported a typical attack: 'The Indian paramilitary police stormed into the Chini Chowk quarter of Anantnag, a town 56 kilometres south of Srinagar. They threw gasoline soaked clothing and gun powder into several brick and wood houses and ignited the explosive mixture.'[48] Among the worst incidents were the burning of several hundred shops and houses in Handwara in October 1990, and of a similar number in the Lal Chowk quarter of Srinagar in April 1993. Finally, the notorious house-to-house searches carried out by the security forces often involve the destruction and/or theft of property.

As mentioned above the security forces are not the only violators of human rights in Kashmir; the militants have also made their 'contribution'. Abuses by the latter are, however, even more poorly chronicled than the patchy records of violations by the Indians and hence it is impossible to give any kind of figures. What one can say is that the pattern of abuse by the militants is very different from that of the security forces. The most common practice is the beating or killing of people suspected of collaborating with the Indian authorities or who refuse to co-operate with the insurgents. The houses of such people may also be burnt or their property otherwise destroyed. As described earlier militants have been known to resort to force in order to get money, food, shelter, etc, from the civilian population. Less common are incidents of rape and sexual molestation.

That human rights abuses take place on a large scale in Kashmir is acknowledged by all the parties involved, and increasingly by the international community. The Indian government is fully aware of the damage such abuses do to its case in international fora that Kashmir is an integral part of India. Hence, since 1993, it has been making efforts to at least give the impression of dealing with the problem. A team of international jurists was allowed to visit the Valley that year, and in October the National Human Rights Commission was set up to investigate abuses. At a press conference in June 1993, Rajesh Pilot, then Minister of State for Home Affairs, claimed that 'the government was taking forceful action to curb violations, and that custodial deaths, in particular, were no longer tolerated.'[49]

In practice, however, there is little evidence to support such Indian claims. International human rights organizations—notably Amnesty International—are still not allowed into the Valley. The National Human Rights Commission set up by the government does not have the power to look into allegations of abuse by the army and paramilitary forces: 'All it can do when faced with complaints of this nature is to call for official reports from the government, effectively functioning as a 'postal box' of official views.'[50] And the allegations of widespread abuse—torture, rape, summary executions, 'disappearances'—continue unabated. Even if only a fraction of these allegations are based on fact, they still paint a very grim picture of human rights in Kashmir.

Effects of the Conflict on the Civilian Population: Public Response

Kashmiri Muslims

The effects of the Kashmir conflict on the people of the Valley can be divided into: financial and material; physical—injuries and fatalities; and psychological. Taking the financial cost of the conflict first, this has been considerable. Prior to 1989 a, if not the, major source of revenue to the State was tourism. The Valley's temperate climate, coupled with its breath-taking scenery attracted both Indian and foreign holidaymakers. But the combination of violent insurgency and hostage-taking has now completely wiped out the State's tourism industry. This has had detrimental consequences both for revenue and employment. Those formerly occupied with catering for tourists—houseboat, hotel and restaurant owners, craftsmen, etc.—have seen the market for their services disappear; they have swollen the already considerable ranks of graduate unemployed in Kashmir. Overall, the standard of living in Kashmir has fallen considerably.

Demands on the State administration have inevitably increased since the conflict began. But at the same time, the State's ability to respond to these has declined. The combination of violent insurgency and lost revenue has made it difficult for the administration to continue providing even the existing (pre-conflict) level of educational, healthcare, and other services. Coping with the extra social problems generated by the conflict, has so far proved impossible.

The city of Srinagar is dusty and dirty, with uncollected rubbish dumped on the roadside for dogs and cows to forage through. The streets are full of potholes... Dal lake is thick and stagnant with weeds... Children have frequently been unable to go to school and the standard of education has declined...many schools have been burnt by 'renegade' militants [or]...occupied by the security forces, who have also installed themselves in university campuses. Official figures maintain that the schools functioned for ninety-three days in 1993–94 and 140 days in 1994–95 and primary school education in general has regressed...[m]edical facilities are insufficient and the hospitals are unhygienic. The doctors are overworked and many have fled...[i]mmunisation programmes for children have fallen behind.[51]

Turning to the human cost of the conflict, this too has been considerable. Estimates vary greatly depending on the source, but according to Amnesty International the number of people killed was in excess of 17,000 at the end of 1995, so must now be well over the 20,000 mark—a recent estimate actually put the figure above 34,000.[52] The number of people who have been injured is, of course, far greater. Wirsing comments that compared to other separatist insurgencies such as the Bangladesh movement in 1971 'the Kashmir uprising so far has taken relatively few lives.' But he goes on to note that 'these figures are substantially magnified in the public's mind...because of the valley's small size, in both territory and population, and unusually strong ethnic solidarity.'[53] The fact that many deaths have been caused by gross human rights abuses has also given them extra potency with respect to their emotional impact.

The psychological trauma induced by the Kashmir conflict will perhaps only be able to be properly assessed once it is over. Some indication of its magnitude can, however, be gauged from the fact that the number of patients seen by the psychiatric department of Srinagar Medical College shot up from 1,528 patients in 1990 to 38,000 in 1994.[54] Abdul Majeed Maalik comments that incidents of suicide, particularly among young Kashmiri women, are becoming more frequent.[55] The reasons for this are understandable: there are very few families in Kashmir that have escaped losing one or more members at the hands of the security forces or the militants. For almost a decade they have been living with the fear that violence could break out at any time—coupled with the over-powering security presence, this makes for very high stress levels. Many, including children, have witnessed highly traumatic incidents such as murder and rape. Even if the fighting in Kashmir were to end tomorrow, its psychological impact will undoubtedly continue to be felt for many years: 'The sad fact is that psychological damage arising out of years of military action and insurgency and militancy...are often irreparable.'[56]

The situation with respect to children in the Valley is particularly worrisome. A recent Amnesty report on children in South Asia noted that those in Kashmir are becoming socialized to violence:

> For the Kashmiri child A stands for arms, B for blood, C for curfew. In one reported incident ten-year old Mushtaq took a bayonet to Burnhall School in Srinagar to show off to friends. He was outdone by another ten-year old boy who had brought a grenade and pistol in his lunchbox. The school's Vice-Principal said that children frequently brought guns to school.[57]

There is a very real danger that a whole generation of children will grow up in Kashmir having known nothing but conflict. Adjusting to peace, assuming that the conflict is eventually resolved, will, therefore, be very difficult for them. The Amnesty report went on 'if this socialisation towards violence continues there will be a large-scale revival of militancy after a decade.'

The effects of the Kashmir conflict described above apply largely to Kashmiri Muslims only because it is they who are 'in the thick of it'—the vast majority of Pandits have left the Valley and hence, while they too have been tremendously affected by the conflict, it has been in different ways. They will be considered separately below.

How do Kashmiri Muslims view the now over ten-year old insurgency? Have their attitudes toward it changed over time? Does the dominance of certain groups in the field accurately reflect public opinion?

As mentioned earlier, Kashmiri Muslims initially supported militant activity. While they expressed disapproval for some of the militants' tactics, their disillusionment with the political process, coupled with the early success of the militants, led them to back them. That was the situation at the beginning of the insurgency, when most people thought it would be resolved within months—few would have predicted then that it would still be going on ten years later. How have Kashmiri attitudes changed since that initial support?

Undoubtedly, there have been factors causing their support to wane. The criminalization and commercialization of the insurgency have already been described. So, too, the generally negative influence of foreign militants. Both of these led to public hostility toward the militants. Add to this the length of the conflict, the massive detrimental effect it has had on their lives, and the fact that as yet no end appears in sight. An element of fatigue, of war-weariness, has definitely crept into the Kashmiri Muslims. Many of them are now tired of the conflict and wish for the restoration of peace and normalcy. The Indian authorities go so far as to claim that what help Kashmiri Muslims do give to the militants is under duress—out of fear of reprisals if they refuse. According to New Delhi, in other words, the insurgency has changed from being one involving militants and the public, to one involving just the former.

But this is not the whole story. While most Kashmiri Muslims do wish for an end to the conflict, this is not at any price. Certainly they are no longer prepared to tolerate any form of Indian rule. By far the most important reason for this has been the widespread abuse of human rights in Kashmir ever since the conflict began. As described above, members of the Indian security forces committed the majority of these. The consequent Kashmiri Muslim hatred of the Indians outweighs their desire for peace. Nonetheless, there are limits on the price they are prepared to pay for such peace.

With respect to the militants, two observations can be made: one, that while Kashmiri Muslims have, at times, felt very hostile toward the militants (some more than others), on the whole, they still support them. The reason for this lies less with the militants themselves, than with the Kashmiri Muslim attitudes toward India. As just mentioned, they are no longer prepared to countenance staying a part of India. But there is no political way for them to secede since, to the limited extent that New Delhi is prepared to make political concessions, this is only in the context of Kashmir staying within the Indian Union. Two, with political change ruled out, the only other means by which Kashmiri Muslims can see Indian control ending is through militancy—hence their continued support of the militants despite militant imperfections.

Evidence for this support is implicit in the nature and continuation of the insurgency. The conflict in Kashmir between militants and security forces is not a guerrilla one, of the type fought in Afghanistan where Soviet forces and *mujahideen* controlled distinct areas, but more of a 'hide-and-seek' one with both parties operating in the same confined area. Ayyub Thakkar claims that in a conflict of this type it would be impossible for militant groups to operate without genuine co-operation from civilians.[58] Moreover, the fact that the insurgency has gone on for more than ten years, implies that it has had public support for this length of time.

Kashmiri Muslims supporting the militants because they are tired of Indian rule, is quite distinct from their supporting the other political aims of the militants (i.e. post-India). As mentioned before, the dominant player in the field is the pro-Pakistan Hizbul-Mujahideen. Do the majority of Kashmiri Muslims share its aspiration to accede to Pakistan? The answer to this question will depend very much on Pakistan's attitude to Kashmir, its own record over the last fifty years, and its role in the current conflict. As seen in Chapter Six on Pakistan and Kashmir, Kashmiri Muslims, in general, still have a favourable view of Pakistan; as in 1947 they see it essentially as a Muslim country—one in which, as Muslims, they too could fit in. Pakistan's slow progress towards an Islamic government, and its poor record on democracy and devolution, has not significantly dented its positive image among Kashmiri Muslims. Pakistan's appeal as a homeland has, of course, grown considerably as their alienation from India has become complete.

Turning to Pakistan's role in the Kashmir conflict, this is the factor that is far more likely to sway Kashmiri Muslims from being pro-accession-to-Pakistan to pro-independence. Chapter Six demonstrated how various elite groups in Pakistan make use of the Kashmir issue to promote their own domestic interests. Whilst the Pakistani public are strongly and genuinely committed to the Kashmiri insurgents' cause, their leaders are less so. Practically, this has been seen in Pakistan's limited support of the militants. Though Pakistan would obviously be placed in a very awkward position internationally if it was to overtly back the militants, covert backing—that has no such negative effects attached—has been far less than it could be. This lack of commitment from the Pakistani authorities has led some Kashmiri Muslims to become disillusioned with that country as well as India—and hence favour Kashmiri independence. The longer Pakistan fails to demonstrate a real commitment to the Kashmir insurgency, the more such thinking will spread. Note that Pakistan's recent involvement in the Kashmir conflict will very likely serve to reverse, or at least halt, this trend.

Pandits

'All communities have suffered during the insurgency.' Victoria Schofield's comment draws attention to the fact that the conflict has also affected the other major population group in the Kashmir Valley—the Pandits. Their suffering and the impact of the conflict on their lives has been different—though arguably no less—than that of the Muslims. In terms of human life, their losses have been fewer. According to Wirsing, up to May 1993 less than 400 Hindus had been killed;[59] these include the notorious shooting of sixteen male Hindu passengers taken off a bus by militants, and the assassination of several prominent Pandits. The numbers of Pandit casualties would undoubtedly have been greater had the community not migrated en masse from their native Valley.

The Pandits' migration has probably been the most obvious effect of the Kashmir conflict upon them; virtually the entire community of more than 150,000 people have now left Kashmir.

By the end of July 1990, almost 49,000 Pandit families were registered as migrants in Jammu, while some 11,500 families were registered as migrants in Delhi.[60] The vast majority of Pandits leaving the Valley for Jammu, Delhi, etc., in 1990 expected their stay there to last no more than a few months. Most took very few possessions with them and made no effort to sell their homes and their businesses before leaving: they merely locked these up, often entrusting the keys to their Muslim neighbours. All this made clear their intention to return. In Jammu too the migrants were accommodated in camps where conditions could only be described as basic—keeping with the conviction that their sojourn was to be of a short duration.

Over a decade later, most of the Pandits who left the Valley in 1990 are still living in camps; what was intended to be temporary accommodation has effectively become—in view of the fact that no end to the conflict is in sight—their permanent home. While some have managed to build new lives for themselves, most have been unable to find employment—certainly not of the standard they left—and remain dependent on aid. Furthermore, after so long their presence has come to be seen as a burden by the local communities into which they migrated. Kumar writes that 'ethnic tensions are gradually surfacing' between Pandits and Jammu Hindus. The stark contrast between their lives now ('in tattered tents and in abject poverty and often without food'[61]...'braving the cold in winter and the searing heat in summer with no proper sanitary facilities and less medical attention'[62]) and what they had in Kashmir ('ancestral orchards, lands and houses') shows very clearly how much the Pandits have suffered as a result of the Kashmir conflict.

It is not surprising, then, that the Pandits feel very bitter about the whole insurgency. Most of their anger is directed towards the militants, whom they see as Pakistani agents and Islamic fundamentalists rather than local Kashmiris (at least at the beginning of the insurgency). Referring to 'the rise of terrorism that Pakistan had injected into the Valley' Kumar goes on: 'It took Pakistan-trained and financed terrorists little time to throw out the Pandits from the Valley to achieve their aim of freeing the Valley from Hindu elements.'[63]

At the beginning of the insurgency, the Pandits appeared to have made a distinction between militants and Kashmiri Muslims. It was fear of the former rather than the latter that drove them from the Valley; had they truly feared Kashmiri Muslims they would hardly have entrusted their property to them when leaving Kashmir. Since then, however, their attitude to the Kashmiri Muslims has changed. This has come about because of Kashmiri Muslim support for the insurgency coupled with the perception that they have abandoned their traditional tolerance and become 'fundamentalist'. The Pandits view their own 'forced' exodus from the Valley as part of a deliberate plan to 'establish an Islamic theocratic State and to secede from India'.[64] And while this might have started off as a Pakistani-militant plan, the Pandits believe it now has the backing of the Muslim community in Kashmir as well. Hence their hostility towards the latter.

As the conflict has dragged on, Pandit anger has increasingly been directed at the Indian government. It is widely seen as having failed and having abandoned them. In 1991, Pandit leaders complained: 'Nothing is being done for us. We are being treated not as human beings, but as herds.'[65] A conference of world Kashmiri Pandits held two years later in New Delhi adopted what became known as the Delhi Declaration. Among other things 'noted with grave concern' were:

The apathy of the Indian Government towards victims of terrorism forced into mass exodus and living under sub-human conditions in refugee camps...the failure of the Indian Administrative and political system to deal with internal subversion and its failure to protect the limb, life, honour and fundamental rights of its citizens in Jammu and Kashmir, the failure of the Indian Foreign Office to effectively project the reality of Kashmir in its true dimension of minority-cleansing, genocide of Hindus and perpetuation of Islamic rule.[66]

It is this anger against India that has perhaps prevented Kashmiri Hindus from being absorbed into the Indian Hindu mainstream. It will be recalled from the introduction that one factor in raising ethnic consciousness is a sense of being treated badly (whether economically, politically or otherwise) by the state. Whilst the Pandits have undoubtedly become more orthodox in their practice of Hinduism, and being Hindu has become a much more significant part of their identity, they have still retained their sense of distinctiveness based on being Kashmiri. The Delhi Declaration of 1993 included a commitment to 'safeguard against cultural disintegration and social obliteration'. Among the measures adopted to do this were the setting up of a 'University in Exile which shall promote studies in Kashmiri language, art, culture, philosophy, literature, [and] history', a Kashmiri Cultural Data Resource Base and a museum of Kashmiri Art and Cultural Heritage.[67]

Political Developments Since the Conflict Began

These can basically be divided into efforts by the militants to establish a united political front, and efforts by the Indian government to restart the political process in Jammu and Kashmir and restore an elected government. Arguably less significant have been growing Pandit demands for their own 'homeland'. Consider each of these in turn.

All Parties Hurriyat Conference

Early attempts by the various groups opposed to Indian rule, to unite in a single organization, fell apart. In February 1993, another attempt was made with the founding of the All Parties Hurriyat Conference (APHC). A conglomeration of more than thirty political parties, this organization encompasses (it is still active) all the major players in the Kashmir conflict, with the exception of Farooq Abdullah's National Conference. Thus it includes both pro-independence groups like the JKLF, and the more numerous pro-Pakistan groups such as Jamaat-i-Islami and the Muslim Conference. A 'neutral' figure was chosen to head the new organization—Omar Farooq, son of the assassinated Maulvi Farooq and heir to his position of Mirwaiz of Kashmir (he has since been replaced by Jamaat leader, Ali Gilani). Through the APHC, the various insurgent groups in Kashmir have been able to present a relatively united political front. The APHC has been able to survive in spite of the fundamental ideological differences among its constituent parties by restricting its political demands to the end of Indian rule and the holding of a free plebiscite to determine the wishes of the Kashmiri people. The latter, if held, would include the option of independence. It may well be that the current unity among the insurgent groups will disintegrate if and when Kashmir secedes from India, but for now the common initial goal of ending Indian rule is holding them together.

Political Initiatives by the Indian Government

These are based on a principle fundamentally opposed to that of the APHC—namely that Jammu and Kashmir is an integral part of the Indian Union and secession, even of only a part of the State, is not an option. When the Kashmir insurgency first began, the Indian response was merely to apply more and more force with the aim of crushing the secessionist movement. However, as time progressed and this approach failed to yield the desired results, thinking in New Delhi turned once again to a political solution. Besides the condition that this had to be found within the existing Indian Union, the Indian government insisted it would only deal with the Kashmiris' elected representatives— effectively ruling out the APHC. New Delhi was keen to restore an elected State government not only to initiate political dialogue but also to counter mounting international criticism of New Dehli and the army's rule in Jammu and Kashmir.

The Indian government had decided, by the end of 1993, on elections as the way forward to a solution of the Kashmir problem. They made clear their intention by releasing several prominent political leaders: Yasin Malik of the JKLF in May 1994, and Shabir Shah, Syed Ali Gilani, Abdul Ghani Lone as well as 276 other political prisoners in October of the same year. Soon after their release, Yasin Malik and Shabir Shah announced that they were renouncing violence. But despite these promising initial moves, it was to take more than two years before elections could actually be held. There were two major obstacles.

One, the need to re-establish some sort of civil administration capable of carrying out an election. Years of conflict had virtually wiped out the State's administrative machinery. So, large numbers of personnel had to be drafted in from other parts of India. In addition, there was a dearth of accurate information about the State's population: the 1991 national census had not been held in Jammu and Kashmir because of the disturbances, and any electoral records that did exist were destroyed by the militants.

Two, and by far the greater obstacle, the opposition of the militant groups and the APHC. The former manifested their antipathy to elections by assassinating Wali Mohammed Yatoo, a National Conference leader and former speaker of the State Assembly, and in the same month (March 1994) attempting to assassinate Farooq Abdullah and Rajesh Pilot when they paid a joint visit to the State. APHC leaders, including the newly released Yasin Malik and Shabir Shah, all made it clear that they were against the proposal and that their respective political parties would stage a boycott if India did push ahead with its plans. Such widespread opposition was already making the idea of holding elections in the spring of 1995 appear difficult. When, in May, the Charar-i-Sharif shrine was burnt down, all hopes of spring elections were effectively quashed. Election speculation renewed in November when the government sent officials into the State to oversee elections the following month, but again massive political opposition within Kashmir, coupled with threats of violence by the militants, forced a postponement.

Elections (of a sort) were finally held in Jammu and Kashmir in May 1996—though for the Lok Sabha rather than a State Assembly. The decision to press ahead with elections was made despite the fact that the APHC's opposition remained unaltered and the militants' threats to sabotage any polls were still in force. The thinking in the Rao government appeared to be that: 'A flawed election is better than no election...rule by any Kashmiri is preferable to continued rule from Delhi.'[68] In the event, the election turned out to be considerably 'flawed.' Either because of complete alienation from India or out of fear of the militants, few Kashmiris showed enthusiasm for voting. In order to ensure a high turnout—vital, if the elections were to have any credibility—the security forces were asked to 'mobilize' the population. Tim McGirk reported in the *Independent*: 'Throughout Kashmir valley, systematic use of intimidation and vote-rigging was carried out by Indian authorities... Everywhere...the story was the same: Indian soldiers and police forced the Kashmiris to vote. It was a fraud of careless transparency and brutality.'[69] Voter turnout in May 1996 was around 40 per cent. Any credibility this high figure gave to the elections was in large measure wiped out by the methods used to achieve it: the *Times* described the exercise as 'a propaganda disaster for India.'[70] With respect to the actual results, four of the State's six Lok Sabha seats went to Congress candidates, with Janata Dal and the BJP winning one each.

In September 1996, elections were held for the State Assembly. As in May, the Hurriyat Conference boycotted the polls so only pro-India parties—notably the National Conference, Congress, Janata Dal and the BJP—contested them. Despite the opposition of the APHC and militants, on this occasion there were far less reports of people being forced by the authorities to vote. The results showed a clear victory for Farooq Abdullah's National Conference; it won 40 out of the Valley's 44 seats, and 57 in total. Abdullah was sworn in as chief minister of Jammu and Kashmir on 8 October.

Pandit Political Demands

As has been observed already, where on the one hand, Pandits have become more 'Hindu' and the gulf between them and

Kashmiri Muslims has widened immensely—to the point of hostility—on the other hand, the Pandits have retained their distinct Kashmiri identity. The political manifestation of this 'new' Kashmiri Hindu identity has been the demand for a homeland in Kashmir exclusively for the Pandits: '*Panun Kashmir*' ('Our own Kashmir'). A resolution adopted by the Kashmiri Pandits Convention at Jammu in December 1991 called for:

> [e]stablishment of a 'Homeland' for the Kashmiri Hindus in the Kashmir Valley, comprising of the regions of the Valley to the East and North of river Jhelum...[t]he 'Homeland' be placed under the Central administration with a Union Territory status, so that it evolves its own economic and political infrastructure.[71]

Support for the 'back home movement' has grown among Pandits. A newspaper article in 1994 stated defiantly: 'Kashmir is the homeland of the Pandits—and so it will remain.'[72] In practice, however, as the conflict in Kashmir drags on, the chances for *Panun* Kashmir becoming a reality become more remote. Kashmiri Muslims are obviously not prepared to countenance such a state, and the Indian Government is more concerned with curbing the separatist movement than appeasing the Pandits. That community's frustration looks set to rise.

Internationalization of Conflict

For almost ten years the Kashmir insurgency remained essentially confined to the Kashmir Valley and LoC. While Pakistan certainly provided more than just moral support to the Kashmiri militants, it refrained from getting directly involved. Hostilities between India and Pakistan in the Siachen Glacier originated in the international Indo-Pak dispute over Jammu and Kashmir, rather than in the internal Kashmiri Muslim insurgency. Recently though, Pakistani forces did become directly involved in the latter. Their doing so marked a further escalation of the Kashmir conflict: having already gone from build-up to insurgency, to full-scale insurgency, it has now (or is seriously threatening to) become an international conflict. How has this come about? In view of the fact that internationalization of the insurgency represents convergence of the two Kashmir issues, international and internal, it is no surprise that the answer lies both in Kashmir and in the domestic politics of India and Pakistan.

Nuclear Rivalry

On 11 May 1998, and again two days later, the BJP government in India stunned the world by conducting a series of nuclear tests. It claimed that these were necessary for Indian security, mentioning the threat from nuclear-armed China, in particular. The failure by the existing nuclear powers, such as the United States, to get rid of their own nuclear arsenals was also cited as a factor: as a country which viewed itself as a world power, claiming a permanent seat on the UN Security Council, India had to be at par militarily. This was how the BJP and Indian 'hawks' justified the decision to go nuclear. The real reasons lie closer to home.

The BJP, like its ideological predecessor Jana Sangh, has always been a strong proponent of India's nuclear weapons programme. Its support does owe something to security considerations. Atal Bihar Vajpayee, addressing the Indian Parliament after China carried out nuclear tests in 1964, declared: 'the answer to an atom bomb is an atom bomb, nothing else.'[73] But it owes more to the party's vision of India as a Hindu state. Moreover, being anti-Muslim, the BJP desires such a state to be—for it has yet to be fully achieved—militarily powerful. As Bidwai and Vanaik explain:

For the BJP...nuclear weapons are an article of faith, part of the essential identity of a powerful, awe-inspiring, militarist 'Hindu India' that can boast of its 'manliness' and 'virility' and thus prove to the world the superiority of Hindu 'civilisation'.[74]

In carrying out nuclear tests, the BJP government sought to impress on the international community that India was a world power, and move closer to realizing its goal of a 'Hindu' India. [Vanaik notes that the alternative ways in which it could have done this, e.g. building up India into an economic tiger, would have taken too long.]

There were also more immediate domestic political reasons behind the BJP's decision. The party, though holding the largest number of seats in the Lok Sabha, did not have an outright majority, and thus headed a coalition government. Consisting of eighteen parties this was always going to be unwieldy and it was no surprise that 'within days of assuming office the fissures in the coalition were evident.' Looking for a way of ending this disunity and holding onto power—and avoiding its 1996 experience of vacating office after just thirteen days—the BJP came up with Operation Shakti (the name given to the nuclear tests). That this strategy worked was evident from the virtually universal political backing the tests received, and the 87 per cent popular support.[75] Riding the nuclear wave, the BJP was, in fact, able to hold on to power until the spring of 1999.

As mentioned above, the professed threat prompting Indian nuclear armament was that posed by China. However, prior to Operation Shakti and the 'deliberate and calculated invocation of China as potential enemy,' Sino-Indian relations had actually improved considerably. The two countries had signed peace agreements in 1991 and 1996, and nothing had changed between then and 1998 to make India feel especially threatened by Beijing. Aside from domestic reasons for going nuclear, the real international threat India was seeking to combat was that posed by its western neighbour, Pakistan. Even here though, the security argument does not seem justified since the balance of firepower in the subcontinent already weighs heavily in India's favour. In all categories of conventional weapons—tanks, artillery, warships, combat aircraft—India's reserves are about double as those of Pakistan; in terms of manpower its 980,000-strong army and 55,000-strong navy are also double as those of Pakistan, the air force almost three times as large.[76] These figures give further credence to the argument that the BJP decided to conduct nuclear tests for domestic political rather than international security reasons.

India's neighbours, however, have little interest in its domestic political intrigues. As far as they were concerned, the country's nuclear tests were directed at them. China, not surprisingly, responded angrily to both the tests and the declared reason behind them. Pakistan's response was more serious. On 28 May 1998, Islamabad conducted the first of its own five nuclear tests. Prime Minister Nawaz Sharif was, of course, urged by much of the international community, notably the United States and Britain, not to do so. However, even if he had been personally inclined toward restraint, the domestic political situation was such that he had no choice but to follow India. Failure to do so would have been seen at home as victory for India. Besides, there were genuine fears among the Pakistani public that India was really threatening Pakistan and should be sent a strong signal to prevent further aggression. As in India, the public loudly applauded the tests in Pakistan.

How does this nuclear rivalry have an impact on Kashmir? The effect on the international Indo-Pak dispute over the State is really quite straightforward. Kashmir has already led India and Pakistan to go to war three times (the 1971 conflict was sparked of by the crisis in East Pakistan). Still unresolved, it is the most likely trigger for a fourth war. Now that India and Pakistan both have nuclear weapons, dangers posed by such a war spinning out of control have hugely increased. 'What would once have been considered a low-key local conflict [*has been developed*] into a matter of grave international concern that could have even more chilling possibilities than the conflict over Kosovo.'[77] Noting Pakistani backing of the Kashmir insurgency, the *Economist* speculates:

> India retaliates only within Kashmir or by firing across a line of control, but it is easy to imagine that a future harder-line government might have other ideas. Pakistan might misinterpret a punitive strike as an attempt to dismember it, and might respond by exploding a

small nuclear weapon over an Indian tank battalion rather than a city...[f]aulty intelligence, mixed signals between governments or within them, or a breakdown in command and control could raise the risk of resorting to nuclear weapons with each step up the ladder.[78]

Furthermore, as Vanaik points out: 'the initiation of such nuclear rivalry both reflects and *qualitatively exacerbates* the hatreds, tensions and suspicions' that have caused such hostile Indo-Pak relations in the past.[79] Going nuclear, in other words, has made the chances of resolution of the Indo-Pak Kashmir dispute far more difficult. At the same time, greater hostility means increased chances of actual conflict starting.

Lahore Declaration

In view of the threats posed by South Asia officially entering the nuclear club, it is not surprising that the international community was greatly alarmed by developments there. Both India and Pakistan were urged to reduce tensions and improve relations with each other. Sanctions were applied to increase pressure on the two countries (as well as, of course, to punish them for going nuclear). The United States 'which controls the flow of money to Pakistan's bankrupt economy' particularly targeted Islamabad. With the BJP government—having achieved its ambition of making India a nuclear power—eager to repair relations with the United States and China and get sanctions lifted, and with Nawaz Sharif, aware that desperately needed foreign aid depended 'largely on progress in peace-making', the international pressure eventually bore fruit.

In February 1999, Prime Minister Atal Bihar Vajpayee made a historic visit to Lahore—historic not just because it was that rare visit by an Indian leader to Pakistan (and the first post-nuclear tests one) but also because, made by bus, it heralded the start of a new Lahore-Delhi bus service. Talks between the two leaders resulted in the Lahore Declaration. Its most significant points were a commitment by the two governments to 'intensify their efforts to resolve all issues, including the issue of Jammu and Kashmir,' and to 'refrain from intervention and interference in each other's internal affairs.' Determination to implement the Simla Agreement was reiterated. The major practical agreement was on measures to reduce accidental war—informing the other side when ballistic missiles were to be tested, and improving lines of communication between the two countries' military chiefs.

It will be apparent that, like the Simla agreement in 1972, the Lahore Declaration of 1999 did little to actually resolve the various disputes between India and Pakistan. In particular it did nothing concrete to settle the Indo-Pak dispute over Kashmir— the most likely cause of future war between them. Nonetheless, it was highly significant. It marked a halt to the escalating tension between the two countries, extremely rapid since the BJP assumed office. And, it de-linked nuclear weapons from the Kashmir issue: efforts to minimize the risk of nuclear war were made despite the Kashmir dispute being unresolved. Nawaz Sharif did make a return visit to Delhi, but within a few months it became clear that the 'bus diplomacy' had failed to improve relations between the two countries. Why was this?

The answer, not surprisingly, lay in each country's domestic politics. Looking at India first, Vajpayee was at pains to make it clear, when he returned from Lahore, that he had not made any compromise on the non-negotiability of Kashmir's status. With Pakistan insisting that the UN resolutions allowing the Kashmiris to decide their own future be implemented, it is difficult to see what the two sides could discuss in the future.

On 11 April 1999, the Indian government tested a new version of its intermediate-range ballistic missile Agni. With a longer range, Agni II is believed to be capable of carrying a nuclear warhead and striking at all of Pakistan and much of China. The government claimed that the new missile would only be used for self-defence. However, the timing of the tests, coming just a few days before the Lok Sabha was due to reconvene, suggests another motive. One of the BJP's key coalition partners was threatening to break away, thereby ending the government's majority and most likely forcing it to vacate office. It seems likely the BJP calculated that the huge popular support testing Agni II would generate would enable it to cling onto power. The fact that missiles of that kind had not been tested for five years lends credence to this view.

Agni II certainly did generate public support for the BJP government but, as with the previous year's nuclear tests, it attracted almost universal international condemnation and caused a rapid deterioration in relations with Pakistan. Also, as in the previous year, Islamabad responded with ballistic tests of its own.

Turning to Pakistan, after the Lahore Declaration the Sharif government faced far greater public hostility than did its Indian counterpart. The mere fact that the Indian Prime Minister had been welcomed by the Pakistan leader caused widespread protests. The Islamic parties, notably Jamaat-i-Islami, were at the forefront of these, and the Pakistan authorities used great force to try and curb their demonstrations. Numerous Jamaat activists were arrested, both during and after the Indian visit. Jamaat opposition was pretty much to be expected. Somewhat more surprising, and far more significant, was the Pakistan army's opposition. The army made no official condemnation of Vajpayee's visit but the fact that the Army Chief chose to fulfil a prior engagement elsewhere with the Chinese Defence Minister, rather than join the welcoming party in Lahore, spoke volumes in itself. As seen in Chapter Six, the army is a very major player in Pakistani politics, and particularly in its foreign and Kashmir policies.

India's testing of Agni II was seen by many Pakistanis as a gesture vindicating the opposition to Prime Minister Vajpayee's visit. The widespread public response was that there was no point in talking to India; Hindus could never be trusted; Pakistan would always be threatened by them. Most people felt Pakistan should react in kind, i.e. be ready to combat force with force, and definitely abandon peace initiatives. In line with this, they greeted Pakistan's Ghauri tests with great enthusiasm.

Kargil Hostilities

India-Pakistan relations deteriorated rapidly from the time the BJP took power in New Delhi. The major factor in this deterioration was the successive nuclear and ballistic missile tests by the two countries. As seen above, these tests were largely prompted by the domestic political situation in each country. The tests greatly increased the already mutually-hostile public opinion, thereby making normalization of relations very difficult. The huge obstacles that needed to be overcome for this to happen, were clearly visible in the reaction to the Lahore Declaration. Furthermore, the fears of the international community that, in such an atmosphere of heightened tension, Kashmir could act as a trigger to wider conflict were to some extent realized.

Pakistani and Indian troops facing each other across the Line of Control have been forced by harsh climate to vacate some parts in winter. It has become an established practice that as soon as the snow melts sufficiently both sides return to their respective positions. This year, 1999, something different happened. Pakistani troops and Kashmiri militants returned before the Indians were expecting them to, crossed the LoC and occupied border posts and considerable mountainous territory, in Kargil, normally under Indian control. This territory included several strategically important peaks that allowed the militants to dominate the main Srinagar-Leh supply route in Indian Kashmir.

India's response was two-fold: on the one hand, the Indian military launched both air and ground offensives to recapture lost territory. Since in many cases militants were lodged on very difficult to approach peaks, this strategy involved considerable Indian casualties. Secondly, New Delhi also launched a diplomatic offensive. Claiming that the intruders were regular Pakistan Army soldiers, it called on the international community to condemn Pakistani aggression and urge Islamabad to withdraw its forces. Before looking at how successful India's diplomatic efforts were, consider whether their accusations of the Pakistan Army involvement were justified.

The *Independent* headline on 28 May 1999—'Muslim militants spearhead Kashmir occupation'—indicates that it at least thought not. Islamabad, of course, persistently refuted Indian charges that its forces had crossed the LoC; it claimed the intruders were all Kashmiri militants over whom it had no control. New Delhi responded by presenting proof of Pakistan Army involvement—ID cards, paybooks, army issued guns, etc. Who was right? The answer, as so often in the Kashmir dispute, is, both. As far as the identity of the men lodged in Kargil's peaks was concerned, while some regular Pakistani soldiers were present, it seems likely that the majority were indeed Kashmiri militants. There is no shortage of these, especially in Azad Kashmir; the Pakistan Army, therefore, does not need to send its own troops.

But this does not mean that it was completely innocent of involvement. Again what seems most likely is that the Army— or rather the ISI—encouraged and facilitated the militants' occupation. The Army's policy on Kashmir was outlined in Chapter Six; as already observed it had no wish to make reconciliatory gestures towards India. Furthermore, the militants in Kargil got there by crossing the LoC from Azad Kashmir. It is extremely difficult to believe that the Afghanistan-seasoned ISI, would, one, not have been aware of such a large-scale operation and two, would not have taken steps to stop it, had they so desired. In summary then, the occupation of Indian territory in the Kargil region was most probably a joint Pak Army/ISI-Kashmiri militants operation.

The noteworthy point in the above assessment of who was behind the push into Kargil is the absence of any mention of the Pakistan government. Most commentators agree that Pakistani involvement in Kargil was limited to the military; it did not extend to the country's political leaders. If correct, this again confirms the relative independence of the army in Pakistan and its dominant role in determining the Kashmir policy.

Of course, after India internationalized the Kargil dispute, Pakistan's politicians did become involved. International bodies such as the United Nations urged the Pakistan government—without overtly agreeing with India's claim that Pakistani soldiers were involved—to exercise its influence and get the militants back on its side of the LoC. Pakistan's response was that, one, it had no control over the militants and two, that the Kargil dispute should not be isolated from the wider Kashmir insurgency.

The Pakistan government was actually caught in a very unenviable position. On the one hand, as discussed above, it probably had no part in initiating the Kargil problem. As explained in Chapter Six, Pakistan's politicians can make full use of the Kashmir issue with just rhetorical support; they have little to gain from practically backing the insurgency. Tremendous international pressure was placed on the Sharif government to end the crisis. If Nawaz Sharif refused to comply, the country faced grave problems: already on the verge of bankruptcy, further international sanctions and the blockage of an IMF loan could have pushed it over the brink. There was also the very real danger of an all-out war with India.

But, on the other hand, his ability to manoeuvre and compromise was severely restricted by a public in no mood to give way to India. The Kargil conflict was portrayed in the Pakistani press as follows: Kashmiri *mujahideen* had already struck a huge blow against India, capturing strategic peaks and blocking the main enemy supply route. Further, they had the ability and were poised to inflict more military defeats on India and even free Kashmir *if they were allowed to do so*. This last point is very significant. Having been told that their country's 'defeats' over Kashmir in the past (particularly 1965 and 1971) were due to their own leaders selling them out—and not due to India militarily overpowering them—this time Pakistanis made clear they would not accept any capitulation by Nawaz Sharif. The dominant message coming across was that Pakistan must seize this opportunity, back the *mujahideen* fully, and liberate Indian Kashmir.

US-Pakistan Statement

From the start, the international community largely—though not always openly—blamed Pakistan for initiating the hostilities in Kargil. As these became more intense, so too did outside pressure on the Pakistan government. On 4 July 1999, Prime Minister Nawaz Sharif met Bill Clinton in Washington, after which the two issued a joint statement on Kashmir. Its main points were:

President Clinton and Prime Minister Sharif...agreed that it was vital for the peace of South Asia that the Line of Control in Kashmir be respected by both parties, in accordance with the Simla Accord. It was agreed between the president and the prime minister that concrete steps will be taken for the restoration of the Line of Control in accordance with the Simla agreement...[t]he president said he would take a personal interest in encouraging an expeditious resumption and intensification of those bilateral efforts [begun in Lahore in February], once the sanctity of the Line of Control has been fully restored.[80]

International pressure, thus, won out over domestic public opinion. Nawaz Sharif effectively agreed to pull out the Kashmiri militants and whatever Pakistan troops were there with them from the Kargil region of Indian Kashmir. Not surprisingly, the joint statement issued in Washington attracted great criticism and hostility in Pakistan. There were mass protests in many of the main cities, condemning the Sharif government and urging continuation of the 'jihad' against India. More worrisomely, the major militant groups—both individually and through their joint body, the United Jihad Council—also condemned Pakistan's government, and declared they would refuse any request by Islamabad to pull back from Kargil. The army, in statements issued by senior officers, also expressed its opposition to withdrawal. However, in practice, both did comply with Islamabad's wishes: by the last week of July, India was able to confirm that the areas occupied by militants/Pakistani forces had been vacated.

The only 'gain' which Nawaz Sharif had to sell the agreement back home, was President Clinton's promise to take an interest in the Kashmir issue. Pakistan government spokesmen claimed that Pakistan had achieved its long-sought target of internationalizing the Kashmir issue and making the world take an interest in resolving it. Opponents countered that India had made no commitment to discuss Kashmir's status. New Delhi, while welcoming Washington's role in persuading Pakistan to withdraw from Kargil, made it clear that it would not welcome the United States as a mediator in the Kashmir issue; it stuck to its old line of bilateral resolution and the non-negotiability of Kashmir's status. Nawaz Sharif's decision to pull out of Kargil and the manner in which he did so—flying to Washington to capitulate to US demands—was deeply unpopular back home. The lack of a strong political opposition meant he did not face much pressure within Parliament. But public dissent was high. Sharif's Kargil surrender was undoubtedly one factor in the Army's decision to overthrow him and take power itself.

Other factors were the growing corruption in the Muslim League administration, the introduction of a Shariah Bill, and (linked to this) Sharif's drive to concentrate more and more power in his own person, e.g. he placed his own appointees in the Supreme Court. But his attempt to replace the Chief of Army Staff, General Pervez Musharraf, with a more pliant commander proved his undoing. The Army responded by staging a coup and seizing power. The date was 12 October 1999.

General Pervez Musharraf carefully refrained from declaring martial law, instead appointing himself Chief Executive. Initially the National and Provincial Assemblies as well as the Senate were just suspended. This led many politicians to believe that the Army only wanted a change in the political leadership and, once a satisfactory replacement was found, they would return to the barracks. Though many offered themselves for that role, such a political switch was not made and Pervez Musharraf stayed in power. In June 2000, Musharraf dismissed then President Rafiq Tarar, dissolved the assemblies and declared himself the new President of Pakistan. At the time of writing

(January 2002) he was still firmly in power, but elections for the provincial and national assemblies were scheduled for October 2002.

Under President Musharraf, Kashmir continued to dominate Indo-Pak relations and the convergence between international dispute and ethnic conflict persisted.

Developments Involving Kashmir: October 1999–July 2001

Almost immediately after the military take-over in Pakistan, the Indian government announced that Prime Minister Vajpayee would not be attending the SAARC Heads of State summit due in November 1999. The reason given was that he did not wish to meet a military leader. The Indian boycott forced the entire summit to be indefinitely postponed. The South Asian Association for Regional Cooperation has never really been significant in its own right: progress on co-operation in economic and other fields between the countries of South Asia has been painfully slow. But, bearing in mind the dearth of bilateral meetings between India and Pakistan, it was highly significant as a forum where the two rivals could meet, discuss and perhaps resolve their differences. India's effective withdrawal from the SAARC process closed off that door.

In December 1999, two months after General Musharraf took power in Pakistan, an Indian Airlines plane was hijacked by Kashmiri militants and flown to Kandahar in Afghanistan. The hijackers demanded the release of several militants being held in Indian jails. After several days, in which the plane remained on the tarmac at Kandahar airport and conditions inside deteriorated, the Indian government gave in to their demands. Among those released was Maulana Masood Azhar, a Punjabi Pakistani who had fought with Hizbul-Mujahideen.

In March 2000, President Bill Clinton made a high-profile visit to South Asia. Any hopes that he might have got involved in resolution of the Kashmir problem were dashed by Indian reluctance and by the change of leadership in Pakistan. Unwilling to be seen as supporting a military take-over, Bill Clinton only spent five hours in Pakistan (compared to five days in India) and did not let pictures of his meeting with Musharraf be released.

Within Indian Kashmir, on 25 July 2000, the main Kashmiri militant group Hizbul-Mujahideen announced a unilateral cease-fire for three months. This announcement was followed by talks in Srinagar between the separatist group and the Indian government on 3 August. Those talks soon collapsed, though, and within two weeks of announcing its cease-fire Hizbul-Mujahideen called it off and ordered its forces to resume fighting with Indian troops.

At the beginning of the Muslim holy month of Ramadan (November 2000), Prime Minister Vajpayee made a similar peace initiative. He announced that Indian security forces would suspend combat operations against militants in Jammu and Kashmir for the duration of Ramadan. This cease-fire was subsequently extended twice. Prime Minister Vajpayee's hope that this move would restart the political process in the state proved forlorn: the All Parties Hurriyat Conference rejected an Indian offer for dialogue in April 2001. Under pressure from military commanders, who thought the cease-fire hampered their ability to crack down on the militants, and with no political gains, Vajpayee called it off in May 2001.

Almost simultaneously, though, he held out the olive branch to Pakistan, inviting General Musharraf to New Delhi for talks. Bearing in mind Prime Minister Vajpayee's earlier refusal to even participate in the same conference as Musharraf, this was indeed a big about-turn. It was probably prompted by India's desire to improve its relations with the United States: Indo-Pak hostility over Kashmir, and the prospect inherent in that of nuclear war, is a great source of concern for Washington. Vajpayee wanted to show that he was striving to resolve the issue. General Musharraf accepted the Indian Prime Minister's invitation.

The two South Asian leaders met in Agra from 14–16 July 2001. The talks started off well and relations between the two sides appeared warm. But the initial optimism was dashed as the talks bogged down over differences on Kashmir. It had been hoped that the Indian and Pakistani leaders would be able to agree on a joint statement at the end of the conference, leaving the path open for further talks. But that proved too much, and President Musharraf flew back to Pakistan empty-handed. The strong stance he had taken in Agra, though, proved very popular at home.

September 11 and its Aftermath

On 11 September 2001, terrorists probably belonging to Osama bin Laden's al-Qaeda network, hijacked four American planes. Two were flown into the twin towers of the World Trade Centre in New York, one into the Pentagon, and one crashed in Pennsylvania. The total death toll is estimated at just over 3000. The ripple effects of the events of 11 September were huge and are still being felt.

In assessing the impact on Kashmir, one needs to focus on the new 'war against terrorism' launched by the Bush administration, and backed by most of the international community. After 11 September there was zero tolerance of terrorism or of—something which it is very difficult to distinguish from it—armed political movements. The use of violence by any kind of non-state actor effectively became unacceptable. Furthermore, just as Bush in his campaign stressed the need to target those who carried out the 11 September attacks (i.e. bin Laden and al Qaeda), so the international war was focused on terrorist groups and the countries that supported them.

India had long been trying to portray the struggle within Indian Kashmir as a problem simply of 'cross-border terrorism', i.e. one exported by Pakistan. As seen in the course of this book, the roots of the conflict within Indian Kashmir arose indigenously. The separatist movement was started and pursued by Kashmiri Muslims, angry at their treatment by India. Pakistan became involved at a later date, backing the Kashmiri movement.

President Musharraf was one of the United States' key allies in the war against terrorism. He provided vital airspace and logistical support to the Americans to help them attack Afghanistan. Though that assistance brought him close to the US, it was only a matter of time before pressure would be applied on him to stop Pakistani backing for Kashmiri militants operating in the Kashmir Valley. Appreciating that reality, the Musharraf government had, as early as October 2001, started taking steps to curb *jihadi* groups in Pakistan, e.g. imposing a ban on fund-raising in public.

On 1 October 2001, unknown assailants carried out an attack on the State Legislative Assembly in Jammu and Kashmir. Thirty-eight people were killed. The Pakistan-based Lashkar-e-Tayyeba initially claimed responsibility for the attack but then denied this. The Indian government reiterated its accusations of cross-border terrorism by Pakistan.

On 13 December 2001, militants carried out a far more audacious, though less successful attack on the Lok Sabha in New Delhi. Five militants and eight Indians died in the gun-fight; a car bomb was defused. India immediately pinned blame for the attack on two groups, Lashkar-e-Tayyeba and Jaish-e-Muhammad, backed by Pakistan's ISI. The Pakistan High Commissioner in New Delhi was issued with a written demand for the leaders of both groups to be arrested and their assets frozen. The Pakistan government, while expressing condolence for the Lok Sabha attack, insisted that it could only take action against individuals or groups based in Pakistan if it was provided with proof of their involvement in terrorist activities. It added that should such evidence be provided, it would take strong action.

The Indian government responded to Pakistan's refusal by recalling its High Commissioner from Islamabad and cutting road and rail links with Pakistan. This was followed by the announcement of sanctions against Pakistan: Indian airspace was closed off to all Pakistani aircraft, the Pakistan High Commission was ordered to halve its staff, and those remaining were ordered not to leave the capital. Pakistan did not recall its High Commissioner from New Delhi, but it did impose identical counter-sanctions against India. These tit-for-tat sanctions were followed by both countries banning transmission of the other's television programmes.

As relations between them deteriorated, both India and Pakistan deployed huge numbers of troops and weapons along the LoC and international border. New Delhi made it clear that war was an option, if Pakistan did not take serious action against those it held responsible for terrorist attacks within India.

As the threat of war grew, so too did international concern. The United States was particularly alarmed at the prospect of a fourth full-scale Indo-Pak war at a time when its troops were deployed in Pakistan, and Pakistani forces were monitoring the border with Afghanistan (to catch fleeing Taliban and al Qaeda forces). President Bush, therefore, urged both sides to exercise restraint, but he also pressed President Musharraf to do his utmost to capture terrorists in Pakistan.

In response to American pressure, Pakistan froze the assets of both groups named by India, and arrested their leaders as well as several dozen more religious extremists. India welcomed some of these moves but dismissed others as cosmetic. New Delhi issued Pakistan a list of twenty alleged terrorists, and demanded their arrest and extradition. Pakistan repeated its demand for evidence of their involvement in terrorist activities.

At the time of writing (January 2002) it was unclear how the situation would evolve. Bearing in mind that the Indian government's hard line stance was motivated by its desire to have international pressure applied on Pakistan to stop supporting Kashmiri militants, together with domestic political considerations, war seemed unlikely. Both New Delhi and Islamabad know another war between them would have disastrous consequences.

By the start of 2002, it was clear that Pakistan had started abandoning its old policy of actively supporting Kashmiri militants fighting in Indian Kashmir. This was largely a consequence of the attacks in the US on 11 September. It marks one of the biggest changes in the Kashmir conflict since 1989. The implications of Pakistan stopping its support will be discussed in the concluding chapter.

NOTES

1. Lamb writes that such groups could have emerged in the wake of Pakistan's unsuccessful 1965 'Operation Gibraltar': 'No doubt one consequence of Operation Gibraltar had been to introduce a large quantity of arms and ammunition into the State; and its abandonment by Pakistan must have left a number of what can only be described as unemployed guerrillas who found it difficult to change their profession and style of life.' She goes on that police authorities in Kashmir certainly blamed the new systematic acts of violence and sabotage in the State on such an 'indigenous terrorist organisation'. Lamb herself expresses the opinion that the activities of this group (Al Fatah?) were probably exaggerated by the authorities to 'damage the reputation of the Plebiscite Front and to provide an excuse for measures against it.' *Op. cit.*, p. 286.
2. Lamb writes that the JKLF actually started life in 1965 as the Plebiscite Front, distinct from the political organization of the same name. 'It had been converted into the Kashmir National Liberation Front (and its objectives more firmly oriented towards sustained guerrilla warfare against the Indians) by Amanullah Khan. An early member had been Maqbool Butt, a charismatic but somewhat mysterious figure, at one time a journalist in Peshawar, who had been crossing regularly the Kashmir cease-fire line since 1958, and in 1966 had been arrested and sentenced to death for the murder of an Indian official during the course of an armed robbery in the Vale of Kashmir. In December 1968 he escaped.' Though this organization had its origins in Pakistan's 'Operation Gibraltar', after 1966: '[t]he members of this Kashmir National Liberation Front...had turned into *ronin* (to use the Japanese concept of the masterless samurai) of covert resistance against Indian rule in Kashmir, responsible to nobody but their own leadership and controlled by no Government.' At some stage, the group's name changed to Kashmir Liberation Army, and then to Jammu and Kashmir Liberation Front. Ibid., pp. 292–3.

3. '[*Maqbool Butt*] had been arrested in 1976 for an offence committed in 1966, and for which he had already been sentenced to death. His re-trial only took place in 1981...[t]he previous sentence of death was confirmed, though execution was postponed for two years because of a temporary suspension of capital punishment in India. When, in early 1984, an execution date was finally fixed, numerous pleas of clemency from throughout the world were ignored.' Ibid., p. 335.

4. Schofield, Victoria, *Kashmir in the Crossfire* (London, Tauris, 1996), pp. 232–3.

5. Schofield, *op. cit.*

6. Ibid., p. 238.

7. Cited in Akbar, *op. cit.*, p. 217.

8. Ganguly, Sumit, *The Crisis in Kashmir: Portents of War and Hopes of Peace* (Cambridge, Cambridge University Press, 1997), p. 104.

9. 'Nor was it possible for me and the advisers to secure the obedience of our orders from local officials who were constantly being fed with the impression that Dr Farooq Abdullah and his colleagues were coming back after the role of "butcher" had been played by the Governor.' Malhotra Jagmohan, *My Frozen Turbulence in Kashmir* (New Delhi, Allied, 1991), pp. 419–420.

10. 'Kashmir: A Deep-rooted Alienation', 5–12 May 1990, p. 978.

11. Akbar, *op. cit.*, p. 219.

12. Schofield, *op. cit.*, pp. 245–6.

13. A report in *Economic and Political Weekly* suggests that Pandits, many of whom were employed in the State service, were encouraged to migrate by the promise that their overdue wages would then be paid to them. 'India's Kashmir War', *op. cit.*, p. 654.

14. Ibid.

15. Wirsing, *op. cit.* (1994), p. 132.

16. Ibid., p. 136.

17. For details of separatist incidents in Jammu and Kashmir, and figures of explosions in public places, see ibid., pp. 128–9.

18. Schofield, *op. cit.*, p. 271.

19. Wirsing, *op. cit.*, pp. 122–3.

20. Ibid., p. 120.

21. E.g. Dr Ayyub Thakkar, President of World Kashmir Freedom Movement; interview with author, London, November 1996.

22. In what started off as a repetition of the Hazratbal siege, a large group of militants holed themselves up in Kashmir's holiest shrine. They were led by an Afghan, Mast Gul, and were believed to be largely of foreign (Afghan and Pakistani) extraction. For several months, the militants remained in the shrine, surrounded by Indian troops. On 7 May, a fire blazed out in the town; it spread rapidly through the wooden buildings,

engulfing the mosque and shrine in the early hours of 8 May. The cause of the fire is disputed. The Indian authorities claim that the Sunni militants deliberately started the fire in order to discredit the Indians and because they were not prepared to surrender—the fire could have covered their escape. Militants and local people, however, claim that it was Indian shellfire that led to the fire. Fighting between Indian soldiers and militants in the aftermath of the fire ended with many of the militants being captured; others were killed, or managed to escape. Destruction of the holy shrine triggered widespread protests throughout Kashmir.

23. This was made clear by JKLF leader Amanullah Khan in an interview to *Newsline* magazine of Pakistan in February 1990: 'We basically stand for reunification of our motherland which has now been divided into four parts: Indian Kashmir; Azad Kashmir and Baltistan—which are currently with Pakistan; and Aksai Chin under the Chinese. We want these parts to be reunified and made a completely independent state. What we are struggling for is independence from both India and Pakistan.' Cited in Bhattacharjea, *op. cit.*, p. 259.

24. Hewitt, Vernon, *Reclaiming the Past? The search for political and cultural unity in contemporary Jammu and Kashmir* (London, Portland, 1995), p. 160.

25. Ibid., p. 162.

26. Wirsing., *op. cit.*, p. 144.

27. Ibid., p. 146.

28. Ibid., p. 154.

29. Schofield, *op. cit.*, p. 271.

30. Wirsing., *op. cit.*, p. 155.

31. Ibid., p. 157.

32. 'Killing Time in Kashmir' in *New Statesman and Society*, 3 September 1993, p. 23.

33. Wirsing., *op. cit.*, p. 156.

34. Schofield, *op. cit.*, p. 265.

35. Ibid., p. 266.

36. Wirsing, *op. cit.*, p. 156.

37. Ibid., p. 158.

38. Hyman, Anthony 'Kashmir: Paths to Peace?' in *The World Today*, July 1994, p. 24.

39. Schofield, *op. cit.*, p. 251.

40. *International Commission of Jurists, Report of a Mission: Human Rights in Kashmir*. Geneva, 1994.

41. Schofield, *op. cit.*, p. 263. For a detailed description of torture methods used by the security forces in Jammu and Kashmir see, Amin, Tahir, *Mass Resistance in Kashmir: Origins, Evolution, Options* (Islamabad, Institute of Policy Studies, 1995), p. 114.

42. Amin, *op. cit.*, p. 115.

43. Interview with author; London, 1998.
44. Victoria Schofield gives the case of Dr Rashid as a typical example of such 'encounters': 'My brother was twenty-five years old. He was running a cosmetics shop. The BSF came and took him. In front of my father and family, he was killed. Someone had pointed him out as being a militant. He was not armed and in the news that evening they gave that there was an encounter, when there was no encounter at all', *op. cit.*, p. 276.
45. Wirsing, *op. cit.*, p. 161.
46. Amin, *op. cit.*, p. 113.
47. Ibid., p. 112.
48. Ibid., p. 117.
49. Wirsing, *op. cit.*, p. 161.
50. Schofield, *op. cit.*, p. 258.
51. Ibid., pp. 276–7.
52. 'Doorstepped by the many Mr Khans' in *The Independent*, 23 November 1998.
53. Wirsing, *op. cit.*, p. 138.
54. 'Hidden Damage' in *Economic and Political Weekly*, 16 December 1995, p. 3185.
55. Interview with author, London, 27 April 1998.
56. 'Hidden Damage'.
57. Amnesty International Report on Abuse of Children in South Asia, cited by Abdul Majeed Maalik in interview with author.
58. Interview with author; London, November 1996.
59. Wirsing, *op. cit.*, p. 140.
60. Kumar, D.P., *Kashmir: Return to Democracy* (New Delhi, Cosmo, 1996), p. 75.
61. Ibid., p. 75.
62. Kamath, M.V., 'The Fate of Kashmiri Pandits' in Wani, Gull Mohammed, (ed.), *Kashmir: From Autonomy to Azadi* (Srinagar, Valley Book House, 1996), p. 406.
63. Kumar, *op. cit.*, p. 74.
64. Ibid., p. 84.
65. *Hindustan Times*, 13 July 1991, ibid., p. 78.
66. Ibid., p. 85.
67. Ibid., p. 87.
68. 'Spoiled Ballot?' in *Economist*, 11 November 1996, pp. 97–8.
69. 'Kashmiris vote at the point of Indian guns' in *The Independent*, 24 May 1996.
70. 'Indian guns force Kashmir voters to the ballot box' in *The Times*, 24 May 1996.
71. Kumar, *op. cit.*, pp. 80–81.
72. *Organiser*, 23 January 1994, cited in Wani, *op.cit.*, p. 408.

73. Sharma, Kalpana, 'The Hindu Bomb'.
74. Bidwai, Praful and Vanaik, Achin, 'A very political bomb'.
75. Sharma, *op. cit.*
76. 'Change of tactics in India's battle to oust guerrillas from Kashmir' in *Daily Telegraph*, 27 May 1999.
77. 'Kashmir: new battle between old rivals', *BBC On-line news*, 1 June 1999.
78. 'The most dangerous place on earth' in *Economist*, 22 May 1999.
79. Vanaik, Achin, 'Danger of an arms race in South Asia'.
80. *BBC On-line news*, 5 July 1999.

CONCLUSION

In the introduction to this book the importance of looking at the Kashmir problem as two issues rather than a single one was stressed. There is Kashmir, the ethnic conflict within India between Kashmiri Muslims, Pandits and the Indian State. And there is Kashmir, the fifty-plus year international dispute between India and Pakistan over control of Jammu and Kashmir. These two issues, while closely inter-linked, are nonetheless quite distinct. Over the previous eight chapters the evolution and development of each Kashmir problem, ethnic conflict and international dispute, was reviewed. Their findings can now be summarized.

Kashmir: Ethnic Conflict

There are two dynamics involved in this: relations between the two main ethnic groups within Kashmir, i.e. Muslims and Pandits, and between these and the Indian State. In order to appreciate why ethnic conflict broke out in the region one must examine both these dynamics. The key factors to look at are perceptions of ethnic identity, factors influencing these and the level of ethnic consciousness, and the political manifestations of ethnicity. Consider each in turn.

Ethnic Identity

Chapter one discussed the 'initial' identity of the Kashmiri people, in particular whether *Kashmiri* Muslims and Pandits shared a common sense of *Kashmiriyat*. It concluded on the basis of the limited interaction between Muslims and Pandits, and their distinctive religious practises, that *Kashmiriyat* was more myth than fact. Both communities had a strong sense of regional identity (Pandits more than Muslims) but this was coupled with a strong religious identity. The latter proved a barrier to unification on the basis of the former.

But chapter one further concluded that the gap between Muslims and Pandits in the Kashmir Valley was far less than that between corresponding communities in other parts of the subcontinent. Inter-communal tolerance arose from the fact that both Muslims and Hindus in the Valley were not very orthodox in their practise of Islam and Hinduism respectively; from the absence of lower castes which necessitated Pandits making use of the services of Muslims; and from the fact that there was little competition between the two communities—they occupied different socio-economic niches. Kashmiri society would thus best be described as a plural society in which relations between the two main ethnic groups, Kashmiri Muslims and Pandits, were good to the extent of functional and economic interaction but did not extend to social interaction.

How could one describe perceptions of ethnic identity and inter-ethnic relations between Kashmiri Muslims and Pandits today?

The first point to note is that among both ethnic groups perceptions of identity are now much more firmly rooted in religion. Pandits are far more conscious of being Hindu, Kashmiri Muslims of being Muslim. Evidence to support this assessment comes from the fact that both communities have become more orthodox in the practise of their respective religions and—in the case of Pandits—their increased proximity to their co-religionists in the rest of India. But the Pandits have also retained their strong sense of being Kashmiri. Among Kashmiri Muslims there is a stronger sense both of being Kashmiri and of being Muslim. Note that the increase is not uniform: some would identify themselves primarily as Kashmiri, others as Muslim.

Turning to relations between Pandits and Kashmiri Muslims today, the gap between the two communities has widened considerably. Apart from increased religious consciousness among both (leading to heightened awareness of the differences between them), this was caused by greater assertiveness on the part of Kashmiri Muslims. They have moved into the occupational niches traditionally occupied by Pandits. Inter-communal competition led to inter-communal tension.

Furthermore, after 1947 and the end of Dogra rule, the Pandits lost the favoured treatment that had counter-balanced their minority position. They suddenly found themselves excluded from the circle of government largesse. Even though prior to the current conflict they had never been targets of Muslim violence, their sense of vulnerability as a minority community increased. The Muslim-Pandit relationship of mutual tolerance and harmony was transformed into one of great tension and—on the part of the Pandits—fear.

Since the conflict within the Valley began the situation has got a lot worse. Few Pandits make the distinction between militants and ordinary Muslims. They blame Kashmiri Muslims in general for the conflict and for the hardships (being uprooted from their homes, having to live in refugee camps, etc.) that they have had to endure as a result of it. Note that this resentment is largely one-way. There is little evidence to suggest that Kashmiri Muslims in general harbour feelings of animosity towards Pandits. Some militants, however, have demanded that the Pandits should make common cause with them or else be regarded like India as the enemy.

Only a tiny proportion of Kashmir's Pandit community still lives in the Valley. Geographical separation has been a major factor in widening the gulf between Kashmiri Muslims and Pandits. As described in chapter one, their main interaction in the Valley had been functional and economic. With that interaction finished, there has really been nothing else to sustain the link between the two communities. The longer the conflict drags on and the Pandits remain outside the Valley, the more the two groups will become complete strangers to one another and the harder it will be to re-establish their old relationship.

Factors Shaping Ethnic Identity and Consciousness

Kashmiri Muslims

Political awakening and mobilization among Kashmiri Muslims in itself influenced their perceptions of themselves and those around them. This is because, as described in chapter two, when Muslims like Sheikh Abdullah and Ghulam Abbas started taking an active part in state politics, e.g. demanding better educational and employment opportunities, they did so as representatives of Kashmir's Muslim community. They used the existing ethnic groupings within Kashmir as the basis for political groupings. In doing so, they helped both to consolidate Kashmiri Muslim identity and raise group consciousness among Kashmiri Muslims. Political mobilization as a spur to ethnic identification is something that has persisted in Kashmir throughout this century.

Prior to Partition, Sheikh Abdullah's adoption of non-communal politics caused at least some of his followers to define themselves primarily as Kashmiris rather than Muslims. Abdullah, as discussed in chapter two, was motivated by political considerations—the desire to win Nehru's and India-wide support, and the desire to supersede Kashmir's religious head Mirwaiz Yusuf as leader of the Muslim community.

After 1947, the political events that undoubtedly had the greatest impact on Kashmiri Muslim thinking were the actions of various state and central governments in Jammu and Kashmir. These can be considered under three main headings: failure to provide democracy, failure to provide regional autonomy, and failure to meet socio-economic expectations.

Taking lack of democracy first, under Dogra rule there had, of course, been negligible opportunities for ordinary Kashmiris to express their will and have a government of their own choosing. After accession to India and Hari Singh's removal from power people expected this situation to change. The blame for its not doing so lies primarily with Sheikh Abdullah and then with New Delhi. The first Sheikh Abdullah-led National

Conference administration was far from an ideal model of free, open government: as described in chapter three political opposition was suppressed, press coverage was highly censored, and the 1951 Constituent Assembly elections were manipulated so as to ensure Abdullah's party won all seventy-five seats. The malpractices of this first 'democratic' government set a precedent which was copied by virtually all succeeding administrations. Press censorship, suppression of political opposition, personalisation of power, rigging elections, etc., became the norm in Kashmir.

While Abdullah is blameworthy for setting this precedent, New Delhi is far more so—firstly for not objecting to what he was doing, and more seriously for adopting those same malpractices itself. For most of Kashmir's post-1947 history, press censorship, electoral rigging, etc., have been used to place and keep in power 'puppet' regimes in the control of India. Furthermore, by removing Abdullah from power in 1953, New Delhi set a precedent of its own—that of central governments ignoring electoral mandates (such as they were) when unhappy with state governments, and using various pretexts to remove them.

Turning to the issue of autonomy, this was supposedly guaranteed to Kashmiris in Article 370 of the Indian Constitution, but it was something that India failed to deliver in practice. The reasons for this are manifold: pressure from Pandits and Jammu Hindus who opposed (feared) Muslim control of their state, fear that autonomous state governments would demand independence, and New Delhi's (particularly under the Gandhis) obsession with keeping absolute control. India was able to bring about rapid erosion of state autonomy in Kashmir through the various 'puppet' rulers it placed in power there. This has been carried out to such an extent, as described in chapters three and four, that Article 370 today has little relevance beyond the paper it is written on.

It should be stressed that a major factor in allowing democracy and autonomy to be pushed aside in Kashmir was weakness in the political leadership there. New Delhi was always able to find political leaders willing to carry out its will. Sheikh Abdullah must also be included in this category. In the initial years after accession he did make a stand for Kashmiri autonomy, but the 1975 Kashmir Accord can be considered as the point at which he too 'sold out' the Kashmiri people in exchange for personal power and gain. His son, Farooq Abdullah, repeated this in 1987 when he allied himself with Congress. Had Kashmiris been served by politicians who put their interests first rather than personal gain, it would have been far harder for India to exercise its will in the state.

Socio-economic policies also served to alienate Kashmiri Muslims from India. The most significant social change was the educational revolution in Kashmir which produced a more demanding society with respect to both political rights and material expectations. Huge numbers of graduates emerged from Kashmiri universities and colleges expecting to get good jobs. When, instead, they found themselves unemployed and with little prospect of their circumstances improving, they, not surprisingly, became frustrated.

The blame for failing to develop Kashmir's economy, and hence to fulfil people's 'lifestyle' expectations, lies both with Kashmir's rulers and New Delhi. The former are guilty of using what money was given to the state to line their own pockets rather than promote economic development. Corruption in government circles has been endemic in Kashmir from the first post-1947 Abdullah administration. Bakshi was probably the one exception, in that whilst filling his own coffers he did also carry out some state projects, but the rest were uniformly single-minded in their accumulation of wealth. This was something that ordinary Kashmiris were well aware of.

India must share the blame for failing to develop Kashmir's economy. Its reasons for not doing so were slightly different to those of the state's leaders. New Delhi had no desire to see Kashmir become self-sufficient since this could have encouraged calls for state autonomy. It suited India for Kashmir to be economically dependent on central government funding. As discussed in chapter four, in the fifty-odd years since accession this dependence has greatly increased. In addition, India has been guilty of economic exploitation in Kashmir: by taking raw goods from the Valley and by keeping it a captive market for its own manufactured products, it has copied the pattern of trade between Britain and the Indian subcontinent in the colonial era.

All of the above—lack of democracy, erosion of state autonomy and economic frustrations, caused Kashmiri Muslims to become disenchanted with India and draw away from it. In doing so, they automatically put more emphasis on the things that distinguished them from other Indians—namely their identity as Kashmiris. They also became more conscious of their Islamic identity. The latter was also influenced by other developments.

Broadly speaking these can be divided into internal (within India) and external. Of the internal influences one was the Indian government's drive to reduce the role of Islam in Kashmir, e.g. through the education curricula. These cultural policies were described in chapter four. It concluded that the evidence to support a concerted Indian policy of secularization/Hinduization is highly debatable, but that many Kashmiri Muslims believed such a policy was being carried out. Furthermore, intentional or otherwise, prior to the 1980s Kashmir was definitely becoming more 'westernised'. Elements within Kashmir responded to this liberal trend by consciously promoting Islam, e.g. through the *madrasas* founded by the Jamaat-i-Islami.

The second major internal development was the rise of political Hinduism as a credible force in India. The BJP's phenomenal growth, culminating in its forming the national government, had a tremendous impact on Kashmiri Muslim thinking. In 1947, secularism had been lauded as the bedrock of a united, multi-religious state. As it weakened and nationalist Hindu rhetoric gained a wider following, it became harder for Kashmiri Muslims to feel they belonged in India. They drew closer to their own religious roots.

Of the external political developments pushing them in this direction, two in particular stand out: the Iranian revolution which brought an Islamic government to power; and the Afghan *'jihad'*.

Kashmiri Muslims, through improved access to and understanding of international news, were aware of other significant events in the Islamic world such as the Palestinian *intifada*, but it was these two events taking place in their immediate neighbourhood that had the most impact on them. The Afghan *jihad* was doubly significant because not only did it make Kashmiris more conscious of their Islamic identity, but it also inspired them to take up arms and try to secede from India by force.

The roots of ethnic conflict in Kashmir are, therefore, clear. For the reasons described above, Kashmiri Muslims had become disillusioned with India and more conscious of their distinct identity both as Kashmiris and as Muslims. It was only a matter of time before they demanded secession from India. The fact that they did so in 1989, by launching a militant secessionist movement, was directly related to events within and outside the state.

Within Kashmir, the 1987 elections had made Kashmiri Muslims completely give up all hope of being treated fairly by India and being allowed to exercise their own will. This was not simply due to the elections being heavily rigged—hardly a new phenomenon in Kashmir—but also to the National Conference, the party that had until then been the champion of Kashmiri autonomy within India, allying itself with Congress. As described in chapter six, this created a vacuum in moderate Kashmiri politics which was soon filled by militant secessionists. The move towards militancy was further encouraged by events outside Kashmir: in neighbouring Afghanistan the *mujahideen* had just got rid of Soviet forces, while in Eastern Europe there was turmoil with communist regimes everywhere being toppled. All these developments were seen in Kashmir.

The conflict itself has served to harden the Kashmiri Muslims' sense of distinctiveness. Human rights abuses by the security forces have been a major factor in this. So too, with respect to the Kashmiri aspect of their identity, has been the role of Pakistan in the insurgency. As discussed in chapter eight, Pakistan's failure to overtly support the militants and to a lesser extent the many problems (ethnic and sectarian conflict, weak democracy, corruption, etc.) within Pakistan itself, have led at least some Kashmiri Muslims to reject that country too, i.e. become more nationalist.

Pandits

Ethnic identity shifts among Pandits have in some ways matched those among Kashmiri Muslims, but in other ways been completely different. The similarity lies in religious identification. Just as Kashmiri Muslims have become far more conscious of their religion, so Pandits have become much more conscious of being Hindu. The difference lies in attitudes to India; while the Muslims have drawn further away from India, Pandits have drawn closer to it.

With respect to the Pandits' 'Hinduization', as with the Muslims, various non-political factors, e.g. the need to preserve traditional values from erosion by Westernization, made them draw closer to their faith. But one can definitely also point to political developments as being influential in this. Most significant have been the various political Hindu groups in India—originally the Mahasabha and currently the BJP. The overtly Hindu imagery and rhetoric employed by these parties raised Hindu consciousness throughout India. But their focus on Pandits, portraying them as a vulnerable *Hindu* minority within *Muslim* Kashmir, meant they have had an especial influence on that ethnic group.

Various other factors led the Pandits to draw further apart from Kashmiri Muslims. The first of these, dating back from the end of the last century, was the act of political mobilization itself. Like Muslims, Pandits from day one took part in politics as a single ethnic group. Furthermore, unlike some Muslims they never attempted to abandon this in favour of Kashmir-wide non-communal politics (with a handful of exceptions such as Prem Nath Bazaz). For Pandits, political activity has thus been a persistent spur to heightened ethnic consciousness.

The Pandits' minority position within Kashmir has been a second major factor. The threat of being submerged in the

Muslim majority forced the Pandits to hold more firmly to their own identity. It acted as a barrier to integration with the Muslims. Political developments enforced the Pandits' 'minority complex'. This was seen in the early part of this century when growing Muslim assertiveness made the Pandits feel vulnerable and led them to campaign to preserve their jobs from Muslim encroachment (described in chapter two). After 1947, when Dogra rule was replaced by National Conference government it became much more apparent. As Sheikh Abdullah and his successors showered favours on their own Muslim cronies, so the Pandits felt discriminated against and afraid for their future.

The Kashmir conflict enforced the direction in which Pandit thinking had been moving until then, i.e. increasing their fears as a minority within Kashmir, making them more consciously 'Hindu' and pushing them closer to India. In addition the conflict has led Pandits to feel not just different and alienated from Kashmiri Muslims, but positively hostile towards them. The reasons for the conflict having these effects hardly need to be spelled out. Migration effectively ended all contact and dealings between Pandits and Kashmiri Muslims, and greatly increased the same with non-Kashmiri Hindus. Living side by side with Hindus outside the Valley (generally more orthodox than Pandits) has led the Pandits to become more orthodox too.

Politics

This is the crux of the Kashmir problem within India: different ethnic groups within the state have different political goals, which, in turn, clash with those of New Delhi.

Kashmiri Muslims

The issues dominating Kashmiri Muslim politics have changed over time. The initial focus of Muslim groups such as the Fateh Kadal Reading Room was to improve the educational and employment opportunities available to Muslims. This brought them into conflict with the Pandits—who were seeking the same for their community, and could only come at the expense of the Pandits, hence the latter's hostility to them.

Turning to 1947, and the question of accession to India or Pakistan, Muslims outside the Valley generally favoured the latter. Within the Valley, though, the main Kashmiri leader Sheikh Abdullah had abandoned communal politics in favour of non-communal 'Kashmiri' politics. Based on his ideal was an independent Kashmir or, if forced to opt for either India or Pakistan, the former. Abdullah's popularity was such that he was able to take the majority of Kashmiri Muslims with him.

Even after Kashmir (the Valley) had joined India, Abdullah continued periodically to call for independence, and more forcefully, for regional autonomy within India. However, his desire for personal power and wealth eventually came to so totally determine his political agenda, that he accepted the state's integration with India. But for the majority of Kashmiri Muslims the desire for autonomy persisted, and as New Delhi strove to bring about greater integration with India, increased. By the late 1980s, Kashmiri Muslim calls for regional autonomy had changed to calls for complete secession from India. Today, this desire is almost universal.

The main political division among Kashmir Muslims now is between those wishing to accede to Pakistan and those wanting an independent Kashmir. At the start of the conflict some ten years ago, the former were almost definitely in the majority. Since then, Pakistan's failure to take a lead in supporting the Kashmiri struggle, coupled to a lesser extent with the situation within Pakistan itself, has led some Kashmiris to switch from favouring accession to Pakistan to independence. Whether supporters of independence now form the majority in the Valley is very difficult to say. One would need to carry out extensive surveys among Kashmir's Muslims in order to be able to determine this—something the Indian authorities will obviously not permit. What one can say is that as the conflict drags on it is the ranks of pro-independence Kashmiris that are being swollen.

Pandits

Pandits entered politics around the turn of the century campaigning to improve and/or preserve their socio-economic status. They demanded better educational facilities, higher job quotas, exclusion of non-Kashmiris from state jobs, etc. As Partition approached, the focus of Pandit political activity shifted. In 1947, Jammu and Kashmir had the choice of joining India or Pakistan—plus the vague possibility of being independent. While the state's Muslims were divided over which option to go for, the Pandits were quite clear that they wanted to accede to India. They felt much more comfortable joining Hindu-majority India than Muslim-majority Pakistan. Within India they would not be a minority but part of the country-wide Hindu majority.

Kashmir's accession to India in 1947 was a great relief to the Pandits. However, even within India they continued to feel vulnerable to the Muslim majority, largely because of the National Conference government's partisanship. It caused the Pandits to demand that Jammu and Kashmir be fully integrated with the rest of India, thereby transferring control of the state from Srinagar to New Delhi. They strongly opposed any moves towards autonomy, e.g. the Delhi Accord of 1952.

Calling for integration with India, opposing regional autonomy, and protesting against state government 'discrimination', have been persistent themes of Pandit political campaigning since 1947. Following the start of the conflict in the Valley some twelve years ago, however, their demands have changed. Instead of full integration they want their own exclusive 'state' within the Valley—*Panun* Kashmir. This would be a region or state within India, autonomous both from central government and Kashmiri Muslim control. If formed, it would allow the Pandits to feel safe as Hindus and yet retain their distinct Kashmiri identity. The chances of *Panun* Kashmir becoming reality, however, are remote. The primary focus of Pandit political activity at the moment is, therefore, more immediate: highlighting their plight as refugees, and pressuring the Indian government to do more for them.

India

New Delhi is the third major player in Kashmir, the ethnic conflict. The goals of the Valley's main ethnic groups have been reviewed above—integration with India or *Panun* Kashmir for the Pandits; secession for the Muslims. What about New Delhi? To a large extent its goals and policies are determined by its position in Kashmir, the international dispute.

In 1947, having finally obtained Hari Singh's signature on the Instrument of Accession and having gained practical control of a large part of the state, India was then faced with the task of consolidating this control, i.e. ensuring that Kashmir would be a permanent part of the Union. Fear of Kashmiri secession has, in fact been a constant determinant of Indian policy towards the state—from 1947 right through to the present day.

India's first Prime Minister, Jawaharlal Nehru, recognised that the Kashmiris could not be retained using indefinite force: they would have to be won over to India. The approach he took to do this was, one, to win the confidence of the main Kashmiri leader Sheikh Abdullah, and two, allow the state a great deal of autonomy within India. He hoped in this way to eradicate all thoughts of secession from Kashmiri minds. But Sheikh Abdullah's continued pursuit of Kashmiri independence forced Nehru to change track. Instead of allowing regional autonomy, bringing the state firmly under central control became the new policy, one that was implemented even more vigorously by Nehru's successors.

It is ironic to note that while the Indian drive for integration was designed to prevent secessionist tendencies emerging, it ended up having precisely the opposite effect. One of the main conclusions drawn in this book is that it was largely Indian policies—eroding autonomy, increasing economic dependence on the centre, imposing 'puppet' rulers—that caused Kashmiri

Muslims to become totally alienated from India and demand secession.

Today, with a full-scale armed movement against Indian rule in Kashmir and with massive numbers of Indian forces stationed in the state to quell this, there can be little doubt that India failed to achieve its 1947 goal of making Kashmiris permanently Indian. However, New Delhi's determination to do this—or at least to ensure Kashmir remains permanently Indian—is undiminished.

Kashmir: International Dispute

The international dispute between Pakistan and India over Jammu and Kashmir started at the time of Partition. Both countries needed the state for economic and strategic reasons and to back their respective nationalist ideologies, Muslim and non-communal. The actual dispute between them arguably arose from the fact that Jammu and Kashmir had a Hindu ruler and a Muslim-majority population. Had both been Hindu, or both Muslim, there would probably never have been a problem deciding its future. As it was, the ruler-people religious dichotomy allowed each country to make a legal claim to the state: India on the basis of the ruler's accession, Pakistan on the basis of the partition principle that all geographically contingent Muslim-majority states should join it. Hari Singh's indecision caused the state to become divided between the two, with each country laying claim to the part under the other's control.

In practical terms, this has pretty much remained the state of affairs for the last fifty years. There have been slight territorial adjustments, with some formerly Indian-controlled territory going to Pakistan and vice versa, and the 'partition line' between the two 'Kashmirs' has become formalized as the Line of Control. On a map this is about as far as the dispute has progressed. But this is not the whole picture.

The Indo-Pak dispute over Jammu and Kashmir has actually got a lot worse during the course of the last fifty years. The reasons lie in each country's domestic politics. As seen in chapters five and six, different groups—politicians, religious fundamentalists, the military, etc.—have made use of the Kashmir issue for their own ends. In doing so, they have hardened public opinion on the dispute: determination to win Kashmir has become entrenched in each country's national psyche.

Worsening of the Indo-Pak dispute on Kashmir can be seen firstly in the way it has been dragged more and more into the overall India-Pakistan relationship. Progress in other spheres, e.g. trade and cultural exchanges, has been held hostage to settlement on Kashmir. Furthermore, it has fuelled a massive arms race between the two countries, one that recently escalated into the nuclear phase.

Worsening of the dispute can also be seen in the fact that it has become harder to resolve. The main reason is the hardening of public opinion just mentioned. Neither the Pakistani nor the Indian public is prepared to accept any compromise on their respective country's traditional position on Kashmir. Political leaders in both countries are well aware of this and hence—even should they wish to do so—they cannot really do anything to resolve the international dispute without committing political suicide. Another factor is the weight of history: maintaining the same position for half a century has effectively set this in concrete. Any flexibility that there might have been in Indian and Pakistani approaches to Kashmir in the late 1940s has long since been eradicated.

Convergence of Ethnic Conflict and International Dispute

A point that has been stressed throughout this book is that while there are two distinct Kashmir issues—ethnic conflict and international dispute—these are closely inter-linked. Pakistani backing for the Kashmiri Muslims' separatist movement marked their convergence. So too did the 1999 fighting in the Kargil sector of Indian Kashmir. Hostilities in Kargil were conducted, on the one hand, between Kashmiri militants and Indian forces as a continuation of their struggle against Indian rule in Kashmir, and on the other, between Pakistani troops/Pakistani-backed militants and Indian forces as a continuation of the international Indo-Pak dispute over Kashmiri sovereignty.

A number of factors brought about this convergence. The most obvious is that Pakistan and the Kashmiri Muslims have the shared goal of ending Indian rule in Kashmir. By supporting the Kashmiri Muslim movement to break away from India, Pakistan is effectively promoting its own cause in its international dispute with India. But Pakistani support, especially among the ordinary public, also derives from their perception of Kashmiris as fellow Muslims being oppressed by non-Muslims. There is a strong ideological component to Pakistani sympathy for the Kashmiris, quite distinct from pure national interest.

India, too, has encouraged convergence—or at least the perception of it. Rather than admit that there are real problems within Indian Kashmir, that the people there have genuine grievances against New Delhi, Indian governments prefer to pin blame for the ethnic conflict in the Valley on Pakistan. They claim that it is simply a problem of 'cross-border terrorism': incited, sponsored and conducted by Pakistan.

That view is widely accepted within India, where people are either ignorant about or choose to turn a blind eye to what is really happening in the Valley. Most believe New Delhi's line that Kashmiri militancy is just a Pakistani export. Their determination to crush it is, therefore, motivated not just by the need to keep Kashmir within India, but also by their desire to 'defeat' Pakistan in the international dispute.

The Indian portrayal of conflict in Kashmir as a Pakistani export has also gained some acceptance in the international community. Pakistani involvement, while helping Kashmiri militants sustain their fight against India, has, therefore, also had a negative effect of giving credence to Indian allegations that the conflict in the Valley is solely due to Pakistani interference. As seen in this book, the Kashmir conflict has quite indigenous roots. But outside involvement makes it hard for the Kashmiris to present their struggle to the international community as a genuine separatist movement.

It would be wrong, though, to conclude that the Kashmiri Muslims' struggle against Indian rule, and Pakistan's opposition to India are now the same thing. There has been co-operation between them because, as mentioned, they have one common goal of ending Indian rule in Jammu and Kashmir. But beyond that, there is divergence. Pakistan wants the state to accede to it. An increasing number of Kashmiri Muslims want independence—anathema to Islamabad. The ethnic conflict in the Valley thus remains distinct from the international dispute between India and Pakistan.

Prospects

Having seen how each Kashmir problem—ethnic conflict and international dispute—developed, a brief note on the prospects of their resolution.

Taking the international Indo-Pakistan Kashmir dispute first, as seen above, a number of factors have made this far harder to resolve now, compared to when it started fifty-odd years ago. Permanent resolution would require compromise by either/both countries on their established positions. Bearing in mind public opposition to this, such compromises could only be made by strong governments—something both countries lack.

Kashmir's internal politics have also made the international dispute far harder to settle. One could reasonably claim that had Pakistan and India reached a mutually acceptable settlement fifty years ago, the Kashmiri people would have accepted it. Today one cannot make such a claim. There are now not two but three parties involved in the Kashmir issue—India, Pakistan and the Kashmiris. Increasingly, the Kashmiris are coming to have an agenda that figures neither Pakistan nor India: independent Kashmir. Thus, even if Pakistan and India were to settle their dispute tomorrow by agreeing on a permanent division of the state between them, it is highly unlikely that the Kashmiri people would accept it.

Uncompromising domestic public opinion, the (uncooperative) Kashmiri element, coupled with—so far anyway—a lack of real resolve on the part of Indian and Pakistani leaders to settle their dispute, means that the most likely future scenario is for the status quo to be maintained. India controlling its part of the state, Pakistan its, and the LoC functioning as the effective international boundary between them. As demonstrated in the recent Kargil episode, international pressure will make it very difficult for either side to alter this status quo unilaterally. And Indian rejection of international mediation means that—despite the Subcontinent's arms race raising international concerns about the Kashmir dispute—the outside world is unlikely to resolve it.

Turning to the Kashmiri ethnic conflict, this has been going on for over a decade. As the chapter on the Kashmir conflict concluded, it has now effectively reached a stalemate. The Kashmiri militants are not sufficiently armed or organised to oust India from the state by force; the Indian forces, despite—or perhaps because of, their utmost efforts have not managed to totally crush the insurgency. This is the way the situation looked set to remain before 11 September 2001.

The attacks on the US on 11 September, however, led Pakistan to abandon its long-standing policy of supporting Kashmiri militants. The withdrawal of Pakistani support will have a profound impact on their ability to fight India. It will be harder for them to inflict damage on the Indian security forces; it will be easier for the Indian security forces to crush the militancy by force. There could, therefore, be a real shift in the almost twelve-year status quo within the Valley, with India emerging the clear victor.

What happens next will depend on New Delhi. It could use the opportunity provided by peace (albeit an involuntary one) to once again engage the Kashmiri Muslims and try to win them over to India, e.g. by providing genuine autonomy, economic investment, etc. In such a scenario, it is likely that the Kashmiri Muslims would accept their inclusion in the Indian Union as unavoidable and come to terms with it. But New Delhi could also use the absence of armed opposition to continue with the policies that led to conflict in the first place. If this is the case, it would only be a matter of time before Kashmiri Muslim frustration and anger again boiled over into militancy.

A final point is that by publicly cutting off the Kashmiri militants, Pakistan's position in the eyes of the international community could be strengthened. It would be relieved of the current criticism and pressure it comes under to stop promoting militancy in India. It would be able to take the 'high moral ground' from India. Pressure would instead shift to India to engage Pakistan in dialogue and find a permanent resolution to their dispute.

So many factors are involved in both Kashmir the ethnic conflict and Kashmir the international dispute, that it is impossible to predict exactly where they will go: whether they will deteriorate or be resolved. Something about which there is no doubt, however, is the need for solutions to be found. Both have dragged on for too long already, both have caused more than enough suffering.

BIBLIOGRAPHY

Interviews

Abdur Rehman, Malik, Deputy Election Commissioner, Azad Jammu and Kashmir. Islamabad, March1997.

Ahmed, Abdul Hadi, Editor, *Jihad-i-Kashmir*. Rawalpindi, March 1997.

Andrabi, Altaf, Pakistan Representative of JKLF (Yasin Malik faction). Rawalpindi, March 1997.

Ashraf, Prof. M. A., Rawalpindi, March 1997.

Ayaz, Ayaz Ahmad, Chief organizer, Pasban. Rawalpindi Division: Islamabad, March 1997.

Gul, General Hameed, Former Head of ISI. Islamabad, February 1997.

Islam, Sheikh Tajammul, Director, Institute of Kashmir Affairs. Rawalpindi, February 1997.

Khan, Amanullah, Chairman, Jammu and Kashmir Liberation Front. Rawalpindi, March 1997.

Khan, Sardar Abdul Qayyum. Former Prime Minister of Azad Kashmir. Rawalpindi, March 1997.

Khan, Zafar, UK Representative of Jammu and Kashmir Liberation Front. Luton, November 1996.

Maalik, Abdul Majeed, Chairman, Human Rights Division of Kashmir Bar Association. London, April 1998.

Mashaddi, Maulana, Tehreek-i-Kashmir. Birmingham, November 1996.

Mehmood, Ershad. Journalist/Reasearch Assistant at Institute of Policy Studies. Islamabad, March 1997.

Rehmani, Farooq, Chairman, Jammu and Kashmir People's League. Rawalpindi, February 1997.

Saleem, A. R., Chief Secretary (retd.), Azad Jammu and Kashmir Government: Rawalpindi, February 1997.

Shawl, Prof. Nazir Ahmed, Chief Editor, *Kashmir Mirror*. Rawalpindi, February 1997.

Thakkur, Dr Ayub, President, World Kashmir Freedom Movement. London, November 1996.

Turabi, Rashid, Amir Jamaat-i-Islami, Azad Kashmir. Islamabad, March 1997.
Wani, Abdul Samad, Editor, *Kasheer*. Rawalpindi, March 1997.

Unpublished Sources

India Office Library Records L/P&S/13
- Collection 23: Jammu and Kashmir
- Collection 48: Indian Independence

Ranganathan, C. S. 'Religion, Politics and the Secular State in India'. PhD thesis, University of Hull, 1993.
'1947-1977 The Kashmir Dispute at Fifty: Charting Paths to Peace'. Report on the visit of an independent study team to India and Pakistan sponsored by the Kashmir Study Group, 1997.

Newspapers and Periodicals

Economic and Political Weekly, India.
The Economist, London.
Far Eastern Economic Review.
India Today, New Delhi.
Newsweek.
Time.
The Daily Telegraph, London.
The Guardian, London.
The Independent, London.
The Times, London.

Books

Abdullah, Sheikh Mohammad. *Flames of the Chinar: An Autobiography.* English translation by Khushwant Singh. New Delhi: Viking, 1993.
Ahmed, Akbar S. *Jinnah, Pakistan and Islamic Identity.* London and New York: Routledge, 1997.

Ahmed, Ishtiaq. *The Concept of an Islamic State: An Analysis of the Ideological Controversy in Pakistan.* London: Frances Pinter, 1987.

Akbar, M. J. *Kashmir: Behind the Vale.* New Delhi: Viking, 1991.

Alavi, Hamza, and Hariss, John, eds. *Sociology of Developing Societies: South Asia.* London, Macmillan, 1989.

Ali, Chaudhri Muhammad. *The Emergence of Pakistan.* New York and London: Columbia University Press, 1967.

Ali, Tariq. *Can Pakistan Survive? The Death of a State.* London: Verso, 1983.

Alter, Peter. *Nationalism* (English translation). London: Edward Arnold, 1989.

Amin, Tahir. *Ethno-national Movements of Pakistan: Domestic and International Factors.* Islamabad: Institute of Policy Studies, 1988.

———— *Mass Resistance in Kashmir: Origins, Evolution, Options.* Islamabad: Institute of Policy Studies, 1995.

Anderson, Benedict. *Imagined Communities: Reflections on the Origin and Spread of Nationalism* (revised edition). London: Verso, 1991.

Bamzai, Prithvi Nath Kaul. *A History of Kashmir* (second edition). New Delhi: Metropolitan, 1973.

Barth, Frederik, ed. *Ethnic Groups and Boundaries: The Social Organization of Culture Difference.* London: George Allen & Unwin, 1969.

Baxter, Craig, and Wasti, Syed Razi, eds. *Pakistan: Authoritarianism in 1980s.* Lahore: Vanguard, 1991.

———— *Government and Politics in South Asia* (third edition). Boulder: Westview, 1993.

Bazaz, Prem Nath. *Kashmir in Crucible.* New Delhi: Pamposh, 1967.

Bhattacharjea, Ajit. *Kashmir: The Wounded Valley.* New Delhi: UBSPD, 1994.

Bjorkman, James, ed. *Fundamentalists, Revivalists and Violence in South Asia.* New Delhi: Manohar, 1988.

Brass, Paul. *Language, Religion and Politics in North India.* London: Cambridge University Press, 1974.

———— *New Cambridge History of India IV-I: Politics of India Since Independence.* Cambridge: Cambridge University Press, 1990.

———— *Ethnicity and Nationalism: Theory and Comparison.* New Delhi: Sage, 1991.

————, ed. *Ethnic Groups and the State.*

Brown, Judith M. *Modern India: The Origins of an Asian Democracy.* Oxford: Oxford University Press, 1985.

Burke, Edmund, and Lapidus, Ira M., eds. *Islam, Politics and Social Movements*. London: I. B. Tauris, 1988.

Burke, S. M., and Ziring, Lawrence. *Pakistan's Foreign Policy: An Historical Analysis* (second edition). Karachi: Oxford University Press, 1990.

Burki, Shahid Javed. *Pakistan Under Bhutto 1971-1977* (second edition). Basingstoke: Macmillan, 1988.

——— *Pakistan: The Continuing Search for Nationhood* (second edition). Boulder: Westview Press, 1991.

Chadda, Maya. *Ethnicity, Security and Separatism in India*. New York: Columbia University Press, 1997.

Chopra, V. D. *Genesis of Indo-Pakistan Conflict on Kashmir*. New Delhi: Patriot, 1990.

Choudhry, G. W. *Pakistan: Transition from military to civilian rule*. Essex: Scorpion, 1988.

——— *Islam and the Contemporary World*. London: Indus Thames, 1990.

Connor, Walker. *Ethnonationalism: The Quest for Understanding*. Princeton: Princeton University Press, 1994.

Das, Veena, ed. *Mirrors of Violence: Communities, Riots and Survivors in South Asia*. Delhi: Oxford University Press, 1992.

Dekmejian, R. H. *Islam in Revolution*. New York: Syracuse University Press, 1985.

Dharamdasani, M. D., ed. *Benazir's Pakistan*. Varanasi: Shalimar, 1989.

Eccleshall, Robert, et al. *Political Ideologies: an introduction* (second edition). London and New York: Routledge, 1994.

Embree, Ainslee. *Imagining India: Essays on Indian History*. Delhi: Oxford University Press, 1989.

Esposito, John, ed. *Voices of Resurgent Islam*. New York: Oxford University Press, 1983.

——— *Islam and Politics*. New York: Syracuse, 1984.

———, ed. *Islam in Asia; Religion, Politics and Society*. New York: Oxford University Press, 1987.

Ganai, Abdul Jabbar. *Kashmir and National Conference and Politics (1975-1980)*. Srinagar: Gulshan, 1984.

Ganguly, Sumit. *The Crisis in Kashmir: Portents of War, Hopes of Peace*. Cambridge: Cambridge University Press, 1997.

Gilani, Syed Ali. *Nawaiy Hurriyat* (Urdu). Islamabad: Institute of Policy Studies, 1994.

Gopal, Sarvepalli, ed. *Anatomy of a Confrontation: Ayodhya and the Rise of Communal Politics in India*. London and New York: Zed Books, 1993.

Graham, B. D. *Hindu Nationalism and Indian Politics: The Origins and Development of the Bharatiya Jana Sangh*. Cambridge: Cambridge University Press, 1990.

Gupta, Jyoti Bhusan Das. *Jammu and Kashmir*. The Hague: Martin Nijhoff, 1968.

Haddad, Y. H.; Haines, Byron; and Findly, Ellison, eds. *The Islamic Impact*. New York: Syracuse Univ. Press, 1984.

Hardgrave, Robert L., and Kochanek, Stanley A. *India: Government and Politics in a Developing Nation* (fifth edition). Fort Worth: Harcourt Brace Jovanovich, 1993.

Harris, Nigel. *National Liberation*. London: Penguin, 1990.

Hasan, Mushir-ul, ed. *India's Partition: Process, Strategy and Mobilization*. Delhi: Oxford University Press, 1993.

―――――. *Legacy of a Divided Nation: India's Muslims since Independence*. London: Hurst & Co., 1997.

Hewitt, Vernon. *Reclaiming the Past? The Search for Political and Cultural Unity in Contemporary Jammu and Kashmir*. London: Portland Books, 1995.

Hobsbawm, E. J. *Nations and Nationalism Since 1870: Programme, Myth and Reality* (second edition). Cambridge: Cambridge University Press, 1992.

Horowitz, Donald. *Ethnic Groups in Conflict*. Berkeley: University of California Press, 1985.

Hussain, Mushahid, and Hussain, Akmal. *Pakistan: Problems of Governance*. New Delhi: Konark, 1993.

Hutchinson, John, and Smith, Anthony, D., eds. *Nationalism*. Oxford: Oxford University Press, 1994.

―――――. *Ethnicity*. Oxford: Oxford University Press, 1996.

Iqbal, S. M., and Niraish, K. L. *The Culture of Kashmir*. New Delhi: Marwah, 1978.

Jaffrelot, Christophe. *The Hindu Nationalist Movement and Indian Politics 1925 to the 1990s*. London: Hurst & Company.

Jagmohan, Malhotra. *My Frozen Turbulence in Kashmir*. New Delhi: Allied, 1994.

Jalal, Ayesha. *The State of Martial Rule: The origins of Pakistan's political economy of defence*. Cambridge: Cambridge University Press, 1990.

———— *Democracy and Authoritarianism in South Asia: A comparative and historical perspective.* Cambridge: Cambridge University Press, 1995.

James, William E., and Roy, Subroto, eds. *Foundations of Pakistan's Political Economy: Towards an Agenda for the 1990s.* New Delhi: Sage, 1992.

Jan, Tarik, and Sarwar, Ghulam, eds. *Kashmir Problem: Challenge and Response.* Islamabad, Institute of Policy Studies, 1990.

Jeffrey, Robin. *What's Happening to India? Punjab, Ethnic Conflict, Mrs Gandhi's Death and the Test for Federalism.* London: Macmillan, 1986.

Kadian, Rajesh. *The Kashmir Tangle: Issues and Options.* Boulder, Westview, 1993.

Kak, B. L. *Kashmir: Problems and Politics.* Delhi: Seema, 1981.

Kakar, Sudhir. *The Colors of Violence: Cultural Identities, Religion and Conflict.* Chicago: University of Chicago Press, 1996.

Kapur, Ashok. *Pakistan in Crisis.* London and New York: Routledge, 1991.

Kapur, M. L. *Kingdom of Kashmir: Political and Cultural History of Kashmir from the Earliest Times to 1586 A.D.* Jammu: Kashmir History Publications, 1983.

Kedourie, Elie. *Nationalism* (fourth edition). Oxford: Blackwell, 1993.

Kellas, James G. *The Politics of Nationalism and Ethnicity.* London: Macmillan, 1991.

Khan, Asghar, ed. *Islam, Politics and the State: The Pakistan Experience.* London, Zed Books, 1985.

Kohli, Atul. *Democracy and Discontent: India's Growing Crisis of Governability.* Cambridge: Cambridge University Press, 1990.

Korbel Josef. *Danger in Kashmir.* Princeton: Princeton University Press, 1954.

Kumar, D. P. *Kashmir: Return to Democracy.* New Delhi: Siddhi Books, 1996.

Lamb, Alastair. *Kashmir: A Disputed Legacy 1846-1990.* Hertingfordbury: Roxford, 1991.

———— *Birth of a Tragedy: Kashmir 1947.* Karachi: Oxford University Press, 1994.

Lawrence, Walter. *The India we served.* London: Cassell and Company, 1928.

Madan, T. N. *Non-renunciation: Themes and Interpretations of Hindu Culture.* Delhi: Oxford University Press, 1987.

———— *Family and Kinship: A Study of the Pandits of Rural Kashmir* (second edition). Delhi: Oxford University Press, 1989.

————,ed. *Muslim Communities of South Asia: Culture, Society and Power* (revised edition). New Delhi: Manohar, 1995.

Malik, Hafeez, ed. *Dilemmas of National Security and Cooperation in India and Pakistan.* New York: St. Martin's Press, 1993.

McLane, John R., ed. *The Political Awakening in India.* Eaglewood Cliffs, New Jersey: Prentice-Hall, 1970.

Mitra, Subrata, ed. *The Post-Colonial State in South Asia.* London and New York: Harvester-Wheatsheaf, 1990.

Mortimer, Edward. *The Politics of Islam.* London: Faber and Faber, 1982.

Newberg, Paula. *Double Betrayal: Repression and Insurgency in Kashmir.* Washington: Carnegie Endowment for International Peace, 1995.

Noman, Omar. *Pakistan: Political and Economic History Since 1947.* London and New York: Kegan Paul International, 1988.

Oommen, T. K. *State and Society in India: Studies in Nation-Building.* New Delhi: Sage, 1990.

Pandey, B. N., ed. *The Indian Nationalist Movement 1885-1947, Select Documents.* London: Macmillan, 1979.

Phadnis, Urmila. *Ethnicity and Nation-Building in South Asia.* New Delhi: Sage, 1990.

Rehmani, Farooq. *Aazadi ki Talash: Kashmir ki Jid-o-Jehd Manzil ba Manzil* (Urdu). Srinagar: Aflaas Publications, 1994.

Rudebeck, Lars, ed. *When Democracy Makes Sense: Studies in the Democratic Potential of Third World Popular Movements.* Uppsala: AKUT, 1992.

Schofield, Victoria. *Kashmir in the Crossfire.* London: I. B. Tauris, 1996

Scruton, Roger. *A Dictionary of Political Thought* (second edition). London: Macmillan, 1996.

Sender, Henry. *The Kashmiri Pandits: A Study of Cultural Choice in North India.* Delhi: Oxford University Press, 1988.

Seton-Watson, Hugh. *Nationalism Old and New.* Sydney: Sydney University Press, 1965.

Singh, Anita Inder. *The Origins of the Partition of India 1936-1947.* Delhi: Oxford University Press, 1987.

Singh, Karan. *Heir Apparent: An Autobiography.* Delhi: Oxford University Press, 1982.

Singh, Nirmal K. *Inter-Communal Relations in Jammu and Kashmir (1846 to 1931)*. Delhi: Jay Kay, 1991.

Singh, Tavleen. *Kashmir: A Tragedy of Errors*. New Delhi: Viking/Penguin, 1995.

Smith, Anthony D. *Nationalist Movements*. London and Basingstoke: Macmillan, 1976.

_____. *Nationalism in the Twentieth Century*. Oxford: Martin Robertson, 1979.

_____. *The Ethnic Origins of Nations*. Oxford: Blackwell, 1986.

_____. *National Identity*. London: Penguin, 1991.

_____, ed. *Ethnicity and Nationalism*. Leiden, The Netherlands: E. J. Brill, 1992.

Stavenhagen, Rodolfo. *Ethnic Conflicts and the Nation-State*. London: Macmillan, 1996.

Stowasser, B. F., ed. *The Islamic Impulse*. London: Croom Helm, 1987.

Syed, Anwar. *Pakistan: Islam, Politics and National Solidarity*. Praeger.

Tariq, M. Sharif. *Kashmir in Strangulation*. Mirpur: M. S. Tariq, 1991.

Taylor, David, and Yapp, Malcolm, eds. *Political Identity in South Asia*. London and Dublin: Curzon, 1979.

Tehreek-i-Kashmir. *Kashmir Mein Paak Lahoo* (Urdu). Lahore: Paramedia Communications, 1994.

Thomas, Raju, ed. *Perspectives on Kashmir: The Roots of Conflict in South Asia*. Boulder: Westview, 1992.

Vajpeyi, D., and Malik, Y., eds. *Religious and Ethnic Minority Politics in South Asia*. Rivedale, 1989.

Vanaik, Achin. *The Painful Transition: Bourgeois Democracy in India*. London and New York: Verso.

_____. *The Furies of Indian Communalism: Religion, Modernity and Secularization*. London: Verso, 1997.

Verma, P. S. *Jammu and Kashmir at the Political Crossroads*. New Delhi: Vikas, 1994.

Wakhlu, Khem Lata and O. N. *Kashmir: Behind the White Curtain 1972-1991*. New Delhi: Konark, 1992.

Wani, Gull Mohammed, ed. *Kashmir: From Autonomy to Azadi*. Srinagar: Valley Book House, 1996.

Wirsing, Robert G. *Pakistan's Security Under Zia 1977-1988*. London: Macmillan, 1991.

———. *India, Pakistan and the Kashmir Dispute: On regional conflict and its resolution*. London: Macmillan, 1994.

Wolpert, Stanley. *Zulfi Bhutto of Pakistan: His Life and Times*. New York: Oxford University Press, 1993.

Woolf, Stuart (ed). *Nationalism in Europe 1815 to the Present: A Reader*. London and New York: Routledge, 1996.

Ziring, L.; Braibanti, R.; and Wriggins, W. H., eds. *Pakistan: the Long View*. Durham: Duke University Press, 1977.

Zutshi, U. K. *Emergence of Political Awakening in Kashmir*. New Delhi: Manohar, 1986.

Articles

AbuKhalil, As'ad. 'Fundamentalism: Arab Islamic Thought at the End of the 20ᵗʰ Century.' *Middle East Journal* 48:4 (Autumn 1994).

Agwani, M. S. 'Islamic Militancy in West Asia.' *Economic and Political Weekly* (19 March 1994): 670–73.

Ahmed, Akbar. 'On the brink of the final bloodbath.' *New Statesman and Society*, 29 January 1993.

Ahmed, Eqbal. 'Soul Struggles.' *New Statesman & Society* (28 June 1991): 23–4.

Amin, Tahir. 'Pakistan in 1994: The Politics of Confrontation.' *Asian Survey* 35:2 (February 1995): 140–46.

Andersen, Walter K. 'India's 1991 Elections: The Uncertain Verdict.' *Asian Survey* 31:10 (October 1991): 976–89.

Andersen, Walter K. 'India in 1994: Economics to the Fore.' *Asian Survey* 35:2 (February 1995): 127–39.

Austin, Dennis, and Lyon, Peter. 'The Bharatiya Janata Party of India.' *Government and Opposition* 28:1 (Winter 1993): 36–50.

Ayoob, Mohammed. 'Dateline India: The Deepening Crisis.' *Foreign Policy*: 166–84.

Azzam, Maha. 'The Gulf Crisis: Perceptions in the Muslim World.'

Bali, Sita. 'India: state elections, national implications. *The World Today*, October 1995.

Ballard, Roger, 'Kashmir Crisis: View from Mirpur.' *Economic and Political Weekly*, 2–9 March 1991.

Baxter, Craig. 'Democracy and Authoritarianism in South Asia.' *Journal of International Affairs*: 307–319.

Bidwai, Praful. 'Jewel without a crown.' *New Statesman and Society*, 31 May 1991.

———. 'Betting on Bhutto.' *New Statesman and Society*, 29 October 1993.

Bose, Tapan; Mohan, Dinesh; Navlakha, Gautam, and Banerjee, Sumanta. 'India's Kashmir War.' *Economic and Political Weekly*, 31 March 1990.

Bray, John. 'Pakistan: the democratic balance-sheet.' *World Today* 46 (June 1990): 111–14.

Burgess, M. Elaine. 'The resurgence of ethnicity: myth or reality?' *Ethnic and Racial Studies* 1:3 (July 1978): 265–83.

Burki, Shahid Javed. 'Pakistan Under Zia, 1977–1988.' *Asian Survey* 28:10 (October 1988): 1082–100.

Chatterjee, Partha. 'History and the Nationalisation of Hinduim.' *Social Research* 59:1 (Spring 1992): 111–49.

Chhibber, Pradeep K., and Misra, Subhash. 'Hindus and the Babri Masjid: The Sectional Basis of Communal Attitudes.' *Asian Survey* 33:7 (July 1993): 666–72.

Chriyankandath, James. 'India: the crisis of secularism.' *The World Today*, March 1993.

Connor, Walker. 'A nation is a nation, is a state, is an ethnic group, is a...' *Ethnic and Racial Studies* 1:4 (October 1978): 377–99.

Copland, Ian. 'Islam and Political Mobilization in Kashmir, 1931-34.' *Pacific Affairs*: 228–59.

Das, P. K. 'The Changing Political scene in India: A Comment.'

Dekmejian, R. Hrair. 'The Rise of Political Islamism in Saudi Arabia.' *Middle East Journal* 48:4 (Autumn 1994).

Dua, Bhagwan D. 'Federalism or Patrimonialism: The Making and Unmaking of Chief Ministers in India.' *Asian Survey* 25:8 (August 1985): 793–804.

Evans, Alexander. 'Subverting the State: Intervention, insurgency and terror in South Asia.' *War Studies Journal* 2:1 (Autumn 1996): 17–29.

Ganguly, Sumit. 'Ethno-religious Conflict in South Asia.' *Survival* 35:2 (Summer 1993): 88–109.

———. 'Wars without End: The Indo-Pakistani Conflict.' *Annals AAPSS* 541 (September 1995): 167–78.

Gordon, Sandy. 'Resources and Instability in South Asia.' *Survival* 35:2 (Summer 1993): 66–87.

Gupta, Dipanker. 'Communalism and Fundamentalism: Some notes on the nature of ethnic politics in India.' *Economic and Political Weekly*, Annual Number, March 1991.

Gupta, Jyotirindra Das. 'India in 1980: Strong centre, weak authority.' *Asian Survey* 21:2 (February 1981): 147–61.

Hadar, Leon T. 'What Green Peril?' Foreign Affairs: 27–42.

Hagerty, Devin T. 'India's Regional Security Doctrine.' *Asian Survey* 31:4 (April 1991): 351–63.

———. 'Nuclear Deterrence in South Asia: The 1990 Indo-Pakistani Crisis.' *International Security* 20:3 (Winter 1995/96): 79–114.

Haq, Farhat. 'Rise of the MQM in Pakistan: Politics of Ethnic Mobilization.' *Asian Survey* 35:11 (November 1995): 990–1016.

Hasan, Mushir-ul. 'In search of Integration and Identity: Indian Muslims since Independence.' *Economic and Political Weekly*, November 1988.

Hasan, Zoya. 'Minority Identity, Muslim Women Bill Campaign and the Political Process.' *Economic and Political Weekly*, 7 January 1989.

Hussain, Altaf. 'Ethnicity, National Identity and Praetorianism: The case of Pakistan.' *Asian Survey* 16 (October 1976): 918–30.

Hussain, Mushirul. 'The Muslim Question in India.' *Journal of Contemporary Asia* 19:3 (1989): 279–96.

Hyman, Anthony. 'Kashmir: paths to peace?' *The World Today*, July 1994.

Inayatullah, Sohail. 'Images of Pakistan's Future.' *Futures* 24 (November 1992): 867–78.

Jalal, Ayesha. 'Kashmir Scars.' *The New Republic*, 23 July 1990.

Joshi, Ram. 'The Shiv Sena: A Movement in Search of Legitimacy.' *Asian Survey* 10:11 (November 1970): 967–78.

'Kashmir and India.' *Economic and Political Weekly*, 24 August 1991.

Kashmir Issue. *Contemporary South Asia* 4:1 (March 1995).

Kaviraj, Sudipta. 'Crisis of the Nation-state in India.' *Political Studies* 42 (1994): 115–29.

Khalidi, Omar. 'Muslims in Indian Political Process: Group Goals and Alternative Strategies.' *Economic and Political Weekly*, 2–9 January 1993.

Kizilbash, Hamid H. 'Anti-Americanism in Pakistan.' *Annals AAPSS* 497 (May 1988): 58–67.

Kolodner, Eric. 'The Political Economy of the Rise and Fall(?) of Hindu Nationalism.' *Journal of Contemporary Asia* 25:2 (1995): 233–53.

Kothari, Rajni. 'The Congress System in India.' *Asian Survey* 4:12 (December 1964): 1161–73.

Kreisberg, Paul H. 'India After Indira.' *Foreign Affairs*: 873–91.

Madan, T. N. 'Secularism in its Place.' *Journal of Asian Studies* 46:4 (November 1987): 747–59.

――― 'Whither Indian Secularism.' *Modern Asian Studies* 27:3 (1993): 667–97.

Mahmood, Cynthia Keppley. 'Rethinking Indian Communalism: Culture and Counter-culture.' *Asian Survey* 33:7 (July 1993): 722–37.

Malik, Iftikhar H. 'Issues in Contemporary South and Central Asian Politics.' *Asian Survey* 32:10 (October 1992): 888–901.

――― 'The Continuing Conflict in Kashmir: Regional Détente in Jeopardy.' Monograph. *Research Institute for the Study of Conflict and Terrorism*: March 1993.

Malik, Yogendra K. 'Indira Gandhi: Personality, Political Power and Party Politics.' *Journal of Asian and African Studies* 22:3–4 (1987): 142–55.

―――, and Singh, V. B. 'Bharatiya Janata Party: An Alternative to the Congress (I)?' *Asian Survey* 32:4 (April 1992): 318–36.

―――, and Vajpeyi, Dhirendra K. 'India: the years of Indira Gandhi.' *Journal of Asian and African Studies* 22:3–4 (1987): 135–140.

――― 'The Rise of Hindu Militancy: India's Secular Democracy at Risk.' *Asian Survey* 29:3 (March 1989): 308–25.

Manor, James. 'How and Why Liberal and Representative Politics Emerged in India.' *Political Studies* 38 (1990): 20–38.

Mathur, Kuldeep. 'The State and the Use of Coercive Power in India.' *Asian Survey* 32:4 (April 1992): 337–49.

Mayer, Peter. 'The Year the Vote-Banks Failed: The 1967 General Elections and the Beginning of the End of Congress Party dominance.'

Mazrui, Ali A. 'The Resurgence of Islam and the Decline of Communism: What is the Connection?'

McKay, James. 'An exploratory synthesis of primordial and mobilizationist approaches to ethnic phenomena.' *Ethnic and Racial Studies* 5:4 (October 1982): 395–416.

Miller, Judith. 'Faces of Fundamentalism: Hassan al-Turabi and Muhammad Fadlallah.' *Foreign Affairs* (Nov/Dec 1994): 121–42.

――――― 'The Challenge of Radical Islam.' *Foreign Affairs*: 43–56.

Mitra, Subrata Kumar. 'Desecularising the State: Religion and Politics in India after Independence.'

Monshipouri, Mahmood. 'Backlash to the Destruction at Ayodhya.' *Asian Survey* 33:7 (July 1993): 711–21.

Monshipouri, Mahmood, and Samuel, Amjad. 'Development and Democracy in Pakistan: Tenuous or Plausible nexus?' *Asian Survey* 35:11 (November 1995): 973–89.

Nasr, Sayyed Vali Reza. 'Democracy and the Crisis of Governability in Pakistan.' *Asian Survey* 32:6 (June 1992): 521–37.

――――― 'Students, Islam, and Politics: Islami Jami'at-I Tulaba in Pakistan.' *Middle East Journal* 46:1 (Winter 1992): 59–76.

Navlakha, Gautam. 'India's Kashmir War.' *Economic and Political Weekly*, 21 December 1991.

Newberg, Paula. 'Dateline Pakistan: Bhutto's Back.' *Foreign Policy* 95 (Summer 1994): 161–74.

Noman, Omar. 'Pakistan and General Zia: era and legacy.' *Third World Quarterly* 11 (January 1989): 28–54.

Omvedt, Gail. 'Hinduism and Politics.' *Economic and Political Weekly*, 7 April 1990.

Osmaston, Henry. 'The Kashmir Problem.' *Geographical Magazine*, June 1990.

Parekh, Bhikhu. 'The concept of national identity.' *New Community* 21:2 (April 1995): 255–68.

――――― 'Ethnocentricity of the nationalist discourse.' *Nations and Nationalism* 1:1 (1995): 25–52.

Parikh, Manju. 'The Debacle at Ayodhya: Why Militant Hinduism Met with a Weak Response.' *Asian Survey* 33:7 (July1993): 674–84.

Rais, Rasul Baksh. 'Pakistan in 1988: From Command to Conciliation Politics.' *Asian Survey* 29:2 (February 1989): 199–206.

――――― 'Pakistan: Hope amidst turmoil.' *Journal of Democracy* 5 (April 1994): 132–43.

Rakisits, C. G. P. 'Centre-Province Relations in Pakistan under President Zia: The Government's and the Opposition's Approaches.' *Pacific Affairs* 61 (Spring 1988): 78–97.

Rao, R. V. R. Chandrasekhara. 'Mrs Indira Gandhi and India's Constitutional Structures: An Era of Erosion.' *Journal of Asian and African Studies* 22:3–4 (1987): 156–75.

Satloff, Robert. 'Islam in the Palestinian Uprising.' *Orbis* (Summer 1989): 389–401.

Scott, George M. Jr. 'A resynthesis of the primordial and circumstantial approaches to ethnic group solidarity: towards an explanatory model.' *Ethnic and Racial Studies* 13:2 (April 1990): 147–70.

Singh, Mahendra Prasad. 'The Dilemma of the New Indian Party System: To Govern or not to Govern?' *Asian Survey* 32:4 (April 1992): 303–17.

Sinha, Dipankar. 'V. P. Singh, Chandra Shekhar, and "Nowhere Politics" in India.' Asian Survey 31:7 (July 1991): 598–612.

Sisson, Richard, and Majmundar, Munira. 'India in 1990: Political Polarization.' *Asian Survey* 31:2 (February 1991): 103–12.

Sivan, Emanuel. 'The Islamic Resurgence: Civil Society Strikes Back.' *Journal of Contemporary History* 25 (1990): 353–64.

Smith, A. D. 'Towards a theory of ethnic separatism.' *Ethnic and Racial Studies* 2:1 (January 1979): 21–37.

————— 'Ethnic Identity and World Order.' *Millenium: Journal of International Studies* 12:2.

————— 'Ethnic and Nation in the Modern World.' *Millennium: Journal of International Studies* 14:2: 127–41.

Spencer, Clare. 'Algeria in Crisis.' *Survival* 36:2 (Summer 1994): 149–63.

Thakur, Ramesh. 'Ayodhya and the Politics of India's Secularism: A Double-Standards Discourse.' *Asian Survey* 33:7 (July 1993): 645–64.

Thapar, Romila. 'Imagined Religious Communities? Ancient History and the Modern Search for a Hindu Identity.' *Modern Asian Studies* 23:2 (1989): 209–31.

Thomas, Raju G. C. 'Secessionist Movements in South Asia.' *Survival* 36:2 (Summer 1994): 92–114.

Tripathi, Deepak. 'India's foreign policy: the Rajiv factor.' *The World Today*, July 1988.

Tremblay, Reeta Chowdhari. 'Nation, Identity and the Intervening Role of the State: A Study of the Secessionist Movement in Kashmir.' *Pacific Affairs* 69:4 (Winter 1996-97): 471–97.

Tully, Mark. 'The Cassandras are Prophesying Again.' *The World Today*, March 1996.

Upadhyaya, Praksh Chnadra. 'The Politics of Indian Secularism.' *Modern Asian Studies* 26:4 (1992): 815–53.

Van der Veer, Peter. "'God must be Liberated!" A Hindu Liberation Movement in Ayodhya.' *Modern Asian Studies* 21:2 (1987): 283–301.

———. 'Ayodhya and Somnath: Eternal Shrines, Contested Histories.' *Social Research.*

Vatikiotis, P. J. 'Islam on the Move? – The Will to Power.'

Vincent, John A. 'Differentiation and resistance: ethnicity in Valle d'Aosta and Kashmir.' *Ethnic and Racial Studies* 5:3 (July 1982): 313–25.

Waseem, Mohammad. 'Pakistan's Lingering Crisis of Dyarchy.' *Asian Survey* 32:7 (July 1992): 617–34.

Whitehead, Andrew. 'Killing Time in Kashmir.' *New Statesman and Society*, 3 September 1993.

Widmalm, Sten. 'The Rise and Fall of Democracy in Jammu and Kashmir.' *Asian Survey* 38:11 (November 1997): 1005–30.

Yasmeen, Samina. 'Pakistan's Cautious Foreign Policy.' *Survival* 36:2 (Summer 1994): 115–33.

Ziring, Lawrence. 'Pakistan in 1989: The Politics of Stalemate.' *Asian Survey* 30:2 (February 1990): 126–35.

———. 'Pakistan in 1990: The Fall of Benazir Bhutto.' *Asian Survey* 31:2 (February 1991): 113–24.

INDEX